T0180669

Lecture Notes in Computer Science 14324

The series Lecture Notes in Computer Science (LNCS), including its subseries Lecture Notes in Artificial Intelligence (LNAI) and Lecture Notes in Bioinformatics (LNBI), has established itself as a medium for the publication of new developments in computer science and information technology research, teaching, and education.

LNCS enjoys close cooperation with the computer science R & D community, the series counts many renowned academics among its volume editors and paper authors, and collaborates with prestigious societies. Its mission is to serve this international community by providing an invaluable service, mainly focused on the publication of conference and workshop proceedings and postproceedings. LNCS commenced publication in 1973.

Lothar Fritsch · Ismail Hassan · Ebenezer Paintsil
Editors

Secure IT Systems

28th Nordic Conference, NordSec 2023
Oslo, Norway, November 16–17, 2023
Proceedings

 Springer

Editors
Lothar Fritsch 🆔
OsloMet – Oslo Metropolitan University
Oslo, Norway

Ismail Hassan 🆔
OsloMet – Oslo Metropolitan University
Oslo, Norway

Ebenezer Paintsil 🆔
OsloMet - Oslo Metropolitan University
Oslo, Norway

ISSN 0302-9743   ISSN 1611-3349 (electronic)
Lecture Notes in Computer Science
ISBN 978-3-031-47747-8   ISBN 978-3-031-47748-5 (eBook)
https://doi.org/10.1007/978-3-031-47748-5

This Springer imprint is published by the registered company Springer Nature Switzerland AG
The registered company address is: Gewerbestrasse 11, 6330 Cham, Switzerland

Paper in this product is recyclable.

Preface

This volume contains the articles presented at the 28th Nordic Conference on Secure IT Systems (NordSec 2023). The conference was held from November 16th to November 17th, 2023, at Oslo Metropolitan University in Norway. The NordSec conference series started in 1996 with the aim of bringing together researchers and practitioners in computer security in the Nordic countries, thereby establishing a forum for discussion and cooperation between universities, industry, and computer societies. The NordSec conference series addresses a broad range of topics within IT security and privacy, and over the years it has developed into an international conference that takes place in the Nordic countries. NordSec is currently a key meeting venue for Nordic university teachers and students with research interests in information security and privacy.

NordSec 2023 received 55 submissions, which were double-blind reviewed each by three members of the 64-person reviewer group. After the reviewing phase, the Program Committee selected 18 of the manuscripts for publication and inclusion in the proceedings (an acceptance rate of 30 per cent).

We were honored to have two keynote speakers:

- Øyvind Ytrehus, Simula UiB and the University of Bergen, who spoke on Post-Quantum Cryptography; and
- Jon Ølnes, Tribe Lead signing and trust services, Signicat, who gave an in-depth talk on Digital Identity.

We sincerely thank everyone involved in making this year's conference a success, including, but not limited to, the authors who submitted their papers, the presenters who contributed to the NordSec 2023 program, the PC members and additional reviewers for their thorough and constructive reviews, OsloMet's supportive administrative staff, and Springer Nature publishers for providing their EquinOCS review and production platform.

November 2023

Lothar Fritsch
Ismail Hassan
Ebenezer Paintsil

Organization

General Chair

Lothar Fritsch · Oslo Metropolitan University and University of Oslo, Norway

Program Committee Chairs

Ismail Hassan · Oslo Metropolitan University, Norway
Ebenezer Paintsil · Oslo Metropolitan University, Norway

Steering Committee

Tuomas Aura · Aalto University, Finland
Aslan Askarov · Aarhus University, Denmark
Mikael Asplund · Linköping University, Sweden
Karin Bernsmed · SINTEF ICT and Norwegian University of Science and Technology, Norway
Billy Bob Brumley · Tampere University, Finland
Sonja Buchegger · KTH Royal Institute of Technology, Sweden
Mads Dam · KTH Royal Institute of Technology, Sweden
Dieter Gollmann · Hamburg University of Technology, Germany
Nils Gruschka · University of Oslo, Norway
Ismail Hassan · Oslo Metropolitan University, Norway
René Rydhof Hansen · Aalborg University, Denmark
Simone Fischer-Hübner · Karlstad University, Sweden
Lothar Fritsch · Oslo Metropolitan University / University of Oslo, Norway
Audun Jøsang · University of Oslo, Norway
Marcel Kyas · Reykjavik University, Iceland
Helger Lipmaa · University of Tartu, Estonia
Antonios Michalas · Tampere University, Finland
Katerina Mitrokotsa · Chalmers University of Technology, Sweden
Hans P. Reiser · Reykjavik University, Iceland
Juha Röning · University of Oulu, Finland
Simin Nadjm-Tehrani · Linköping University, Sweden
Nicola Tuveri · Tampere University, Finland

Program Committee

Aws Naser Jaber Al-Zaraqawee	KTH Royal Institute of Technology, Sweden
Anders Andersen	University of Tromsø - The Arctic University of Norway, Norway
Diego F. Aranha	Aarhus University, Denmark
Mikael Asplund	Linköping University, Sweden
Tuomas Aura	Aalto University, Finland
Karin Bernsmed	SINTEF ICT and Norwegian University of Science and Technology, Norway
Svetlana Boudko	Norwegian Computing Center, Norway
Patrick Bours	Norwegian University of Science and Technology, Norway
Bruno Dzogovic	Telenor ASA and Oslo Metropolitan University, Norway
Laszlo Erdodi	University of Oslo, Norway
Sigurd Eskeland	Norwegian Computing Center, Norway
Boning Feng	Oslo Metropolitan University, Norway
Ulrik Franke	RISE Research Institutes of Sweden, Sweden
Lothar Fritsch	Oslo Metropolitan University and University of Oslo, Norway
Christian Gehrmann	Lund University, Sweden
Dieter Gollmann	Hamburg University of Technology, Germany
Nils Gruschka	University of Oslo, Norway
René Rydhof Hansen	Aalborg University, Denmark
Ismail Hassan	Oslo Metropolitan University, Norway
Hårek Haugerud	Oslo Metropolitan University, Norway
Kirsi Helkala	Norwegian Defence University College, Norway
Erik Hjelmås	Norwegian University of Science and Technology, Norway
Leonardo Iwaya	Karlstad University, Sweden
Meiko Jensen	Karlstad University, Sweden
Pontus Johnson	KTH Royal Institute of Technology, Sweden
Michael Kubach	Fraunhofer Institute for Industrial Engineering, Germany
Joakim Kävrestad	Jönköping University, Sweden
Marcel Kyas	Reykjavik University, Iceland
Leonardo Martucci	Karlstad University, Sweden
Nuno Marques	Oslo Metropolitan University, Norway
Antonis Michalas	Tampere University, Finland
Nurul Momen	Blekinge Institute of Technology, Sweden
Tomas Olovsson	Chalmers University of Technology, Sweden

Michaela Padden	Karlstad University, Sweden
Samuel Pagliarini	Tallinn University of Technology, Estonia
Ebenezer Paintsil	Telenor Asa and Oslo Metropolitan University, Norway
Paolo Palmieri	University College Cork, Ireland
Aleksi Peltonen	Aalto University, Finland
Danny Poulsen	Aalborg University, Denmark
Siddharth Prakash Rao	Aalto University and Nokia Bell Labs, Finland
Hans Peter Reiser	Reykjavik University, Iceland
Jenni Reuben	Swedish Defence Research Agency, Sweden
Juha Röning	University of Oulu, Finland
Einar Snekkenes	Norwegian University of Science and Technology, Norway
Åvald Åslaugson Sommervoll	University of Oslo, Norway
Nicola Tuveri	Tampere University, Finland
Simin Nadjm-Tehrani	Linköping University, Sweden
Nils Petter Wien	University of Oslo, Norway
Sule Yildirim Yayilgan	Norwegian University of Science and Technology, Norway
Rose-Mharie Åhlfeldt	University of Skövde, Sweden

Additional Reviewers

Mohamed Abomhara	Norwegian University of Science and Technology, Norway
Mahdi Akil	Karlstad University, Sweden
Levent Aksoy	Tallinn University of Technology, Estonia
Andre Büttner	University of Oslo, Norway
Alejandro Cabrera Aldaya	Tampere University, Finland
Thomas Dangl	Passau University, Germany
Simon Gökstorp	KTH Royal Institute of Technology, Sweden
Malik Imran	Tallinn University of Technology, Estonia
Nikolaos Kakouros	KTH Royal Institute of Technology, Sweden
Marko Kivikangas	Tampere University, Finland
Akif Mehmood	Tampere University, Finland
Emre Süren	KTH Royal Institute of Technology, Sweden
Samuel Wairimu	Karlstad University, Sweden

Contents

xii   Contents

Privacy and Data Protection

Analysis of a Consent Management Specification and Prototype Under the GDPR

Jonas Palm[1] and Meiko Jensen[2]([⊠]) [iD]

[1] Kiel University of Applied Sciences, Kiel, Germany
[2] Karlstad University, Karlstad, Sweden
Meiko.Jensen@kau.se

Abstract. Consent requests for the processing of personal information are ubiquitous for users of web services across the European Union (EU). However, their form and contents differ greatly, and often include deceptive design patterns (so-called dark patterns) meant to influence users' choices.

In this paper, we provide the results of a research project to define a new specification that can be used to handle consent requests based on cookies in a standardized and GDPR-compliant manner. We define and evaluate a set of requirements for consent management systems and we illustrate the advantage of our proposed specification to the state of the art based on a prototype implementation and evaluation. Based on a small usability study, we found our solution to reduce the necessary interactions with respect to consenting, consent withdrawal, and consent configuration by far.

Keywords: consent management · usability · requirements elicitation

1 Introduction

When the GDPR came into effect in 2018, consent requests regarding the processing of personal data became ubiquitous in the sphere of internet related services across the EU [9, p. 10]. While small and unobtrusive "cookie banners" at the website's corners were introduced several years earlier with the ePrivacy Directive [11], the unequivocal consent definition of the GDPR resulted in new user interfaces requirements. These include allowing the user to reject requests without refusing service, providing specific information for each request, as well as requiring an explicit affirmative action. With the omnipresence of advertisement, user behavior analysis and inclusion of third party contents (see e.g. [27, p. 7]), it has become a continuous task for the user to interact with consent management interfaces while using internet services. Service providers utilize psychological methods to influence users, often successfully, to accept all consent requests regardless of their own preferences [6,25]. These methods include requiring the user to interact with multiple control elements, hiding preferences behind multiple layers, or threaten the loss of functionality when rejecting requests [25]. Being overwhelmed by the amount of requests [26] or pressured by indicated notifications, such as unread messages, and without an option to ignore the requests, users might just choose the interface controls they expect will close the consent interface fastest and let them continue to the website's content [25, pp. 27–31].

From a privacy perspective this clearly is not an ideal solution. While courts and Data Protection Authorities (DPAs) continue to limit the legal use of these psychological methods (see e.g. [8, 10]), the fundamental problem of answering very similar requests across many websites, remains. First steps in the automated objection to data processing were taken with the development of the Global Privacy Control (GPC) standard [1]. Proposals for unified consent management platforms exist [23], but none that is developed by a leading actor in the development of web standards (see e.g. [14, p. 2]). These proposals only offer solutions for individual problems such as request presentation with Advanced Data Protection Control (ADPC) [24] or standardization with the Transparency and Consent Framework (TCF) [15]. But even these limited approaches have obvious shortcomings, as ADPC's requests only consist of a single description attribute [24, Sect. 6.1] and TCF's requests standardization was ruled insufficient for legal compliance due to being too vague [5, para. 535]. With many current DPAs and court decisions prohibiting established methods and enforcing a privacy-centric interpretation of the General Data Protection Regulation (GDPR) (see e.g. [5, 8, 16]), new approaches to consent management become necessary. Features like preventing manipulative design and descriptions and reducing the amount of user interaction across websites appear to be fundamental to ensure that responses to consent requests actually reflect upon the user's preferences.

In this paper, we provide the results of a research project on defining and evaluating a novel policy exchange specification for the web (see [20]). Based on this specification, users can manage their consent, i.e. give, reject, or withdraw their consent, in general or for selected categories of cookies. In particular, we analyze the state of the art in consent management on the web, and derive a set of functional, legal, and interface requirements for consent management systems that comply with the GDPR. We then provide a technical description of the prototype developed in this project based on these requirements, which is implemented as a browser plugin, and we analyze its utility and effectiveness in selected real-world scenarios and against the set of requirements elicited. We then provide the results of a usability study, comparing our prototype to said state of the art frameworks for a set of scenarios and websites typically representing today's Internet landscape.

The paper is organized as follows. The next section briefly iterates over the state of the art in consent management frameworks and related work. Section 3 then describes the methodology followed during the project, explaining the main concepts and artifacts elaborated. Section 4 then provides the set of requirements elicited, which are evaluated against the prototype (which is described in Sect. 5) in Sect. 6. The results of our usability study are provided in Sect. 7, and the paper concludes with future research indications in Sect. 8.

2   Background

2.1   Consent Management Frameworks

HTTP Privacy Headers (DNT/GPC). Do Not Track (DNT) and Global Privacy Control (GPC) are Hypertext Transfer Protocol (HTTP) headers that can be set by a user agent to indicate that users do not want to be traced across visited websites, respectively that they do not want their personal data shared with, or sold to third parties. Both settings default to not-enabled, meaning that while their presence indicates the user's preference, their absence does not [22, Sect. 4], [21, Sect. 3.2]. DNT was proposed in 2009 as an approach to regulate user tracking by voluntarily acknowledging the header [7]. The responsible World Wide Web Consortium (W3C) working group was closed in January 2019, citing insufficient deployment of the header and support from third parties to justify further advancements [4]. Apple removed DNT support from its Safari web browser in 2019 to "prevent potential use as a fingerprinting variable" [3]. In 2020, GPC was introduced as a replacement, aiming to accommodate the legal requirements of the GDPR and California Consumer Privacy Act (CCPA), for service providers to accept automated objection from their users [1]. To make this system comparable with the other Consent Management Platforms (CMPs), the specifications and Firefox's implementation of the DNT header settings are evaluated together.

Transparency and Consent Framework (TCF). The Transparency and Consent Framework (TCF) (see [15]) is a standard for consent management in the advertisement industry. It defines policies and categories for data processing (so-called *purposes*) to request and store user consent across participating CMP vendors. Noteworthy, the developer, Interactive Advertising Bureau Europe (IAB Europe), was recently fined due to compliance issues of TCF version 2.1 with the GDPR (see [5]). A new version, 2.2., was published recently.

Advanced Data Protection Control (ADPC). ADPC (see [23]) is a proposed mechanism to request user consent for privacy decisions in a simple JSON format. It uses HTTP headers and a JavaScript interface for requests and responses and depends on the HTTP client to process these. The prototype implementation has the form of a browser extension and presents the user with a unified interface on websites implementing the specification.

CookieBlock (see [2]) is a browser extension that automatically manages browser cookies and deletes unwanted ones. Neither does it process requests from a service provider nor does it send any information about user's choices to service providers. Therefore, CookieBlock cannot be used for consent management, but this comparison can still help to understand challenges and solutions regarding categorization of consent requests and the reduction of necessary user interaction.

2.2   Deceptive Design

Deceptive design patterns, sometimes also referred to as *dark patterns*, are User Interface (UI) patterns that are used to influence users into doing things that are not in their own interest, but in the interest of the service provider [6].

In their report "Deceived by Design", the Norwegian consumer council (Forbrukerraadet) analyzed CMPs of Facebook, Google and Microsoft with regard to consumer privacy and the right to make informed choices [25], which provides a list of such deceptive design patterns of relevance for this paper:

Default settings: setting defaults in the interest of the service provider,

Ease: make the provider-friendly option more easy, e.g. by hiding other options in multiple layers, or using deceptive coloring,

Framing: use of positive and negative wording to influence the user's choice towards the provider-favored option,

Rewards and punishment: rewarding certain choices with (perceived) more or better functionality, or other benefits,

Forced action and timing: increase pressure on users based on timing or urgency indicators, and

Illusion of control: exploiting the fact that users become less cautious if they perceive to have control over their data.

All of these qualify as deceptive design patterns, and most of these are either directly or indirectly violating the GDPR. For a detailed analysis of these patterns with respect to GDPR compliance, see [20].

2.3   Related Work

In [9], Degeling et al. compared changes in privacy policy and cookie consent banners in top 500 websites for each European Union (EU) country before and after the GDPR came into effect. They found that the overall prevalence of privacy policies and consent banners increased from 79.6% before January 2018 to 84.5% in end of May 2018 [9, p. 7] and from 46.1% to 62.1% respectively [9, p. 10]. Additionally, they analyzed different types of consent interfaces regarding their ability to reject requests. From websites with consent banners, a large majority gave users no choice or a confirmation only option, and only a minority allowed for any choice at all [9, p. 11, without exact numbers]. Furthermore, they identified technical problems with the deletion of third party cookies due to same-origin browser policies, misuse of libraries by adding all requests to a "strictly necessary" category and general information deficits of the requests.

In [14], Human et al. introduced an interdisciplinary set of classifiers to compare consent management in web browsers and used it to analyze ADPC and GPC. They found various problems with both samples, including validity of use under the GDPR and insufficient information [14, p. 7], as well as legal challenges regarding standardization and technical challenges regarding the use in non-HTTP settings [14, p. 8]. They conclude that further research and development in this field is warranted and that their classification system can be used to analyze progress thereof [14, p. 8].

In [27], Utz et al. analyzed the use of third party services on websites and their impact on user privacy. They surveyed website creators and maintainers for websites they currently worked on and collected a set of 361 unique websites [27, p. 6]. They found that on average each website contacted 6.2 third party domains, and only 80 websites (about 22%) did not contact any third party domain at all. Identified reasons for the preferred inclusion of third party resources are mainly ease of integration and familiarity with the solution [27, p. 9]. Only about a quarter of the participants indicated that they employed specific measures to protect user's privacy [27, p. 9] and, while they displayed a good understanding of data collection regarding the core functionality of a third party service, they commonly lacked awareness about data collection that happens by just including third party resources, such as Internet Protocol (IP) addresses [27, pp. 10–11].

3   Methodology

For the project described in this paper, a mixed evaluation approach was chosen, consisting of a qualitative and a quantitative part. The qualitative part includes the development of requirements, the analysis of existing consent management systems, the development of an exploratory prototype, and the evaluation of the prototype using the requirements. This is described in the next 3 sections.

The quantitative part compares the prototype to existing systems by measuring and comparing user interaction and deceptive patterns to determine whether and to what degree this prototype approach actually improves consent management for the user. This is described in Sect. 7.

For the first part, the requirements elicitation process started with the identification of the project scope, actors and requirement sources. From these, user stories were produced that highlight different approaches to consent management and helped to identify new requirements. The requirements were updated throughout the research process, and especially after each evaluation step. The resulting requirements are detailed in [20] and listed in the next section.

The evaluation of existing systems was done by a comparative analysis of different samples based on these requirements. They were selected by reviewing proposed and referenced solutions in the analyzed literature (see e.g. [9,14]) and by searching for appropriate terms via Google and GitHub. Outdated standards and user-side programs with repetitive functionality were dismissed, resulting in a remaining total of four samples. These consist of two existing standards (DNT/GPC and TCF), one proposed standard (ADPC) and one user-side program (CookieBlock).

Based on the requirements and findings from this study, we defined a *policy exchange specification*, which we then evaluated based on a prototype implementation (see [20] for details on the policy exchange specification). In short, the policy exchange specification defines a standardized file format that declares intended processing of personal information and supports workflows for consent requests, as well as for objection to and information about the processing. The prototype was realized as a browser extension that implements these workflows and allows the user to react to them via a unified interface. Combined, they provide a measurable advancement over the previously discussed state-of-the-art solutions.

The developed prototype was analyzed qualitatively using the established requirements, and core features were tested with automated unit tests and manual system testing.

4 Requirements

Resulting from the requirements elicitation process discussed above, the following set of requirements was derived (for more details on this process, see [20]).

4.1 Functional Requirements

The system must provide the following functionalities.

FR1: Request categorization: The system must organize consent requests into a defined set of categories. It should limit the number of categories to an amount that does not discourage users from making a conscious choice about each category. As this depends on the specific implementation, no exact number is given.

FR2: Preset configuration: The system must allow the user to configure their preferences regarding the processing of personal data globally and in defined categories so that no further consent requests for the configured categories are required.

FR3: Preset exceptions: The system must allow for site and data processor specific exceptions to to the general category settings.

FR4: Controller notice: The system must inform the controller about the user's acceptance of consent requests and objection to processing. It may inform the controller about rejection of consent requests.

FR5: Third party resources: The system should specify consent requests for the loading of third party media and other web resources.

FR6: First/third party differentiation: The system should differentiate between the processing of personal data through the controller or other processors and allow the user to configure presets accordingly.

FR7: Request-resource relationship: The system should specify all relevant relationships between a request and locally stored data, accessing third party contents or first party contents that impact the processing of personal data.

FR8: Active protection: The system should react to known request-resource relationships and protect the user against unwanted resources.

4.2   Legal Requirements

The system must abide by the following legal requirements.

LR1: Consent for all locally stored data: The system must allow consent requests for all data stored locally on the user's device in accordance to [11, art. 5(3)].

LR2: Affirmative action for consent: The system must request consent in such a way that only affirmative action by the user will result in accepting the request in accordance to [12, art. 4(11)]. Specifically, the system must not interpret pre-selected options as consent or derive such from similar requests.

LR3: Rejection equally easy as consenting: The system must make rejection of a consent request equally easy as accepting it in accordance to [12, art. 4(11)]. Specifically, the system must not require more user interactions with the CMP (such as scrolling, deselecting options, opening a new layer) to reject the request, than it would for accepting it.

LR4: Purpose limitation of requests: The system must allow for individual requests for each purpose of the processing of personal data in accordance to [12, art. 5(1)(b)]. Accepting or rejecting each purpose individually must be possible.

LR5: Proof of consent possible: The system must inform the data controller about the user's choice regarding the acceptance of consent requests so that the controller can use this answer for the demonstration of consent as required by [12, art. 7(1)]. The system may inform the controller about the user's rejection of a consent request.

LR6: Requests in clear and plain language: The system must allow requests in clear and plain language in accordance to [12, art. 7(2)]. It should support standardization of user facing texts so that at a minimum the general purpose of the request becomes clear to the user.

LR7: Withdrawal of consent at any time: The system must allow for consent to be withdrawn at any time in accordance to [12, art. 7(3)]. It must provide a mechanism to inform the controller about the withdrawal in real-time.

LR8: Withdrawal equally easy as consenting: The system must make the withdrawal of consent equally easy as giving it as required by [12, art. 7(3)]. It should provide an obvious way for accessing the CMP again. The CMP must not be hidden behind multiple user interactions or in large amounts of options.

LR9: Required information given: The system must allow consent requests to contain all information required by [12, art. 13–14]. It should provide a specification on providing this information to the user in a structured way that makes it easy for the user to access information relevant for their decision.

LR10: Objection to processing possible: The system must provide a way for users to object to the processing of personal data in cases where previous consent is not required in accordance to [12, art. 21(1)].

LR11: Objection by automated means: The system must provide a way for users to object to the processing of personal data by automated means in accordance to [12, art. 21(5)].

4.3 Interface Requirements

The system must abide by the following UI requirements.

IR1: Uniform interface: The system must use uniform control elements across consent requests and service providers.

IR2: Uniform explanations: The system should use uniform explanations across consent requests and service providers.

IR3: Minimal contents: The system must not show unnecessary information for individual requests or anywhere else in the CMP. Especially, the system must not show associated data processors who do not take part in the current requests.

IR4: No default settings: The system must not use the *default settings* pattern, as discussed in Sect. 2.2. Particularly, the legal requirement on affirmative action for consent must be enforced by the interface.

IR5: No ease: The system must not use the *ease* pattern. Particularly, the legal requirements that Withdrawal and Rejection must be equally easy as consenting must be enforced by the interface.

IR6: No framing: The system must not use the *framing* pattern.

IR7: No rewards and punishments: The system must not use the *rewards and punishments* pattern.

IR8: No forced action and timing: The system must not use the *forced action and timing* pattern.

IR9: No illusion of control: The system must not use the *illusion of control* pattern.

5   Prototype

The prototype of the browser plugin to enforce the developed policy exchange specification was built using the WebExtension API that is supported by all major browsers [17]. It was designed with the following functionality in mind:

- Fulfillment of all of the requirements above,
- Adherence to the policy exchange specification described in [20],
- Reduction of the amount of interactions necessary to achieve the desired responses to data processing requests to a minimum,
- Provision of a freely configurable automation logic that allows for personalized responses to data processing requests,
- Support for a configuration preset that enables automatic privacy by default responses, and
- Adherence to known UI patterns used in the Firefox web browser to provide a familiar experience.

As an exploratory prototype, the implementation demonstrates the capabilities of the specification, but does not claim to be employable for everyday use as a finished product. For this, it was deemed sufficient to implement only a subset of interaction methods to demonstrate its capabilities. The prototype's interfaces were developed to fulfill the identified interface requirements. They are not meant as an ideal solution from the perspective of the average internet user, but to demonstrate capabilities of the specification and possible solutions for concrete problems.

The prototype consists of the following components:

- The *content script* that accompanies each tab, loads and parses the manifest file, receives and responds to Data Processing Item (DPI).
- The *background script* that is responsible for communication between components.
- The *options* page that provides the interface to inspect and manage automation rules.
- The *popup* that provides an interface to review and answer the requests for a website supporting the specification (Fig. 1).

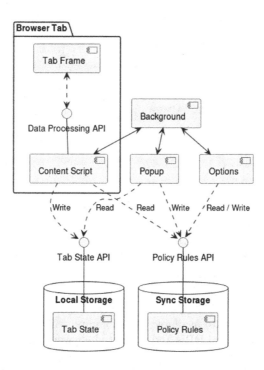

Fig. 1. Browser extension components

Table 1. Comparison of consent technologies *(entries marked with ∗ depend on the CMP vendor (TCF) or the service provider (ADPC, prototype), but it is allowed by the specification. Blank entries are out of scope for the particular sample).*

Requirement	DNT/GPC	TCF	ADPC	CookieBlock	Prototype
Functional					
FR1: (Request categorization)		✓	✗	✓	✓
FR2: (Preset configuration)	✓	✗	✗	✓	✓
FR3: Preset exceptions	✗	✓	✗	✓	✓
FR4: Controller notice	✓	✓	✓	✗	✓
FR5: Third party resources	✓	∗	∗		✓
FR6: First/third party differentiation	✗	✗	∗	✗	✓
FR7: Request-resource relationship		∗	✗		✓
FR8: Active protection	✗	∗	✗	✓	✗
Legal					
ePrivacy Directive					
LR1: Consent for all locally stored data	✓	∗			✓
GDPR					
LR2: Affirmative action for consent		✓	✓	✓	✓
LR3: Rejection equally easy as consenting		∗	✓	✓	✓
LR4: Purpose limitation of requests		✓	∗	✗	✓
LR5: Proof of consent possible		✗	✓		✓
LR6: Requests in clear and plain language		✗	∗	✓	∗
LR7: Withdrawal of consent at any time		✓	✓	✓	✓
LR8: Withdrawal equally easy as consenting		∗	✓	✓	✓
LR9: Required information given		✗	∗		✓
LR10: Objection to processing possible	✓	✓	✓		✓
LR11: Objection by automated means	✓	✗	✓		✓
Interface					
IR1: Uniform interface	✓	✗	✓	✓	✓
IR2: Uniform explanations	✓	✓	✗	✓	✗
IR3: Minimal contents	✓	∗	∗	✓	✓
Deceptive Design Patterns					
IR4: No default settings	✗	∗	✓	✓	✓
IR5: No ease	✓	∗	✓	✓	✓
IR6: No framing	✓	✓	∗	✓	∗
IR7: No rewards and punishments	✓	✓	∗	✓	∗
IR8: No forced action and timing	✓	∗	✓	✓	✓
IR9: No illusion of control	✓	∗	✓	✓	✓

The WebExtension API supports multiple storage locations. Local storage is used to make the tab state available for all components, including the current loaded manifest, additional DPIs and evaluated answers. Sync storage is used to store the custom and site specific decisions permanently, and can be synchronized between browser instances on different devices.

6   Requirements Evaluation

In order to evaluate the fulfillment of requirements, we compared our prototype to the most common state-of-the-art solutions in the market, as described in Sect. 2.1. The overall results in terms of fulfillment of requirements in comparison to these other approaches is shown in Table 1.

On the functional level, the prototype sufficiently satisfies requirements FR1-FR7 directly. Requirement FR8, active protection against unwanted resources, is possible by analyzing the DPI's list of resources and blocking cookies or the loading of other resources, but was not yet implemented in the prototype due to time constraints.

Similarly, all legal requirements are fulfilled satisfactorily, where LR6 depends on the texts provided by the controller, obviously.

Concerning the user interface, most requirements were satisfied (IR1, IR3-5, IR8, IR9) sufficiently by the prototype in each scenario. For IR2, the purpose of processing and list of processed data are not standardized and can be freely formulated by the service provider, hence this one is not satisfied immediately. Similarly, as the specification does not come with uniform explanations, the framing as well as the rewards and punishment patterns are possible, but hampered with the initial presentation of processing categories (making both IR6 and IR7 dependent on the controller).

7   Usability Study

In order to soundly evaluate the usability of our prototype, three evaluation scenarios were developed and evaluated against samples from 10 randomly selected websites (taken from the 500 most popular websites according to [18]). This study was performed in summer 2022.

The following scenarios were chosen:

Scenario 1: The user wants to find the fastest way to close the CMP while rejecting all consent requests ("Reject all").

Scenario 2: The user chose the "accept all" option on the CMP in the past and tries to re-open it again to withdraw all given consent ("Withdraw all").

Scenario 3: The user wants to reject and object to all processing perceived as tracking, advertising, or third party performance analytics ("Reject unnecessary").

We used these scenarios to measure the usability of the specification and prototype in two metrics: the steps necessary to fulfill the scenario and the amount of encountered deceptive design patterns. Steps are any user interactions on a website, specifically clicking on or hovering over UI elements with the mouse cursor, or scrolling the current page. Each scenario starts with the loading of the sample page and is finished after all consent requests were answered according to the scenarios aims and the initial website is displayed in the browser.

The websites used in this study are:

amazon.co.uk An American operating shopping platform, using a custom CMP. Their British site was selected.

bbc.com The British national broadcasting service, using a TCF based CMP with unknown vendor and a second, custom CMP.

cnbc.com An American business news channel, using a TCF based CMP by OneTrust.

elpais.com A Spanish daily newspaper, using a TCF based CMP by Didomi.

google.es An American search engine provider, using a custom CMP. Their Spanish site was selected.

mailchimp.com An American e-mail marketing service, using a cookie specific CMP by OneTrust.

parallels.com An American visualization provider, using a cookie specific CMP by OneTrust.

sciencedaily.com An American science news aggregator, using a TCF based CMP with unknown vendor.

spotify.com A Swedish audio streaming service, using a TCF based CMP with unknown vendor.

thetimes.co.uk A British newspaper, using a TCF based CMP with unknown vendor.

All scenarios were simulated in a new private instance of the Chrome web browser in version 103. In private instances, all local data, such as cookies and browser storage, is deleted after the browser window is closed [13], resulting in a clean environment for each scenario. While it was not tested explicitly in a scenario setting, it is worth noting that the option to accept all requests was available for each sample with a single click.

The amount of necessary user interactions and encountered deceptive patterns to reach the scenario's goals for each website was documented and compiled into a list. These representative measurements were then compared to the scenarios' results for the prototype. This approach is derived from usability metrics testing to track interface improvements as described in [19].

Table 2 shows the results of applying the scenarios to each website. The numbers given under "Prototype" refer to the number of steps necessary when utilizing our browser plugin, and these numbers result from the following usage: Scenario 1 is completed by clicking "Reject All" in the popup. Scenario 2 is completed by opening the popup again, selecting the drop-down menu and clicking "Withdraw all given consent". Scenario 3 is analogous to having the "Reject unnecessary data processing" preset selected and is completed by clicking "Accept All" in the popup for the remaining requests. Each scenario can be completed without inspecting individual requests, thus also preventing deceptive design patterns that could be used in the custom purpose text for each DPI.

It shows that both, the amount of steps, i.e. user actions necessary, and the number of deceptive design patterns encountered to fulfill each scenario, differs widely. The sample *mailchimp.com* has shown the best result by only requiring 7 steps and deploying 2 patterns across all scenarios. In contrast, the samples *bbc.com* and *amazon.co.uk* have shown the worst results by requiring 27

Table 2. Measured steps and Deceptive Design patterns

Sample	Scenario 1 (reject all)		Scenario 2 (withdraw all)		Scenario 3 (reject unnecessary)		Total	
	Steps	Patterns	Steps	Patterns	Steps	Patterns	Steps	Patterns
amazon.co.uk	**6**	**6**	8	**5**	6	**6**	20	**17**
bbc.com	3	2	12	2	12	3	**27**	7
cnbc.com	2	2	7	1	2	2	11	5
elpais.com	2	4	**16**	1	2	4	20	9
google.es	1	2	7	1	4	2	12	5
mailchimp.com	1	1	3	0	3	1	7	2
parallels.com	1	0	7	1	3	1	11	2
sciencedaily.com	1	1	4	1	4	1	9	3
spotify.com	3	3	13	1	5	1	21	5
thetimes.co.uk	2	4	3	1	**13**	5	18	10
Average	2.2	2.5	8.0	1.4	5.4	2.6	15.6	6.5
Prototype	1	0	3	0	1	0	5	0

steps and are deploying 17 patterns respectively. Low step numbers for the first scenario show that it is usually possible to reject all consent in 1 or 2 clicks (in 7 samples), but these numbers more than double when a custom selection is made by the user, as is shown in scenario 3. Choosing the minimum necessary data for the desired functionality (scenario 3) requires an average of 5.4 steps and requires the user to overcome 2.6 deceptive patterns. On average, the sampled websites require more than 3 times as many steps (15.6) as the prototype (5) to fulfill all scenarios while confronting the user with 6.5 patterns. Only one sample in scenario 1 (*parallels.com*) and scenario 2 (*mailchimp.com*) achieved the same results as the prototype. Every other sample required more steps or presented the user with one or more deceptive design patterns.

The substantial difference between *amazon.co.uk* and the other samples in scenario 1 stems from hiding preferences for personalized advertisements on a different settings page than their default "Cookie Preferences" page. The large step numbers in scenario 2 are mainly caused by websites hiding their CMP after it was closed (*amazon.com, bbc.com, google.es, parallels.com*) or requiring users to withdraw their consent individually for multiple items (*cnbc.com, elpais.com, spotify.com*). Notably, the samples *amazon.co.uk* and *bbc.com* are using two instead of one CMP, making it especially difficult for users to answer them according to their preferences.

8   Conclusion

As we have demonstrated, the proposed policy exchange specification in [20] reasonably implements the set of requirements elicited for GDPR-compliant consent management frameworks—in contrast to the most commonly utilized state of the art frameworks. Moreover, the prototype implementation as a browser plugin demonstrates real-world utility of the approach, and the evaluation and usability study results clearly show the advantages of this approach over the state of the art.

The evaluation of the specification and prototype has shown that the proposed system works as expected and can be used to replace web based CMPs reasonably. With its capability of preventing many forms of user manipulation through deceptive design patterns and substantially reducing user interaction across websites, it provides a novel way to effectively answer consent requests in accordance to user preferences. Providing a simple way to reject the processing of personal data for purposes of personalized advertisement and user behavior analysis is presumably desired by many users and would be a great improvement to the current situation from a privacy perspective.

Concerning future work, the completion of the prototype into a fully developed browser plugin has highest priority. Once completed, public release and standardization are intended. On the concept level, it remains to be evaluated more precisely to what extent such a semi-automated consent management system actually can be fully compliant to the GDPR, to what extent it actually is desired by the users, and to what extent website operators are willing to adhere to such a specification. Here, more quantitative studies are planned.

References

1. Announcing Global Privacy Control: Making it Easy for Consumers to Exercise Their Privacy Rights. https://globalprivacycontrol.org/press-release/20201007
2. CookieBlock Browser Extension. https://github.com/dibollinger/CookieBlock
3. Safari 12.1 Release Notes (2019). https://developer.apple.com/tutorials/documentation/safari-release-notes/safari-12_1-release-notes
4. Archive of DNT deliverables - README.md. World Wide Web Consortium (2021). https://github.com/w3c/dnt/blob/master/README.md
5. Autorité de protection des données / Gegevensbeschermingsautoriteit: DOS-2019-01377 (2022). https://www.autoriteprotectiondonnees.be/publications/decision-quant-au-fond-n-21-2022-english.pdf
6. Brignull, H.: Deceptive design - home. https://www.deceptive.design/
7. Soghoian, C.: The history of the do not track header. http://paranoia.dubfire.net/2011/01/history-of-do-not-track-header.html
8. Commission Nationale de l'Informatique et des Libertés (CNIL): Cookies: GOOGLE fined 150 million euros (2022). https://www.cnil.fr/en/cookies-google-fined-150-million-euros
9. Degeling, M., Utz, C., Lentzsch, C., Hosseini, H., Schaub, F., Holz, T.: We value your privacy ... now take some cookies: measuring the GDPR's impact on web privacy. In: Proceedings 2019 Network and Distributed System Security Symposium (2019). https://doi.org/10.14722/ndss.2019.23378
10. European Court of Justice (Grand Chamber): Case C-673/17: Bundesverband der Verbraucherzentralen und Verbraucherverbände - Verbraucherzentrale Bundesverband e.V. v Planet49 GmbH. (2019). https://eur-lex.europa.eu/legal-content/EN/TXT/?uri=CELEX:62017CJ0673
11. European Parliament, Council of the European Union: Directive 2002/58/EC of the European Parliament and of the Council of 12 July 2002 concerning the processing of personal data and the protection of privacy in the electronic communications sector (2002). https://eur-lex.europa.eu/eli/dir/2002/58/oj

12. European Parliament, Council of the European Union: Regulation (EU) 2016/679 of the European Parliarment and of the Council of 27 April 2016 on the protection of natural persons with regard to the processing of personal data and on the free movement of such data, and repealing Directive 95/46/EC (General Data Protection Regulation) (2016). http://data.europa.eu/eli/reg/2016/679/oj
13. Google: How private browsing works in Chrome - Computer. https://support.google.com/chrome/answer/7440301
14. Human, S., et al.: Data protection and consenting communication mechanisms: current open proposals and challenges. In: 2022 IEEE European Symposium on Security and Privacy Workshops (EuroS&PW), Genoa, Italy (2022). https://doi.org/10.1109/EuroSPW55150.2022.00029
15. IAB Europe: Transparency and Consent Framework Policies (2022). https://iabeurope.eu/wp-content/uploads/2021/09/TransparencyConsentFramework-_Policies_version_TCF-v2.0-2021-06-22.3.4.docx.pdf
16. Landgericht München: 3. Zivilkammer: 3 O 17493/20 (2022). https://rewis.io/s/u/zH2/
17. MDN Contributors: Browser Extensions. https://developer.mozilla.org/en-US/docs/Mozilla/Add-ons/WebExtensions
18. Moz Inc: Top 500 Most Popular Websites. https://moz.com/top500
19. Nielsen, J.: Usability metrics: tracking interface improvements. IEEE Softw. **13**(6), 1–2 (1996). https://doi.org/10.1109/MS.1996.8740869
20. Palm, J.: Protecting user privacy by automating consent in web browsers. Master's thesis, Kiel University of Applied Sciences, Kiel, Germany (2022)
21. Berjon, R., Zimmeck, S., Soltani, A., Harbage, D., Snyder, P.: Global privacy control (GPC) proposal (2022). https://globalprivacycontrol.github.io/gpc-spec/
22. Fielding, R.T., Singer, D.: Tracking preference expression (DNT) W3C working group note (2019). https://www.w3.org/TR/tracking-dnt/
23. Human, S., Schrems, M., Toner, A., Gerben, Wagner, B.: How it works | advanced data protection control. https://www.dataprotectioncontrol.org/about/
24. Human, S., Schrems, M., Toner, A., Gerben, Wagner, B.: Advanced data protection control specification (ADPC) unofficial draft (2021). https://www.dataprotectioncontrol.org/spec/
25. The Consumer Council of Norway (Forbrukerraadet): Deceived By Design (2018). https://fil.forbrukerradet.no/wp-content/uploads/2018/06/2018-06-27-deceived-by-design-final.pdf
26. UK Information Commissioner's Office: ICO to call on G7 countries to tackle cookie pop-ups challenge (2021). https://ico.org.uk/about-the-ico/media-centre/news-and-blogs/2021/09/ico-to-call-on-g7-countries-to-tackle-cookie-pop-ups-challenge/
27. Utz, C., Amft, S., Degeling, M., Holz, T., Fahl, S., Schaub, F.: Privacy rarely considered: exploring considerations in the adoption of third-party services by websites (2022)

No Place to Hide: Privacy Exposure in Anti-stalkerware Apps and Support Websites

Philippe Mangeard[✉], Xiufen Yu, Mohammad Mannan, and Amr Youssef

Concordia University, Montreal, QC, Canada
{p_mangea,y_xiufe,mmannan,youssef}@ciise.concordia.ca

Abstract. Stalkerware is malicious software found in mobile devices that monitors and tracks a victim's online and offline activity. This harmful technology has become a growing concern, jeopardizing the security and privacy of millions of victims and fostering stalking and Intimate Partner Violence (IPV). In response to this threat, various solutions have emerged, including anti-stalkerware apps that aim to prevent and detect the use of monitoring apps on a user's device. Organizations dedicated to assisting IPV victims have also enhanced their online presence, offering improved support and easy access to resources and materials. Considering how these tools and support websites handle sensitive personal information of users, it is crucial to assess the privacy risks associated with them. In this paper, we conduct a privacy analysis on 25 anti-stalkerware apps and 323 websites to identify issues such as PII leaks, authentication problems and 3rd-party tracking. Our tests reveal that 14/25 apps and 210/323 websites share user information with 3rd-party services through trackers, cookies or session replay. We also identified 44 domains to which sensitive data is sent, along with 3 services collecting information submitted in forms through session replay.

1 Introduction

A recent report [19] published by the Bureau of Justice Statistics revealed that approximately 1.3% (3.4 million) of all U.S. residents age 16 or older were victims of stalking in 2019. Intimate Partner Violence can take various forms, from physical violence to psychological harm, and can occur in several contexts including households, and long distance relationships. As indicated by a 2022 Kaspersky report [13], there is an undeniable correlation between online and offline abuse; 25% of surveyed people confirmed experience of IPV, and 24% confirmed incidents of cyber-stalking within their relationship. Such experiences can lead to severe emotional distress and physical harm with extreme cases being homicides (15% of the 2020 homicides in Canada were committed by spouses or former intimate partners [2]). Given the serious nature of stalking, its growth in the past few years [3] and its detrimental effects on victims, there are a variety of physical and online resources available to help victims, especially against digital

L. Fritsch et al. (Eds.): NordSec 2023, LNCS 14324, pp. 18–36, 2024.
https://doi.org/10.1007/978-3-031-47748-5_2

tools fostering abusive behaviors like stalkerware. In today's digital era, anti-stalking websites/apps help victims to prevent, identify, report, and respond to stalking incidents.

Anti-viruses or anti-malware apps are generally widely known as they offer a large set of services regarding malware mitigation, but other apps claim to focus on protecting the user from stalkerware specifically, and can be found more easily than other general detection tools when looking for stalking-related keywords on app markets. Victims suspicious that a stalkerware could be installed on their phone might be more likely to download an app claiming to be specifically conceived for this case. Through our work, we aim to understand whether and how user data privacy is ensured in detection apps, as well as their reliability in combating stalkerware. Additionally, we examine websites that provide online resources and support materials to IPV victims. These resources may include hot-line numbers, support center addresses, chat rooms, and general guidelines for various victim situations. Considering that these websites may be accessed by individuals in danger, it is crucial to carefully assess how they handle private user information to prevent exposing sensitive data to unauthorized parties or networks. Our focus is to identify 3rd-party trackers and potential leaks of personally identifiable information (PII), as they pose a threat to the anonymity that should be inherent to these websites.

Numerous studies related to anti-malware apps have been conducted, notably on new malware detection methods and rogue mitigation apps being hidden malware [6,11,15,22]. Other work in spyware detection [16] does not focus on mobile environment. Similarly, privacy issues on websites have been extensively analyzed, with large scale studies of privacy protection on the web, including specific areas like government websites [23] and hospital websites [29]. Han et al. [11] developed a framework specifically designed for stalkerware detection, using active learning on the in-store app description to classify the stalkerware's capabilities. This method is efficient against potentially harmful apps available on the Play Store without the help of a threat list, but is unfit for apps downloaded from other sources. The specific case of anti-stalkerware apps, however, has not been thoroughly studied yet. More specifically, their privacy footprint and effectiveness have not been measured. The same applies for IPV victims helping websites.

In this paper, we perform a privacy and security study on 25 anti-stalkerware Android apps and 323 victim support websites. Out of 25 Android apps, we downloaded 18 from the Google Play Store and 7 from a Chinese website dedicated to downloading Chinese apps.[1] We chose to look at Chinese apps because of their unique app ecosystem, which is arguably the second largest after the Google Play Store one. We divided our analysis into three parts, each addressing a specific challenge: (i) Identifying privacy issues that could jeopardize user anonymity, such as the collection and distribution of Personally Identifiable Information, (ii) Identifying security issues that could enable malicious actors to gather user data or compromise user accounts, and (iii) Understanding the func-

---

[1] http://www.downcc.com.

tionality of these apps and evaluating their effectiveness in detecting stalkerware. Our research contributions and findings encompass the following:

1) We design analysis frameworks to identify privacy related issues in apps and websites, and use them to assess the privacy footprint of 25 anti-stalkerware apps for Android devices and 323 IPV victim support websites. We detected 1206 third-party scripts in IPV victim support websites, 603/1206 (50.0%) of them were identified as known trackers.

2) Our privacy analysis reveals that 14/25 apps transmit data to 3rd-party services, including sensitive information like device ID or GPS location in 4 cases. 13 apps are also found using trackers for advertisements or user experience purposes. We also identify 44 distinct 3rd-party domains that tested apps communicate with during user interaction. 210/323 (65.0%) of victim support websites include 3rd-party trackers. We list 40 unique 3rd-party hosts that gather the user's browsed web pages and the keywords used in the Search functionality. We detect 3 session replay services (Yandex, Hotjar and Clarity) on 17 victim support websites, which apparently collect usage information, user PII and other sensitive data (when a data submission form is available). Our analysis also reveals that the Chinese tracker hm.baidu.com collects users sensitive information on 2 Chinese websites.

3) 2/4 apps incorporating a login feature with account management use dangerous authentication practices, which could lead to account takeover in one of these cases. One anti-stalking website uses HTTP protocol for their online chat service, exposing users' names, emails and messages.

4) We identify one company developing a stalkerware (KidsGuard) and an anti-stalkerware (ClevGuard), promoting both apps on their website and publishing their mitigation tool on the Google Play Store. The anti-stalking tool detects the malicious app but requires a premium subscription to see it. We also observe 3 apps from separate companies using the same detection framework on their back-end infrastructure when scanning the phone.

2   Related Work

Anti-stalkerware Apps. Fassl et al. [10] compared the users' reviews of 2 anti-stalkerware apps to understand users' perception and the apps' capabilities. They also performed reverse engineering to understand their detection features. Their results suggests that app capabilities do not correspond to the users' expectations. In order to detect spyware systems, Qabalin et al. [22] employed machine learning algorithms to create a multi-class classification model for network traffic, which achieved good detection accuracy. Kaur et al. [15] proposed a hybrid approach of description analysis, permission mapping and interface analysis to detect malicious applications in Android. The works mentioned above deal with spyware detection, instead of privacy and security issues related to such detection methods. In addition to academic research, the specific topic of stalkerware also caught the attention of people in the industry. ESET research group published a white paper [25] which analyzed Android stalkerware vulnerabilities. A group of collaborators also compiled all information about known stalkerware apps and built the Stalkerware-indicators [8] GitHub repository to make the detection of spyware easier in both Android and iOS systems. Another detection solution, TinyCheck [14] is currently in development by Kaspersky to assist non-technical individuals to detect stalkerware on their device. Because of its early development stage, the tool currently lacks features thus making it less effective than more standard solutions. However, its main end goal quality would be to allow stalkerware detection without installing or interacting with anything on the compromised phone, thus making it harder for the stalker to notice that the victim is being suspicious.

IPV Victim Support Websites. Eterovic et al. [9] conducted a review of the technologies used by stalkers and technologies used against stalkers. They pointed out the following possible future research directions: improving existing privacy and anti-stalker techniques as well as developing methods to detect stalking behavior on social media and blogging platforms. Samarasinghe et al. [23] performed a privacy measurement on government websites and Android apps. They found numerous commercial trackers on these services; 27% of government Android apps leak sensitive information to 3rd-parties. Senol et al. [24] performed a measurement of data exfiltration from online forms. Their study showed that users' email addresses were collected by 3rd-parties before form submission and without giving consent on both US and EU websites. Similarly, password on 52 websites were found to be leaked to 3rd-party session replay scripts. Yu et al. [29] analyzed the privacy issues on hospital websites and observed that users credentials were sent to session replay services. Ischen et al. [12] investigated the privacy issues of chatbots used on websites. Their results showed that users are more inclined to share personal information with a human-like chatbot rather than with a machine-like chatbot.

Other Relevant Work. Several other recent studies also explored topics related to IPV technologies and victims, although not directly the privacy implications of victim-support apps and websites. For example, Chatterjee et al. [5] studied the intimate partner stalking (IPS) spyware ecosystem, and identified several hundred of such IPS-relevant apps (from app stores and beyond). The authors showed that existing anti-virus and anti-spyware tools mostly fail to identify these dual-use apps as a threat. More recently, Almansoori et al. [1] identified 854 dual-use apps available on the Google Play Store, many of which do not provide English descriptions and cannot be found via English search queries (i.e., available in other languages, which are not as well-monitored by Google as the apps in English). Liu et al. [17] analyzed 14 Android apps outside of Google Play, and studied the mechanisms used for spying. ESET [25] performed a comprehensive security analysis of 86 stalkerware applications, and reported several critical vulnerabilities in the apps that may allow victim data compromise via other third-party attackers.

Beyond stalkerware apps, Stephenson et al. [27] identified how various common IoT devices (32 types in total) including home thermostats, smart speakers, cameras, smart toys, and Bluetooth item trackers, can be abused by IPV attackers. From interviews with 20 IPV victims of such IoT abuse, in another study, Stephenson et al. [26] identified various instances of abuse cases involving such devices. Ceccio et al. [4] evaluated commercial devices and apps that claim to detect such spy IoT devices, and found that these detectors are very ineffective in real-world abuse scenarios.

3   Methodology

3.1   Anti-Stalkerware Apps

We conduct our analysis of solutions against stalkerware apps with three goals in mind: evaluating data privacy and identifying security issues of stalkerware detection tools available for Android, as well as assessing their effectiveness in a realistic context. To collect apps we look through the Google Play Store and web-based Android app databases for keywords such as "anti-stalkerware", "anti-stalking", "stalk detector", as they would be most probably used by a victim looking for such apps. We gather a sum of 25 victim support apps, with 18 from the Google Play Store, and 7 from Chinese app markets. See Fig. 1 for our methodology diagram.

Privacy and Security Analysis. We focus our analysis on 4 distinct vectors through which users' security and privacy could be violated. We chose these specific vectors as they represent a threat to the user's anonymity, which is crucial in the context of IPV and stalkerware detection.

Authentication Mechanisms. In cases where the app offers a login feature and account management functionalities, we identify the mechanisms used for authentication and verify their security. Such methods include username & password validation, session management and authentication tokens. We examine network traffic related to user login to check if credentials are properly secured and sent. We also look at how the user session is kept alive over time and if token replay attacks allow unauthorized users to hijack the user's account.

Personal Identifiable Information (PII) Leaks. Apps can sometimes upload information about the device they are installed on, or the device's user. If such personal data is transmitted without proper encryption, pieces of information such as names, addresses, phone numbers or IMEI number could be extracted by attackers and used to identify, track or impersonate individuals. These leaks can be unintentional or malicious, in cases where the app transmit data to other parties without the consent of the user. Unintentional leaks can be caused by faulty security protocols during uploads, or accidental exposure through error messages or debug logs.

Third-Party Libraries. Through static code analysis, we identify 3rd-party libraries used by anti-stalking apps. Then, by examining the traffic generated by user interactions, we can discern requests related to first-party and 3rd-party libraries. Like with PII leaks, these 3rd-party libraries used by the app could be a threat to the user's privacy by accessing device information or personal data. We identify the presence of libraries and trackers and verify the data they collect through static code analysis and traffic monitoring. We then compare them to a list of well-known trackers (Easylist) for classification.

Insecure Custom Encryption. In addition to potentially insecure implementations of standard encryption channels (like HTTPS), some apps use non-standard protocols, additional channels and encryption layers. We used ThirdEye [21] to identify custom encryption used by the apps and assess their security.

Effectiveness Tests. Proper functioning of anti-stalkerware apps is crucial to the safety of IPV victims, it is thus important to assess the effectiveness of such apps and verify that they are not being wrongfully advertised as "highly effective spyware detectors". We tested the reliability of anti-stalkerware solutions by manually installing each app on a purposefully compromised Android device and verifying whether the app could flag the installed stalkerware. Each app is tested against 10 different free stalkerwares. We utilize only free stalkerware apps for our test to avoid purchasing such apps due to ethical concerns about supporting stalkerware companies. Among the 10 chosen stalkerware apps, *iKeyMonitor* and *AndroidSpy* are treated as special cases, as they provide weekly builds of their app's package. The APK available on their website is recompiled every week with a different package name. This effectiveness test allows us to identify the different detection mechanisms used by anti-stalkerware apps as well as the amount of details they give about detected apps. This includes information such as the permissions required by the detection app to function properly, or flags assigned to potentially dangerous apps giving details to the user (e.g., labelling the detected app as a stalkerware or just a malware). We note that our tests do not include any attempt to trick the anti-stalkerware apps, by changing the stalkerware package names or signature. However, the inclusion of weekly built apps approximates this behaviour.

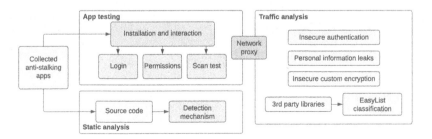

Fig. 1. Privacy analysis methodology of anti-stalkerware apps

3.2 Privacy Analysis of Victim Support Websites

Our methodology comprises three key elements. We collect the URLs of anti-stalking websites through keyword searches such as "anti-stalking", "stalking victims" or "stalking support" in both Google and Baidu search engines. We then use OpenWPM [20] to crawl the websites, which saves crawled information in a SQLite database. We then filter it through Easylist and EasyPrivacy [7] to categorize 3rd-party scripts/cookies and check whether there are session replay services on the websites or not. We manually fill online forms on those websites to identify users' sensitive information leaks; see Fig. 2.

Collecting Victim Support Websites. We start with the resources mentioned on the stopstalkerware website[2] which includes 25 domains in 13 different countries. We then manually extended our victim support website collection by searching for keywords, like, "anti-stalking", "stalking victims", "stalking support" and "stalking help". In total, we collect 323 victim support websites; including 120 from China, 77 from Canada, 34 from the USA, 22 from Europe, 14 from Hong Kong, 13 from the UK, 12 from South America, 7 from Australia, 24 others from Egypt, Turkey, Malaysia, Russia, Ukraine, India and 1 from the UN. This set might not be exhaustive but it includes the most relevant websites that we were able to find online. Note that the collect websites can be either dedicated to anti-stalking or related to anti-stalking, so they can be any websites that provide support or advice to victims, e.g., anti-stalking websites, government websites, university websites, websites for legal help, websites offering shelters to victims or non-profit organizations. Chinese websites are collected on Google and Baidu, however if we search keywords related to anti-stalking or domestic violence for China, most of the results tend to be news reports rather than websites or resources directly related to the topic. We choose Women's Federation's websites[3] for our Chinese dataset. The Women's Federation is a women's rights organization divided in subgroups across China, providing online resources for each city. They offer guidelines for victims of domestic violence or any form of IPV. In total, we collect 108 Women Association websites and 12 online legal support websites in China.

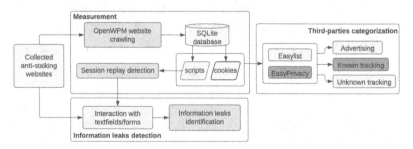

Fig. 2. Privacy analysis methodology of victim support websites

[2] https://stopstalkerware.org/resources.

[3] https://www.bjwomen.gov.cn/, https://hnflw.gov.cn/, https://www.sxwomen.org.cn/, https://www.womenvoice.cn/.

Privacy Measurements. We configure OpenWMP [20] web privacy measurement framework with 10 parallel browser instances in headless mode. We explicitly enable OpenWPM instrumentations for HTTP requests, Javascript, cookies, DNS requests, callbacks and page navigations. We use a physical machine running Ubuntu 22.04 LTS for our measurements in Feb. 2023. A total of 323 victim support websites are crawled using OpenWPM from a North American university campus. We save the crawling result in a SQLite database for further analysis. The saved information contains both stateful (i.e., scripts/cookies), and stateless forms of tracking metrics. We then examine the saved tracking scripts/cookies for 3rd-party domains, i.e., domains of scripts/cookies that do not match the domain of the websites that they are on.

We use filtering rules [7] that block 3rd-parties to identify three categories of 3rd-party domains: ad-related 3rd-parties blocked by EasyList; known trackers blocked by EasyPrivacy; Unknown trackers, or any 3rd-party service that is not blocked by either lists. We manually browse those websites to find pages containing user-filled forms, which include registration/login, contact-us, and search. We tested 220 unique URLs of such web pages on victim support websites.

4 Results

4.1 Results of Victim Support Apps Analysis

Tested apps gathered on the Google Play Store are listed in Table 3. We refer to their common names (or company names) in the following sections. For Chinese apps, we refer to their package names.

Authentication and Session Management. Out of the tested 25 anti-stalkerware apps, only 4 of them allow the user to register an account and login with their credentials (Protectstar AntiSpy and Clevguard on Google Play, as well as cn.lslake.fangjianting and uni.UNI1898B51 on Chinese app markets). Protectstar uses API calls to perform actions, and authenticate as a specific default user when no account is used. This user account called "psapi" is automatically logged into by the app on launch, using seemingly hard-coded credentials to request a session token. This session token appears to be usable for any regular API call, except the ones reserved for getting premium subscription licenses and account management. On the other hand, the Chinese app uni.UNI1898B51 assigns session tokens on login that are not modified nor deleted after logging out. Even though a new token is generated if the user logs in again, an attacker could replay this token even after a user disconnected from their account and call the API on their behalf. The second Chinese app, cn.lslake.fangjianting, allows login through either Tencent QQ or Wechat and thus leaves authentication responsibility to these apps.

Encryption Mechanisms and PII Leaks. Upon manual inspection of the network traffic generated by anti-stalkerware apps, we identified 3 cases where data is being sent to 3rd-party hosts. Com.arcane.incognito shares hardware and OS information with Facebook, data including memory usage, OS version or the phone's model, whether the device is rooted or not, and if it is identified as an emulator. We also noticed the user's email being sent to a first party host (incognitotheapp.zendesk.com), even though the app does not feature user accounts. Skibapps also shares hardware information like the device type, alongside OS type and version, only this time to Adloox. The app spyware.detector.remove.antihacker communicates with Yandex, a Russian ad provider, and sends hardware information along with the google_aid (advertising ID), device-id (IMEI or MEID) and userid.

In addition to these manual checks, we gathered network traffic from all 25 anti-stalkerware apps using ThirdEye [21], and identified 21 additional instances of user/device information being shared to 3rd-party hosts by 14 apps. The data includes 13 cases disclosing the phone model, 4 with OS information, and others sharing cookies or tokens. We identified 3 first-party destination hosts (for Foxbyte Code, Incognito and Cb Innovations), the others being 3rd-party; see Table 1.

Table 1. Information shared per app to 3rd-party services.

App	Item	Destination address
cn.lslake.fangjianting	build	pangolin.snssdk.com (custom encryption)
Foxbyte Code	build	www.foxbytecode.com
com.txjjy.fjtjc	build	pangolin.snssdk.com (custom encryption)
Clevguard	cookie	apipdm.imyfone.club
com.yyyx.fjtws	cookie	fjt.4fqp.com
Incognito Security Solutions	device-email	incognitotheapp.zendesk.com
cn.lslake.fangjianting	model	ulogs.umeng.com
Cb Innovations	model	firebase-settings.crashlytics.com
Certo	model	certo-scan-results-ingestion.azurewebsites.net
Cyber Tor	model	cdn.liftoff-creatives.io
Malloc Privacy	model	firebase-settings.crashlytics.com
Protectstar Antivirus	model	firebase-settings.crashlytics.com
com.txjjy.fjtjc	model	privacy.viterbi-tech.com
com.txjjy.fjtjc	model	ulogs.umeng.com
World Globle	model	adtubeservices.co.in
World Globle	model	cdn.liftoff-creatives.io
com.yyyx.fjtws	model	ulogs.umeng.com
Coolrepairapps	model	yastatic.net
cn.lslake.fangjianting	token	tool.sqcat.cn (custom encryption)
Mahika Developers	token	graph.facebook.com

Table 2. Number of anti-stalkerware apps reaching 3rd-party hosts

Destination host	#App
Google	18
DoubleClick	7
Umeng, app-measurement.com, cdn.liftoff-creatives.io, s0.2mdn.net	3
graph.facebook.com, dt.adsafeprotected.com, fw.adsafeprotected.com, impression-east.liftoff.io, mobile.adsafeprotected.com, my-api.protectstar.com, pangolin.snssdk.com, rr4—sn-gpn9-t0as.gvt1.com, sf3-fe-tos.pglstatp-toutiao.com, static.adsafeprotected.com, toblog.ctobsnssdk.com, api-access.pangolin-sdk-toutiao.com	2
adexp.liftoff.io, adtubeservices.co.in, Android.bugly.qq.com, api.revenuecat.com, app.adjust.com, app.viterbi-tech.com, assets.mintegral.com, click.liftoff.io, cdnjs.cloudflare.com, dsum-sec.casalemedia.com, ec2-18-116-59-188.us-east-2.compute.amazonaws.com, fjt.4fqp.com, ib.adnxs.com, lf6-ad-union-sdk.pglstatp-toutiao.com, maps.wikimedia.org, privacy.viterbi-tech.com, settings.crashlytics.com, sf3-ttcdn-tos.pstatp.com, techcrunch.com, tnc3-bjlgy.snssdk.com, tool.sqcat.cn, us01.rayjump.com, https://www.facebook.com/, https://www.lslake.cn/, yastatic.net	1

Third-Party Libraries. Since all anti-stalkerware apps in our analysis are free, most of them rely on 3rd-party ad providers and trackers to generate income. Others offer premium versions of their app with additional features, but still make the device scan available for free. During the course of our analysis, we kept track of each request being sent to a 3rd-party and compiled all of them into Table 2. We can see the majority of apps use Google APIs (e.g., 11 using Firebase) for various reasons. However, specific apps like spyware.detector.remove.antihacker send data to unique known tracking/advertisement companies like Yandex, adjust or Doubleclick (owned by Google). We also notice the presence of Facebook hosts in 3 apps, 2 of them specifically reaching graph.facebook.com, often used to get data in or out of the platform (in our case, both requests were sending data to Facebook).

Out of 121 separate get requests for .js files found in the apps' network traffic, we found 95 are used by "advertisers" according to EasyList. The other 26 URLs were unknown to the blocklist we used for comparison, but we then manually identified 3 domains associated with Yandex (in spyware.detector.remove.antihacker), and 5 related to a Chinese advertisement platform (pglstatp-toutiao.com, hosted by ByteDance).

Detection Methods and Effectiveness. From the effectiveness tests, we found that 15 out of 25 anti-stalking apps could detect at least one malicious app; see Table 3. Surprisingly, 10 out of 25 anti-stalkerware apps (i.e., 7 Chinese apps and 3 Google Play Store apps) completely failed to detect any of the stakerware apps; these 10 apps are omitted in the result table. Overall, stalkerware apps present in open source threat lists and featured in online web articles were the most detected, with TheTruthSpy being found by 13 out of the 25 mitigation tools and CatWatchful by 11 out of 25. Only 4 tools flagged the weekly build of iKeyMonitor as suspicious, but none identified it as a stalkerware. Similarly, AndroidSpy was flagged in 6 cases, but only once as a malware. 7 tools reported apps with risky permissions, but Malloc Privacy and Incognito needed the stakerware to be entirely configured (not just installed and disabled) to flag it.

10 anti-stalkerware apps required a total filesystem access (READ, WRITE and MANAGE_EXTERNAL_STORAGE permissions) and 6 of them requested media access only (among which 3 of them were requesting total access as well). Notification access is required by 11 apps. This is mostly to send notifications rather than to analyze them, as many apps use them to warn the user that a scan is in progress, or that a problem has been found. These permissions are all required by apps performing application signature checks.

Other anti-stalkerware apps function by monitoring the phone's main tools (e.g., camera, microphone, GPS) and sending a notification when an app uses either of these. One app (World Globle Apps) from the Google Play Store claims to use this "active" detection method, recording camera, microphone and GPS usage and alerting the user if it is accessed by another app. However it raised only 1 flag when one stalkerware was being configured (warning that the camera was being used). This means that this anti-stalkerware needs to be on the phone before the malicious app is installed. Other than that, no alerts were raised, even after multiple hours of phone usage. Unlike Google Play Store apps, all Chinese ones implement this monitoring method and thus require related permissions. Access to camera and microphone was requested by 7 apps, and GPS usage was needed in 6 apps. App usage access was only requested twice. This detection mechanism didn't prove to be the most efficient, even if it detects stalkerware upon installation, as the abuser would be the one seeing the notification.

During our analysis, we noticed that 4 different apps use the exact same backend framework to perform their malware scan (Protectstar Antispy, Protectstar Antivirus, Cb Innovations and Foxbyte Code). We note that only the first two apps are developed by the same company. When scanning the device, these apps send two batches of information to an API responding with a list of identified threats. The first batch contains package names of apps installed on the phone, the second one contains their cryptographic hashes. This means that the actual comparison of installed apps to the malware database is done remotely.

Additionally, we found that the company developing com.clevguard.guard also offers on their website a "parental control" app that is advertised as a remote monitoring tool (in other words, a stalkerware). The anti-stalkerware developed by ClevGuard hides most of its functionalities behind paywalls. The free version displays the number of detected threats but does not give information about flagged apps. We tested this anti-stalkerware against the spyware developed by the same company. Even though the free version prevented us from seeing the name of the flagged app, the fact that it detected one threat confirmed that it was not ignoring it.

Table 3. Anti-stalkerware apps detection results. ●: flagged as stalkerware. ⊘: flagged as malware. ○: flagged because of critical permissions detected. ⊙: flagged because of trackers detected. ◐: Combination of permissions and trackers. ⊖: Flagged as a hidden/fake system app. Empty: not flagged

Company name (package name)	Version	SpyPhoneLabs	Mobilespy	TheTruthSpy	Snoopza	OwnSpy	CatWatchful	iKeyMonitor	MeuSpy	Cerberus	AndroidSpy
Malloc Privacy (com.mallocprivacy.antistalkerfree)	2.49	○	⊙	●	○	○	◐	●	⊙	○	●
World Globle Apps (com.world.globle.mobileantistalker.rs)	1.0.3					○					
Incognito Security Solutions (com.arcane.incognito)	3.0.0.15	●	○	○	○	●			○	○	○
Protectstar antispy (com.protectstar.antispy.android)	5.0.3	●		●	⊘	●	●				
Cb innovations (com.cbinnovations.antispy)	2.0.1	●		●	⊘	●	●			●	⊘
Protectstar antivirus (com.protectstar.antivirus)	1.2.5	⊙		●	⊘	●	●			⊘	●
Certo (com.certo.Android)	2.1.2	●		●		●	●			●	●
Own effect (com.owneffect.spyware.detector)	1.0.4	○									
Foxbyte Code Inc. (com.foxbytecode.spywarescanner)	1.4	⊘		●	⊘	⊘	⊘			⊘	⊘
Coolrepairapps (spyware.detector.remove.antihacker)	5.0.0.1	⊘	⊙	○	⊙	○	○	◐		⊘	○
Skibapps (com.skibapps.antispyforAndroid)	3.43			●	⊘	●	●			⊘	⊖
Lighthouse (net.hobbyapplications.privacyscanner)	1.8.29	●	●	●	○	○	●	○	○	●	○
Mahika Developers (com.whotrackmyphonehmk)	1.0.6	○	○	○	○	○	○	○	○	○	○
Safety Apps (com.spyscanner.spyware.antispywaredetector)	3.0		⊖		○			⊖		○	
Cyber Tor (com.cyber genius.cyber tor)	5.6		⊖		○					○	

4.2   Results of Victim Support Websites Analysis

Third-Party Tracking JavaScript/Cookies.   We found that 169/323 (52.3%) of victim support websites include at least one known 3rd-party tracking script; 31/323 (9.6%) victim support websites use 3rd-party tracking cookies. The proportion of websites with 3rd-party tracking cookies is much lower than websites with 3rd-party tracking scripts. This might be because the EasyList Cookies list we used[4] does not include extensive rules for cookies on Chinese websites.

To better understand 3rd-party scripts/cookies, we grouped them into three categories. We found that 53/1206 (4.4%) 3rd-party scripts were flagged as advertising; 603/1206 (50.0%) 3rd-party scripts were identified as known trackers; 550/1206 (45.6%) were not recognized by Easylist [7], we labelled them as unknown trackers. Similarly, 49/694 (7.1%) 3rd-party cookies were identified as advertising cookies; 266/694 (38.3%) 3rd-party cookies were categorized as known trackers; 379/694 (54.6%) were unknown trackers.

We listed the top-10 domains of tracking scripts and tracking cookies. We can see that the top tracking scripts are googlemanager.com (107/323

---

[4] https://easylist.to/.

(33.1%)), google-analytics (115/323 (35.6%)), Facebook (30/323 (9.3%)) and Baidu (25/323 (7.7%)). We observed Baidu tracker only on Chinese websites; see Fig. 3. Top tracking cookies are addthis.com (10/323 (3.1%)), clarity.com (6/323 (1.9%)), and demdex.net (8/323 (2.5%)). Addthis is used for a free social bookmarking service integrated in websites, making sharing content across social web; clarity.ms is Microsoft session replay service [18]; Sharethis collects data on user behavior advertising and analytics; see Fig. 4.

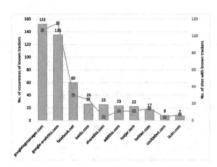

Fig. 3. Top-10 known tracking scripts on victim support sites.

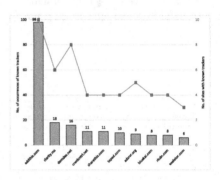

Fig. 4. Top-10 known tracking cookies on victim support sites.

Third-Party Hosts Tracking Users' Operations. We also listed some 3rd-party hosts that track web pages victims browse and the keywords used in the websites search functionality (if available); see Table 4. We found 7 hosts belonging to Google (https://marketingplatform.google.com/about/analytics/, https://www.google.ca/, googleads.g.doubleclick.net, https://www.googleadservices.com/, analytics.google.com, adservice.google.com, and ssl.google-analytics.com); 2 hosts owned by Twitter (syndication.twitter.com, analytics.twitter.com); and 3 Chinese hosts (hm.baidu.com, sp0.baidu.com, analytics.tiktok.com). We observed that hm.baidu.com and sp0.baidu.com only tracks Chinese websites while analytics.tiktok.com tracks 5 Canadian websites along with 1 South Africa website.

Online Chat Tracking. We noticed that the online chat service on three websites (diamondlaw.ca, lawyersuae.com, dubaipolice.gov.ae) tracked users. Diamondlaw.ca is a law firm with physical offices in Canadian provinces including British Columbia, Ontario and Alberta, which offers legal services related to stalking. The website employed chat-api.intaker.com for customer online chat service. However, the customer online chat service tracks the user's navigation through the website. Similarly, lawyersuae.com and dubaipolice.gov.ae, both UAE websites, use online chat services tracking the victims' page navigation (on their websites). Lawyersuae.com uses gateway.botstar.com for online chat while dubaipolice.gov.ae used api.livechatinc.com.

Table 4. Third-party hosts tracking users' operations in more than 10 different websites

Third-party Host	#Sites
https://marketingplatform.google.com/about/analytics/	130
https://www.google.ca/	52
googleads.g.doubleclick.net	42
https://www.facebook.com/	37
https://www.googleadservices.com/	26
hm.baidu.com	25
https://www.youtube.com/	23
analytics.google.com	15
syndication.twitter.com	13
m.addthis.com	11
px.ads.linkedin.com	11

We found that two Chinese websites for online legal support (user.maxlaw.cn and https://www.66law.cn/) leak users' information to hm.baidu.com. Both websites claim that users do not need to worry about the information they provide, because all data is encrypted, so they can provide as much detailed information as possible for online legal support. Although user's sensitive data is encrypted, it is sent to hm.baidu.com without the user's consent through a tracking pixel with the url *hm.baidu.com/hm.gif*. The script from s.canddi.io tracks the functionalities of mailing list subscription and contact on https://www.suzylamplugh.org/; as a result, victims' first name, last name, email, message title and message were disclosed to s.canddi.io. The website https://www.workspacesrespond.org/ provides help to victims of domestic and sexual violence in the USA. All the private information filled in the contact web page (e.g., first/last name, email, organization, subject, message) is sent to the workspacesrespond server as well as to another non-profit organization (go.futurewithoutviolence.org), apparently another anti-violence organization; however, this information sharing is not visible to users.

Expiration of Tracking Cookies. We examined the validity duration of top-10 tracking cookies, and found that clarity.ms set cookies on 4 victim support websites were valid for more than 1000 years. Known tracking cookies that expire within 1 to 5 years were addthis.com (90), clarity.ms (4), sharethis.com (8) and adsrvr.org (9); see Table 5.

Session Replay. Session replay services are used to replay a visitor's session on the browser, to get a deeper understanding of a user's browsing experience; information replayed includes user interactions on a website such as typed inputs, mouse movements, clicks, browsed pages, tapping and scrolling events. During

Table 5. The top-10 known tracking cookies and their expiry periods (m = month, y = year).

Tracker	Cookie Expiry Duration				
	#Sites	<1m	1m-1y	1y-5y	>1000y
addthis.com	98		8	90	
clarity.ms	18	6	4	4	4
demdex.net	16		16		
crwdcntrl.net	11		11		
sharethis.com	11	3		8	
tapad.com	10		10		
adsrvr.org	9			9	
bluekai.com	8		8		
rlcdn.com	8		8		
exelator.com	6		6		

this process, users' sensitive information can be exposed to 3rd-party servers that host session replay scripts. We identified 3 session replay services in the analyzed 323 victim support websites: Clarity on 6 websites (Canada (4), UAE (1), USA (1)), Hotjar on 9 websites (Canada (4), USA (3), South-Africa (1), UK (2), India (1)) and Yandex on 2 in Russia; see Table 7.

We found that 2 victim support websites in Russia expose victims' information to Yandex [28] session replay servers. One of the websites is wcons.net (i.e., the Consortium of Women's Non-Governmental Associations website), which provides legal support for victims of domestic violence in Russia. Users are asked to fill an online form for support; all the victims' sensitive information in the form is sent to Yandex, including, name, email address, phone number, year of birth, location, the presence of minor children, reasons to contact, who inflicts violence as well as a custom message. The other website, i.e., nasiliu.net provides legal assistance, psychological help and support to victims. We noticed that when victims use the website's search engine, searched keywords are collected by Yandex. Users' names and email addresses are also leaked through money donations; see Table 6. Note that safehorizon.org includes two session replay services: Hotjar and Clarity. Clarity initializes scripts from https://www.clarity.ms/eus-sc/s/0.7.2/clarity.js to track users' interactions with the DOM elements on a web page and the collected data is uploaded to o.clarity.ms. Hotjar uses web sockets to transfer collected data to ws4.hotjar.com. Both session replay services collect elements and web pages that users interacted with, as well as mouse events.

HTTP Plaintext Traffic. We observed that 4 websites use HTTP protocol for their core functions; these include connectnetwork.ca https://www.tandemlaw.ca/, https://www.alberta.ca/ and https://www.dfac.ae/. On https://www.

Table 6. Sensitive information leaks in victim support websites

Website	Country	Leaked data	Feature	Destination	Cause
wcons.net	Russia	Name, email address, birthyear, phone number, location, minor children presence, custom message, name of the abuser	Report a crime	mc.yandex.ru	Session Replay
		Keywords	Search		
nasiliu.net					
		Name	Donate		
lawyersuae.com	UAE	Keywords	Search	botstar.com	Online Chat
dubaipolice.gov.ae				api.livechatinc.com	
diamondlaw.ca	Canada			chat-api.intaker.com	
suzylamplugh.org	UK	Name, email address	User Sign-in	s.canddi.io	Tracker
		Name, email address, phone number, job title, company name, custom message	Contact		
workplacesrespond.org	USA	Name, email address, company name, custom message	Contact	go.futurewithoutviolence.org	
www.maxlaw.cn	China	Chat messages	Online Chat	hm.baidu.com	
www.66law.cn				hm.baidu.com	
www.dfac.ae	UAE	Name, email address, chat messages		www.chat.dfwac.ae	HTTP
www.alberta.ca	Canada	Name, email address, location, gender, agegroup	Online Chat sign-in	m2.icarol.com	

Table 7. Session replay services (SRS) on victim support websites.

SRS	Websites
Yandex	wcons.net (Russia), nasiliu.net(Russia)
Hotjar	getsafeonline.org (USA), safehorizon.org (USA), onlineharassmentfieldmanual.pen.org (USA), domesticshelters.org(USA, CAN), canadianwomen.org (CAN), member.psychologytoday.com (USA), lawrato.com (India), mysupportspace.org.uk (UK), legalwise.co.za (South-Africa)
Clarity	legaladviceme.com (UAE), getsafeonline.org (USA), diamondlaw.ca (CAN) calgarydefence.com (CAN), ualberta.ca (CAN), lawcentralalberta.ca (CAN)

alberta.ca/, users are required to fill in their email, first and last name, location data, gender and age group to create an online chat server account. However, the chat registration (provided by the 3rd-party domain m2.icarol.com), use HTTP, exposing all provided information to any on-path attacker. The online chat service (https://www.chat.dfwac.ae/Customer/Start) for the Dubai Foundation for Women and Children (DFWAC) used the HTTP protocol. Victims are required to enter name, email and questions before sending a chat request. Victims sensitive information (e.g., name, email, and chat logs) is leaked because of the use of HTTP. We found that 72/120 (60.0%) of websites in China only support HTTP protocol, they however do not handle sensitive information (no forms to fill).

The Use of Third-Party Services for Core Functionality. We observed two websites (safehorizon.org and rainn.org) in the USA using a 3rd-party service for the sign-up functionality. Safehorizon.org utilizes go.pardot.com for this functionality, consequently sending user's email address, first and last name to 3rd-party servers. We noticed that three websites in Canada (canadianlabour.ca, iheartmob.org and https://www.kruselaw.ca/) use a 3rd-party service during user sign-up, leading to victims' sensitive information being sent to the 3rd-party domain, instead of the website's domain. Consequently, on canadianlabour.ca, victims' first and last name, email address, phone number and location data are sent to actionnetwork.org; their first and last name, email address and country are also sent to the same address when asking for support on iheartmob.org.

5   Conclusion

The limited number of efficient anti-stalkerware app makes it difficult for users to rely on such tools. In addition, based on our experiments, more than half of the analyzed apps share sensitive data to other parties and use tracking services for advertisement. Similarly, 65% of the websites dedicated to IPV victim support use 3rd-party trackers, with 8% of them collecting PII. It should be noted, however, that using only free stalkerware apps for our tests might not give a thorough picture of anti-stalkerware effectiveness, as premium stalkerware apps could use more advanced techniques to evade detection. Our analysis provides a lower bound of the help these solutions can provide, and makes it easy to extrapolate to a larger testing set the effectiveness of apps that fail to detect free stalkerware. Testing such paid apps would provide more insights into this problem. Detection tools providers and developers should be aware of the data gathered by 3rd-party libraries and avoid using them for their apps and/or websites; it is crucial to ensure that no PII is used or collected by these apps. Improving the detection rate should also be a priority. We recommend using multiple trusted, up-to-date package name databases (like Echap's repository of stalkerware indicators [8]) and relying more on local analysis rather than cloud-based ones. Similarly, anti-stalkerware websites' developers should ensure that 3rd-party scripts they use are not performing any user tracking. As victims' data is highly sensitive, these support websites should avoid using any tracking services, like session replay services. Finally, we hope that our work provides insight for developers to improve these platforms and make them as safe and useful as possible for IPV victims in need of help.

Acknowledgements. This research was funded by the Office of the Privacy Commissioner of Canada (OPC), we thank them for their trust and support.

References

1. Almansoor, M., Gallardo, A., Poveda, J., Ahmed, A., Chatterjee, R.: A global survey of android dual-use applications used in intimate partner surveillance apps. In: Proceedings on Privacy Enhancing Technologies Symposium, Lausanne, Switzerland (2022)
2. Armstrong, A., Jaffray, B.: Homicide in Canada. Canadian Centre for Justice Statistics, Juristat (2020)
3. Bracewell, K., Hargreaves, P., Stanley, N.: The consequences of the covid-19 lockdown on stalking victimisation. J. Family Viol. 1–7 (2020)
4. Ceccio, R., Stephenson, S., Chadha, V., Huang, D.Y., Chatterjee, R.: Sneaky spy devices and defective detectors: the ecosystem of intimate partner surveillance with covert devices. In: USENIX Security Symposium, Anaheim, CA, USA (2023)
5. Chatterjee, R., et al.: The spyware used in intimate partner violence. In: 2018 IEEE Symposium on Security and Privacy (SP), pp. 441–458. IEEE (2018)
6. Conti, M., Rigoni, G., Toffalini, F.: Asaint: a spy app identification system based on network traffic. In: Proceedings of ARES 2020, pp. 1–8 (2020)
7. EasyList. EasyList 2023 (2023). https://easylist.to
8. Echap. Stalkerware indicators of compromise (2022). https://github.com/AssoEchap/stalkerware-indicators
9. Eterovic-Soric, B., Choo, K.-K.R., Ashman, H., Mubarak, S.: Stalking the stalkers-detecting and deterring stalking behaviours using technology: a review. Comput. Secur. **70**, 278–289 (2017)
10. Fassl, M., Anell, S., Houy, S., Lindorfer, M., Krombholz, K.: Comparing user perceptions of anti-stalkerware apps with the technical reality. In: SOUPS 2022, pp. 135–154 (2022)
11. Han, Y., Roundy, K.A., Tamersoy, A.: Towards stalkerware detection with precise warnings. In: Annual Computer Security Applications Conference, pp. 957–969 (2021)
12. Ischen, C., Araujo, T., Voorveld, H., van Noort, G., Smit, E.: Privacy concerns in chatbot interactions. In: Følstad, A., et al. (eds.) CONVERSATIONS 2019. LNCS, vol. 11970, pp. 34–48. Springer, Cham (2020). https://doi.org/10.1007/978-3-030-39540-7_3
13. Kaspersky. New kaspersky stalkerware report confirms the link between online and offline violence (2022). https://www.kaspersky.com/about/press-releases/2022_new-kaspersky-stalkerware-report-confirms-the-link-between-online-and-offline-violence
14. KasperskyLab. Tinycheck (2021). https://github.com/KasperskyLab/TinyCheck
15. Kaur, P., Sharma, S.: Spyware detection in android using hybridization of description analysis, permission mapping and interface analysis. Procedia Comput. Sci. **46**, 794–803 (2015)
16. Kirda, E., Kruegel, C., Banks, G., Vigna, G., Kemmerer, R.: Behavior-based spyware detection. In: Usenix Security Symposium, p. 694 (2006)
17. Liu, E., et al.: No privacy among spies: assessing the functionality and insecurity of consumer android spyware apps. Proc. Priv. Enhanc. Technol. **1**, 1–18 (2023)
18. Microsoft Clarity. Microsoft clarity (2023). https://clarity.microsoft.com

19. B. of Justice Statistics. Stalking victimization (2019). https://bjs.ojp.gov/library/publications/stalking-victimization-2019
20. OpenWPM. OpenWPM (2023). https://github.com/openwpm/OpenWPM
21. Pourali, S., Samarasinghe, N., Mannan, M.: Hidden in plain sight: exploring encrypted channels in android apps. In: Proceedings of the 2022 ACM SIGSAC CCS, pp. 2445–2458 (2022)
22. Qabalin, M.K., Naser, M., Alkasassbeh, M.: Android spyware detection using machine learning: a novel dataset. Sensors **22**(15), 5765 (2022)
23. Samarasinghe, N., Adhikari, A., Mannan, M., Youssef, A.: Et tu, brute? privacy analysis of government websites and mobile apps. In: Proceedings of the ACM Web Conference 2022, pp. 564–575 (2022)
24. Senol, A., Acar, G., Humbert, M., Borgesius, F.Z.: Leaky forms: a study of email and password exfiltration before form submission. In: USENIX Security Symposium, pp. 1813–1830 (2022)
25. Stefanko, L.: Android stalkerware vulnerabilities (2021). https://www.welivesecurity.com/wp-content/uploads/2021/05/eset_android_stalkerware.pdf
26. Stephenson, S., Almansoori, M., Emami-Naeini, P., Chatterjee, R.: "it's the equivalent of feeling like you're in jail": lessons from firsthand and secondhand accounts of iot-enabled intimate partner abuse. In: USENIX Security Symposium, Anaheim, CA, USA (2023)
27. Stephenson, S., Almansoori, M., Emami-Naeini, P., Huang, D.Y., Chatterjee, R.: Abuse vectors: a framework for conceptualizing IoT-enabled interpersonal abuse. In: USENIX Security Symposium, Anaheim, CA, USA (2023)
28. Yandex. Yandex (2023). https://metrica.yandex.com/about
29. Yu, X., Samarasinghe, N., Mannan, M., Youssef, A.: Got sick and tracked: privacy analysis of hospital websites. In: 2022 IEEE EuroS&PW, pp. 278–286. IEEE (2022)

From Whistle to Echo: Data Leaks in Web-Based Whistleblowing Channels

Esko Vuorinen, Panu Puhtila, Sampsa Rauti[(✉)], and Ville Leppänen

University of Turku, 20014 Turku, Finland
{etvuor,papuht,sjprau,ville.leppanen}@utu.fi

Abstract. Whistleblowing refers to reporting misconduct to responsible authorities. With accelerating digitalization and the European Union's new whistleblower directive, large numbers of whistleblowing channels and company web pages that act as gateways to these services have been deployed. At the same time, on modern websites rife with third-party services such as web analytics, this development introduces privacy challenges. In the current study, we analyze websites of 15 Finnish companies and the whistleblowing services they employ in order to assess whether they inadvertently reveal identifying personal data to the employee's company and third parties. Results indicate there is reason for serious concern about the privacy of whistleblowers who report wrongdoings online.

Keywords: Whistleblowing · reporting channels · data leaks · third-party services · online privacy

1 Introduction

Whistleblowing is the act of disclosing illegal, unethical, or unsafe activities within an organization to the parties that are able to take corrective action [7,16]. Whistleblowers play an important part in exposing wrongdoing, fraud, corruption, as well as other types of misconduct in an organization or company. A whistleblower is typically an employee, former employee, or insider who discloses wrongdoing or misconduct that may involve violations of laws or regulations.

Whistleblowing is recognized as a pivotal mechanism for exposing wrongdoing within organizations, promoting transparency and protecting public interest [22]. In Finland, for instance, the Whistleblower Act has been enacted to implement the European Union's whistleblower directive. Private sector employers that regularly employ at least 250 employees and public sector employers with at least 50 employees now have the obligation to maintain a confidential internal whistleblowing channel[1]. Moreover, a new centralized reporting channel has been adopted among authorities[2].

---

[1] https://www.twobirds.com/en/trending-topics/the-eu-whistleblowing-directive/implementation-status/finland.

[2] https://oikeuskansleri.fi/en/centralised-external-reporting-channel.

L. Fritsch et al. (Eds.): NordSec 2023, LNCS 14324, pp. 37–53, 2024.
https://doi.org/10.1007/978-3-031-47748-5_3

Data protection and confidentiality are very important when whistleblowers use reporting channels [3, 28]. As modern websites are rife with various embedded third-party services such as web analytics tools, it is fair to ask whether these third parties are also present in the context of whistleblowing channels and whether the online privacy of whistleblowers is adequately safeguarded. At the same time, the organization or the company itself should not be able to identify the whistleblowers. After all, organizations may perceive whistleblowers as a potential threat [14]. No identifying personal data on users of these reporting channels should leak to the company or any third parties.

This study explores the privacy implications of third-party services that may be present in either 1) the company web page leading to the whistleblowing channel, or 2) the whistleblowing channel itself. We study the websites of 15 large Finnish companies and their whistleblowing channels. We analyze the network traffic to see whether identifying personal data and data revealing the intent to use the whistleblowing services is leaked to third parties or to the company that is being reported. Additionally, we also analyze the dark patterns on the websites' cookie notices and assess the transparency of privacy policies on the company websites. By examining these aspects, we shed light on the potential risks whistleblowers face when using reporting channels and offer insights into safeguarding their privacy.

To the best of our understanding, no actual peer-reviewed research on the subject of third-party data leaks in whistleblowing services has thus far been published. However, there have been master's level theses that touch upon this topic. Lehtola [18] presents a case study on a whistleblowing web application and analyzes its network traffic to ensure there are no third-party data leaks. Uddholm [26] also discusses the threat of third parties in whistleblowing services and proposes an approach based on cryptography to protect the submission sent by whistleblowers. The scarcity of studies on this topic is most likely due to the fact that the regulations mandating corporations to have these kinds of channels are quite recent. Our analysis of third-party data leaks in company pages leading to reporting channels as well as in actual whistleblowing services fills this research gap.

The remainder of the paper is structured as follows. Section 2 explains how the analyzed company websites were selected and outlines the used study methods. Section 3 presents the results of the study. Section 4 summarizes the key findings of the study and discusses the potential consequences of data leaks in whistleblowing channels. From the viewpoint of software engineering, the section also explores ways to ensure personal data is not leaked to third-party services. Finally, Sect. 5 concludes the paper.

2 Method and Study Setting

In this study, we assess the privacy of the whistleblowing services of 15 Finnish companies. In each case, this includes both the page on the company website linking to the whistleblowing service and the reporting channel itself. The company websites were selected to be studied from a list of largest corporations in

Finland maintained by Asiakastieto[3], a Finnish company providing information on businesses. A couple of companies chosen from the list were omitted from the study, as they did not appear to have whistleblowing channels that could be openly accessed by non-employees. In the current study, we will refer to the selected companies anonymously using labels such as Corporation 1.

To assess the privacy of the selected company websites and analyze potential data leaks to the company and third-party services, a short testing sequence was run on the company websites. First, all cookies and data collection were consented to on the studied websites. We then navigated from the landing page of the web service to the page leading to the web-based whistleblowing channel. The reporting channel was then opened and information was filled in to see whether there were any leaks of reported data. However, the reporting process was aborted before submitting any information.

Recording of the network traffic was carried out with Google Chrome's Developer Tools. Recording was performed with the cache disabled to prevent distortion of test results due to previously cached data. The network traffic recorded during this testing sequence was saved in log files for further review. As the log files were analyzed, we extracted two types of personal data from web requests:

- *Identifying information*: Personal data that can be used to identify the visitor of the website, such as IP address or other user or device specific identifiers.
- *Contextual information*: Data containing sensitive contextual information, for instance data showing that the user has visited a page leading to the whistleblowing service or clicked a link leading to this service. Obviously, the whistleblowing service itself leaking the information about a visitor using it (e.g. the URL of the service) is also highly sensitive data.

We also assessed the dark patterns present in cookie consent banners of the studied websites. The presence of these deceptive design practices that aim to persuade the user to give their consent to third-party cookies and data collection can have adverse effects for the privacy of the whistleblowing process. To evaluate dark patterns, we used selected dark pattern descriptions from "Report of the work undertaken by the Cookie Banner Taskforce" by European Data Protection Board[4]. The document outlines various poor practices in cookie banner design that are considered as dark patterns. In this study, we look at the four specific dark patterns: 1) missing rejection button on the first layer of the cookie banner, 2) pre-ticked selection boxes when choosing to give consent, 3) deceptive button colors, and 4) deceptive button contrasts. These dark pattern types were singled out for study due to their simplicity in analysis and the absence of significant ambiguity. Moreover, we also observed whether the studied websites completely failed to ask for consent to use cookies.

In addition to network traffic analysis and assessment of dark patterns, the privacy policies of the studied websites were also looked into. These documents

---

[3] https://www.asiakastieto.fi/yritykset/top-listat.

[4] https://edpb.europa.eu/our-work-tools/our-documents/other/report-work-undertaken-cookie-banner-taskforce_en.

were perused to see whether sharing of data to third parties was adequately reported and transparency of these documents was gauged by examining how well their contents corresponded to the actual network traffic. Specifically, we wanted to see whether there were any mentions about personal data related to the use of whistleblowing services.

Finally, as "personal data" is a central concept in this paper, this term needs to be briefly defined. We adopt the definition given in GDPR and also used by the Finnish Office of the Data Protection Ombudsman. Therefore, *personal data* is "all data related to an identified or identifiable person"[5] Following this definition, technical information such as IP addresses, device identifiers, accurate location data or any data point that identifies the user of the services counts as personal data. It must also be noted that while many technical details such as device type or screen resolution alone are not sufficient to identify someone, a combination of these data items can be used for identification. Therefore, they are also included in the definition of personal data.

3   Results

Our results indicate several and severe flaws in the privacy of the company websites, specifically sub-pages which link to whistleblowing services. Most strikingly, we discovered one whistleblowing channel that actually leaked sensitive data to a third party, but in addition to this, a large majority of the pages which were used to access these services from the corporation websites did also leak data. In total, 13 out of the 15 corporations (86.7%) leaked the data about clicking the link leading to the whistleblowing service to a third-party actor, while 14 websites (93.3%) revealed that the user was at least interested in the whistleblowing (as they either visited the whistleblowing-themed page or clicked the link to a reporting channel). Some of the corporations leaked this information to more than one of the third parties involved. Also, on 2 websites (13.3%), the link clicks also leaked internally to the corporation in question. In what follows, we will delve deeper into these findings.

3.1   Types of Data Leaks

We discovered there were three main types of contextual data leaks on the researched corporation websites:

- *The visited URL leaks.* In this first leak type, the address of the current page leaks. This information, combined with identifying details on the user, can be used to deduce that the user is interested in the whistleblowing channel, provided that the page is dedicated to the whistleblowing service (e.g. a corporation page discussing the whistleblowing process and containing a link to a whistleblowing channel).

---

[5] See the definitions at https://gdpr.eu/eu-gdpr-personal-data/ and https://tietosuoja.fi/en/what-is-personal-data.

- *The link click leaks.* The second leak type discloses the fact that the user has clicked on a specific link leading to a whistleblowing channel. Therefore, the leak gives a definite confirmation that the user has accessed the whistleblowing channel and likely intends to file a report.
- *The link address leaks.* In the third leak type, the destination address of the clicked link is leaked, which usually directly contains the name of the used whistleblowing service.

As we will see in this section, in most cases these leaks are relevant in the context of third-party services that receive the data. These leaks take place on a corporation page linking to a whistleblowing service. The leaks can also happen internally when the information leaks to the corporation running the website. In the case of the first leak type, however, it is quite self-evident that the corporation can always track visited pages on its own websites, even without using third-party analytics services. The third leak type, link address leak, is not that relevant internally either, because the company knows the whistleblowing service it uses. The second type, however, is highly relevant: if the company gets to know who clicks the link to access the whistleblowing service, the employee reporting the misconduct may be in serious trouble. Finally, aside from the company website, the visited URL can also leak inside a whistleblowing channel along with identifying technical details on the user. This data leak type is also addressed in our study.

3.2   Third Parties and Contextual Data Leaks

The total number of different third-party analytics services identified in the study was as high as 31. This gives us the average of 2.1 data collection tools per corporation, but it should be noted that the majority of the corporations used more than 3, with one corporation deploying even as much as 11 different analytics services on their website. However, there was a significant degree of overlap among the tools used, with Google, for instance, being present in the vast majority of the inspected websites.

Figure 1 shows the third-party tools that were found to leak personal data outside the company domain. It also displays the total number of three types of third-party data leaks we discussed in Sect. 3.1: 1) leaks of visited URLs, 2) link click leaks, and 3) link URL leaks. Figure 2 provides a different overview of these data leak types: it shows the numbers of the data leaks per corporation and data leak type.

Among the found analytics services were the globally largest analytics providers such as Google Analytics and Facebook, but also smaller and less well-known services such as 2o7.net (used by Adobe Systems for their web analytics and tracking services). There was exactly one company (Corporation 10) whose website did not leak any data belonging to the three categories above. In addition, there was one other company (Corporation 3) that did not leak the link click to third parties. In other words, 13 corporation websites leaked link

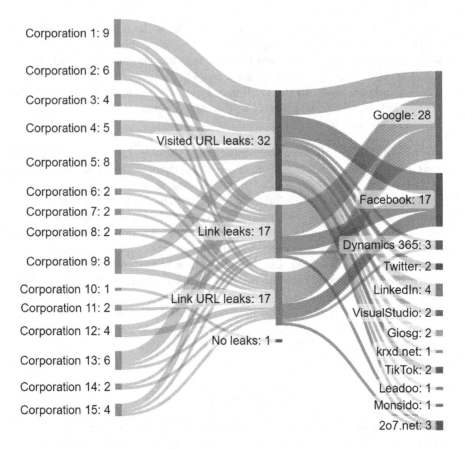

Fig. 1. Corporations, data leak types, and third parties data leaked to. On the left, the figure shows number of data leaks for each corporation. The sums of three different data leak types are presented in the middle. Finally, the right side shows the number of data leaks going to each third party.

clicks to at least one third party. There were also five company websites (Corporations 6, 7, 8, 11, 12) that did not leak information about visiting the page to access the whistleblowing service, but still leaked the critical information about clicking the link and the address of the whistleblowing service.

As shown by Fig. 1, Google Analytics was the most common third-party service that was used, being present in 14 out of 15 (93.3%) of the studied websites. It alone accounted for 28 out of 66 (42.42%) of all data leaks found in this study, when all three categories of data leaks are accounted for, which demonstrates the extensive reach of Google as an operator in the field of data collection in general. The second largest source of leaks was Facebook (Meta), which accounted for 15 out of 66 (22.73%) of all leaks detected, which is not surprising either, as Facebook is also a major actor in data collection industry. All the rest of the data analytics tools that leaked data outside corporation domains

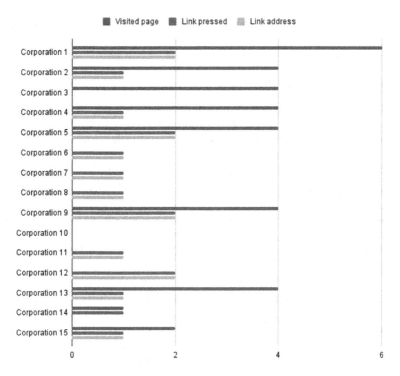

Fig. 2. Corporations with numbers of different types of data leaks.

had shares ranging from 1 (1.4%) to 4 (6.06%) out of 66, with the largest among these being LinkedIn (4 leaks), followed closely by Dynamics 365/Microsoft and 2o7.net (3 leaks each).

What is important to consider is that while the study found 31 analytics tools in total among the 15 corporations inspected, only 38% of them leaked contextual data that was of interest in this study, suggesting that there are ways to deploy these tools with relative safety in regards to user privacy, and that there are tools which are safer than others in this aspect. Likewise, in several instances it was found that the same tool leaked data from one corporation, but not the other, which implies that the other major culprit in the data leakages we found are the specific configurations of these services.

It is worth noting that the absolute number of URL leakages was higher than just those we have focused on in this study. For example, while some websites leaked the URL of a page linking to the whistleblowing service, the URL was often too generic to indicate that the user is interested in using the whistleblowing channel. For instance, www.company.fi/contact is too generic and includes other topics and functionalities in addition to the link to a whistleblowing channel. On the other hand, URLs such as www.company.fi/whistleblowing quite clearly indicates that the page is about whistleblowing. Therefore, generic pages such as "contact information" pages were not counted as leaked URLs as it is impossible to deduce the user's intention to use whistleblowing service based on the URL or the page contents.

3.3   Identifying Personal Data

While this research has focused mainly on whether the current URL, clicking of the whistleblowing service link and the link URL were leaked to third parties, it bears mentioning that all of the surveyed tools did leak personal data that can be used for the identification of the user. These data points included cid numbers (client ID, a unique identifier for the combination of a device and browser), IP address, device screen size, operating system, and other technical details. While some of these items (such as screen size and operating system) in themselves cannot be used to definitely pinpoint any single person, other details such as cid numbers and IP addresses usually can. When combined, all these details can be used to build a digital fingerprint of the user, which can then be used to identify the user using the service.

Recital 26 of the GDPR states that when determining if an individual can be identified, "account should be taken of all the means reasonably likely"[6] to lead to an individual's direct or indirect identification. This includes assessing factors such as the costs and time involved in identifying a person, as well as the existing technological capabilities and advancements. For instance, IP addresses can be considered personal data in accordance with the decision of the Court of Justice of the European Union in the Breyer case [1,5], even in the cases where additional information must be obtained from a third party, such as a internet service provider, to identify a specific individual.

Together, this identifying information and the contextual information such as link click event tell a third-party service – and in some cases to the company – who has potentially used the whistleblowing service. Especially technology giants like Google and Facebook are very likely to have a good understanding about whom certain IP addresses and device identifiers belong to. For example, the user just has to log into their services and a connection between IP address and person can be made.

However, the companies we have studied may be able to make this connection as well, even without obtaining information from a third party. For instance, this may be the case if the whistleblowing service is accessed from a corporation-owned and issued (work laptops, smartphones and tablets) device, especially if the whistleblowing channel is accessed from a corporation network. Obviously, corporations should never be able to learn the identities of whistleblowers.

---

[6] https://www.privacy-regulation.eu/en/recital-26-GDPR.htm.

3.4 Leaky Whistleblowing Service

As stated before, only one actual whistleblowing service was found to leak data to a third party – all the other leaks were on company pages leading to the actual reporting channels. This service was used by the Corporation 5, and it leaked the data to New Relic, which is a web analytics service company headquartered in the USA. It seems the whistleblowing solution used by Corporation 5 and implemented by a Finnish software company, includes the New Relic analytics service as a built-in component. The URL of the whistleblowing channel and the user's IP address were leaked to New Relic, which is a grave privacy violation considering the nature of this kind of reporting channel. Since the software company behind the whistleblowing solution themselves advertises their service as "safe and compliant with EU directives", it seems safe to assume that the corporation that deployed this service is not aware of the deficiency in their whistleblowing channel.

Naturally, the fact that this kind of a data leakage combining the IP address and URL exists in a whistleblowing channel is a cause for grave concern. It should be noted that this particular whistleblowing channel was implemented using a service obtained from a vendor that is known to incorporate the New Relic analytics tool into their products, which is likely to be the reason for the leakage. Other inspected whistleblowing channels, implemented in more appropriate ways for this kind of service, did not have such flaws.

While it is a good result that 14 out of 15 whistleblowing channels were free of third-party data leaks, the leak we found clearly shows that even developers specifically designing highly confidential whistleblowing channels make mistakes by including third-party services and not testing their software products properly. In addition, the corporation using the whistleblowing channel has also failed to assess the privacy of the product in question.

3.5 Internal Leaks to Corporations

Internal leaks to corporations are more difficult to track with our test setup than third party leaks. Any website owner can track the IP addresses of visitors as well as the pages they visit, so the visits to the page which links to a whistleblowing service can potentially always be tracked on the server side (which cannot be studied here). However, the information on link clicks have to be specifically sent to the company. We found that this happened in 2 out of 15 cases (13.3%). The address of the clicked link was also sent to the company server in both cases. With this information, the company can be sure that a user has not only visited the page concerning the whistleblowing procedure, but also knows for sure that the user has accessed the whistleblowing channel and intends to make a report. While it has been well understood that some trusted external party, and not the company itself, should implement and maintain the reporting channel, the pages hosted by the company leading to whistleblowing channels remain a significant problem in terms of privacy.

46   E. Vuorinen et al.

Table 1. Dark patterns on cookie banners of the studied company websites.

Website	Type A No reject button on first layer	Type B Pre-ticked consent boxes	Type D Deceptive colors	Type E Deceptive contrast
Corporation 1				
Corporation 2				
Corporation 3				
Corporation 4				
Corporation 5				
Corporation 6				
Corporation 7				
Corporation 8				
Corporation 9				
Corporation 10				
Corporation 11				
Corporation 12				
Corporation 13				
Corporation 14				
Corporation 15				

3.6 Dark Patterns and Privacy Policies

Table 1 shows the results of our evaluation of the dark patterns found in the cookie consent banners of the corporation websites. The red color indicates a deceptive pattern was present, while the green color signifies that the website adheres to a user-friendly practice. As can be seen here, there were several deficiencies in these banners, mainly of the type that exhibited psychologically misleading use of color and contrast in accept and reject buttons. In total, 14 out of the 15 (93.4%) studied corporations used these deceptive patterns in their cookie consent banners. Corporations 4, 11 and 13 fared slightly worse than the rest when it comes to dark patterns, with all three of these lacking obvious rejection button for cookies in the first layer of the banner, and number 13 using preticked consent boxes, which per the GDPR[7] are not considered to be sufficient to grant consent. Only one website (Corporation 7) in the study fared obviously better than the rest, and exhibited none of the design principles which could be seen as dark patterns.

The discrepancies between the stated privacy policy and the actual data collection practiced by the corporation websites are detailed in Table 2. The red

---

[7] https://www.privacy-regulation.eu/en/recital-32-GDPR.htm.

Table 2. Transparency of the studied privacy policies.

Website	Tells about collecting identifying personal data	All 3rd parties mentioned	Informs that data about link clicks is collected
Corporation 1			
Corporation 2			
Corporation 3			
Corporation 4			
Corporation 5			
Corporation 6			
Corporation 7			
Corporation 8			
Corporation 9			
Corporation 10			
Corporation 11			
Corporation 12			
Corporation 13			
Corporation 14			
Corporation 15			

color implies a discrepancy, while green indicates the privacy policy informs the user properly. Our inspection of the privacy policies yielded quite similar results to what other studies on privacy policies [9,12,13,24] in general have found out. In practice, there are very common discrepancies between what is said in the privacy policy and how the data collection actually happens. Privacy policies were quite often, but not always, full of opaque and ambiguous wordings, the intent of which was hard to decipher. Due to this, 6 out of 15 corporation websites failed to clearly inform the user about identifying data collection in general and 14 out of 15 failed to inform that all link clicks will also be tracked. It was also quite common that the third parties to which the data was leaked to were not clearly named in the privacy policy, with only 7 out of 15 (46.6%) corporations sufficiently naming all third parties. Only one (6.6%) of the studied corporations (Corporation 3) had a privacy policy that – in terms of the criteria we assessed here – adequately disclosed the extent of the data processing activities on their website, while all of the rest (93.4%) did not.

4   Discussion

4.1   Key Findings

Outlined below are the key takeaways from our results:

- *Prevalence of data leaks.* Majority of the corporation websites (86.6%) studied in this research were found to leak data to third parties that could be used to identify that a visitor had accessed the whistleblowing channel of the corporation.
- *Internal leaks about using the whistleblowing channel.* In two of the studied websites, it was observed that the corporation itself obtained information about the use of the link leading to whistleblowing service.
- *Whistleblowing channel leak.* One actual whistleblowing channel leaked its URL address along with identifying user information, revealing its use to a third party.
- *Discrepancy in the data leakages across websites that used similar tools.* We found that due to different configurations, there were clear differences in the severity of the data leaks between corporation websites that used similar data analytics tools.
- *Google's pervasive influence.* Google Analytics was the most common analytics service to be used by the corporation websites, being found deployed on 14 out of the 15 (93.3%) observed websites. It also accounted for 28 out of 66 (42.42%) of all data leaks found in the current study.

4.2   Implications for Whistleblowers

If the personal data leaked to the company or third parties contains identifying details on the whistleblower, their anonymity can be compromised. The disclosure of such data can have various severe consequences, including retaliation, loss of trust, and negative impacts on ongoing investigations and society in general [15].

First, data leaks in whistleblowing channels can lead to a danger of retaliation. If the identity of the whistleblower is revealed to the implicated individual or company, they can engage in reprisals or intimidation tactics against the whistleblower [27]. This can have the effect of deterring potential future whistleblowers from using reporting channels. This is because whistleblowers can be considered a threat by companies and organizations [20], and seen as individuals who refuse to abide by the organizational norms [4,14]. Therefore, whistleblowing carries substantial personal risks and can have negative consequences for one's career progression [17].

These consequences, in turn, can have a chilling effect on whistleblowing activities as a whole [10]. As potential whistleblowers see the effects of data leaks on people reporting wrongdoings, it is likely they will be discouraged from using the reporting channel. This undermines the whole whistleblowing process and hampers uncovering important information. Whistleblowing services are built on trust and confidentiality [19] and a data leak to third-party services erodes this trust. Users hesitate to report cases of misconduct if they do not believe their personal data is safe, which may also have adverse effects on the reputation of the company, as well as the provider of the whistleblowing service.

Moreover, ongoing investigations or legal cases may rest on details reported in the whistleblowing service. In these cases, a data leak can endanger those efforts. Upon learning that the reporting channel has been used by a specific individual, the parties under investigation may attempt to evade scrutiny or cover up evidence. Likewise, data leaks may have an impact on public interest in general. Whistleblowers often report information that is of public concern, such as fraud, corruption, or safety violations [2,21]. Accountability of companies and organizations can be hindered if information is prevented from reaching the public due to a third-party data leak. Consequently, this can have profound negative repercussions for society.

Aside from these negative consequences discussed above, it is simply ethically questionable that such sensitive personal data is leaking to third parties. Third parties can use the data to further refine profiles they may be building for users. The more third parties get hold of the personal data and store it somewhere, the more likely it is that some "fourth party" also comes to possess the collected data at some point.

4.3   Recommendations for Web Developers

While maintaining user privacy in websites is always important, developers of whistleblowing websites should take several important things into account due to the special nature of these websites. The most important of these considerations is whether third party analytics services should even be included into the website design, as it is very questionable whether they bring any added value to whistle-blowing services. After all, these kinds of websites are built to be used by people who are intent on exposing secrets of often criminal or at least of highly question-able nature, of wrongdoings by those in positions of power and of other kinds of workplace misconduct. This can involve reporting actions such as financial fraud, violations of corporate social responsibility principles, harassment, dis-crimination, and workplace safety violations. Bringing such actions to light puts the whistleblower in a position where remaining anonymous is paramount, for the compromization of this secrecy can lead to dire consequences, both socially, career-wise and even physically.

Web analytics, on the other hand, are meant for observing the user actions, usually in the name of "improving the user experience" of the website. On the other hand, web-based whistleblowing services are – at least hopefully – websites that users do not visit often. In the best case scenario, no one has to ever use these services, and those using them are ultimately interested only in their practical usability and securing their own anonymity. Both requirements can be met appropriately without any constant user surveillance. Several other studies on privacy violations in other types of websites have shown that third-party analytics services are very prone to leaking sensitive information that can be utilized in identifying the user, usually to the private enterprises developing these tools [6,11,23]. When large corporations are involved, as they are in the case of whistleblowing websites inspected in this research, it is not outside the realm of possibility that such actors could access this leaked information to decipher the identity of whistleblower amidst their ranks.

All of the aforementioned factors combined speak strongly against using third-party analytics services at all in these websites. Even if for some reason they must be used, these tools should be locally deployed or even custom-made specifically for the website in question. Previous research (see e.g. [9,11]) has clearly shown that the presence of third-party analytics services at any website or other online application has a strong correlation with data leakages to these third-parties themselves, and such potential privacy violations can not be allowed to happen in the case of whistleblowing services.

Apart from not using the analytics services at all, certain other precautions should also be implemented by the developers working on such projects. First of all, a thorough network traffic analysis should be conducted at the testing phase of the website in question, similar in methodology to what we have used in this paper, to ensure that no data leakages occur. Objections to such practices might be raised by either the development team, for increased workload, or by the customer due to increased costs. It should be noted, however, that performing this kind of analysis is not very laborious, requiring neither specialized tools, specific expertise nor many hours of work. Therefore, both cost and time constraints should not be obstacles. The lack of, or active rejection of performing, such testing can be considered a form of gross negligence.

The avoidance of dark patterns in both the website and cookie consent banner design is especially important when building services of this nature. The propagation of such unsavory design practices has become all too common in contemporary web development, and previous research [8,25] on this phenomenon has revealed that the stark majority of website cookie consent banners exhibit at least some characteristics that can be defined as dark patterns. The developers should consult the recommendations agreed upon by the European Data Protection Board, which has produced a report (See footnote 4) detailing several common practices that can be considered intentionally and actively misleading to the users, tricking them to give consent to data collection they would not otherwise agree to. These elements include psychologically manipulative use of colors and contrast, pre-ticked consent boxes which are often "hidden" to the next layer of the banner, clear absence of rejection button and such. Several studies [9,12,13,24] conducted on privacy policies have also concluded that it is not just the cookie consent banners that are problematic in this sense, but also the privacy policy declarations detailing the data collection practices used by the service. This research has shown that in the majority of cases, privacy policies are either erroneous, actively misleading or expressed with both ambiguous and overly technical terms. Therefore, a layperson, not accustomed to legal or technical jargon, can hardly be required to correctly understand the contents of these documents.

This study very clearly highlights the fact that the privacy of whistleblowing channels is not just about the privacy of the channel itself. It is very important to address the confidentiality of the company website that links to this channel, and specifically the sub-page containing the link to the whistleblowing service. As our research suggests, all too often clicking these links leaks information to the deployed analytics tools, which in itself could jeopardize the privacy and safety of the users of the service. As we saw in Sect. 3, 13 out of 15 (86.7%) of inspected websites leaked the information of clicking this link to third parties. In 2 cases (13.3%) the information about clicking this link was even leaked internally to the company in whose website the whistleblowing service was operated. In 9 out of 15 (60.0%) websites the URL of the page where the link to whistleblowing was positioned was leaked. While even the leakage of visiting these pages to outside actors is not acceptable, it is needless to say that leaking such information internally to the company in question is quite alarming. These findings should serve as stark examples of how not to plant web analytics in the pages linking to whistleblowing services, and underline the need to seriously deliberate whether such tools should be deployed at all.

All of the various recommendations brought forth in this section lead us to the root issue at the heart of this problem, namely that the web analytics have become so commonplace, and that there is an ongoing trend to deploy as many of these tools to the contemporary websites as is possible. Many of the inspected websites, both in this study and in previous research [9], have several analytics tools operating simultaneously, essentially collecting similar data about their users. Even if there would be an initial need to have some kind of analytics present in the website, it is hard to see the reason for deploying several almost identically operating services at the same time, especially since many of them collect basically the same data points about the user. The more there are analytics services in use, the more there are potential points of leakage that may elude the developers and administrators of the website even if proper precautions are in place. The reason for this overpropagation of analytics services is most likely born out of the current internet climate, in which the use of analytics services and tracking tools is regarded as being completely normal, even when there would be very little actual reason for doing so. Specifically in the case of whistleblowing websites, such needs are dubious under the best of the circumstances, and both the developers and the companies should take this to heart when designing and developing these services. Generally, encouraging developers to adopt ethical web development practices such as Ethical Web Dev[8] would be beneficial.

---

[8] https://edri.org/our-work/ethical-web-dev-2/.

5 Conclusion

We have provided an overview of the data leaks related to whistleblowing in the websites of 15 large Finnish corporations and the external whistleblowing services they utilize. The results strongly indicate that the analytics services planted in pages leading to reporting channels are the main culprits of these data leaks. An external analytics service received a clear indication of the user accessing the whistleblowing channel in 13 out of 15 cases (86.7%). In one case, even the whistleblowing channel itself leaked data revealing its use to a third party. Moreover, on 2 occasions the corporation being reported also received the information about the user accessing the whistleblowing service. This can be especially dangerous for an individual if the company is able to link the identifying technical information to them. Lastly, we also found that 14 out of 15 (94.4%) had dark patterns in their cookie consent banners, persuading the user to accept data collection, further enabling data leaks. We hope these results serve as a reminder to website developers to be more mindful of the third parties when planning their websites and especially critical pages such as ones discussing whistleblowing and linking to reporting channels.

Acknowledgements. This research has been funded by Academy of Finland project 327397, IDA – Intimacy in Data-Driven Culture.

References

1. Case C-582/14, Patrick Breyer v. Bundesrepublik Deutschland [2016] ECLI:EU:C:2016:779, paragraph 49
2. Bowden, P.: In the Public Interest: Protecting Whistleblowers and Those Who Speak Out. Tilde Publishing and Distribution (2014)
3. Devine, S.: Protecting whistleblower information. USENIX Association, Santa Clara (2023)
4. Dozier, J.B., Miceli, M.P.: Potential predictors of whistle-blowing: a prosocial behavior perspective. Acad. Manag. Rev. **10**(4), 823–836 (1985)
5. Finck, M., Pallas, F.: They who must not be identified-distinguishing personal from non-personal data under the GDPR. Int. Data Priv. Law **10**(1), 11–36 (2020)
6. Friedman, A.B., Bauer, L., Gonzales, R., McCoy, M.S.: Prevalence of third-party tracking on abortion clinic web pages. JAMA Intern. Med. **182**, 1221–1222 (2022)
7. Greenwood, C.A.: Killing the messenger: a survey of public relations practitioners and organizational response to whistleblowing after Sarbanes-Oxley. Ph.D. thesis, University of Oregon (2011)
8. Gunawan, J., Pradeep, A., Choffnes, D., Hartzog, W., Wilson, C.: A comparative study of dark patterns across web and mobile modalities. Proc. ACM Hum.-Comput. Interact. **5**(CSCW2) (2021). https://doi.org/10.1145/3479521
9. Heino, T., Carlsson, R., Rauti, S., Leppänen, V.: Assessing discrepancies between network traffic and privacy policies of public sector web services. In: ARES 2022. Association for Computing Machinery, New York (2022). https://doi.org/10.1145/3538969.3539003
10. Høedt-Rasmussen, I., Voorhoof, D.: Whistleblowing for sustainable democracy. Neth. Q. Hum. Rights **36**(1), 3–6 (2018)

11. Huo, M., Bland, M., Levchenko, K.: All eyes on me: inside third party trackers' exfiltration of phi from healthcare providers' online systems. In: Proceedings of the 21st Workshop on Privacy in the Electronic Society, WPES 2022, pp. 197–211. Association for Computing Machinery, New York (2022). https://doi.org/10.1145/3559613.3563190

12. Iwaya, L., Babar, A., Rashid, A., Wijayarathna, C.: On the privacy of mental health apps. Empir. Softw. Eng. **28**, 2 (2023)

13. Jiang, K.: Mental health mobile apps and the need to update federal regulations to protect users. Mich. Technol. Law Rev. **28**, 421 (2022)

14. Jubb, P.B.: Whistleblowing: a restrictive definition and interpretation. J. Bus. Ethics **21**, 77–94 (1999)

15. Khan, J., et al.: Examining whistleblowing intention: the influence of rationalization on wrongdoing and threat of retaliation. Int. J. Environ. Res. Public Health **19**(3), 1752 (2022)

16. Kiziloglu, M.: The relationship between whistleblowing and organizational citizenship behaviour in textile sector. Int. J. Organ. Leadersh.-IJOL (2018)

17. Kvalnes, Ø.: Whistleblowing. In: Kvalnes, Ø. (ed.) Communication Climate at Work: Fostering Friendly Friction in Organisations, pp. 119–126. Springer, Cham (2023). https://doi.org/10.1007/978-3-031-28971-2

18. Lehtola, T.: Security, privacy, and legislation adherence assessment of a whistleblowing web application. University of Turku Department of Computing, Faculty of Technology Master of Science in Technology Thesis Information and Communication Technology (2022)

19. Lewis, D.: The contents of whistleblowing/confidential reporting procedures in the UK: some lessons from empirical research. Empl. Relat. **28**, 76–86 (2006)

20. Martin, B., Rifkin, W.: The dynamics of employee dissent: whistleblowers and organizational Jiu-Jitsu. Public Organ. Rev. **4**, 221–238 (2004)

21. Roberts, P.: Motivations for whistleblowing: personal, private and public interests. In: International Handbook on Whistleblowing Research, pp. 207–229. Edward Elgar Publishing (2014)

22. Santoro, D., Kumar, M.: A justification of whistleblowing. Philos. Soc. Criticism **43**(7), 669–684 (2017)

23. Schnell, K., Kaushik, R.: Hunting for the privacy policy - hospital website design (2022)

24. Singh, S., Sagar, R.: Time to have effective regulation of the mental health apps market: maximize gains and minimize harms. Indian J. Psychol. Med. **44**, 399–404 (2022)

25. Soe, T.H., Nordberg, O.E., Guribye, F., Slavkovik, M.: Circumvention by design - dark patterns in cookie consent for online news outlets. In: Proceedings of the 11th Nordic Conference on Human-Computer Interaction: Shaping Experiences, Shaping Society, NordiCHI 2020. Association for Computing Machinery, New York (2020). https://doi.org/10.1145/3419249.3420132

26. Uddholm, J.: Anonymous Javascript cryptography and cover traffic in whistleblowing applications. Master's thesis at NADA (2016)

27. Van Portfliet, M., Irfan, M., Kenny, K.: When employees speak up: human resource management aspects of whistleblowing. In: The Emerald Handbook of Work, Workplaces and Disruptive Issues in HRM, pp. 533–547. Emerald Publishing Limited (2022)

28. West, J.P., Bowman, J.S.: Whistleblowing policies in American states: a nationwide analysis. Am. Rev. Public Adm. **50**(2), 119–132 (2020)

Cryptography, Protocols, Analysis

Small Private Key Attack Against a Family of RSA-Like Cryptosystems

Paul Cotan[1,2] and George Teşeleanu[1,2(✉)]

[1] Advanced Technologies Institute, 10 Dinu Vintilă, Bucharest, Romania
{paul.cotan,tgeorge}@dcti.ro
[2] Simion Stoilow Institute of Mathematics of the Romanian Academy,
21 Calea Grivitei, Bucharest, Romania

Abstract. Let $N = pq$ be the product of two balanced prime numbers p and q. Elkamchouchi, Elshenawy and Shaban presented in 2002 an interesting RSA-like cryptosystem that uses the key equation $ed - k(p^2 - 1)(q^2 - 1) = 1$, instead of the classical RSA key equation $ed - k(p - 1)(q-1) = 1$. The authors claimed that their scheme is more secure than RSA. Unfortunately, the common attacks developed against RSA can be adapted for Elkamchouchi *et al.*'s scheme. In this paper, we introduce a family of RSA-like encryption schemes that uses the key equation $ed - k(p^n - 1)(q^n - 1) = 1$, where $n > 0$ is an integer. Then, we show that regardless of the choice of n, there exists an attack based on continued fractions that recovers the secret exponent.

1 Introduction

In 1978, Rivest, Shamir and Adleman [29] proposed one of the most popular and widely used cryptosystems, namely RSA. In the standard RSA encryption scheme, we work modulo an integer N, where N is the product of two large prime numbers p and q. Let $\varphi(N) = (p-1)(q-1)$ denote the Euler's totient function. In order to encrypt a message $m < N$, we simply compute $c \equiv m^e \bmod N$, where e is generated a priori such that $\gcd(e, \varphi(N)) = 1$. To decrypt, one needs to compute $m \equiv c^d \bmod N$, where $d \equiv e^{-1} \bmod \varphi(N)$. Note that (N, e) are public, while (p, q, d) are kept secret. In the standard version of RSA, also called balanced RSA, p and q are of the same bit-size such that $q < p < 2q$. In this paper, we only consider the balanced RSA scheme and its variants.

In 2002, Elkamchouchi, Elshenawy and Shaban [15] extend the classical RSA scheme to the ring of Gaussian integers modulo N. A Gaussian integer modulo N is a number of the form $a+bi$, where $a, b \in \mathbb{Z}_N$ and $i^2 = -1$. Let $\mathbb{Z}_N[i]$ denote the set of all Gaussian integers modulo N and let $\phi(N) = |\mathbb{Z}_N^*[i]| = (p^2 - 1)(q^2 - 1)$. To set up the public exponent, in this case we must have $\gcd(e, \phi(N)) = 1$. The corresponding private exponent is $d \equiv e^{-1} \bmod \phi(N)$. In order to encrypt a message $m \in \mathbb{Z}_N[i]$, we simply compute $c \equiv m^e \bmod N$ and to decrypt it $m \equiv c^d \bmod N$. Note that the exponentiations are computed in the ring $\mathbb{Z}_N[i]$.

L. Fritsch et al. (Eds.): NordSec 2023, LNCS 14324, pp. 57–72, 2024.
https://doi.org/10.1007/978-3-031-47748-5_4

The authors of [15] claim that this extension provides more security than that of the classical RSA. In the following paragraphs we present a series of common attacks that work for both types of cryptosystems.

Small Private Key Attacks. In order to decrease decryption time, one may prefer to use a smaller d. Wiener showed in [33] that this is not always a good idea. More exactly, in the case of RSA, if $d < N^{0.25}/3$, then one can retrieve d from the continued fraction expansion of e/N, and thus factor N. Using a result developed by Coppersmith [12], Boneh and Durfee [5] improved Wiener's bound to $N^{0.292}$. Later on, Herrmann and May [19] obtain the same bound, but using simpler techniques. A different approach was taken by Blömer and May [3], whom generalized Wiener's attack. More precisely, they showed that if there exist three integers x, y, z such that $ex - y\varphi(N) = z$, $x < N^{0.25}/3$ and $|z| < |exN^{-0.75}|$, then the factorisation of N can be recovered. When an approximation of p is known such that $|p - p_0| < N^{\delta}/8$ and $\delta < 0.5$, Nassr, Anwar and Bahig [25] present a method based on continued fractions for recovering d when $d < N^{(1-\delta)/2}$.

In the case of Elkamchouchi *et al.*, a small private key attack based on continued fractions was presented in [7]. Using lattice reduction, the attack was improved in [28,34]. The authors obtained a bound of $d < N^{0.585}$. A generalization of the attack presented in [7] to unbalanced prime numbers was presented in [9]. Considering the generic equation $ex - y\phi(N) = z$, the authors of [8] describe a method for factoring N when $xy < 2N - 4\sqrt{2}N^{0.75}$ and $|z| < (p - q)N^{0.25}y$. An extension of the previous attack was proposed in [27].

Multiple Private Keys Attack. Let $\ell > 0$ be an integer and $i \in [1, \ell]$. When multiple large public keys $e_i \simeq N^{\alpha}$ are used with the same modulus N, Howgrave-Graham and Seifert [20] describe an attack against RSA that recovers the corresponding small private exponents $d_i \simeq N^{\beta}$. This attack was later improved by Sarkar and Maitra [30], Aono [1] and Takayasu and Kunihiro [31]. The best known bound [31] is $\beta < 1 - \sqrt{2/(3\ell + 1)}$. Remark that when $\ell = 1$ we obtain the Boneh-Durfee bound.

The multiple private keys attack against the Elkamchouchi *et al.* cryptosystem was studied by Zheng, Kunihiro and Hu [34]. The bound obtained by the authors is $\beta < 2 - 2\sqrt{2/(3\ell + 1)}$ and it is twice the bound obtained by Takayasu and Kunihiro [31]. Note that when $\ell = 1$ the bound is equal to 0.585.

Partial Key Exposure Attack. In this type of attack, the most or least significant bits of the private exponent d are known. Starting from these, an adversary can recover the entire RSA private key using the techniques presented by Boneh, Durfee and Frankel in [6]. The attack was later improved by Blömer and May [2], Ernst *et al.* [16] and Takayasu and Kunihiro [32]. The best known bound [32] is $\beta < (\gamma + 2 - \sqrt{2 - 3\gamma^2})/2$, where the attacker knows N^{γ} leaked bits.

Zheng, Kunihiro and Hu [34] describe a partial exposure attack that works in the case of the Elkamchouchi *et al.* scheme. The bound they achieve is $\beta < (3\gamma + 7 - 2\sqrt{3\gamma + 7})/3$. When $\gamma = 0$, the bound is close to 0.569, and thus it remains an open problem how to optimize it.

Small Prime Difference Attack. When the prime difference $|p - q|$ is small and certain conditions hold, de Weger [14] described two methods to recover d, one based on continued fractions and one on lattice reduction. These methods were further extended by Maitra and Sakar [22,23] to $|\rho q - p|$, where $1 \leq \rho \leq 2$. Lastly, Chen, Hsueh and Lin generalize them further to $|\rho q - \epsilon p|$, where ρ and ϵ have certain properties. The continued fraction method is additionally improved by Ariffin *et al.* [21].

The small prime difference attack against the Elkamchouchi *et al.* public key encryption scheme was studied in [11]. Note that when the common condition $|p-q| < N^{0.5}$ holds, their bound leads to the small private key bound $d < N^{0.585}$.

Related Work. It is worth noting that our current undertaking shares similarities with a prior work of ours [13], where we explored a cryptographic system closely related to our own. Specifically, we studied the implications of generalizing the Murru-Saettone cryptosystem [24], and the effect of using continued fractions to recover the private key.

1.1   Our Contributions

We first remark that the rings $Z_p = \mathbb{Z}_p[t]/(t+1) = GF(p)$ and $Z_p[i] = \mathbb{Z}_p[t]/(t^2 + 1) = GF(p^2)$, where GF stands for Galois field. Therefore, we can rethink the RSA scheme as working in the $GF(p) \times GF(q)$ group instead of $\mathbb{Z}_N$. Also, that the Elkamchouchi *et al.* scheme is an extension to $GF(p^2) \times GF(q^2)$ instead of $Z_N[i]$. This leads to a natural generalization of RSA to $GF(p^n) \times GF(q^n)$, where $n > 1$. In this paper we introduce exactly this extension. We wanted to see if only for $n = 1$ and $n = 2$ the common attacks presented in the introduction work or this is something that happens in general. In this study we present a Wiener-type attack that works for any $n > 1$. More, precisely we prove that when $d < N^{0.25n}$, we can recover the secret exponent regardless the value of n. Therefore, no matter how we instantiate the generalized version, a small private key attack will always succeed.

Structure of the Paper. We introduce in Sect. 2 notations and definitions used throughout the paper. Inspired by Rivest *et al.* and Elkamchouchi *et al.*'s work [15,29], in Sect. 3 we construct a family of RSA-like cryptosystems. After proving several useful lemmas in Sect. 4, we extend Wiener's small private key attack in Sect. 5. Two concrete instantiations are provided in Sect. 6. We conclude our paper in Sect. 7.

2 Preliminaries

Notations. Throughout the paper, λ denotes a security parameter. Also, the notation $|S|$ denotes the cardinality of a set S. The set of integers $\{0, \ldots, a\}$ is further denoted by $[0, a]$. We use $\simeq$ to indicate that two values are approximately equal.

2.1 Continued Fraction

For any real number ζ there exists a unique sequence $(a_n)_n$ of integers such that

$$\zeta = a_0 + \cfrac{1}{a_1 + \cfrac{1}{a_2 + \cfrac{1}{a_3 + \cfrac{1}{a_4 + \cdots}}}},$$

where $a_k > 0$ for any $k \geq 1$. This sequence represents the continued fraction expansion of ζ and is denoted by $\zeta = [a_0, a_1, a_2, \ldots]$. Remark that ζ is a rational number if and only if its corresponding representation as a continued fraction is finite.

For any real number $\zeta = [a_0, a_1, a_2, \ldots]$, the sequence of rational numbers $(A_n)_n$, obtained by truncating this continued fraction, $A_k = [a_0, a_1, a_2, \ldots, a_k]$, is called the convergents sequence of ζ.

According to [18], the following bound allows us to check if a rational number u/v is a convergent of ζ.

Theorem 1. *Let* $\zeta = [a_0, a_1, a_2, \ldots]$ *be a positive real number. If* u, v *are positive integers such that* $\gcd(u, v) = 1$ *and*

$$\left| \zeta - \frac{u}{v} \right| < \frac{1}{2v^2},$$

then u/v *is a convergent of* $[a_0, a_1, a_2, \ldots]$.

2.2 Quotient Groups

In this section we will provide the mathematical theory needed to generalize the Rivest, Shamir and Adleman, and the Elkamchouchi, Elshenawy and Shaban encryption schemes. Therefore, let $(\mathbb{F}, +, \cdot)$ be a field and $t^n - r$ an irreducible polynomial in $\mathbb{F}[t]$. Then

$$\mathbb{A}_n = \mathbb{F}[t]/(t^n - r) = \{a_0 + a_1 t + \ldots + a_{n-1}t^{n-1} \mid a_0, a_1, \ldots, a_{n-1} \in \mathbb{F}\}$$

is the corresponding quotient field. Let $a(t), b(t) \in \mathbb{A}_n$. Remark that the quotient field induces a natural product

$$
\begin{aligned}
a(t) \circ b(t) &= \left(\sum_{i=0}^{n-1} a_i t^i \right) \circ \left(\sum_{j=0}^{n-1} b_j t^j \right) \\
&= \sum_{i=0}^{2n-2} \left(\sum_{j=0}^{i} a_j b_{i-j} \right) t^i \\
&= \sum_{i=0}^{n-1} \left(\sum_{j=0}^{i} a_j b_{i-j} \right) t^i + r \sum_{i=n}^{2n-2} \left(\sum_{j=0}^{i} a_j b_{i-j} \right) t^{i-n} \\
&= \sum_{i=0}^{n-2} \left(\sum_{j=0}^{i} a_j b_{i-j} + r \sum_{j=0}^{i+n} a_j b_{i-j+n} \right) t^i + \sum_{j=0}^{n-1} a_j b_{n-1-j} t^{n-1}.
\end{aligned}
$$

3   The Scheme

Let p be a prime number. When we instantiate $\mathbb{F} = \mathbb{Z}_p$, we have that $\mathbb{A}_n = GF(p^n)$ is the Galois field of order p^n. Moreover, $\mathbb{A}_n^*$ is a cyclic group of order $\varphi_n(\mathbb{Z}_p) = p^n - 1$. Remark that an analogous of Fermat's little theorem holds

$$
a(x)^{\varphi_n(\mathbb{Z}_p)} \equiv 1 \bmod p,
$$

where $a(x) \in \mathbb{A}_n^*$ and the power is evaluated by $\circ$-multiplying $a(x)$ by itself $\varphi_n(\mathbb{Z}_p) - 1$ times. Therefore, we can build an encryption scheme that is similar to RSA using the $\circ$ as the product.

Setup(λ): Let $n > 1$ be an integer. Randomly generate two distinct large prime numbers p, q such that $p, q \geq 2^\lambda$ and compute their product $N = pq$. Select $r \in \mathbb{Z}_N$ such that the polynomial $t^n - r$ is irreducible in $\mathbb{Z}_p[t]$ and $\mathbb{Z}_q[t]$. Let

$$
\varphi_n(\mathbb{Z}_N) = \varphi_n(N) = (p^n - 1) \cdot (q^n - 1).
$$

Choose an integer e such that $\gcd(e, \varphi_n(N)) = 1$ and compute d such that $ed \equiv 1 \bmod \varphi_n(N)$. Output the public key $pk = (n, N, r, e)$. The corresponding secret key is $sk = (p, q, d)$.

Encrypt(pk, m): To encrypt a message $m = (m_0, \ldots, m_{n-1}) \in \mathbb{Z}_N^n$ we first construct the polynomial $m(t) = m_0 + \ldots + m_{n-1} t^{n-1} \in \mathbb{A}_n^*$ and then we compute $c(t) \equiv [m(t)]^e \bmod N$. Output the ciphertext $c(t)$.

Decrypt(sk, c(t)): To recover the message, simply compute $m(t) \equiv [c(t)]^d \bmod N$ and reassemble $m = (m_0, \ldots, m_{n-1})$.

Remark 1. When $n = 1$ we get the RSA scheme [29]. Also, when $n = 2$, we obtain the Elkamchouchi *et al.* cryptosystem [15].

4   Useful Lemmas

In this section we provide a few useful properties of $\varphi_n(N)$. Before starting our analysis, we first note that plugging $q = N/p$ in $\varphi_n(N)$ leads to the following function

$$f_n(p) = N^n - p^n - \left(\frac{N}{p}\right)^n + 1,$$

with p as a variable. The next lemma tells us that, under certain conditions, f_n is a strictly decreasing function.

Proposition 1. *Let N be a positive integer. Then for any integers $n > 1$ and $\sqrt{N} \leq x < N$, we have that the function*

$$f_n(x) = N^n - x^n - \left(\frac{N}{x}\right)^n + 1,$$

is strictly decreasing with x.

Proof. Computing the derivative of f we have that

$$f'(x) = -n\left(x^{n-1} - \frac{1}{x^{n+1}} \cdot N^n\right).$$

Using $x \geq \sqrt{N}$ we obtain that

$$x^{2n} > N^n \Leftrightarrow x^{n-1} > \frac{1}{x^{n+1}} \cdot N^n \Leftrightarrow f'(x) < 0,$$

and therefore we have f is strictly decreasing function.   □

Using the following result from [26, Lemma 1], we will compute a lower and upper bound for $\varphi_n(N)$.

Lemma 1. *Let $N = pq$ be the product of two unknown primes with $q < p < 2q$. Then the following property holds*

$$\frac{\sqrt{2}}{2}\sqrt{N} < q < \sqrt{N} < p < \sqrt{2}\sqrt{N}.$$

Corollary 1. *Let $N = pq$ be the product of two unknown primes with $q < p < 2q$. Then the following property holds*

$$\left(\sqrt{N}^n - 1\right)^2 > \varphi_n(N) > N^n\left(1 - \frac{2^n + 1}{\sqrt{2N}^n}\right) + 1.$$

Proof. By Lemma 1 we have that

$$\sqrt{N} < p < \sqrt{2}\sqrt{N},$$

which, according to Proposition 1, leads to

$$f_n(\sqrt{N}) > f_n(p) > f_n(\sqrt{2}\sqrt{N}).$$

This is equivalent to

$$\left(\sqrt{N}^n - 1\right)^2 > \varphi_n(N) > N^n \left(1 - \frac{2^n + 1}{\sqrt{2N}^n}\right) + 1,$$

as desired.   □

When $n = 1$ and $n = 2$, the following results proven in [10] and [7] respectively become a special case of Corollary 1.

Corollary 2. *Let $N = pq$ be the product of two unknown primes with $q < p < 2q$. Then the following property holds*

$$(\sqrt{N} - 1)^2 > \varphi_1(N) > N + 1 - \frac{3}{\sqrt{2}}\sqrt{N}.$$

Corollary 3. *Let $N = pq$ be the product of two unknown primes with $q < p < 2q$. Then the following property holds*

$$(N - 1)^2 > \varphi_2(N) > N^2 + 1 - \frac{5}{2}N.$$

We can use Corollary 1 to find a useful approximation of φ_n. This result will be useful when devising the attack against the generalized RSA scheme.

Proposition 2. *Let $N = pq$ be the product of two unknown primes with $q < p < 2q$. We define*

$$\varphi_{n,0}(N) = \frac{1}{2} \cdot \left(\sqrt{N}^n - 1\right)^2 + \frac{1}{2} \cdot \left[N^n \left(1 - \frac{2^n + 1}{\sqrt{2N}^n}\right) + 1\right].$$

Then the following holds

$$|\varphi_n(N) - \varphi_{n,0}(N)| < \frac{\Delta_n}{2}\sqrt{N}^n,$$

where

$$\Delta_n = \frac{(\sqrt{2}^n - 1)^2}{\sqrt{2}^n}.$$

Proof. According to Corollary 1, $\psi_{n,0}(N)$ is the mean value of the lower and upper bound. The following property holds

$$|\psi_n(N) - \psi_{n,0}(N)| \le \frac{1}{2}\left[\left(\sqrt{N}^n - 1\right)^2 - N^n \left(1 - \frac{2^n + 1}{\sqrt{2N}^n}\right) - 1\right]$$

$$= \frac{1}{2}\left(N^n - 2\sqrt{N}^n + 1 - N^n + N^n \cdot \frac{2^n + 1}{\sqrt{2N}^n} - 1\right)$$

$$= \frac{1}{2}\sqrt{N}^n \left(\frac{2^n + 1}{\sqrt{2}^n} - 2\right)$$

$$= \frac{\Delta_n}{2}\sqrt{N}^n,$$

as desired. □

When $n = 1$ and $n = 2$, the following property presented in [10] and [7] respectively become a special case of Proposition 2.

Corollary 4. *Let $N = pq$ be the product of two unknown primes with $q < p < 2q$. Then the following holds*

$$|\varphi_1(N) - \varphi_{1,0}(N)| < \frac{3 - 2\sqrt{2}}{2\sqrt{2}}\sqrt{N}.$$

Corollary 5. *Let $N = pq$ be the product of two unknown primes with $q < p < 2q$. Then the following holds*

$$|\varphi_2(N) - \varphi_{2,0}(N)| < \frac{1}{4}N.$$

5   Application of Continued Fractions

We further provide an upper bound for selecting d such that we can use the continued fraction algorithm to recover d without knowing the factorisation of the modulus N.

Theorem 2. *Let $N = pq$ be the product of two unknown primes with $q < p < 2q$. If $e < \varphi_n(N)$ satisfies $ed - k\varphi_n(N) = 1$ with*

$$d < \sqrt{\frac{\sqrt{2^n}N^n(\sqrt{N}^n - \delta_n)}{e(\sqrt{2^n} - 1)^2}}, \tag{1}$$

where

$$\delta_n = \frac{2\sqrt{2}^n}{(\sqrt{2^n} - 1)^2} + \frac{2(2^n + 1)}{\sqrt{2^n}},$$

then we can recover d in polynomial time.

Proof. Since $ed - k\varphi_n(N) = 1$, we have that

$$\left|\frac{k}{d} - \frac{e}{\varphi_{n,0}(N)}\right| \leq e\left|\frac{1}{\varphi_{n,0}(N)} - \frac{1}{\varphi_n(N)}\right| + \left|\frac{e}{\varphi_n(N)} - \frac{k}{d}\right|$$
$$= e\frac{|\varphi_n(N) - \varphi_{n,0}(N)|}{\varphi_{n,0}(N)\varphi_n(N)} + \frac{1}{\varphi_n(N)d}.$$

Let $\varepsilon_n = N^n - \sqrt{N}^n(2^n + 1)/\sqrt{2}^n + 1$. Using $d = (k\varphi_n(N) - 1)/e = 1$ and Proposition 2 we obtain

$$
\begin{aligned}
\left| \frac{k}{d} - \frac{e}{\varphi_{n,0}(N)} \right| &\leq \frac{\frac{\Delta_n}{2}e\sqrt{N}^n}{\varphi_{n,0}(N)\varphi_n(N)} + \frac{e}{\varphi_n(N)(k\varphi_n(N) - 1)} \\
&\leq \frac{e\sqrt{N}^n(\sqrt{2}^n - 1)^2}{2\sqrt{2}^n \varepsilon_n^2} + \frac{e}{\varepsilon_n(k\varepsilon_n - 1)} \\
&\leq \frac{e\sqrt{N}^n(\sqrt{2}^n - 1)^2}{2\sqrt{2}^n \varepsilon_n^2} + \frac{e}{\varepsilon_n^2} \\
&= \frac{e[\sqrt{N}^n(\sqrt{2}^n - 1)^2 + 2\sqrt{2}^n]}{2\sqrt{2}^n \varepsilon_n^2} \\
&\leq \frac{e[\sqrt{N}^n(\sqrt{2}^n - 1)^2 + 2\sqrt{2}^n]}{2\sqrt{2}^n(N^n - \frac{2^n+1}{\sqrt{2}^n}\sqrt{N}^n)^2}.
\end{aligned}
$$

Note that

$$
\begin{aligned}
\frac{[\sqrt{N}^n(\sqrt{2}^n - 1)^2 + 2\sqrt{2}^n]}{2\sqrt{2}^n(N^n - \frac{2^n+1}{\sqrt{2}^n}\sqrt{N}^n)^2} &= \frac{(\sqrt{2}^n - 1)^2[\sqrt{N}^n + \frac{2\sqrt{2}^n}{(\sqrt{2}^n-1)^2}]}{2\sqrt{2}^n N^n(\sqrt{N}^n - \frac{2^n+1}{\sqrt{2}^n})^2} \\
&\leq \frac{(\sqrt{2}^n - 1)^2}{2\sqrt{2}^n N^n(\sqrt{N}^n - \delta_n)},
\end{aligned}
$$

which leads to

$$
\left| \frac{k}{d} - \frac{e}{\varphi_{n,0}(N)} \right| \leq \frac{e(\sqrt{2}^n - 1)^2}{2\sqrt{2}^n N^n(\sqrt{N}^n - \delta_n)} \leq \frac{1}{2d^2}.
$$

Using Theorem 1 we obtain that k/d is a convergent of the continued fraction expansion of $e/\varphi_{n,0}(N)$. Therefore, d can be recovered in polynomial time. □

Corollary 6. *Let $\alpha < 1.5n$ and $N = pq$ be the product of two unknown primes with $q < p < 2q$. If we approximate $e \simeq N^\alpha$ and $N \simeq 2^{2\lambda}$, then Eq. 1 becomes*

$$
d < \frac{2^{(n-\alpha)\lambda + \frac{n}{4}}\sqrt{2^{n\lambda} - \delta_n}}{\sqrt{2}^n - 1} < \frac{2^{(1.5n-\alpha)\lambda + \frac{n}{4}}}{\sqrt{2}^n - 1}
$$

or equivalently

$$
\log_2(d) < (1.5n - \alpha)\lambda + \frac{n}{4} - \log_2(\sqrt{2}^n - 1) \simeq (1.5n - \alpha)\lambda
$$

When cases $n = 1$ and $n = 2$ are considered the following properties presented in [10] and [7] respectively become a special case of Corollary 6. Note that when $n = \alpha = 1$ we obtain roughly the same margin as Wiener [4,33] obtained for the classical RSA.

Corollary 7. *Let $\alpha < 1.5$ and $N = pq$ be the product of two unknown primes with $q < p < 2q$. If we approximate $e \simeq N^\alpha$ and $N \simeq 2^{2\lambda}$ then Eq. 1 is equivalent to*

$$\log_2(d) < (1.5 - \alpha)\lambda - 0.25 + 1.27 \simeq (1.5 - \alpha)\lambda.$$

Corollary 8. *Let $\alpha < 3$ and $N = pq$ be the product of two unknown primes with $q < p < 2q$. If we approximate $e \simeq N^\alpha$ and $N \simeq 2^{2\lambda}$ then Eq. 1 is equivalent to*

$$\log_2(d) < (3 - \alpha)\lambda - 0.5 \simeq (3 - \alpha)\lambda.$$

The last corollary tells us what happens when e is large enough. We can see that n is directly proportional to the secret exponent's upper bound.

Corollary 9. *Let $N = pq$ be the product of two unknown primes with $q < p < 2q$. If we approximate $e \simeq N^n$ and $N \simeq 2^{2\lambda}$ then Eq. 1 is equivalent to*

$$\log_2(d) < 0.5n\lambda + \frac{n}{4} - \log_2(\sqrt{2}^n - 1) \simeq 0.5n\lambda.$$

6   Experimental Results

We further present an example for the $n = 3$ and $n = 4$ cases. Examples for $n = 1$ and $n = 2$ cases are provided in [10] and [7] respectively, and thus we omit them.

6.1   Case $n = 3$

Before providing our example, we first show how to recover p and q once $\varphi_3(N) = (ed - 1)/k$ is recovered using our attack.

Lemma 2. *Let $N = pq$ be the product of two unknown primes with $q < p < 2q$. If $\varphi_3(N) = N^3 - p^3 - q^3 + 1$ is known, then p and q can be recovered in polynomial time.*

Proof. We will rewrite $\varphi_3(N)$ as

$$\varphi_3(N) = N^3 - p^3 - 3p^2q - 3pq^2 - q^3 + 1 + 3p^2q + 3pq^2$$
$$= N^3 - (p + q)^3 + 3N(p + q) + 1,$$

which is equivalent to

$$(p + q)^3 - 3N(p + q) + \varphi_3(N) - N^3 - 1 = 0.$$

Finding $S = p + q$ is equivalent to solving (in $\mathbb{Z}$) the following cubic equation

$$x^3 - 3Nx + (\varphi_3(N) - N^3 - 1) = 0. \tag{2}$$

which can be done in polynomial time as it is presented in [17]. In order to find p and q, we compute $D = p - q$ using the following remark

$$(p - q)^2 = (p + q)^2 - 4pq = S^2 - 4N.$$

Taking into account that $p > q$, D is the positive square root of the previous quantity, and thus we derive the following

$$\begin{cases} p = \frac{S+D}{2} \\ q = \frac{S-D}{2} \end{cases}.$$

□

The following lemma shows that in order to factor N we only need to find one solution to Eq. 2, namely its unique integer solution.

Lemma 3. *Eq. 2 always has exactly two non-real roots and an integer one.*

Proof. Let x_1, x_2 and x_3 be Eq. 2's roots. Using Vieta's formulas we have

$$x_1 + x_2 + x_3 = 0,$$
$$x_1 x_2 + x_2 x_3 + x_3 x_1 = -3N,$$
$$x_1 x_2 x_3 = -(\varphi_3(N) - N^3 - 1).$$

From the first two relations we obtain

$$x_1^2 + x_2^2 + x_3^2 = (x_1 + x_2 + x_3)^2 - 2(x_1 x_2 + x_2 x_3 + x_3 x_1)$$
$$= 6N.$$

If we assume that $x_1 = p + q$ and x_2, x_3 are both real, we get the following system

$$\begin{cases} x_2 + x_3 = -(p + q) \\ x_2^2 + x_3^2 = 6N - (p + q)^2 \end{cases} \Rightarrow \begin{cases} (x_2 + x_3)^2 = (p + q)^2 \\ 2(x_2^2 + x_3^2) = 12N - 2(p + q)^2 \end{cases} \Rightarrow$$

$$(x_2 - x_3)^2 = 12N - 3(p + q)^2$$
$$= 6pq - 3p^2 - 3q^2$$
$$= -3(p - q)^2 < 0.$$

Therefore, we obtain a contradiction, and hence we conclude that Eq. 2 has one real root, which is $p + q \in \mathbb{Z}$, and two non-real roots.   □

Now, we will exemplify our attack for $n = 3$ using the following small public key

$$N = 3014972633503040336590226508316351022768913323933,$$
$$e = 8205656493798992557632452332926222819762435306999$$
$$ 0124626035612517563005998895654688526643002715434$$
$$ 2511202062827811962381704432052232 8087505650969.$$

Remark that $e \approx N^{2.989}$. We use the Euclidean algorithm to compute the continued fraction expansion of $e/\varphi_{3,0}(N)$ and obtain that the first 25 partial quotients are

$$[0, 3, 2, 1, 16, 5, 3, 5, 1, 5, 1, 11, 2, 6, 1, 3, 1, 4, 1, 1, 1, 267, 1, 1, 4, \ldots].$$

According to Theorem 2, the set of convergents of $e/\varphi_{3,0}(N)$ contains all the possible candidates for k/d. From these convergents we select only those for which $\varphi_3 = (ed - 1)/k$ is an integer and the following system of equations

$$\begin{cases} \varphi_3 = (p^3 - 1)(q^3 - 1) \\ N = pq \end{cases}$$

has a solution as given in Lemma 2. The 2nd, 3rd and 21st convergents satisfy the first condition, however only the last one leads to a valid solution for p and q. More precisely, the 21st convergent leads to

$$\varphi_3 = 27406282078929532070187021740774838075632644408773$$
$$7057963987757509374280517157259708222994487763446$$
$$9466218555656009272154715655458071982989539333036,$$

$$\frac{k}{d} = \frac{514812488}{1719435401},$$

$$p = 211977819903685906870781819,$$

$$q = 142230570862221395680680807.$$

6.2   Case $n = 4$

As in the previous case, we first show how to factorize N once φ_4 is known.

Lemma 4. Let $N = pq$ be the product of two unknown primes with $q < p < 2q$. If $\varphi_4(N) = N^4 - p^4 - q^4 + 1$ is known, then

$$p = \frac{1}{2}(S + D) \qquad and \qquad q = \frac{1}{2}(S - D),$$

where $S = \sqrt{2N + \sqrt{(N^2 + 1)^2 - \varphi_4(N)}}$ and $D = \sqrt{S^2 - 4N}$.

Proof. We will rewrite $\varphi_4(N)$ as

$$\varphi_4(N) = N^4 - p^4 - 4p^3q - 6p^2q^2 - 4pq^3 - q^4 + 1 + 4p^3q + 6p^2q^2 + 4pq^3$$
$$= N^4 - (p + q)^4 + 4N(p^2 + 2pq + q^2) - 2p^2q^2 + 1$$
$$= N^4 - (p + q)^4 + 4N(p + q)^2 - 2N^2 + 1$$

which is equivalent to

$$(p + q)^4 - 4N(p + q)^2 + \varphi_4(N) - (N^2 - 1)^2 = 0.$$

Finding $S' = p + q$ is equivalent to solving (in $\mathbb{Z}$) the following biquadratic equation

$$x^4 - 4Nx^2 + \varphi_4(N) - (N^2 - 1)^2 = 0 \Leftrightarrow$$
$$(x^2)^2 - 4N(x^2) + \varphi_4(N) - (N^2 - 1)^2 = 0.$$

The previous equation can be solved as a normal quadratic equation. Computing the discriminant Δ, we have that

$$\Delta = 4(N^2 + 1)^2 - 4\varphi_4(N) > 0.$$

Thus, the roots of the quadratic equation, $x'_{1,2}$, are

$$x'_{1,2} = 2N \pm \sqrt{(N^2 + 1)^2 - \varphi_4(N)}.$$

The roots of the biquadratic equation are the square roots of the previous quantities.

$$x_{1,2} = \pm\sqrt{2N + \sqrt{(N^2 + 1)^2 - \varphi_4(N)}}$$
$$x_{3,4} = \pm\sqrt{2N - \sqrt{(N^2 + 1)^2 - \varphi_4(N)}}$$

The roots $x_{3,4}$ are pure imaginary since

$$\sqrt{(N^2 + 1)^2 - \varphi_4(N)} > 2N \Leftrightarrow$$
$$(N^2 + 1)^2 - \varphi_4(N) > 4N^2 \Leftrightarrow$$
$$N^4 + 2N^2 + 1 - N^4 + p^4 + q^4 - 1 - 4N^2 > 0 \Leftrightarrow$$
$$(p^2 - q^2)^2 > 0.$$

The root $x_2 = -\sqrt{2N + \sqrt{(N^2 + 1)^2 - \varphi_4(N)}} < 0$, thus we get $S' = S = x_1 = \sqrt{2N + \sqrt{(N^2 + 1)^2 - \varphi_4(N)}}$. The values of p and q can be recovered by using the algorithm from Lemma 2.   □

We will further present our attack for $n = 4$ using the following small public key

$$N = 30149726335030403365902265083163510227689133239 33,$$
$$e = 3886649078157217512540781268280213360319970133145$$
$$6396788273204320283738850302214441484301356047280$$
$$9980074678226938065582620857819830171139174634897$$
$$69731055010977380039512575106301590600391232847.$$

Note that $e \approx N^{3.993}$. Applying the continued fraction expansion of $e/\varphi_{4,0}(N)$, we get the first 25 partial quotients

$$[0, 2, 7, 1, 15, 6, 1, 2, 4, 1, 1, 2, 1, 1, 3, 1, 1, 1, 2, 38, 1, 2, 1, 45, 8, \ldots].$$

In this case, we consider the convergents of $e/\varphi_{4,0}(N)$, and we select only those for which $\varphi_4 = (ed-1)/k$ is an integer and the following system of equations

$$\begin{cases} \varphi_4 = (p^4-1)(q^4-1) \\ N = pq \end{cases}$$

has a solution as given in Lemma 4. The $2nd$ and $23rd$ convergents satisfy the first condition, however only the last one leads to a valid solution for p and q. More precisely, the $23rd$ convergent leads to

$\varphi_4 = 8262919045403735048878111025050137547018067986718$
$6489272861711603139280409749776405912009959512474$
$1225965967573968605037596274853618481302754457480$
$6787891184267004832506535094151626645227 1040000,$

$\dfrac{k}{d} = \dfrac{799532980}{1699787183},$

$p = 2119778199036859068707819,$

$q = 1422305708622213956806807.$

7 Conclusions

In this paper we introduced a family of RSA-like cryptosystems, which includes the RSA and Elkamchouchi *et al.* public key encryption schemes [15, 29] (*i.e.* $n = 1$ and $n = 2$). Then, we presented a small private key attack against our family of cryptosystems and provided two instantiations of it. As a conclusion, the whole family of RSA-like schemes allows an attacker to recover the secret exponent via continued fractions when the public exponent is close to N^n and the secret exponent is smaller that $N^{0.25n}$.

Future Work. When $n = 1, 2, 3, 4$, in Sect. 6 and [4, 7, 10] a method for factoring N once φ_n is known is provided. Although we found a method for particular cases of n we could not find a generic method for factoring N. Therefore, we leave it as an open problem. Another interesting research direction, is to find out if the attack methods described in Sect. 1 for the RSA and Elkamchouchi *et al.* schemes also work in the general case.

References

1. Aono, Y.: Minkowski sum based lattice construction for multivariate simultaneous coppersmith's technique and applications to RSA. In: Boyd, C., Simpson, L. (eds.) ACISP 2013. LNCS, vol. 7959, pp. 88–103. Springer, Heidelberg (2013). https://doi.org/10.1007/978-3-642-39059-3_7
2. Blömer, J., May, A.: New partial key exposure attacks on RSA. In: Boneh, D. (ed.) CRYPTO 2003. LNCS, vol. 2729, pp. 27–43. Springer, Heidelberg (2003). https://doi.org/10.1007/978-3-540-45146-4_2

3. Blömer, J., May, A.: A generalized wiener attack on RSA. In: Bao, F., Deng, R., Zhou, J. (eds.) PKC 2004. LNCS, vol. 2947, pp. 1–13. Springer, Heidelberg (2004). https://doi.org/10.1007/978-3-540-24632-9_1
4. Boneh, D.: Twenty years of attacks on the RSA cryptosystem. Notices AMS **46**(2), 203–213 (1999)
5. Boneh, D., Durfee, G.: Cryptanalysis of RSA with private key d less than $N_{0.292}$. In: Stern, J. (ed.) EUROCRYPT 1999. LNCS, vol. 1592, pp. 1–11. Springer, Heidelberg (1999). https://doi.org/10.1007/3-540-48910-X_1
6. Boneh, D., Durfee, G., Frankel, Y.: An attack on RSA given a small fraction of the private key bits. In: Ohta, K., Pei, D. (eds.) ASIACRYPT 1998. LNCS, vol. 1514, pp. 25–34. Springer, Heidelberg (1998). https://doi.org/10.1007/3-540-49649-1_3
7. Bunder, M., Nitaj, A., Susilo, W., Tonien, J.: A new attack on three variants of the RSA cryptosystem. In: Liu, J.K., Steinfeld, R. (eds.) ACISP 2016. LNCS, vol. 9723, pp. 258–268. Springer, Cham (2016). https://doi.org/10.1007/978-3-319-40367-0_16
8. Bunder, M., Nitaj, A., Susilo, W., Tonien, J.: A generalized attack on RSA type cryptosystems. Theor. Comput. Sci. **704**, 74–81 (2017)
9. Bunder, M., Nitaj, A., Susilo, W., Tonien, J.: Cryptanalysis of RSA-type cryptosystems based on Lucas sequences, Gaussian integers and elliptic curves. J. Inf. Secur. Appl. **40**, 193–198 (2018)
10. Bunder, M., Tonien, J.: A new attack on the RSA cryptosystem based on continued fractions. Malays. J. Math. Sci. **11**, 45–57 (2017)
11. Cherkaoui-Semmouni, M., Nitaj, A., Susilo, W., Tonien, J.: Cryptanalysis of RSA variants with primes sharing most significant bits. In: Liu, J.K., Katsikas, S., Meng, W., Susilo, W., Intan, R. (eds.) ISC 2021. LNCS, vol. 13118, pp. 42–53. Springer, Cham (2021). https://doi.org/10.1007/978-3-030-91356-4_3
12. Coppersmith, D.: Small solutions to polynomial equations, and low exponent RSA vulnerabilities. J. Cryptol. **10**(4), 233–260 (1997)
13. Cotan, P., Teşeleanu, G.: Continued fractions applied to a family of RSA-like cryptosystems. In: Su, C., Gritzalis, D., Piuri, V. (eds.) Information Security Practice and Experience. ISPEC 2022. LNCS, vol. 13620, pp. 589–605. Springer, Cham (2022). https://doi.org/10.1007/978-3-031-21280-2_33
14. De Weger, B.: Cryptanalysis of RSA with small prime difference. Appl. Algebra Eng. Commun. Comput. **13**(1), 17–28 (2002)
15. Elkamchouchi, H., Elshenawy, K., Shaban, H.: Extended RSA cryptosystem and digital signature schemes in the domain of Gaussian integers. In: ICCS 2002, vol. 1, pp. 91–95. IEEE Computer Society (2002)
16. Ernst, M., Jochemsz, E., May, A., de Weger, B.: Partial key exposure attacks on RSA up to full size exponents. In: Cramer, R. (ed.) EUROCRYPT 2005. LNCS, vol. 3494, pp. 371–386. Springer, Heidelberg (2005). https://doi.org/10.1007/11426639_22
17. Fujii, K.: A Modern Introduction to Cardano and Ferrari Formulas in the Algebraic Equations. arXiv Preprint arXiv:quant-ph/0311102 (2003)
18. Hardy, G.H., Wright, E.M., et al.: An Introduction to the Theory of Numbers. Oxford University Press, Oxford (1979)
19. Herrmann, M., May, A.: Maximizing small root bounds by linearization and applications to small secret exponent RSA. In: Nguyen, P.Q., Pointcheval, D. (eds.) PKC 2010. LNCS, vol. 6056, pp. 53–69. Springer, Heidelberg (2010). https://doi.org/10.1007/978-3-642-13013-7_4

20. Howgrave-Graham, N., Seifert, J.-P.: Extending wiener's attack in the presence of many decrypting exponents. In: CQRE 1999. LNCS, vol. 1740, pp. 153–166. Springer, Heidelberg (1999). https://doi.org/10.1007/3-540-46701-7_14

21. Kamel Ariffin, M.R., Abubakar, S.I., Yunos, F., Asbullah, M.A.: New cryptanalytic attack on RSA modulus N = pq using small prime difference method. Cryptography **3**(1), 2 (2018)

22. Maitra, S., Sarkar, S.: Revisiting wiener's attack – new weak keys in RSA. In: Wu, T.-C., Lei, C.-L., Rijmen, V., Lee, D.-T. (eds.) ISC 2008. LNCS, vol. 5222, pp. 228–243. Springer, Heidelberg (2008). https://doi.org/10.1007/978-3-540-85886-7_16

23. Maitra, S., Sarkar, S.: Revisiting Wiener's Attack - New Weak Keys in RSA. IACR Cryptology ePrint Archive 2008/228 (2008)

24. Murru, N., Saettone, F.M.: A novel RSA-like cryptosystem based on a generalization of the Rédei rational functions. In: Kaczorowski, J., Pieprzyk, J., Pomykała, J. (eds.) NuTMiC 2017. LNCS, vol. 10737, pp. 91–103. Springer, Cham (2018). https://doi.org/10.1007/978-3-319-76620-1_6

25. Nassr, D.I., Bahig, H.M., Bhery, A., Daoud, S.S.: A new RSA vulnerability using continued fractions. In: AICCSA 2008, pp. 694–701. IEEE Computer Society (2008)

26. Nitaj, A.: Another generalization of wiener's attack on RSA. In: Vaudenay, S. (ed.) AFRICACRYPT 2008. LNCS, vol. 5023, pp. 174–190. Springer, Heidelberg (2008). https://doi.org/10.1007/978-3-540-68164-9_12

27. Nitaj, A., Pan, Y., Tonien, J.: A generalized attack on some variants of the RSA cryptosystem. In: Cid, C., Jacobson Jr., M. (eds.) Selected Areas in Cryptography – SAC 2018. SAC 2018. LNCS, vol. 11349, pp. 421–433. Springer, Cham (2019). https://doi.org/10.1007/978-3-030-10970-7_19

28. Peng, L., Hu, L., Lu, Y., Wei, H.: An improved analysis on three variants of the RSA cryptosystem. In: Chen, K., Lin, D., Yung, M. (eds.) Inscrypt 2016. LNCS, vol. 10143, pp. 140–149. Springer, Cham (2017). https://doi.org/10.1007/978-3-319-54705-3_9

29. Rivest, R.L., Shamir, A., Adleman, L.: A method for obtaining digital signatures and public-key cryptosystems. Commun. ACM **21**(2), 120–126 (1978)

30. Sarkar, S., Maitra, S.: Cryptanalysis of RSA with more than one decryption exponent. Inf. Process. Lett. **110**(8–9), 336–340 (2010)

31. Takayasu, A., Kunihiro, N.: Cryptanalysis of RSA with multiple small secret exponents. In: Susilo, W., Mu, Y. (eds.) ACISP 2014. LNCS, vol. 8544, pp. 176–191. Springer, Cham (2014). https://doi.org/10.1007/978-3-319-08344-5_12

32. Takayasu, A., Kunihiro, N.: Partial key exposure attacks on RSA: achieving the Boneh-Durfee bound. In: Joux, A., Youssef, A. (eds.) SAC 2014. LNCS, vol. 8781, pp. 345–362. Springer, Cham (2014). https://doi.org/10.1007/978-3-319-13051-4_21

33. Wiener, M.J.: Cryptanalysis of short RSA secret exponents. IEEE Trans. Inf. Theory **36**(3), 553–558 (1990)

34. Zheng, M., Kunihiro, N., Hu, H.: Cryptanalysis of RSA variants with modified Euler quotient. In: Joux, A., Nitaj, A., Rachidi, T. (eds.) AFRICACRYPT 2018. LNCS, vol. 10831, pp. 266–281. Springer, Cham (2018). https://doi.org/10.1007/978-3-319-89339-6_15

Fair Distributed Oblivious Polynomial Evaluation via Bitcoin Deposits: Compute-as-a-Service

Amirreza Hamidi[✉] and Hossein Ghodosi

James Cook University, Townsville, QLD, Australia
amirreza.hamidi@my.jcu.edu.au, hossein.ghodosi@jcu.edu.au

Abstract. Distributed oblivious polynomial evaluation (DOPE) is a special case of two-party computation where the sender party P_1 holds a polynomial $f(x)$ of degree k and the receiver party P_2 has a value α. They wish to perform a secure computation with the help of n designated cloud servers such that P_2 obtains the value $f(\alpha)$ while the privacy of their inputs is maintained.

We present the first *fair* DOPE scheme using Bitcoin deposit transactions in the presence of n cloud servers where n is independent of the polynomial degree k. The fairness property ensures that an honest server gains the reward for conducting a computation service while a corrupt server has to pay some penalty amount to an honest party. Our protocol consists of two separate phases: *setup* and *computation*. The cloud servers are involved with P_1 in the setup phase while P_2 communicates with the servers in the computation phase which means that the actual computation can be implemented at any time after the setup phase. Any corrupt party/server can be detected using the non-interactive Pedersen's commitment scheme. Our protocol preserves the security against an active adversary corrupting a coalition of P_1 and at most t cloud servers in the setup phase and a coalition of up to t servers in the computation phase in the presence of honest majority of the servers. The communication complexity is bounded to $O(kt)$ which is the same as that in the previous DOPE studies while the fairness feature is also achieved in our scheme.

Keywords: Distributed Oblivious Polynomial Evaluation · Fairness via Bitcoin Deposits · Cloud Servers · Cloud Computing Service

1 Introduction

Secure two-party computation enables two participants, with their private inputs x and y, to jointly execute some secure computation process to obtain the outputs $f_1(x, y)$ and $f_2(x, y)$, respectively. Oblivious polynomial evaluation (OPE), introduced by [21], is a variant of two-party computation where a sender party P_1 has a polynomial of degree k as $f(x) = a_0 + a_1x + a_2x^2 + \ldots + a_kx^k$ and a receiver party P_2 holds a value α. The parties wish to perform a secure computation such

© The Author(s), under exclusive license to Springer Nature Switzerland AG 2024
L. Fritsch et al. (Eds.): NordSec 2023, LNCS 14324, pp. 73–86, 2024.
https://doi.org/10.1007/978-3-031-47748-5_5

that P_2 gains the value $f(\alpha)$ and P_1 gets nothing while the privacy of the parties' inputs is preserved. The inputs and the output are over a pre-determined field $\mathbb{F}_q$ and the system can be denoted by the functionality $(f(x), \alpha) \to (\perp, f(\alpha))$. One may think of using multi-party computation solutions in OPE systems, however, these solutions are generic and very inefficient, especially when large inputs are involved. As a more formal definition:

Definition 1. *In a secure OPE system, two parties with their private inputs participate in the system with the field $\mathbb{F}_q$ where the sender party P_1 holds a polynomial $f(x)$ of degree k and the receiver party P_2 has a value α. They wish to execute a secure computation procedure such that P_2 obtains the value $f(\alpha)$. The system is said to be securely implemented such that:*

- *P_1 cannot distinguish α from a value α' randomly chosen over the field.*
- *P_2 can gain no information in relation to the P_1's polynomial $f(x)$ except the output $f(\alpha)$.*

There may exist two types of adversaries in this system: either passive (semi-honest) or active (malicious). The former follows the protocol but aims to learn as much information as possible about the private inputs. The latter takes full control of a party and (in addition to being semi-honest) deviates from a protocol in an arbitrary fashion to change the output correctness without being caught. A malicious party is detected in a fully secure protocol in which the security can be either unconditional or computational. Furthermore, in a *fair* protocol the detected corrupt party gets penalized for conducting the malicious behaviour.

OPE is a building block of many cryptographic models and security fields such as RSA keys generation [12], privacy-preserving data mining [1], scalar product [13], oblivious keyword search [9], oblivious neural networking [6], set intersection [10] and electric voting [22]. It also plays an important role in privacy-preserving machine learning where a client wishes to execute a secure protocol with a server/company to gain private information in the classification phase of a machine learning algorithm [8]. An example of this application is in healthcare where a patient intends to obtain a prediction of his health status from a healthcare company holding a trained model without revealing any information about his personal health records [14].

The recent development of cloud computing has made it possible to outsource main bottleneck computations to cloud servers. This is where distributed oblivious polynomial evaluation (DOPE) emerges where the main two parties P_1 and P_2 communicate with a set of remote distributed cloud servers to outsource and conduct their OPE computation in a secure fashion. This system offers higher flexibility as the main two parties do not communicate directly, i.e., they can remain anonymous. Also, another important point of this method is that any user with low computation power is able to outsource the heavy computation operations to the cloud servers. However, here the main challenge is that this approach incurs obvious security and privacy breaches.

1.1   Background

In the literature, some studies have investigated the idea of employing either one cloud third party [4,11,14,16] or a set of distributed ($t \geq 2$) servers [7,15,19] in their protocols. With regards to OPE using a third party, [14] presented a verifiable privacy-preserving monitoring scheme for mobile health systems with one cloud-assisted server. Also, [11] proposed a verifiable and private OPE protocol, by employing homomorphic feature of Paillier cryptosystem and a trusted server, to record medical datasets. [4] formally defined the notion of private polynomial evaluation with a designated server.

Using just one cloud server offers lower communication complexity, however, the serious problem could be that corrupting only one server causes a central point of failure breaking the whole security of the system. Hence, DOPE gives higher security as corrupting the total t number of servers is less likely which can be denoted as the *security parameter*. [19] conducted the first unconditionally secure DOPE study in the presence of semi-honest adversaries. The main problem of their protocol is that the privacy of the parties' inputs is not maintained against the maximum possible number $t - 1$ servers. To deal with this issue, they introduced some publicly known information raising the communication overhead. Another private DOPE protocol was proposed by [7] with passive adversaries and the communication complexity $O(kt)$. However, their protocol requires that the main two parties P_1 and P_2 directly communicate with each other which does not meet the condition that the two parties are allowed to interact only with the cloud servers. Recently, [15] presented the first verifiable secure DOPE protocol in the presence of an active adversary corrupting a coalition of $t-1$ servers and the party P_1 with the communication complexity $O(kt)$. Although any inconsistency in the output correctness can be detected in their protocol, a corrupt server/party can fail the protocol without being penalized for conducting such this malicious behaviour. In order to make the DOPE system more practical in the cloud computing service, where the parties pay for the outsourced computation service to the servers, the notion of *fairness* is required such that any corrupt party/server must compensate as well.

1.2   Our Contribution

We present the first *fair* secure DOPE scheme where the sender party P_1, having a polynomial $f(x)$ of degree k, and the receiver party P_2, holding the input α, conduct a secure outsourced computation service with a set of n cloud servers such that P_2 obtains the output $f(\alpha)$. The number of cloud servers is $n \geq 2t+1$ where t can be considered the security parameter and it is independent of the polynomial degree k. The fairness property ensures that an honest server/party never has to pay any penalty and also, if a server/party does not deliver the correct output to P_2 or aborts the protocol, it compensates to an honest party. This can be achieved by the features of *scripts* and *time-lock* in Bitcoin transactions such that an honest server gains the reward for the computation service it performs while each corrupt party/server gets penalized as well. Note that we choose Bitcoin network, as a decentralised ledger without the need of a third trusted party, since the market price is less volatile compared to the other cryptocurrencies with smart contracts. With regards to the outsourced computation service, each server computes an encrypted share of the output using homomorphic feature of Paillier cryptosystem. In detail, our scheme consists of two phases:

- **Setup Phase**: P_1 distributes the shares of his polynomial among the servers. He also commits to the shares using the Pedersen's non-interactive verifiable secret sharing scheme. The servers check the commitments and if the honest majority complain, P_1 is dishonest and compensates to the servers. Otherwise, P_1 penalizes every corrupt server and eliminates it from the protocol.
- **Computation Phase**: P_2 encrypts his inputs and broadcasts them. Each server employs one round of homomorphic encryption to compute the encrypted share of the output and sends it back to P_2 who checks the commitment. If P_2 detects any faulty server, he eliminates it and gets compensated from it. Otherwise, he pays to the honest servers for the computation service they have executed.

We assume that the communication channels are asynchronous, and if a server/party does not perform the computation and communicate by the timelock t_l, it is corrupt and makes the compensation for that. Moreover, the servers/parties send the Bitcoin deposits before commencing each phase. Note that an honest server gets back its deposit after completing the service in each phase. Our scheme holds the full security against a static active adversary corrupting a coalition of t cloud servers and P_1 in the presence of the major honest servers (i.e., $t + 1$). The privacy of the P_1's inputs is preserved by the unconditional security of secret sharing while the privacy of the P_2's inputs is maintained with IND-CPA security of Paillier cryptosystem. The communication complexity is bounded to $O(kt)$ which is the same as the previous studies in this field.

2   Preliminaries

2.1   Secret Sharing

In Shamir's secret sharing scheme in the field $\mathbb{F}_q$, a dealer distributes the secret s among the participants by a random polynomial $p(x) = \sum_{j=0}^{t} a_j x^j$, where $a_0 = s$ and q is a prime number, such that each party is given a share $p_i \leftarrow p(i)$ [25]. In order to reconstruct the secret, a set of at least $t + 1$ participants (which is said $(t + 1, n)$) pools their shares and reconstructs the secret using Lagrange interpolation method. With regards to the privacy level, this scheme is information-theoretically secure against a passive adversary corrupting up to t parties.

The secret sharing is linear and the parties can reconstruct any linear function with no interaction. We denote the t-sharings $[s]_t$ as a set of $t + 1$ shares of a random polynomial $p(x)$ with the threshold/degree t and the secret s.

2.2   Pedersen's Verifiable Secret Sharing

We also employ the non-interactive secret sharing commitment approach of Pedersen [24] over the integers to detect any corrupt party in our protocol. Note that the Pedersen's verifiable secret sharing is *unconditionally hiding* and *computationally binding* under the assumption of discrete logarithm with the information rate $\frac{1}{2}$.

Namely, a dealer chooses two large prime numbers p and q such that q divides $p-1$, i.e., the order q is a subgroup of the field $\mathbb{Z}_p$. The dealer picks two random generators g and h over the field $\mathbb{F}_q$ such that $\log_g h$ is unknown. The dealer, holding a secret s in $\mathbb{Z}_q$, shamir-shares the secret among the participants using a random polynomial $p(x) = s + b_1 x + b_2 x^2 + \ldots + b_t x^t \bmod q$ where $b_j \in \mathbb{Z}_q$ (for $j = 1, \ldots, t$). He also chooses a random companion polynomial $p'(x) = s' + b'_1 x + b'_2 x^2 + \ldots + b'_t x^t \bmod q$ where $s', b'_j \in \mathbb{Z}_q$ and distributes the shares among the participants. Thus, each party P_i is given two shares $[s]_t$ and $[s']_t$. The dealer computes:

$$A_0 = g^s \cdot h^{s'} \bmod p$$

and publishes it. He also computes $A_j = g^{a_j} \cdot h^{a'_j} \bmod p$ and broadcasts them. Each share-holder P_i checks that whether the dealer has committed to the correct share $[s]_t$ as follows:

$$g^{[s]_t} \cdot h^{[s']_t} = \prod_{j=0}^{t} (A_j)^{i^j} \bmod p$$

P_i accepts the share $[s]_t$ if the check is *OK*, otherwise he broadcasts a complaint.

2.3   Paillier Cryptosystem

The Paillier cryptosystem [23], which is based on composite degree residuosity, works under the assumption of decisional composite residuosity (DCR). Namely, given two plaintexts and the corresponding ciphertexts encrypted under the DCR assumption, a probabilistic polynomial-time adversary can guess either of the plaintexts with any negligible advantage. As a result, the security of this cryptosystem is said indistinguishability against chosen function attack (IND-CFA) under the DCR assumption. More formally:

Definition 2. *Let x_0 and x_1 be encrypted using a k-bits cryptosystem under the DCR assumption. Let a probabilistic polynomial-time adversary $\mathcal{A}$ gain the encryption of x_β for a randomly chosen $\beta \in \{0,1\}$. Suppose $\mathcal{A}$ can guess the plaintexts x_0 and x_1 with the probabilities denoted by $p_0(\mathcal{A}, k)$ and $p_1(\mathcal{A}, k)$, respectively. The encryption system is said to be IND-CFA secure if $|p_0(\mathcal{A}, k) - p_1(\mathcal{A}, k)| \leq \varepsilon$ for any ε negligible in k.*

This encryption system includes main three algorithms: keys generation, encryption and decryption.

Keys Generation: The dealer invokes a probabilistic algorithm $\mathsf{Gen}(1^k)$, with the security parameter k, to generate the keys pair $(pk, sk) \leftarrow \mathsf{Gen}(1^k)$. The public key pk is an RSA modulus $pk \leftarrow N$ where $N = p_c \cdot q_c$ such that p_c and q_c are two large prime numbers with k/2 bits, e.g., each at least 1024 bits. The private key sk is the Euler's totient $sk \leftarrow \phi(N)$ where $\phi(N) = (p_c - 1)(q_c - 1)$ such that $\gcd(N, \phi(N)) = 1$.

Encryption: The dealer invokes a probabilistic algorithm $\mathsf{Enc}_{pk}(m, r)$ to encrypt the message m and computes the ciphertext $c \leftarrow \mathsf{Enc}_{pk}(m, r)$ as:

$$\mathsf{Enc}_{pk}(m, r) = g^m \cdot r^N \bmod N^2$$

where the simplest value for $g \in Z_{N^2}^*$ can be $g = N + 1$ and r is a random number chosen in Z_N^*.

Homomorphism. A very useful feature of this cryptosystem is homomorphism which can be applied to the ciphertexts. Namely, let m_1 and m_2 be two plaintexts in Z_N which are encrypted with the same public key denoted by $\mathsf{Enc}_{pk}(m_1)$ and $\mathsf{Enc}_{pk}(m_2)$, respectively. It is trivial to show that $\mathsf{Enc}_{pk}(m_1) \times \mathsf{Enc}_{pk}(m_2) = \mathsf{Enc}_{pk}(m_1 + m_2)$ and also $\mathsf{Enc}_{pk}(m_1)^d = \mathsf{Enc}_{pk}(d \cdot m_1)$ for any random $d \in Z_N$.

Decryption: To decrypt the ciphertext c, a deterministic algorithm $\mathsf{Dec}_{sk}(c)$ is invoked to obtain the plaintext $m \leftarrow \mathsf{Dec}_{sk}(c)$. In detail, one raises the ciphertext to the private key $\phi(N)$ which, based on the Euler's totient function, can be simplified as:

$$[(N + 1)^m \cdot r^N]^{\phi(N)} \bmod N^2 = N \cdot \phi(N) \cdot m + 1$$

proven by the means of binomial coefficients in modulo N^2. Let the function $L(x)$ be $L(x) = \frac{x-1}{N}$, the plaintext m can be obtained as follows:

$$\mathsf{Dec}_{sk}(c) = L[c^{\phi(N)} \bmod N^2] \cdot \phi(N)^{-1} \bmod N$$

2.4   Bitcoin Transactions

Bitcoin is a decentralized peer-to-peer electronic cash system which was designed and developed by an anonymous person or group of people [20] as the first innovative idea of cryptocurrency. The transactions are stored in blockchain (as a public ledger) which helps to achieve agreement in decentralized scenarios without a trusted third party and also can avoid the single point of failure attack. Due to this property, Bitcoin has attracted some studies of multi-party computation to add fairness to their protocols, see e.g., [2,3,17,18]. The data consistency in blockchain is maintained using a consensus algorithm called proof of work. Namely, the first node solving a difficult computation puzzle (which generally takes roughly 10 mins) is selected to record a block of transactions. Moreover, the security of the Bitcoin network is preserved by the honest majority of computing power. Note that one may choose any other cryptocurrency with smart contract which can be applicable to our scheme, nevertheless, we employ Bitcoin since the market price and the transaction fee is less volatile and, thus, it is more reliable.

In detail, the system consists of addresses and transactions between them. An address is the hash of a public key and a transaction works with asymmetric cryptography. Each block can have several transactions in the body section. A sender signs a transaction with his private key and the recipient verifies the signature by the sender's public key. A transaction can have some inputs, i.e., it can accumulate money from several past transactions. Each transaction T_x includes the index of the previous transaction y, the scripts, the value $d\,\mathcal{B}$ and the time-lock t_l. The scripts of a transaction have a very useful feature where the users have much more flexibility in defining the condition on how the transaction T_x can be redeemed. This is achieved by the *input-scripts* and *output-scripts*. The output-script of the transaction T_x is a description function π_x with a boolean output. The transaction T_x is redeemed successfully and is valid if π_x evaluates to true, and then it is taken to the input-script of the next transaction. In other words, the input-script σ_x is a witness that is used to make the output-script π_y of the last transaction T_y evaluates to true on the current transaction T_x. One may think of an input-script as a signature of the transaction and the output-script as a verification algorithm of the signature. Moreover, if the time-lock t_l of the transaction T_x is reached, the transaction is redeemed automatically. So, the time-lock tells at what time the transaction becomes valid. Figure 1 shows the structure of the current transaction T_x with the value $d_2\,\mathcal{B}$ and the last redeemed transaction T_y.

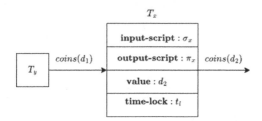

Fig. 1. The structure of the transaction T_x

To summarize, a transaction is valid if 1) the output-script evaluates to true or 2) the time-lock is reached. In our case, we employ the script and time-lock properties such that an honest party has the authority to redeem a transaction deposit. This can be either making a payment to an honest cloud server for the computation service it has performed or penalizing a corrupt server. Note that an honest server gets back its deposit after conducting the computation service.

2.5   Security Model

We discuss ideal/real security model of a fair DOPE scheme in this section. In a simulation-based model, it is assumed that there exists a simulator S playing the role of an adversary in the ideal model. The simulator takes the inputs of the corrupt parties and implements the functionality $\mathcal{F}$ such that the participants do not communicate directly. As a result, the ideal model achieves the highest level of security. We denote the ideal model by $IDEAL_{\mathcal{F},S}$ and the view of the simulator by $VIEW_S$. On the other hand, a probabilistic polynomial-time adversary $\mathcal{A}$ corrupts a coalition of the parties in the real model where the protocol Π is executed. The real model is denoted by $REAL_{\Pi,\mathcal{A}}$ with the adversary's view $VIEW_{\mathcal{A}}$. The protocol Π is said to be securely implemented if the ideal and the real models, $IDEAL_{\mathcal{F},S}$ and $REAL_{\Pi,\mathcal{A}}$, are computationally indistinguishable [5].

Initially, we mention the conditions of a secure DOPE system and, then, we discuss about adding fairness to it. Namely, in a secure DOPE protocol with n cloud servers, where P_1 holds a polynomial $f(x)$ of degree k and P_2 has a value α, the privacy and the correctness requirements must be satisfied as follows:

- **Receiver's Privacy:** The adversary $\mathcal{A}$ corrupts a coalition of P_1 and a number of maximum t cloud servers. The protocol maintains the privacy of the P_2's input, if for any α' in the field, the $VIEW_{\mathcal{A}}$ for α and that for α' are computationally indistinguishable in the real model.
- **Sender's Privacy:** The adversary $\mathcal{A}$ controls a coalition of P_2 and up to t cloud servers. The simulator S executes the functionality with a random value α' in the field to gain the output $f(\alpha')$. The privacy of the sender's polynomial is held if $f(\alpha')$ is computationally indistinguishable from any value randomly chosen over the field. In other words, $VIEW_{\mathcal{A}}$ must get no information about the polynomial $f(x)$ except the output $f(\alpha)$. It should be stated that P_2 is only allowed to obtain at most $k-1$ outputs from the same sender P_1, otherwise, he would be able to gain the polynomial $f(x)$ and break the sender's privacy.
- **Correctness:** Here, a static active adversary $\mathcal{A}$ takes the full control of a coalition of P_1 and up to t cloud servers. P_2 implements the protocol to gain the value $f(\alpha)$ while $\mathcal{A}$ deviates from the protocol trying to change the output to $f(\alpha')$ without being detected for any α' over the field. The protocol preserves the correctness if $f(\alpha)$ and $f(\alpha')$ are computationally indistinguishable.
- **Fairness:** In addition to the conditions above, we add the *fairness* property to our scheme to propose the first robust DOPE system. Namely, in a fair DOPE scheme:
  - An honest cloud server gets paid for the computation service it performs.
  - An honest party/server never has to pay any penalty.
  - If a party/server does not deliver the correct output to P_2 or it aborts the protocol before the computation finishes, it compensates for conducting the malicious behaviour.

Note that we assume the receiver party P_2 is always honest and does not deviate from the protocol as he wishes to obtain the correct output. Furthermore, in order to detect a malicious sender P_1, the majority of the cloud servers are honest in our scheme, i.e., $n \geq 2t + 1$ servers with at most t corrupt servers.

3 Our Scheme

We discuss our DOPE protocol in this section. Our protocol consists of two phases: setup and computation.

We assume that the parties have access to a perfect clock and the communication between the parties takes no time, unless the adversary delays. In particular, the parties and the servers have agreed on a time-lock t_l for the computation delay before the protocol begins.

3.1 Setup Phase

The sender party P_1 is involved with n cloud servers ($n \geq 2t + 1$) in this phase. We assume that P_1 and the servers have already posted their deposits via the Bitcoin network and their transactions are already on the ledger before this phase starts. Figure 2 depicts the setup phase of our protocol Π_{DOPE}.

Note that in order to incentivise and prevent the servers from cheating, the reward value for each server's computation service must be greater than its initial deposit, i.e., $D_1 > d$. Of course, an honest server gets back its deposit at the end of this phase.

3.2 Computation Phase

The receiver P_2 starts this phase while the corrupt servers in C in the setup phase have been eliminated. So, P_2 communicates with a set of $S \subseteq n - C$ servers where $|S| \geq t + 1$. Similarly, the players post their deposit transactions to the ledger before commencing this phase. Each server computes an encrypted share of the output and P_2 verifies the shares using the Pedersen's commitments published in the setup phase. P_2 detects any corrupt server, gets the compensation from it and eliminates it. Figure 3 shows the computation phase of our protocol Π_{DOPE}.

Note that an honest servers gets back its deposit after accepting its computation service by P_2. Similar to the setup phase, due to the incentive mechanism and to prevent the cloud servers from cheating, the reward amount $D_2 \text{\Bitcoin}$ has to be greater than each server's deposit $d_2 \text{\Bitcoin}$. The communication complexity of our protocol is $O(kt)$ which is the same as that in the previous DOPE protocols [7,15]. However, our DOPE holds the *fairness* with the same communication overhead.

Input: P_1 holds the polynomial $f(x) = a_0 + a_1 x + \ldots + a_k x^k = \sum_{j=0}^{k} a_j x^j$ where $a_j \in Z_q$.

- P_1 has already made the deposit $D_1 \text{\B}$ for each server. Also, Each server $S_i \in S$ has posted the deposit $d\,\text{\B}$ to the ledger.

- P_1 distributes t-sharings $[a_0]_t, [a_1]_t, \ldots, [a_k]_t$, denoted by $[a_j]_t$ among the servers. Also, as described in the section 2.2, he distributes random companion t-sharings $[a'_j]_t$ over the field $\mathbb{Z}_q$. He picks a large prime p and two generators g and h in $\mathbb{F}_q$ such that $\log_g h$ is unknown, and he commits to the shares $[a_j]_t$ using the Pedersen's VSS scheme. Namely, P_1 computes the commitments $A_{j0}, A_{j1}, \ldots, A_{jt}$ in $\mathbb{F}_p$ (see section 2.2) denoted by A_{je} for $e = 0, \ldots, t$. P_1 broadcasts the commitments A_{je}, i.e., totally $(k+1) \times (t+1)$ commitments.

- Each server $S_i \in S$ checks for its share $[a_j]_t$ that:

$$g^{[a_j]_t} \cdot h^{[a'_j]_t} = \prod_{e=0}^{t} (A_{je})^{i^e} \mod p \qquad (1)$$

and accepts the share $[a_j]_t$ if the commitment is OK and receives the P_1's deposit $D_1 \text{\B}$, otherwise it broadcasts a complaint.
If the server does not respond about the check by the time-lock t_l, it is tagged as corrupt.

- If more than t servers complain, the sender P_1 is dishonest and the protocol *fails*. Each server gets compensated and redeems the deposit $D_1 \text{\B}$ from P_1.

- If equal or less than t servers complain, they are tagged as corrupt. Let C denote the set of corrupt servers ($|\mathsf{C}| \le t$). P_1 penalises each server in C redeeming its corresponding transaction $d\,\text{\B}$ and eliminates it from the protocol.

Fig. 2. The setup phase of the protocol Π_{DOPE}

4   Security Evaluation

We assess the security of our scheme based on the security model described in Sect. 2.5.

Theorem 1. *The protocol Π_{DOPE} is robust against a static active adversary corrupting a coalition of P_1 and at most t cloud servers. The security is unconditional for the P_1's polynomial and semantic for the P_2's input.*

Proof. Let H and C denote the honest and the corrupt parties/servers in the ideal model, respectively. Let $\{P_1, (S_1, \ldots, S_t)\} \in \mathsf{C}$ and $\{S_{t+1}, \ldots, S_{2t+1}\} \in \mathsf{H}$ in the setup phase. The simulator $\mathcal{S}$ broadcasts wrong commitments $A_{je\delta}$ to the functionality which is analogous to the situation where the adversary $\mathcal{A}$ introduces the errors $A_{je\delta} = A_{je} + \delta_A$ to the real model. $\mathcal{S}$ runs the function-

Input: P_2 has the value $\alpha \in Z_q$.
Output: P_2 obtains $f(\alpha)$ in $\mathbb{Z}_q$.

- P_2 has already posted the deposits $D_2\ ฿$ for each server. Also, each server $S_i \in S$ has sent the deposit transaction $d\ ฿$ to the ledger.

- P_2 invokes the keys generation algorithm $\mathsf{Gen}(1^k)$ of the Paillier cryptosystem to produce the keys (pk, sk) where the public key is $N = p_c \cdot q_c$ as described in section 2.3. He encrypts the values α^j (for $j = 0, 1, \ldots, k$) to obtain the ciphertexts $c_j \leftarrow \mathsf{Enc}_{pk}(\alpha^j)$ and publishes them.

- Each S_i employs the homomorphic feature to compute an encrypted share of the output as:

$$c_i = \prod_{j=0}^{k} c_j^{[a_j]_t} \mod N^2$$

similarly, it computes an encrypted share of the companion polynomials, which it receives in the setup phase as:

$$c_i' = \prod_{j=0}^{k} c_j^{[a_j']_t} \mod N^2$$

and sends them to P_2. If S_i delays and does not send the corresponding c_i and c_i' to P_2 by the time-lock t_l, P_2 tags it as a corrupt server.

- P_2 decrypts c_i and c_i' to open the share $[f(\alpha)]_t$ of the output and the companion share $[v']_t$ of the companion polynomials, respectively. Let $E_j = \prod_{e=0}^{t} A_{je}^{i^e} \mod p$ which can be computed by P_2 for each server S_i. He checks for S_i that whether:

$$g^{[f(\alpha)]_t} \cdot h^{[v']_t} = \prod_{j=0}^{k} E_j^{\alpha^j} \mod p \tag{2}$$

if it is Ok, he accepts the computation of the share $[f(\alpha)]_t$ from the server S_i. Otherwise S_i is corrupt.

- P_2 penalizes every corrupt servers in this phase, redeems its deposit $d\ ฿$ and eliminates it. Finally, P_2 obtains $f(\alpha)$ using the t-sharings $[f(\alpha)]_t$.

Fig. 3. The computation phase of the protocol Π_{DOPE}

ality and the servers in H do not accept the t-sharings $[a_j]_t$ using the non-interactive Pedersen's VSS (Eq. 1). Thus, they detect the corrupt P_1, penalize him by redeeming his deposit transaction $D_1\ ฿$ and get back their own deposits $d\ ฿$. Let $\{S_1, \ldots, S_t\} \in C$ and $\{P_1, (S_{t+1}, \ldots, S_{2t+1})\} \in H$ in the setup phase. S delays by the time-lock t_l or broadcasts wrong complains regarding the P_1's commitments A_{je}. This is similar to the same condition in the real model. P_1 eliminates the servers in C and gets compensated by redeeming the deposit $d\ ฿$

from each server in that set. Moreover, each server in H gains the reward $D_1 \text{\BitcoinSign}$ from P_1 and gets back its own deposit $d\,\text{\BitcoinSign}$.

Let $\{S_1, \ldots, S_t\} \in C$ and $\{P_2, (S_{t+1}, \ldots, S_{2t+1})\} \in H$ in the computation phase. The simulator $\mathcal{S}$ sends the wrong encrypted shares $c_{i\delta}$ and $c'_{i\delta}$ to P_2. This is analogous if $\mathcal{A}$ introduces the errors $c_{i\delta} = c_i + \delta_c$ and $c'_{i\delta} = c'_i + \delta_{c'}$ in the real model. $\mathcal{S}$ executes the functionality and P_2 detects a faulty server using the extension of the Pedersen's commitments in Eq. 2 which can be written as:

$$\prod_{j=0}^{k} E_j^{\alpha^j} \bmod p = \prod_{j=0}^{k} g^{\alpha^j \cdot [a_j]_t} \cdot h^{\alpha^j \cdot [a'_j]_t} \bmod p$$

$$= g^{[f(\alpha)]_t} \cdot h^{[v']_t} \bmod p$$

P_2 redeems the deposit transaction $d\,\text{\BitcoinSign}$ of each server in C and eliminates it. Also, each server in H achieves the reward transaction $D_2\,\text{\BitcoinSign}$ and gets back its own deposit $d\,\text{\BitcoinSign}$.

P_2 accepts c_i from an honest server after the verification stage which can be shown as:

$$c_i \leftarrow \mathsf{Enc}_{\mathsf{pk}}\left(\sum_{j=0}^{k} \alpha^j \cdot [a_j]_t\right)$$

which clearly is an encrypted share of the output. P_2 invokes the decryption algorithm to gain the share $[f(\alpha)]_t \leftarrow \mathsf{Dec}_{\mathsf{sk}}(c_i)$. He gathers at least $t+1$ shares from the honest servers and reconstructs the output $f(\alpha)$.

P_1 maintains the privacy of his polynomial $f(x)$ using the unconditional security of the secret sharing and the Pedersen's VSS scheme, and P_2 employs the IND-CFA security of the Paillier cryptosystem to preserve the privacy of his input α. Note that a P_2 is only allowed to evaluate at most $k-1$ values from the same sender P_1.

5   Conclusion

DOPE is a variant of two-party computation which is the significant building block of many cryptographic models and privacy-preserving algorithms. We present the first fair DOPE protocol where an honest cloud server gains reward for performing a computation service while a corrupt server has to pay some penalty for conducting the malicious behaviour via Bitcoin deposit transactions. This can be achieved by using the properties scripts and time-lock in a Bitcoin transaction as a decentralised means of electronic payment without the need of a trusted third party. Our scheme includes two separate phases: setup and computation. The sender party P_1 interacts with the cloud servers in the setup phase while the receiver party P_2 communicates with the servers in the computation phase. This implies that the computation phase can be implemented at any time well in advance of the setup phase. P_1 distributes his polynomial among the servers and commits to the shares using the non-interactive Pedersen's commitment scheme which are checked by the servers. Each server employs one round of homomorphic feature of the Paillier cryptosystem to compute an encrypted share of the output, and P_2 verifies the share and detects any corrupt party.

Our protocol maintains the security against an active adversary corrupting a coalition of P_1 and up to t cloud servers in the setup phase and a coalition of maximum t servers in the computation phase in the presence of honest majority of the servers. The communication complexity is bounded to $O(kt)$ which is the same as that in the previous DOPE protocols [7,15], while the fairness property is also achieved in our scheme.

References

1. Agrawal, R., Srikant, R.: Privacy-preserving data mining. In: Proceedings of the 2000 ACM SIGMOD International Conference on Management of Data, pp. 439–450 (2000)
2. Andrychowicz, M., Dziembowski, S., Malinowski, D., Mazurek, Ł: Fair two-party computations via bitcoin deposits. In: Böhme, R., Brenner, M., Moore, T., Smith, M. (eds.) FC 2014. LNCS, vol. 8438, pp. 105–121. Springer, Heidelberg (2014). https://doi.org/10.1007/978-3-662-44774-1_8
3. Andrychowicz, M., Dziembowski, S., Malinowski, D., Mazurek, Ł: Secure multi-party computations on bitcoin. Commun. ACM **59**(4), 76–84 (2016)
4. Bultel, X., Das, M.L., Gajera, H., Gérault, D., Giraud, M., Lafourcade, P.: Verifiable private polynomial evaluation. In: Okamoto, T., Yu, Y., Au, M.H., Li, Y. (eds.) ProvSec 2017. LNCS, vol. 10592, pp. 487–506. Springer, Cham (2017). https://doi.org/10.1007/978-3-319-68637-0_29
5. Canetti, R.: Universally composable security: a new paradigm for cryptographic protocols. In: Proceedings 42nd IEEE Symposium on Foundations of Computer Science, pp. 136–145. IEEE (2001)
6. Chang, Y.-C., Lu, C.-J.: Oblivious polynomial evaluation and oblivious neural learning. In: Boyd, C. (ed.) ASIACRYPT 2001. LNCS, vol. 2248, pp. 369–384. Springer, Heidelberg (2001). https://doi.org/10.1007/3-540-45682-1_22
7. Cianciullo, L., Ghodosi, H.: Unconditionally secure distributed oblivious polynomial evaluation. In: Lee, K. (ed.) ICISC 2018. LNCS, vol. 11396, pp. 132–142. Springer, Cham (2019). https://doi.org/10.1007/978-3-030-12146-4_9
8. David, B., Dowsley, R., Katti, R., Nascimento, A.C.A.: Efficient unconditionally secure comparison and privacy preserving machine learning classification protocols. In: Au, M.-H., Miyaji, A. (eds.) ProvSec 2015. LNCS, vol. 9451, pp. 354–367. Springer, Cham (2015). https://doi.org/10.1007/978-3-319-26059-4_20
9. Freedman, M.J., Ishai, Y., Pinkas, B., Reingold, O.: Keyword search and oblivious pseudorandom functions. In: Kilian, J. (ed.) TCC 2005. LNCS, vol. 3378, pp. 303–324. Springer, Heidelberg (2005). https://doi.org/10.1007/978-3-540-30576-7_17
10. Freedman, M.J., Nissim, K., Pinkas, B.: Efficient private matching and set intersection. In: Cachin, C., Camenisch, J.L. (eds.) EUROCRYPT 2004. LNCS, vol. 3027, pp. 1–19. Springer, Heidelberg (2004). https://doi.org/10.1007/978-3-540-24676-3_1
11. Gajera, H., Giraud, M., Gérault, D., Das, M.L., Lafourcade, P.: Verifiable and private oblivious polynomial evaluation. In: Laurent, M., Giannetsos, T. (eds.) WISTP 2019. LNCS, vol. 12024, pp. 49–65. Springer, Cham (2020). https://doi.org/10.1007/978-3-030-41702-4_4

12. Gilboa, N.: Two party RSA key generation. In: Wiener, M. (ed.) CRYPTO 1999. LNCS, vol. 1666, pp. 116–129. Springer, Heidelberg (1999). https://doi.org/10.1007/3-540-48405-1_8

13. Goethals, B., Laur, S., Lipmaa, H., Mielikäinen, T.: On private scalar product computation for privacy-preserving data mining. In: Park, C., Chee, S. (eds.) ICISC 2004. LNCS, vol. 3506, pp. 104–120. Springer, Heidelberg (2005). https://doi.org/10.1007/11496618_9

14. Guo, L., Fang, Y., Li, M., Li, P.: Verifiable privacy-preserving monitoring for cloud-assisted mhealth systems. In: 2015 IEEE Conference on Computer Communications (INFOCOM), pp. 1026–1034. IEEE (2015)

15. Hamidi, A., Ghodosi, H.: Verifiable dope from somewhat homomorphic encryption, and the extension to dot. In: Science of Cyber Security: 4th International Conference, SciSec 2022, Matsue, Japan, 10–12 August 2022, Revised Selected Papers, pp. 105–120. Springer, Heidelberf (2022). https://doi.org/10.1007/978-3-031-17551-0_7

16. Hanaoka, G., Imai, H., Mueller-Quade, J., Nascimento, A.C.A., Otsuka, A., Winter, A.: Information theoretically secure oblivious polynomial evaluation: model, bounds, and constructions. In: Wang, H., Pieprzyk, J., Varadharajan, V. (eds.) ACISP 2004. LNCS, vol. 3108, pp. 62–73. Springer, Heidelberg (2004). https://doi.org/10.1007/978-3-540-27800-9_6

17. Kiayias, A., Zhou, H.-S., Zikas, V.: Fair and robust multi-party computation using a global transaction ledger. In: Fischlin, M., Coron, J.-S. (eds.) EUROCRYPT 2016. LNCS, vol. 9666, pp. 705–734. Springer, Heidelberg (2016). https://doi.org/10.1007/978-3-662-49896-5_25

18. Kumaresan, R., Vaikuntanathan, V., Vasudevan, P.N.: Improvements to secure computation with penalties. In: Proceedings of the 2016 ACM SIGSAC Conference on Computer and Communications Security, pp. 406–417 (2016)

19. Li, H.D., Yang, X., Feng, D.G., Li, B.: Distributed oblivious function evaluation and its applications. J. Comput. Sci. Technol. **19**(6), 942–947 (2004)

20. Nakamoto, S.: Bitcoin: a peer-to-peer electronic cash system. Decentralized Bus. Rev. 21260 (2008)

21. Naor, M., Pinkas, B.: Oblivious transfer and polynomial evaluation. In: Proceedings of the Thirty-First Annual ACM Symposium on Theory of Computing, pp. 245–254 (1999)

22. Otsuka, A., Imai, H.: Unconditionally secure electronic voting. In: Towards Trustworthy Elections: New Directions in Electronic Voting, pp. 107–123 (2010)

23. Paillier, P.: Public-key cryptosystems based on composite degree residuosity classes. In: Advances in Cryptology-EUROCRYPT'99: International Conference on the Theory and Application of Cryptographic Techniques Prague, Czech Republic, 2–6 May 1999, Proceedings 18, pp. 223–238. Springer, Heidelberg (1999). https://doi.org/10.1007/3-540-48910-x_16

24. Pedersen, T.P.: Non-interactive and information-theoretic secure verifiable secret sharing. In: Feigenbaum, J. (ed.) CRYPTO 1991. LNCS, vol. 576, pp. 129–140. Springer, Heidelberg (1992). https://doi.org/10.1007/3-540-46766-1_9

25. Shamir, A.: How to share a secret. Commun. ACM **22**(11), 612–613 (1979)

Smart Noise Detection for Statistical Disclosure Attacks

Marc Roßberger$^{(\boxtimes)}$ and Doğan Kesdoğan

University of Regensburg, Regensburg, Germany
{marc.rossberger,dogan.kesdogan}@ur.de

Abstract. While anonymization systems like mix networks can provide privacy to their users by, e.g., hiding their communication relationships, several traffic analysis attacks can deanonymize them. In this work, we examine Statistical Disclosure Attacks and introduce a new implementation called the Smart Noise Statistical Disclosure Attack. This attack can improve results by examining how often other users send together with the attacker's target to better filter out the noise caused by them. We evaluate this attack by comparing it to previous variants in various simulations and thus show how it can improve upon them. Further, we demonstrate how other implementations can be improved by combing them with our approach to noise calculation. Finally, we critically review used evaluation metrics to determine their significance.

Keywords: Statistical Disclosure Attack · Anonymity · Intersection Attack · Mix Network

1 Introduction

The increasing research and use of data science techniques (i.e., statistics and data analytics) is leading to increasingly stringent requirements for confidentiality and privacy, which are essential in our information society. Above all, the provision of confidentiality is hard to prove. If someone can analyze and learn personal data, one cannot be sure that this data will not be (mis)used. However, this "being sure" is essential with respect to privacy and data protection.

Therefore, one of today's biggest problems is, on the one hand, to keep the data of individuals as secret as possible so that they can be sure about their privacy, and, on the other hand, to serve the user with valuable contextual knowledge. So, the general question is: How can information be learned without violating the privacy of individuals?

This question seems to be answered by anonymity techniques. Anonymity techniques are based on the general idea that profiles of groups, rather than individual profiles, are learned. Individuals can thus be hidden within a group, and only the group's behavior is visible and learnable. The next question is to what extent this approach is effective.

© The Author(s), under exclusive license to Springer Nature Switzerland AG 2024
L. Fritsch et al. (Eds.): NordSec 2023, LNCS 14324, pp. 87–103, 2024.
https://doi.org/10.1007/978-3-031-47748-5_6

Anonymity is usually equated with the anonymity set. Generally, it was assumed that the larger the anonymity set and the more evenly distributed the sending or receiving behavior within that set, the stronger the provided anonymity [14]. For example, metrics such as entropy have been used to measure the distribution within anonymity sets [4,16]. However, in these works, only individual anonymity sets were considered when evaluating anonymity. Successful de-anonymization is demonstrated through disclosure attacks using a different model [7]. There, multiple anonymity sets were analyzed using set theory, and the corresponding information flows were accumulated until anonymity could be broken. Thus, it can be shown that the use of simple anonymity sets alone does not guarantee anonymity.

It depends on how the anonymity function hides the individual traces of the target (Alice) in the set of other objects (we use the term noise for other objects that cover Alice's behavior). The cover function of noise needs to be further explored by investigating the disclosure attack to allow for the construction of secure anonymity systems. There are many studies on statistical disclosure attacks in the literature. We will give an overview of them and present and evaluate our extension, which improves the attack's effectiveness by considering present co-senders in the noise calculation. In particular, we contribute with:

- An overview of previous disclosure attacks and their calculation of noise.
- A novel attack called the Smart Noise Statistical Disclosure Attack.
- An extensive evaluation, introducing new scenarios.
- A critical review of the evaluation metrics previously used.

The remainder of this paper is structured as follows: Sect. 2 gives an overview of related literature and how this work extends upon them, with the relevant system model and formulas being explained in Sect. 3. We propose our new approach in Sect. 4 by highlighting previous shortcomings and evaluating its performance under different scenarios in Sect. 5. Afterward, Sect. 6 critically reviews evaluation metrics used when measuring different statistical disclosure attack variations. We conclude this work in Sect. 7 and show directions for possible future work.

2   Related Work

In 1981, David Chaum introduced the concept of mixes [1] for anonymous communication. A mix is a router employed between a message's sender and its recipient, providing anonymity by preventing outsiders from linking the two communication partners. For this purpose, the first mix implementation was a so-called threshold mix (or batch mix), which collects packets from multiple senders until its threshold (batch size) is reached and then forwards them to their recipients. All packets follow a standardized packet format, ensuring equal length, and undergo cryptographic operations and shuffling by the mix to prevent outsiders from reidentifying packets by their appearance or their time of arrival/departure. Multiple mixes can be combined into a network, providing anonymity as long as one mix does not cooperate with the attacker.

However, this approach still gives adversaries information, which can be used to deanonymize communication behavior. In each round, i.e., one batch of messages, an adversary can see the senders and recipients involved. This knowledge can be employed in the Disclosure Attack [7] and its improvement, the Hitting Set Attack [9]. This attack assumes that every time a target user Alice sends a packet to a mix, one of Alice's communication partners receives a message from the corresponding batch leaving the mix. Once enough observations are made, Alice's communication partners can be identified by determining the unique minimal hitting set, which can explain every observation, i.e., the smallest set of recipients, where at least one of them appears in every batch of recipients in rounds in which Alice participated. However, this attack ignores the noise, i.e., the other users' traffic. Even though the authors mention that the attack could be applied in parallel to the other users, thus also considering each participant individually, the authors' goal was to show the principal weakness of the anonymity set.

This attack can provide deterministic results but does suffer from two problems. First, finding the unique minimal hitting set is an NP-complete problem, resulting in too complex computation for large systems. Second, the attack relies on the assumption that Alice only communicates with her fixed set of communication partners and that at least one of them appears in the recipient list each time Alice participates in the system. This assumption is problematic, as more complex types of mixes, such as Stop&Go-Mixes [8], do not generate distinct batches with the target's message. Similarly, Alice sending dummy messages (cover traffic) can also prevent this attack by diluting the recipient sets since her recipients must no longer appear in them each round.

These problems can be circumvented by the Statistical Disclosure Attack (SDA) [2], which provides de-anonymization at the expense of accuracy and determinability. The SDA approximates Alice's sending behavior by determining which recipients appear most often when Alice sends messages. This approach has a linear runtime complexity, allowing its use against large networks. Furthermore, many different extensions have been proposed to improve the SDA. Among them are approaches that employ it against Pool Mixes [12].

Since this approach tries to filter out the target's contacts among the noise caused by other senders present in the network, one line of research has tried to improve the attack's efficiency by enhancing the noise calculation. For this purpose, Mathewson and Dingledine [12] look at rounds in which Alice is not sending any messages (background rounds) and calculate the average background noise of these rounds in contrast to the previously assumed uniform background noise. Emamdoost et al. [5] further improve this approach by defining cloak users, i.e., senders that sent at least once together with Alice (in any round). Background rounds are only used for noise calculation if at least one cloak user is present as a sender since the noise in that round was otherwise caused by users who are not responsible for the noise that this attack tries to filter out during the target's active rounds. In this work, we extend this approach by weighting cloak users based on the frequency of their co-occurrence as senders together with Alice, as shown in Sect. 4. We also implicitly weight background rounds, depending on the cloak users present and their respective weights.

Another direction for improving the attack is by considering the sending behavior of users other than the target. Troncoso et al. [17] proposed a variant called the Perfect Matching Disclosure Attack (PMDA). In the first step, the existing SDA is employed against all users in the network. Then, using the estimated communication profiles, they calculate the likeliest sender-recipient pairs for each round where the target user was active. In another approach, the Two-Sided Statistical Disclosure Attack (TS-SDA), Danezis et al. [3] assume a symmetric system model where users answer messages. To improve the SDA, they calculate the likelihood of messages being replies to previous messages since this allows for intersection attacks between the original message's senders and the reply's recipients. A further approach considering a (semi-)symmetrical model is the Reverse Statistical Disclosure Attack (RSDA) [11], which calculates the regular SDA for all other users. Afterward, it determines Alice's partners by using her possible recipients (as previously) and the possible senders of messages Alice received, weighting the two directions depending on how many messages Alice sent and received.

These three approaches either calculate the regular SDA as a basis for their attack (PMDA, RSDA) or the background noise according to original SDA (TS-SDA). Thus by improving the calculation of the background noise, all of these variants can be improved, as will be demonstrated by integrating our approach into the Reverse SDA.

While this line of research is primarily focused on mix networks, it should be noted that these attacks are relevant for all kinds of anonymization systems that protect their users' privacy. As long as an attacker can make some observations regarding user activity, like observing senders and recipients, these attacks may be possible, as shown by Gaballah et al. [6] by employing them against anonymous microblogging systems.

3   Background - The Usage of Context for Statistical Disclosure Attacks

In this section, we will give an overview of the system model and show how the Statistical Disclosure Attack evolved by using more and more background information.

3.1   System Model

A system using multiple mixes should still provide anonymity even if all but one are under the control of an attacker. Thus, in this work, we consider a single batch mix node with batch size b and a global passive adversary who can observe all senders and recipients of messages entering and leaving the mix. Once enough (b) packets are inside the mix, they get shuffled and forwarded to their recipients. Collecting and delivering these messages is considered a round i, and the system is active for t rounds. If the attacker's target user Alice participates as a sender in a round, we call it a target round. Otherwise, it is a background round. There are t_t target rounds and t_{bg} background rounds, so $t = t_t + t_{bg}$. For every round i, S_i defines the list of senders, and R_i the list of recipients[1]. Each list is of size b and contains users n_j, all part of the global user set U of size N. Every user can act as a sender and recipient. Alice (n_A) has m partners she sends messages to, and her sending behavior is defined by the vector $\vec{v}$, which displays the probability of a message sent by Alice being directed towards a specific user. For example, if Alice only communicates with the users n_1 and n_3 with the same likelihood (50%), her vector looks like this: $\vec{v} = (\frac{1}{2}, 0, \frac{1}{2}, 0, ..., 0)$.

3.2 Statistical Disclosure Attacks Using Noise

The original Statistical Disclosure Attack [2] tries to determine Alice's sending behavior $\vec{v}$ by using the following logic. In every target round, one message originates from Alice and $b - 1$ from other users, whose combined sending behavior is represented by the vector $\vec{u}$ and is assumed to be uniform, i.e., $\vec{u} = (\frac{1}{N}, ..., \frac{1}{N})$. Thus all observations $\vec{o}_i$, i.e., the distribution of recipients observed in target rounds, can be explained by Eq. (1), where $\bar{O} = \frac{1}{t_t} \sum_{i=1}^{t_t} \vec{o}_i$ represents the average observation across all target rounds.

$$\bar{O} \approx \frac{\vec{v} + (b-1)\vec{u}}{b} \tag{1}$$

Thus, Alice's communication behavior can be approximated as displayed in Eq. (2) by filtering out the noise $\vec{u}$ caused by other users from the total signal $\bar{O}$ to determine the relevant signal $\vec{v}$ originating from Alice.

$$\vec{v} \approx \frac{b}{t_t} \sum_{i=1}^{t_t} \vec{o}_i - (b-1)\vec{u} \tag{2}$$

Note that this approach assumes a uniform background noise and only considers target rounds like the preceding Disclosure Attack [7]. However, this assumption does not hold very well in the real world, where people, based on, e.g., their social status or job, receive more or fewer messages, causing a non-uniform background noise. This results in the SDA identifying any people receiving many messages as Alice's partners. To solve this issue, Mathewson and Dingledine [12] extended the SDA by calculating the noise based on background rounds. Thus the vector $\vec{u}$ is no longer uniform but calculated as the average of $\vec{u}_i$, which represent the distribution of recipients in background rounds, analog to $\vec{o}_i$. This can be seen in Eq. (3).

$$\vec{u} = \frac{1}{t_{bg}} \sum_{i=1}^{t_{bg}} \vec{u}_i \tag{3}$$

---

[1] We allow senders and recipients to appear multiple times per round. Thus we talk about lists, not sets.

Taking this one step further, Emamdoost et al. [5] filter the background observations $\vec{u}_i$ by defining cloak users. A cloak user n_c is a user who sent at least once in the same round as Alice, i.e., there is a round i such that $n_c, n_A \in S_i$. The background noise $\vec{u}$ is calculated as previously but uses only cloak rounds $\vec{c}_i$ containing at least one cloak user in their sender set S_i. This is displayed in Eq. (4). There are t_c cloak rounds, where $t_c \leq t_{bg}$.

$$\vec{u} = \frac{1}{t_c} \sum_{i=1}^{t_c} \vec{c}_i \tag{4}$$

In the next section, we will show the shortcomings of this approach and how we solve them and improve this variant by extending it.

As mentioned in the previous section, some approaches extend the SDA by calculating other users' communication profiles. One example of this is the Reverse Statistical Disclosure Attack [11]. It calculates the regular SDA for every user n_j and saves their results as $\vec{v}_j$, where $\vec{v}_A$ represents Alice's vector, previously just denoted as $\vec{v}$. It then builds the vector $\vec{v}_R$ from each user other than Alice by taking their calculated probabilities of communicating with Alice. That means that if user n_1, according to the SDA result $\vec{v}_1$, sends 30% of their messages to Alice and user n_2 50%, then the resulting vector will at first look like this: $\vec{v}_R = (0.3, 0.5, ...)$. This vector is then normalized. For the final calculation of the target communication behavior $\vec{v}$ as displayed in Eq. (5), the attack counts how many messages Alice sent (msg_{out}) and how many she received (msg_{in}) to weight both sides.

$$\vec{v} = \frac{msg_{out}\vec{v}_A + msg_{in}\vec{v}_R}{msg_{out} + msg_{in}} \tag{5}$$

Using our approach from Sect. 4 for calculating the SDA results $\vec{v}_j$ and thus both $\vec{v}_A$ and $\vec{v}_R$, we can improve the Reverse SDA and other variants, as shown in Sect. 5.

4   Approach

In this section, we will present our new approach to calculating background noise caused by users other than the attacker's target. For this purpose, we will demonstrate the issues of the SDA-IER approach shown in the last section and how we resolve them to create a new and improved version of the SDA, called the Smart Noise Statistical Disclosure Attack (SN-SDA).

4.1   Shortcomings in the SDA-IER Approach

The SDA-IER [5] improves upon previous versions of the SDA by only using background rounds that contain cloak users. That means that other background rounds, which contain no cloak users as senders, are ignored. This makes sense, as those ignored rounds contain no senders who are responsible for the noise in target rounds that needs to be filtered out. However, this approach is restricted to binary decisions. Every sender is either a cloak user or not. Similarly, every background round gets labeled as a cloak round or not. We want to highlight two problems with this approach.

First, as soon as a user sends at least once together with Alice, he is considered a cloak user. This low requirement leads to many users turning into cloak users very quickly. Furthermore, since the appearance of just one cloak user in a background round's sender list turns the round into a cloak round, most background rounds will be cloak rounds very quickly, leaving little to no non-cloak background rounds to filter out, thus producing results nearly identical to the SDA without this improvement. We demonstrate this problem in Fig. 1 using the parameters used by the original authors in their evaluation ($N = 20000, b = 50, m = 20$), assuming independent senders. It can be seen that after just 25 observations (rounds with Alice sending), 6% of users are cloak users, reducing the chance of a non-cloak background round appearing to 4.7%[2]. After 50 rounds, the chance is reduced to 0.2%. Thus the approach will not be able to filter out a significant number of background rounds.

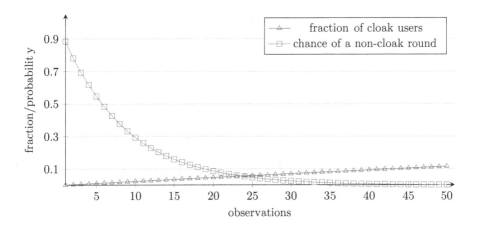

Fig. 1. The fraction of cloak users and the resulting chance of a non-cloak background round appearing after x observations, using the SDA-IER [5] approach.

Second, the approach's binary classification system leaves room for improvement. There is no distinction between cloak user n_1, who only sends together with Alice once, and cloak user n_2, who sends every time Alice is active. This method should be changed since the second user is responsible for significantly

---

[2] This assumes random and independent senders. Thus the chance of a non-cloak background round appearing can be calculated (with values for round 25) as $(fraction\ of\ non-cloak\ users)^b = (1 - \frac{cloakusercount}{N})^b = (1 - (\frac{1183}{20000}))^{50} \approx 0.047$. Note that there can be small but insignificant differences in the simulated results due to senders appearing multiple times per round, reducing the number of distinct cloak users.

more noise present in the recipient lists R_i of observations $\vec{o}_i$. Furthermore, every cloak round is treated the same, even though the number and relevance of cloak users in their sender lists S_i may differ drastically. This leads to no distinction between different cloak rounds, even though they might be more or less accurate approximations of the noise that needs to be filtered out.

4.2   The Smart Noise Approach

We solve the above-mentioned issues by implementing a version of the previous approach that weights cloak users depending on their appearance rate together with Alice. Furthermore, we weight background rounds depending on the number of cloak users in their sender lists and these users' relevance. When reviewing the formula for the SDA in Eq. (2), notice that this approach only changes how the background noise $\vec{u}$ is calculated. Equation (6) shows how this weighted noise is calculated. w_j represents the weight of (cloak) user n_j, depending on how often they appear together with Alice, the weight of all users adding up to one. $\vec{d}_j$ represents the distribution of recipients observed for user n_j.

$$\vec{u} = \sum_{n_j \in U \setminus \{n_A\}} w_j \vec{d}_j \qquad (6)$$

Table 1. Example rounds to explain the smart noise calculation

round i	senders S_i	recipients R_i
1	1, 2, 3	4, 5, 6
2	1, 2, 4	4, 7, 8
3	2, 2, 3	6, 6, 9

Table 2. Weights and distributions calculated by the SN-SDA based on the rounds from Table 1

user n_j	co-sender weight w_j	user profile $\vec{d}_j$
2	0.5	$(0,0,0,\frac{2}{12},\frac{1}{12},\frac{5}{12},\frac{1}{12},\frac{1}{12},\frac{2}{12})$
3	0.25	$(0,0,0,\frac{1}{6},\frac{1}{6},\frac{3}{6},0,0,\frac{1}{6})$
4	0.25	$(0,0,0,\frac{1}{3},0,0,\frac{1}{3},\frac{1}{3},0)$
5–9	0	N/A

We will now explain the equation above using example rounds from Table 1. The target user Alice ($n_A = 1$ in the table) is active in rounds 1 and 2. In these two rounds, 6 messages are sent (since $b = 3$), and 2 of them originate from Alice, 4 from other users. Since user 2 is responsible for 2 out of these 4 messages, they are assigned weight $w_2 = \frac{2}{4}$. Users 3 and 4 both sent one message and thus are assigned weights $w_3 = w_4 = \frac{1}{4}$. When calculating users' sending behavior $\vec{d_j}$, all rounds, i.e., target and background rounds, are considered. Since user 4 only appears as a sender in round 2, their distribution of recipients $\vec{d_4}$ is based purely on that round's recipient list R_2. Since users 4, 7, and 8 each appear once in R_2, their corresponding values in $\vec{d_4}$ are all $\frac{1}{3}$. User 2 sent two messages in round 3, so the recipients occurring in that round are counted twice for their profile $\vec{d_2}$. Table 2 gives an overview of all calculated weights w_j and recipient distributions $\vec{d_j}$, with the calculation of the total background noise $\vec{u}$ being shown in Eq. (7). For simplicity's sake, users 5 to 9 are excluded from the equation since their weights of $w_j = 0$ would result in them not impacting the calculation.

$$\vec{u} = \sum_{n_j \in U \setminus \{n_A\}} w_j \vec{d_j} = w_2 \vec{d_2} + w_3 \vec{d_3} + w_4 \vec{d_4} + \ldots = 0.5\vec{d_2} + 0.25\vec{d_3} + 0.25\vec{d_4}$$

$$\approx (0, 0, 0, 0.21, 0.08, 0.33, 0.13, 0.13, 0.13) \tag{7}$$

This approach solves both identified issues with the SDA-IER approach. The problem of differently significant cloak users gets solved explicitly by assigning them weights depending on their co-occurrence rate with Alice. The other problem of all users turning into cloak users and thus not being able to filter out non-cloak background rounds is solved implicitly, as there no longer is a binary classification between cloak and non-cloak background rounds since their relevance now depends on the present senders. A background round without any cloak users present effectively gets filtered out just as in the previous approach since its recipient list R_i does not contribute to any cloak users' profiles $\vec{d_j}$.

A difference in this strategy compared to all previous approaches trying to improve the calculation of the background noise $\vec{u}$ is the fact that the recipient lists R_i of target rounds are used for the calculation of the sending profiles $\vec{d_j}$. In our evaluation, we also tried calculating these profiles using only background rounds but could not find significant differences. Thus, this version of the implementation is the only one considered in the remainder of this work.

5 Evaluation

In this section, we perform an extensive evaluation of our new approach, comparing it to existing variants in different scenarios. At first, we will examine how it performs against previous versions of the SDA that improved the calculation of the background noise. Afterward, we will analyze scenarios with symmetrical user behavior to evaluate the approach's performance under conditions it can not take advantage of and how well it can be integrated into existing solutions.

5.1   Comparison of Noise Calculation Approaches

Our approach is designed to take advantage of context information not previously used by considering the senders' co-appearance rates with Alice and the distribution of said co-senders in background rounds. For this purpose, we will evaluate our approach (SN-SDA) by comparing it to the SDA-IER [5], on whose idea it builds upon and show the SDA calculating background noise (SDA (bg) [12], see Eq. (3)) for completeness. The evaluation is performed under the conditions described in Sect. 3.1, i.e., one batch mix with senders independent of each other and with random uniform contact profiles. Table 3 gives an overview of the default parameters used for the evaluation. We examine the impact of changing m, N, and b to analyze how the performance of the attacks changes for different anonymization systems. Each evaluation was performed in 25 random simulations, and the mean results are displayed in the following sections.

Table 3. Overview of default parameters used for the evaluation

Parameter	Default Value	Explanation
N	100	number of users
b	10	batch size
m	10	target contact count
c	10	other users' contact count
t^{max}	50000	time (round) limit for the attacks

At first, we assume a model with randomly chosen senders and show the results in Table 4. The metric used is the mean number of rounds required to identify all of the target's contacts. Both the SDA-IER and our SN-SDA can not achieve significant improvements unless Alice only has one contact. However, this is to be expected since both approaches expect a not completely random distribution of senders so that they can take advantage of certain co-senders appearing more often.

Table 4. Evaluation results for different values of m assuming random senders

m	mean rounds required		
	SDA (bg)	SDA-IER	SN-SDA
1	29.5	27.6	23.4
2	77.4	78.1	76.1
5	506.0	506.0	507.6
10	2131.1	2131.1	2075.6
20	7710.7	7710.7	7626.2

For this purpose, we change the system model by distributing the senders worldwide and choosing them depending on the time of day. The effect of this change is that senders with similar indices are closer to each other and send together more often[3], as can be expected in real-world scenarios where peoples' online activity depends on local time and other factors, e.g., their religion, culture, or job. We now draw senders from a normal distribution with mean i mod N (i is the current round number) and standard deviation $N/6$. This setup impacts the activity of senders and their co-occurrence rate. Every sender, however, still has a set of recipients chosen uniformly randomly from all users. This scenario is used for the remainder of this section.

Table 5 shows the results of performing the previous attacks on the global sender scenario. It can be seen that even in this scenario, the SDA-IER approach does not achieve improvements compared to the regular SDA (bg). This is caused by the problems explained in Sect. 4.1, and we will not display its result in the following evaluations as it could not improve upon its predecessor. The Smart Noise approach, however, does perform better than the other variants, and its advantage (except for the case $m = 1$) seems to increase for a growing m, and thus, a more difficult scenario for the attacker. When an attack cannot identify all contacts in all scenarios within the given time limit t^{max}, it is denoted in braces how many scenarios it could solve. In the case $m = 20$, the SDA (bg) could only identify all of the target's recipients in 12 out of 25 cases, and in those, it did so in an average of 19281 rounds. If the other scenarios, where it reached the time limit, are counted with a value of $t^{max} = 50000$, its mean rounds required metric comes out at 35255.

Table 5. Evaluation depending on m

m	mean rounds required							
	SDA (bg)		SDA-IER		SN-SDA		SN-SDA/SDA (bg)	
	perfect (#)	all	perfect (#)	all	perfect (#)	all	perfect	all
1		20.7		21.0		13.7		66.2%
2		93.4		93.4		90.1		96.5%
5		605.6		605.6		568.1		93.8%
10		2551.6		2551.6		2108.8		82.6%
20	19281 (12)	35255	19281 (12)	35255	12140 (24)	13654	63.0%	38.7%

Next, we examined the attack's performance for networks of different sizes. The results in Table 6 show a clear advantage in smaller networks, which does shrink considerably for growing networks.

Finally, Table 7 shows results for varying batch sizes, a security parameter that can be easily changed. Except for the edge case $b = 2$, which is too insecure

---

[3] E.g., senders n_0 and n_1 are closer and send together more often than n_0 and n_{50}. Note that senders n_0 and n_{99} are neighbors for $N = 100$.

to use in realistic scenarios, the SN-SDA approach improves significantly on previous versions. It can still identify all of the target's contacts for $b = 20$, while the SDA (bg) only manages that in 14 scenarios. The reduced number of rounds required when moving from $b = 2$ to $b = 5$ can be explained by the increased batch size leading to more messages from Alice, which are needed for the attack's success.

Table 6. Evaluation for differing network sizes N

N	mean rounds required					
	SDA (bg)		SN-SDA		SN-SDA/SDA (bg)	
	perfect (#)	all	perfect (#)	all	perfect	all
20	4922 (7)	37378	2210 (19)	13680	44.9%	36.6%
50	5065 (22)	10457		2093	41.3%	20.0%
100		2928		2292		78.3%
200		3135		3039		97.0%

Table 7. Evaluation for different batch sizes b

b	mean rounds required					
	SDA (bg)		SN-SDA		SN-SDA/SDA (bg)	
	perfect (#)	all	perfect (#)	all	perfect	all
2		3149		3094		98.3%
5		2406		2105		87.5%
10		2860		2240		78.3%
20	5150 (14)	24884		3842	74.6%	15.4%

We also performed a longer simulation for larger system parameters ($N = 1000$, $b = 100$) to address concerns about the system parameters being chosen as too small. The results in Table 8 demonstrate that the attack's advantage is even more significant than in the default scenario from Table 5.

Table 8. Evaluation for a larger anonymity system

m	mean rounds required					
	SDA (bg)		SN-SDA		SN-SDA/SDA (bg)	
	perfect (#)	all	perfect (#)	all	perfect	all
10	14638 (9)	37269.7		7758	53.0%	20.8%

These evaluations considered the mean number of rounds required to identify Alice's contacts. However, the SN-SDA approach only changes how the background noise $\vec{u}$ is calculated. Thus, we also include a repeat of the first evaluation but limit the attacker to a fixed number of target rounds to more accurately determine our approach's impact on the number of background rounds required to identify contacts. The limit to target rounds t_t^{max} was chosen based on the previous evaluation results as the maximum number of required target rounds to complete the attack across all attack variants and simulations per value m to not prevent the success of attacks by decreasing their available information too much. It can be seen in Table 9 that the SN-SDA fulfills its expectations of calculating noise more efficiently since it requires fewer background rounds.

Table 9. Evaluation when limiting target rounds available

m	t_t^{max}	mean rounds required					
		SDA (bg)		SN-SDA		SN-SDA/SDA (bg)	
		perfect (#)	all	perfect (#)	all	perfect	all
1	8		21.8		9.0		41.3%
2	16		40.0		26.9		67.3%
5	151		232.2		198.5		85.5%
10	410		1134.0		715.0		63.1%
20	3549	9384 (11)	32129	7492 (23)	10893	79.8%	33.9%

5.2 Symmetrical User Behavior

The previous section has shown that the SN-SDA can improve upon previous versions by calculating noise more intelligently. However, several different SDA variants also enhance their efficiency by employing other strategies. To demonstrate how our approach can improve these variants, we will integrate it into the Reverse SDA (RSDA) [11] by calculating the vector $\vec{v}_A$ using our smart noise technique. The RSDA assumes symmetrical user behavior, i.e., if Alice sends messages to Bob, Bob also sends messages to Alice. For this reason, we change the previous system model. Senders are still chosen randomly depending on the time of day, but to create symmetrical relationships, we employ the Watts-Strogatz model [18] to build a communication graph. This graph has N nodes and a mean degree of c, though we ensure that every node is connected to at least one other node and that Alice has exactly m connections. We use $p = 0.5$ to allow for both local and global communication relationships. The evaluation results in Table 10 show that by integrating our approach into the RSDA to build the Reverse SDA with smart noise (RSDA (SN)), further improvements can be achieved. Not depicted in the table, it also performed better than just the SN-SDA, and all approaches performed significantly better than the regular SDA (bg).

Table 10. Evaluation results for the symmetrical communication model

m	mean rounds required					
	RSDA		RSDA (SN)		RSDA (SN)/RSDA	
	perfect (#)	all	perfect (#)	all	perfect	all
1		17.0		17.0		100%
2		94.8		87.6		92.4%
5		647.2		551.7		85.2%
10		4371.8		2432.0		55.6%
20	N/A (0)	50000	17096 (14)	31574	N/A	63.1%

6   Critical Review of Evaluation Metrics Used for SDAs

After this evaluation, we want to discuss the validity of the metrics used to determine the effectiveness of these attacks and argue why we chose the rounds required metric in our evaluation. We shortly examine other possible metrics and the impact of SDA results on peoples' anonymity.

6.1   The Metric Rounds Required

The metric "rounds required to identify all (or a fraction of) Alice's partners" is the metric used in the two works we try to extend (SDA-IER [5]) and integrate into (RSDA [11]). Thus we chose this metric for comparable results. However, there are some shortcomings to using this metric.

For one, the result of the SDA, since it is only a statistical approximation, can fluctuate a lot in early rounds. This can lead to the correct result being found for one round by a "lucky hit," only to be discarded in the next round. We have introduced a confirmation threshold of five rounds to prevent this issue. This threshold requires the attack to correctly identify Alice's partners for five rounds in a row until it is halted. However, the first of these five rounds is used in the evaluation analysis to avoid skewing results.

When analyzing evaluation results, one should consider their meaning in a real-world scenario. Currently, attacks are halted once the attack correctly identifies the target's partners. However, "identified" is a strong word since the attack only assigned higher probabilities to Alice's partners than all other users. Consider a scenario where the SDA's result is $\vec{v} = (0.31, 0.19, 0.23, 0.05, ...)$. If the users n_1 and n_3 who got assigned the highest probabilities are Alice's partners, the attack is halted for evaluation purposes. If they are not, the attack continues, analyzing more rounds. However, in a real scenario, where an attacker only has limited observations and must wait for more communication from Alice or other users in the network, he has to decide when he is sure about the target's contacts. This is further complicated by the fact that he does not know the number of Alice's partners. Possible approaches for confirming the intermediate results of the SDA might include a threshold between assumed contacts and non-contacts or combining it with the Hitting Set Attack [9]. However, this still does not address the issue that a few of Alice's partners may be identified earlier, possibly caused by them engaging in conversation more often. This is discussed by Mallesh and Wrigth [10], highlighting the delay caused by identifying the last recipient.

Lastly, while this metric does confirm when the attack is finished, it does not provide details about its progress, i.e., how close the attack is to fulfilling the halting condition. Such information could be helpful, especially when simulating bigger scenarios where the attack may not finish within a reasonable number of observations, and the rounds required metric would not provide any information. We will show two such metrics in the next section. However, even after examining all these possible problems, this metric is still useful. It can provide an estimated lower bound for the observations necessary to deanonymize communication partners and thus assess an anonymization system's strength.

When discussing these metrics, one should consider the meaning of SDA attack results. For this purpose, we will borrow the degrees of anonymity scale by Reiter and Rubin [15], which ranks how close an attacker is to breaking anonymity, ranging from *absolute privacy* to *provably exposed*. No intersection attacks presented in this work can result in the target being *provably exposed* since Alice always has plausible deniability by claiming to communicate with everyone at random. However, depending on the attack results, an attacker can be confident about having identified the target's contacts. When employing the Hitting Set Attack [9], provided its assumptions are met, the target's partners can be *exposed* if one unique minimal hitting set is identified. At this point, we introduce a new marker, called *probably exposed*, and place it between *possible innocence* and *exposed*. We argue that the SDA can only result in the partners being *probably exposed* because its results are only approximations and the attacker's lack of knowledge of m. Similarly, the Hitting Set attack also only achieves *probably exposed* (at best) if no unique minimal hitting set is identified.

6.2   Metrics for Ongoing Attacks

Another metric that can be employed to evaluate SDA attacks is the mean rank of target users [3]. The SDA assigns probabilities to users, estimating the chance that Alice's next message will be directed towards them[4]. For this purpose, all users are ordered, depending on the probabilities in the result vector $\vec{v}$. If the attack rates Alice's contacts in the ranks 1 and 5, the mean rank of the attack result would be $(1+5)/2 = 3$. In general terms, a perfect result would lead to a mean rank of $(m+1)/2$, while a random guess would have an expected average result of $(N+1)/2$ (the mean of the first m, respectively N, natural numbers).

This metric, however, should not be mindlessly used. Let us assume, for example, that the attack ranked Alice's partners in places 1, 2, 3, and 100 ($m = 4, N = 100$). This results in a mean rank of 26.5. The same mean rank would also have been calculated if the attack had ranked recipients as 25, 26, 27, and 28.

---

[4] Or in the case of symmetrical communication, that her next communication (including messages received) will be performed with this user.

In the first scenario, the attack correctly identified three of Alice's four contacts while not identifying any in the second. This example demonstrates why looking only at the mean rank is not an adequate measure when evaluating attack results. This difficulty is caused by the metric interpreting all ranks and their distances equally, even though the difference between, e.g., rank 1 and 10 (for any $m < 10$) is more significant than between 51 and 60 as the first case decides if the recipient is classified as a contact while the second does not.

Another metric for evaluation purposes is the mean squared error of the SDA result [13]. Displayed in Eq. (8), it calculates how close the attack's estimated vector $\vec{v}'$ is to Alice's actual sending behavior $\vec{v}$. Possible modifications might include restricting the error calculation to the target's partners. However, that variant would be unable to identify false positives, i.e., non-contacts being calculated as more likely than real contacts. In our experiments, we could not definitively assess this metric's accuracy and often observed results similar to the mean rank metric, though they were sometimes slightly contradicting. Thus, we did not rely on this new metric for evaluation purposes, and it should be studied further to determine its adequacy for SDA evaluation.

$$\left\| \vec{v}_i - \vec{v}_i{}' \right\|^2 = \sum_{i=1}^{N} (\vec{v}_i - \vec{v}_i{}')^2 \tag{8}$$

7   Conclusion

In this work, we have presented the Smart Noise Statistical Disclosure Attack (SN-SDA). Our approach uses more information available compared to previous implementations by examining other users' co-occurrence frequency with the target user to more efficiently filter out their noise. We have shown in an extensive evaluation how different factors impact the attack's performance and that it can improve upon its predecessors while not resulting in worse results, even when its assumptions are not met (see Table 4). Furthermore, since this approach improves the noise calculation used in nearly every SDA variant, we have demonstrated that it can be integrated into other implementations to improve their effectiveness.

We have also reviewed the metrics used to evaluate Statistical Disclosure Attacks, highlighting shortcomings and other factors to consider when analyzing different versions. In future work, we want to revisit these metrics, possibly combining them, to allow for a more thorough evaluation of intermediate and final results to give better insights when users' anonymity is endangered.

References

1. Chaum, D.L.: Untraceable electronic mail, return addresses, and digital pseudonyms. Commun. ACM **24**(2), 84–90 (1981)
2. Danezis, G.: Statistical disclosure attacks: traffic confirmation in open environments. In: Gritzalis, D., De Capitani di Vimercati, S., Samarati, P., Katsikas, S. (eds.) SEC 2003. ITIFIP, vol. 122, pp. 421–426. Springer, Boston, MA (2003). https://doi.org/10.1007/978-0-387-35691-4_40

3. Danezis, G., Diaz, C., Troncoso, C.: Two-sided statistical disclosure attack. In: Borisov, N., Golle, P. (eds.) PET 2007. LNCS, vol. 4776, pp. 30–44. Springer, Heidelberg (2007). https://doi.org/10.1007/978-3-540-75551-7_3

4. Díaz, C., Seys, S., Claessens, J., Preneel, B.: Towards measuring anonymity. In: Dingledine, R., Syverson, P. (eds.) PET 2002. LNCS, vol. 2482, pp. 54–68. Springer, Heidelberg (2003). https://doi.org/10.1007/3-540-36467-6_5

5. Emamdoost, N., Dousti, M.S., Jalili, R.: Statistical disclosure: improved, extended, and resisted. arXiv preprint arXiv:1710.00101 (2017)

6. Gaballah, S.A., Abdullah, L., Tran, M.T., Zimmer, E., Mühlhäuser, M.: On the effectiveness of intersection attacks in anonymous microblogging. In: Reiser, H.P., Kyas, M. (eds.) NordSec 2022. LNCS, vol. 13700, pp. 3–19. Springer, Cham (2022). https://doi.org/10.1007/978-3-031-22295-5_1

7. Kedogan, D., Agrawal, D., Penz, S.: Limits of anonymity in open environments. In: Petitcolas, F.A.P. (ed.) IH 2002. LNCS, vol. 2578, pp. 53–69. Springer, Heidelberg (2003). https://doi.org/10.1007/3-540-36415-3_4

8. Kesdogan, D., Egner, J., Büschkes, R.: Stop- and- Go-MIXes providing probabilistic anonymity in an open system. In: Aucsmith, D. (ed.) IH 1998. LNCS, vol. 1525, pp. 83–98. Springer, Heidelberg (1998). https://doi.org/10.1007/3-540-49380-8_7

9. Kesdogan, D., Pimenidis, L.: The hitting set attack on anonymity protocols. In: Fridrich, J. (ed.) IH 2004. LNCS, vol. 3200, pp. 326–339. Springer, Heidelberg (2004). https://doi.org/10.1007/978-3-540-30114-1_23

10. Mallesh, N., Wright, M.: Countering statistical disclosure with receiver-bound cover traffic. In: Biskup, J., López, J. (eds.) ESORICS 2007. LNCS, vol. 4734, pp. 547–562. Springer, Heidelberg (2007). https://doi.org/10.1007/978-3-540-74835-9_36

11. Mallesh, N., Wright, M.: The reverse statistical disclosure attack. In: Böhme, R., Fong, P.W.L., Safavi-Naini, R. (eds.) IH 2010. LNCS, vol. 6387, pp. 221–234. Springer, Heidelberg (2010). https://doi.org/10.1007/978-3-642-16435-4_17

12. Mathewson, N., Dingledine, R.: Practical traffic analysis: extending and resisting statistical disclosure. In: Martin, D., Serjantov, A. (eds.) PET 2004. LNCS, vol. 3424, pp. 17–34. Springer, Heidelberg (2005). https://doi.org/10.1007/11423409_2

13. Pérez-González, F., Troncoso, C.: Understanding statistical disclosure: a least squares approach. In: Fischer-Hübner, S., Wright, M. (eds.) PETS 2012. LNCS, vol. 7384, pp. 38–57. Springer, Heidelberg (2012). https://doi.org/10.1007/978-3-642-31680-7_3

14. Pfitzmann, A., Köhntopp, M.: Anonymity, unobservability, and pseudonymity— a proposal for terminology. In: Federrath, H. (ed.) Designing Privacy Enhancing Technologies. LNCS, vol. 2009, pp. 1–9. Springer, Heidelberg (2001). https://doi.org/10.1007/3-540-44702-4_1

15. Reiter, M.K., Rubin, A.D.: Crowds: anonymity for web transactions. ACM Trans. Inf. Syst. Secur. (TISSEC) 1(1), 66–92 (1998)

16. Serjantov, A., Danezis, G.: Towards an information theoretic metric for anonymity. In: Dingledine, R., Syverson, P. (eds.) PET 2002. LNCS, vol. 2482, pp. 41–53. Springer, Heidelberg (2003). https://doi.org/10.1007/3-540-36467-6_4

17. Troncoso, C., Gierlichs, B., Preneel, B., Verbauwhede, I.: Perfect matching disclosure attacks. In: Borisov, N., Goldberg, I. (eds.) PETS 2008. LNCS, vol. 5134, pp. 2–23. Springer, Heidelberg (2008). https://doi.org/10.1007/978-3-540-70630-4_2

18. Watts, D.J., Strogatz, S.H.: Collective dynamics of 'small-world' networks. Nature 393(6684), 440–442 (1998)

Cyber Security

Cybersecurity Challenges and Smart Technology Adoption in Norwegian Livestock Farming

Karianne Kjønås and Gaute Wangen[✉]

Department of Information Security and Communication Technology,
Norwegian University of Science and Technology, 2815 Gjøvik, Norway
{karinanne.kjonaas,gaute.wangen}@ntnu.no
http://www.ntnu.no

Abstract. The importance of cybersecurity in agriculture has grown significantly due to the increasing use of technology, which brings about vulnerabilities in farm systems. This study investigates the technology usage and cyber attack susceptibility on Norwegian cow and pig farms while focusing on impacts to food production. Employing a phenomenological approach, we conducted 14 one-on-one interviews with cattle and pig farmers in Norway, complemented by two interviews with domain experts in widely-used milking robot brands for dairy farms. The findings indicate that dairy cow farms heavily rely on the milking robot for production, pig farms are highly dependent on feeding systems, while suckler cow farms have the lowest digital technology dependence. However, targeting a single farm is unlikely to cause significant consequences for the entire society. For threat actors aiming to disrupt food production on a national scale, the focus might shift towards suppliers of raw materials, machinery, data processors, and regulatory bodies for meat and dairy. Attacks at this level could have widespread implications for farms across the country, making it a critical area for future research and attention.

Keywords: Cybersecurity · Food production · Norway

1 Introduction

The agricultural sector uses a lot of technology in their day-to-day operations [2], and digital technology are a part of many different aspects, such as water management, crop fertigation, livestock monitoring and e-commerce to name a few [2,3]. Internet of Things (IoT) sensors are placed all around the farm and can also be used for specialized tasks such as detecting plant illness, or they can be placed on equipment such as tractors and drones [5]. The use of technology has also increased in recent years along with the rise of smart farming and precision agriculture [25]. Increased digitization also increases the potential consequence of cyber attacks. To illustrate this issue, in late 2021, the Norwegian butchery and meat production company Nortura was hit by a ransomware attack [20]. The attackers managed to impact the production line with the consequences from the attack manifesting in the physical world going both ways in the supply chain:

L. Fritsch et al. (Eds.): NordSec 2023, LNCS 14324, pp. 107–125, 2024.
https://doi.org/10.1007/978-3-031-47748-5_7

Through less available goods in the stores the following weeks for consumers, but also impacted meat suppliers as they experienced trouble delivering live stock to the butchery as digital records were lost. The said attack illustrates food production process IT dependency and vulnerability, and the need for gathering knowledge of digital risks in agricultural value chains.

A review of cybersecurity in agriculture and smart farming highlighted gaps in the research, particularly in understanding farmers' knowledge, perspectives, and technological dependencies [9]. This study is a first step to filling this knowledge gap by investigating the technology use and digital risks of farms. Knowing the consequences for farmers in different attack scenarios can give a clearer view of the true threats to Norwegian agriculture technology. Understanding the threats to one of the main components of the supply chain can highlight what threats are important to protect against from a societal point of view. In order to find the societal consequences of cyber attacks to agriculture technology, the first step is to look at what technologies are used by farmers today, and mapping the dependency on them. While there are multiple avenues for researching this topic, such as looking at specific farm production systems in detail, or looking at the technological dependencies of the whole supply chain, this research will focus on the farm in general. Examining multiple farms, their use of technology and reliance on suppliers will give insight into what kind of damage a cyber attack can do. Cattle and pig farms are the chosen types in this research because of their role in the Norwegian food production. This leads to three research questions:

- *What technologies are used by Norwegian cattle and pig farmers to produce and deliver their product?*
- *What are the main cyber risks to the production and delivery of produce on these Norwegian farms?*
- *How can a threat exploit the vulnerabilities of individual farms to affect food production on a national scale?*

This paper begins by providing essential background information to help readers understand the problem space. It then outlines the applied method and demographics used in the research. The results concerning technology usage are presented separately for three surveyed farm types: Dairy Cows, Suckler Cows, and Pig farms. Subsequently, the key IT assets, vulnerabilities, and risks associated with smart farm types are summarized. Following this, we engage in a discussion about the identified risks and their potential to impact food production on a national scale in Norway. The paper concludes with suggestions for future work, including the possibility of conducting similar research on other farm types and exploring additional research opportunities within the agricultural sector. A more detailed description of this research and results can be found in Karianne Kjønås's master thesis [10].

2   Background and Related Work

Smart farming uses software and hardware to enhance farm operations and involves various technologies like sensors, IoT, AI, machine learning, and unmanned vehicles [2,15]. These technologies enable tasks such as precise weeding and pesticide application [15]. Farming technology has undergone four revolutions [15]: Initially, manual labour and basic tools were used. The first industrial revolution introduced steam-based machinery, leading to a shift from agriculture to manufacturing [22]. The second industrial revolution brought powered machinery, replacing manual and animal labor [4]. The third revolution involved automation using electronics and IT [22], while the fourth revolution integrated big data, AI, IoT, and unmanned vehicles into agriculture [4].

Unmanned farms have emerged, utilizing IoT, AI, robots, and big data for production [23]. Sensors and IoT devices collect data, enabling smart collars for livestock to track health and fertility [23]. Precision feeding calculates the exact amount of feed needed, and milking robots cater to individual cow settings [23]. Automatic barn ventilation with sensor-based control optimizes conditions for livestock [8].

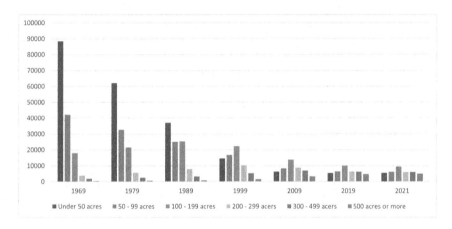

Fig. 1. The change in farm size from 1969 to 2021 showing trend towards centralization. Data from Statistics Norway (SSB) [21]

2.1   Farming in Norway

This study aims to investigate the first part of the food production value chain, namely the technology use and digital risks of farms. Scoping such a study is challenging as the issue is complicated by the many types of farms and food production, geographical differences in altitude and latitude, climate, and individual technology adoption among the farmers. We narrowed the scope to Norwegian farms. According to Statistics Norway [21], there were 38 076 farms in Norway in 2021. The amount of farms in Norway has been steadily decreasing since 1979 when there were 125 302 farms. The trend tends towards centralisation with fewer and larger farms. There were 5 031 large farms (over 500 acres of land) in 2021 compared to 709 in 1979. The most common size of a farm in 2021 was between 100 and 199 acres. Figure 1 shows a comparison of the amount of farms in different size categories over the years.

The are more animal farms than plant producing farms in Norway today. In 2020, there where 11 421 plant producing farms, 23 636 milk and meat producing farms and 1 451 that produce both animal and plant products [21]. Meat production has increased drastically in Norway from 1950 until more recent years [11]. The largest increase happened up until 1984 because of the agricultural revolution which improved the efficiency of the farmers. This also meant that less people were needed to work on the farms, and over time this has led to a significant reduction in the amount of employees on each farm, even though the size of the farms have increased.

2.2   Previous Work on Risks and Vulnerabilities in Smart Farming

A literary review of cybersecurity within agriculture and smart farming research papers revealed several gaps in the research [9]: Topics such as threats and vulnerabilities in the technology was quite well covered, but research into farmers' knowledge and perspectives, as well as their technological dependencies is lacking. The consequences of potential incidents are discussed in terms of confidentiality, integrity and availability (CIA), but the practical implications of such a consequence is not discussed [25]. For example, Gupta et al. mention that a denial of service (DoS) attack will lead to loss of availability, but does not discuss how this may affect the farmer [6]. A full risk assessment that considers the consequences for the farmer and the likelihood of cyber attacks is not present in the research, even though some of the components of a risk assessment are. There is a need for an overview of assets, supply chains and dependencies in order to implement the correct protective measures against various threat actors. Farmers must also deal with food traceability and integrity risks as a crucial part of safety [1].

3   Research Method

The overarching research approach for this study is the phenomenological approach, where the researchers try to understand a situation from the data subjects' perspectives [13]. The farmers' experience and knowledge will affect their dependency on a technology, which in turn will affect the consequence of a potential cyber attack, and is therefore important to include in the collected data. The experienced consequence will also be somewhat subjective as different farmers can have different economical backgrounds and other differences that leads to variations in acceptable risk levels. This study was conducted using sixteen unstructured interviews with a set of pre-prepared questions, fourteen with farmers and two with milk robot experts. There are two major suppliers of milking robots that are used in Norway, Lely and DeLaval, and this study includes one interview with each. Look to Karianne Kjønås's master thesis [10] for a more detailed method description including interview design.

3.1   Sampling

Phenomenological studies typically involve a relatively small sample size, usually less than 25 participants [13]. The focus is on the quality and depth of data rather than the quantity of participants and than the breadth of generalization. Inclusion and exclusion criteria for this study was:

- Participants with Direct Experience: The sample should consist of individuals who have direct and relevant experiences with the phenomenon being investigated. These participants should be able to provide rich and meaningful descriptions of their experiences.
- Homogeneity and Diversity: The sample should be homogeneous in terms of the phenomenon under study, meaning participants should share similar experiences related to the research topic. However, some level of diversity within the sample can also be beneficial to capture various perspectives and nuances.
- Information Richness: Phenomenological studies aim to gain in-depth insights into the experiences of participants. Therefore, the sample should consist of individuals who can provide detailed and information-rich accounts of their experiences.
- Data Saturation: Phenomenological studies often continue until data saturation is reached. Data saturation occurs when no new or relevant information is emerging from additional participants, indicating that the sample size is sufficient to capture the essence of the phenomenon.
- Farm selection and scoping: This study does not include farms that do not produce food or farms that do not work with animals. Cattle was chosen as Norway was 98% self sufficient for milk and milk products in 2022, and pigs were chosen as that was the most produced type of meat in 2022 [12]. The study prioritised farms with a basic level of technology adoption.

3.2   Participant Recruitment

Interview participants were recruited through existing contact networks, from farmer related organizations (e.g. Norsk Bondelag) and their county offices to see if they knew anyone who could participate. This yielded another set of contacts, and some recommendations of other organizations to contact that could help both to understand more of some of the technologies used by farmers, but also give recommendations for farmers to contact for interviews. Contacting the organizations that produced some of the equipment used on the farms yielded contacts that knew more technical details about the equipment, as well as regular contacts to farms that used that organization's equipment.

3.3   Interviews and Data Collection

The main medium used to perform the interviews was online meetings and telephone. Before the interview, the participant was sent the interview questions so they could prepare if they wished to. The participant was asked if audio recording of the session was permitted, and if not, notes were to be taken during the interview. The interview participant was asked the first question to start, and were allowed to talk freely about the topic. Whenever they were done answering the questions, follow up questions were asked to gather the necessary details. Which follow up questions were asked depended on what the participant said, and when they were interviewed. The first interviews were longer and more general, and the participants were asked more clarifying questions than ones about specific details. As the data collected was analyzed along the way, it became clearer which details where needed to perform the case study and risk assessment.

3.4 Data Analysis

The data analysis was performed mainly using Creswell's data analysis spiral [13]. The method consists of four steps that are repeated several times until the data analysis is complete: Firstly, the data was organized using qualitative study analysis tools (Nvivo), and labeled according to type of farm [18]. The second step is perusal, where the entire dataset is perused to get an overview, and figure out potential categories, note down thoughts and comments in general. The third step is classification, where the data is sorted into subcategories and coded. The fourth step is synthesis, where the data is integrated and summarized for readers. The spiral was followed using the data currently available, and repeated whenever new data was added to the set.

3.5 Risk Assessment Method

The risk assessment in this study adhered to the ISO/IEC 27005 standard [7], which is considered a best practice in the field [24]. An asset-based approach was employed, taking into account threats and vulnerabilities for information security assessments. The assessment began with evaluating assets based on their levels of confidentiality, integrity, and availability. Consequence and probability levels were approximated using four distinct levels for each, derived from the data collected during interviews. Threats to the assets were then identified, drawing from a comprehensive list of example threats provided in the ISO 27005 standard [7]. These threat actions were further linked to specific threat agents, adding more detail to the analysis. To gauge the likelihood of these threat actions, the capability and capacity of the threat agents were assessed. Capability pertains to the threat actor's knowledge and abilities, while capacity refers to their available resources [24]. Due to the project's scope and limitations, other characteristics of threat agents were not considered in the assessment.

4   Sample Demographics

In total, 14 farmers were interviewed about their use of technology on the farm. Of these, eight were dairy farms, two were suckler cow farms, and four were pig farms. The 14 farms are described in Table 1 by type of farm, the county the farms is located in, and information related to the size of the farm. The amount of animals on the farm is an approximation in most cases, as it varies throughout the year. Therefore, the capacity of the milking tank is included for the dairy farms to give a more precise picture. There are five different counties represented in the study. Innlandet county is represented most heavily due to being in close proximity to the researchers.

Table 1. Demographics of the smart farms included in the study

No.	Type	Location	Size
1	Dairy farm	Trøndelag	2000 l 40 dairy cows - 80 young cows
2	Dairy farm	Innlandet	6000 l capacity 40 dairy cows - 164 in total
3	Dairy farm	Viken	72 dairy cows 120 calves and heifers
4	Dairy farm	Troms og Finnmark	3000 l 40 dairy cows
5	Dairy farm	Rogaland	8000 l capacity 475 cows - 80 suckle cows
6	Dairy farm	Innlandet	Up to 5000 l
7	Dairy farm	Innlandet	Up to 10 000 l 115 dairy cows
8	Dairy farm	Innlandet	42 dairy cows
9	Suckler cow	Innlandet	50 mother cows
10	Suckler cow	Viken	50 mother cows
11	Pig	Innlandet	1200–1600 during a year
12	Pig	Trøndelag	Up to 1000 at a time
13	Pig	Innlandet	600 at a time
14	Pig	Innlandet	1600 currently

In addition to the 14 farmers, we also interviewed two service technicians who specialize in dairy farm technology. These technicians were associated with the two largest milking robot manufacturers in Norway, namely Lely and DeLaval. Since these manufacturers dominate the Norwegian market, their insights were invaluable for understanding the technologies, how they provide service for the machines, potential vulnerabilities, and gaining some understanding of the data collected by their respective organizations.

5   Dairy Cow Farms

Figure 2 shows a summary of all the technologies used on the eight dairy farms that were interviewed, and how they are connected to the Internet. Each technology is marked with how many of the eight specifically mentioned using that technology. All farms that produce cow's milk depend on a milking robot. This is connected to a farm PC where the machine management software is located. This PC is often used to manage other machines such as feeding robots, as well as ordering supplies, uploading data to relevant websites and accessing software used to manage production.

Some of these programs are also connected to the farmers' mobile phone so that they can check on progress remotely, and set alarms for events such as equipment failure or a power outage. All the farms also have a fire alarm system that will call the farmers' phone in case of fire. A dedicated robot is used by some of the farmers to remove manure, but the machine runs on its own system and is not managed through the farm PC. Overall, the only technologies all the dairy farmers use is the milking robot, farm PC, and a milking robot identification solution. The use of other technologies varies by size and farm house layout as well as location and simply choice.

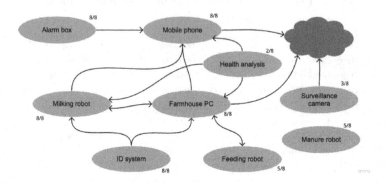

Fig. 2. Overview of use of technology on the dairy farms

The Milking Robot. During the milking process, cows in the milking robot are provided with concentrate as an incentive to remain in place. This feeding is controlled alongside the milking process from the farmhouse PC. To manage milking settings and keep track of which cows have been milked and their milk's destination, each cow wears identification, such as an RFID chip in an ear tag or a necklace. These ID tags categorize cows based on milking needs and can also regulate access to specific areas, such as preventing cows on antibiotics from accessing the main milking robot. Smart gates are also used to direct cows to designated locations for health checks and insemination, with the farmer being able to control this process through the machine software, and the milking robot having its own mobile modem to communicate directly with the farmer.

Lely and DeLaval offer their own software solutions for managing farm machines. Lely has the T4C management system, specifically designed for milking machines, while DeLaval offers DelPro, which not only manages milking but can also be connected to feeding and manure robots. These solutions aim to streamline farm activities and tasks into a unified system, providing substantial decision support. Farmers regularly use these software systems to monitor milking status, ensure all machines are functioning correctly, check the supply in feeding robots (if used), and synchronize data with other software, such as Kukontrollen, utilized by the farmers. The milking robot software is remotely updated and maintained by both Lely and DeLaval through the farming computer.

Manure and Feeding Robots. On Norwegian dairy farms, two common types of robots are used: manure removal robots and feeding robots. Five out of eight farms have a robot to manage manure, either connected to the farm PC or operating on a predetermined route, while the others use a hydraulic draft for manure removal, with some using both methods. During milking, cows are primarily fed concentrate in limited quantities, while fodder or forage is provided at feeding stations within their living areas, accessible to them at all times. Feeding robots are utilized by five dairy farmers to distribute this feed, while the remaining three use a machine connected to the back of a tractor. The feeding robots are managed either through software on the farmhouse PC or by predetermined settings that keep them separate from the LAN. Two farms have an automatic feeder for calves, which can be connected to the same software as the milking robot or programmed manually.

Alarms, Surveillance, and Mobile Connections. The farms have different levels of alarm functions, both emergency functions such as a fire alarm, and alarms related to problems with the milking and feeding robots. Both the fire alarms and the milking robots have the ability to call the farmers' mobile phone in cases of emergency. The farmer can set up as few or many alarm scenarios as they wish for the milking and feeding robots, and some have chosen to get alerts though text message instead. Some of the applications can also give notifications directly to the mobile phone, especially for those systems that have a phone application to access services remotely. Three of the farms also had remote access surveillance cameras to keep an eye on the farm house and the cows.

Common Software. Farmers in Norway use a variety of software and websites for farm management, including mandatory and optional solutions. They report crucial information to the Norwegian food authority through the national livestock register, maintaining records of cows with unique identification numbers. The farmers also keep detailed journals about each cow on the farm, ensuring control over production, animal rights, and traceability in disease outbreaks.

In addition to required systems, approximately 97% of dairy farmers in Norway use Tine's Kukontrollen, a data processing solution that compiles and analyzes animal data from different sources. This includes Geno, a breeding website, and Dyrhelseportalen by Animalia, which provides health and insemination information. Other online services, like Felleskøpet for purchasing animal feed and the chosen slaughterhouse's website, are essential for the supply chain and product delivery.

Health analysis services, such as Lely's system that connects to cow necklaces, have become popular among Norwegian dairy farmers. These sensors analyze various aspects of cows, enabling early detection of health issues and optimal insemination. However, only two farmers mentioned using these solutions, and they were among the largest farms in terms of milking tank capacity.

6   Suckler Cow Farms

The use of technology on suckler cow farms differs from dairy cow farms mostly by the lack of the milking robot. Both types of farms produce cattle for beef production, but the dairy farmers produce cattle to induce milk production, whilst the suckler cow farms produces calves to sells them to other beef or dairy farms. Some of the calves are kept for beef production, others are kept for breeding, and the rest are sold to other farms.

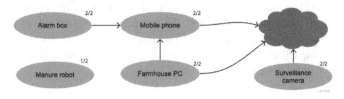

Fig. 3. Overview of the use of technology on suckler cow farms

Technology, Software, and Third Parties. Figure 3 shows an overview of the technologies used by the two suckler cow farmers interviewed in this study. There is also less use of software systems because they do not have the same need to optimize milking, but they are still required to give information to the national livestock register, and do use solutions such as Cattle Meet Control (Storfekjøttkontrollen) to keep track of beef cattle. The cows still have ID tags as required by the national food authority, but they do not use RFID to control access rights and keep track of the cows in the same manner as the dairy farms. The farms still have a farmhouse PC for ordering food, keeping track of the herd, ordering slaughter, and accessing the applications and websites of various other online services.

One of the farms also used the surveillance cameras to monitor heat. The two farms do insemination in different ways, where one farm orders semen online, the other farm purchases the sire and does the insemination naturally. Because they work with the same animals, the suckler cow farms use many of the same services as the dairy farms. Both farmers need to order feed and sell the cows to a slaughterhouse. As they produce calves, they also need to sell the calves, which both farms do through Nortura.

None of the two suckler cow farms used a feeding robot, but one of them does used manure robot. As feeding and cleaning is needed for both dairy and suckler cow farms, the use of robots for these functions is more about preference than difference in the use cases.

Alarms, Surveillance, and Mobile Connections. When it comes to alarm functions, there is less need for it on suckler cow farms as they did not have any robots or machines they are critically dependent on. Both farmers had fire alarms similarly to the dairy farms. Both farmers used surveillance cameras to monitor the cows, especially during calving season, to make sure that things go smoothly.

7   Pig Farms

Figure 4 shows the use of technologies on the four included pig farms. The feeding systems are the most critical technologies, and they are controlled through a dedicated management computer. The other main technology used is the ventilation system, which is also managed through a dedicated computer. The barns are required to have alarm functions in place in case the temperature or humidity reaches unsafe levels, or there is a power outage. The feeding station is also connected to the alarm system in cases of malfunction or power outages. The pig farmers also rely on online solutions to manage the farm, and purchase from and sell to other companies in the supply chain.

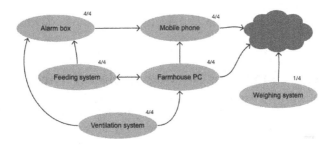

Fig. 4. Overview of the use of technology on pig farms

Feeding Systems. Pigs are either fed dry or liquid feed, and in some cases a combination. The different types of feed requires different machines, because in liquid feeding, the concentrate is mixed with water, whilst the dry feeding machines distributes the feed mix directly. Two of the farmers in this study uses both, one uses only dry feed, and the fourth uses only liquid feed. The pigs are fed twice a day, and the law requires that the feeding system is checked once daily to make sure it works [14]. Three of the four have one feeding station which can be controlled through a separate screen connected to the machine. Some of the feeding machines are connected to the Internet, whilst others are not, but all are connected to an alarm system that will alert the farmer in cases of power outages or malfunctions.

Ventilation Systems. The ventilation systems are generally more mechanical, where not all can be connected to the Internet. The surveyed ventilation systems primarily did not have remote access control configured. The ventilation systems are critical for pig farming, as poor air quality and temperature will affect the animals' welfare. Therefore, the farms are required by law to have emergency openings that are battery operated in case of power outages if the farmhouse itself does not have sufficient natural ventilation [14]. The ventilation systems are also controlled through a separate computer, and this is connected to the alarm system, so that the farmer is alerted if the humidity or temperature is too high.

Animal Identification. Pigs do have ear tags that they are required by law to wear for identification, but they are not used in connection with machines such as the cows are connected to the milking robot. Also, none of the pig farmers used sensors to monitor animal health. One of the farmers mentioned using an automatic weighing system connected to the internet to monitor growth and gather data.

Software and Third Parties. Three of the four pig farmers uses Ingris to keep track of the animals and register production results. Nortura and other slaughterhouses are used to sell products. Two of the farms used Norsvin to order semen for insemination. The other two farms purchased the young pigs through for example Nortura. Felleskjøpet also sells feed to pig farmers, which is where three of the interviewed farmers purchase their feed, whilst the fourth uses a local mill.

8   Risk Assessment for Norwegian Smart Farms

This sections starts by providing a brief evaluation of the ICT assets for the three farm types. The evaluation is followed by a threat and a vulnerability assessments for the smart farms, and ends with a risk assessment.

8.1   Information Asset Evaluation for the Three Farm Types

On a dairy farm, the milking robot is the most critical element, as its unavailability can halt milk production and harm the animals. Breaching the integrity of the milking robot could lead to contaminated milk or fines for the farmer. The farmhouse PC and mobile phone are essential tools but not critical for production, while feeding and manure robots are less critical since manual routines can be used in case of failure. Machine ID tags are crucial for milking and must be fixed if unavailable, as mislabelling cows could lead to economic losses. The alarm box is essential for emergencies, and surveillance cameras and health sensors are not necessary for production but can impact animal well-being if relied upon. Additionally, software integrity, particularly for the milking robot and related applications, is crucial, as incorrect information can affect production planning and meat disposal.

The asset evaluation for the technologies used on suckler cow farms is very similar to the dairy farms. They do rely on surveillance cameras more in their business, but other than that, the use cases are very similar. Other than the alarm box, there are no critical consequences in terms of availability, because they do not rely on technology in order to produce cows, only to manage and optimize production. Similarly, breaches of integrity will not have critical consequences economically, but it can affect traceability. Only Husdyrregisteret has a critical integrity consequence, because this can affect production if the meat has to be discarded.

The feeding systems are critical for pig farmers in their everyday operations, as the pigs require regular access to food. While short periods of unavailability can be managed, extended downtime (more than 12 h) can cause problems, and manual feeding would be challenging. Integrity is not as important, because the farmer will quickly notice if the pigs have received too little food. Too much feed will lead to some economic loss for the farmer. The alarm function is also crucial for emergency situations to ensure the well-being of the animals. The farmhouse PC and mobile phone play essential roles, similar to dairy and suckler cow farms, and software solutions are necessary for production planning, although they do not need to be available at all times. Correct data on these sites is vital for smooth production. While farmers are dependent on supply chain organizations, some can still function with phone orders in case of cyber attacks or other disruptions.

8.2   Threat Assessment

Various actors pose threats to Norwegian farmers, summarized in Table 2. Cyber criminals pose a threat to smart farms due to their malicious intentions and potential financial gain through activities like ransomware attacks. They have medium-level capabilities as they dedicate time and resources to hacking, aiming to earn money and sustain their livelihoods, making them more likely to perform cyber attacks, particularly if it leads to financial gains.

State actors may be motivated by geopolitical reasons, seeking to sabotage food production or gather valuable information through cyber attacks. They have high capabilities and capacities due to state support. Activists may target farmers to portray the food industry negatively or disrupt production, but their capabilities and capacities vary depending on their goals and resources. Natural causes, like power supply disruptions or equipment damage, also pose a threat to farming, with high capacity to cause severe damage, although their capabilities are generally low due to infrequent occurrences.

8.3   Vulnerability Assessment

Table 3 lists some potential vulnerabilities identified from the interviews, as well as findings from Nikander, Manninen and Laajalahti's work on dairy farms in Finland [17]. The vulnerabilities in Norwegian farming vary depending on equipment, farmer knowledge, farm size, and other factors. Many farms have remotely accessible equipment, which is beneficial as it allows for remote access, but also makes them susceptible to unauthorized access and tampering. Several of the websites and software solutions used in Norwegian farming, such as Kukontrollen, Geno, Animalia and Nortura, are logged into through Produsentregisteret, a national register over agricultural producers [19]. The benefit of such a solution is that the farmers need fewer unique login credentials, however, this can cause issues if Produsentregisteret is unavailable, and the farmers can not access all the services they rely on. Transportation of goods is also a vulnerability for farmers, as product, such as milk, spoil after a period, and emergency slaughter requires urgency.

Table 2. Threat assessment for Smart Farming

Threat actor	Capability	Capacity	Threat action
Cyber criminal	Medium	Medium	Intentional denial of service event
			Corruption of data
			Theft of digital identity or credentials
State actor	High	High	System sabotage or software failure or malfunction
			Sabotage of supply system
			Theft of media or documents
Activist	Low	Low	Eavesdropping and interception of data
			Theft of equipment and sensitive media through unauthorized physical access
			Unchecked data viewing or alteration
Natural	Low	High	Equipment damage or destruction due to natural causes (fire, lightning, etc.)
			Loss of power

The protection of farmhouse PCs and network architecture in Norwegian farming depends on the farmer's security awareness, training, economic resources, and personal experience. One dairy farmer, having experienced a ransomware attack, implemented stricter security regulations to prevent future incidents. Vulnerabilities in software and network categories are common in small businesses without dedicated security personnel, aligning with findings from Nikander et al. [17]. Inadequate physical access control is a vulnerability, as many farmhouses in Norway are unlocked. Location will affect how vulnerable the farm is to attacks conducted through physical access, as highly trafficked areas are more exposed. Farmhouse PCs and data cards are susceptible to lightning damage, as mentioned by a technician.

Table 3. Vulnerability assessment for Smart farming

Category	Vulnerability description
Software	Remote access control
	Same login service on multiple sites
	Lack of malware protection
Network	Unprotected communication lines
	Insecure network architecture
	Lack of equipment maintenance
Personnel	Lack of security awareness
	Insufficient security training
Site	Inadequate physical access control and security
	Susceptible to damage in cases of lightning

8.4   Risk Evaluation for the Smart Farms

In the risk analysis conducted for different types of farms, including dairy farms, suckler cow farms, and pig farms, various key risks were identified.

For dairy farmers, the main critical risks involved the milking robot's integrity and availability. A virus on the milking robot, physical sabotage, unauthorized access to milking robot software, and power outages were potential risk scenarios. These risks were deemed unacceptable as the milking robot is crucial for dairy production and cannot be easily replaced manually. Other risks for dairy farmers were less critical and had lower risk scores.

Suckler cow farmers faced lower critical risks, as they were less reliant on digital technology in their production. The identified risks included a ransomware attack on Animalia and a denial of service attack on the farmhouse network.

Pig farmers also had lower critical risks, with a virus on the feeding system control computer being the highest-risk scenario. While a power outage, ransomware attack on Animalia, and denial of service attack on the farmhouse network were also significant risks, pig farmers could potentially go longer without feeding machines compared to dairy farmers and still manage production.

Overall, attacks on confidentiality were not prioritized by the farmers as they saw little consequence tied to confidentiality breaches. The risk of power outages varied depending on the farm's location, with some farmers more prepared with generators and manual alternatives due to their location. Dairy farms and pig farms faced some critical risks, while suckler cow farms had non-critical but high-scoring risk scenarios. The severity of risks varied based on farm reliance on technology and existing mitigating measures and redundancies.

9   Risk Evaluation for Smart Farms on a National Scale

As the risk analysis shows, it is possible to hinder farm production through a cyber attack, but an attack on one or a couple of farms will not have a widespread effect when there are over 38 thousand farms in Norway. On a national scale our investigation found:

- Local Attacks vs. Supplier Attacks: To impact food production on a national scale, the attacks must be aimed towards the suppliers the farmers heavily depend on in various parts of the supply chain.
- Different Types of Attacks on Suppliers: The supply chain involves entities that deliver services or products to farms, those to whom farms deliver their products, and those that receive, analyze, and deliver data. Potential targets for cyber attacks include power suppliers, milking robot manufacturers with remote access control, food suppliers like Felleskjøpet, and data processors such as Nortura, Norsvin, and Tine.
- Effects of Supplier-Targeted Attacks: The outcomes of cyber attacks on suppliers can vary significantly. For instance, power outages may affect farms differently depending on their location and level of preparedness. An attack on milking robot software can be particularly detrimental to dairy farmers'

production, while attacks on data processors can lead to economic and animal welfare consequences for farmers who rely on their services. In cases where certain segments of the value chain are monopolized or exhibit limited competition, the presence of single points of failure increases overall vulnerability

– Data Processors and Authentication Services: Shared login services like Produsentregisteret and Landbrukets Dataflyt are potential targets for cyber attacks, allowing hackers to gain access to multiple organizations and data. Understanding the data flow between organizations in the food production chain is crucial for assessing vulnerabilities.
– General Data Attacks: Attacks focused on data integrity, such as altering data in Husdyrregisteret, can create uncertainty and impact national food planning and self-sufficiency analysis.
– Loss of Cloud Connectivity: Smart farming systems, which depend on cloud platforms for data storage and analysis, would suffer from interrupted data flow and real-time monitoring. A milking robot can do business a few days without cloud connection, however, the connected logistics for dairy and meat processing is vulnerable to collapse such as with the Nortura attack.

Supply chain protection is of strategic national importance, but safeguarding individual farms against cyber attacks can contribute to overall defense. The UK National Cyber Security Centre (NCSC) has collaborated with the National Farmers Union to develop a specialized cybersecurity guide for farmers [16].

10   Limitations and Future Work

As a qualitative study, the data presented here does not fully represent the entire agriculture industry: Although different farmers employ diverse technologies, the findings still hold value and relevance at a general level. The study primarily focused on medium and large-sized cow and pig farm, leaving room for investigating smaller farms in future efforts. There are other critical sectors, such as Norwegian food readiness, supply chains, salmon farming, and the fish trawling fleet, that are as important as dairy and pork farming in Norway. Automation technology in aquaculture was not within the scope of this research, but it represents an area for potential future exploration.

While dairy and pig farms were the primary focus, it is essential to extend research to other farm types, such as chicken farms, which heavily rely on technology for temperature control. Additionally, a deeper exploration of plant-based food production is warranted, as disruptions to technology is feasible in this sector. Understanding specific vulnerabilities and consequences, particularly their impact on the food supply chain, is crucial. Another critical aspect lies in precision agriculture's reliance on satellite systems such as GNSS and Kartverket's CPOS. Further investigation is needed to assess the risks and consequences of cyber attacks in this area.

The research identified potential targets within the supply chain, emphasizing the importance of studying critical organizations like Felleskjøpet, whose disruption could lead to waste and impact food production. Comprehensive research into the entire supply chain, including services like Landbrukets Dataflyt, is necessary to unveil potential weaknesses and vulnerabilities.

While the study outlined potential scenarios affecting food production, feasibility analysis is essential to evaluate the likelihood and extent of damage each scenario could cause. Understanding the criticality of different agricultural sectors and their emergency storage capacity will help differentiate the consequences of potential attacks. The threat and attacker models used in this study were based on the farmer's own statements, resulting in a relatively narrow attacker model in Table 2. Criminals, state actors, and activists were presented as the attackers, but it's important to consider a more intricate list of actual threats against smart tags, communication links, and infrastructure around smart farming, such as cyber sabotage with the application of fertilizers and pesticides, digital controllers in greenhouse systems that can grow or destroy all vegetable or fruit produce, and irrigation systems in grain farming that can water, flood, or dry out large areas when attacked.

11   Conclusion

The research findings highlighting Norwegian cattle and pig farm IT system dependencies. Dairy cow farms rely heavily on the milking robot and its connected ID tag, while pig farms consider the feeding system crucial due to their large number of pigs. Suckler cow farms also use similar technologies but do not view them as critical for their production. The risk assessment for dairy farms identified 10 critical risk scenarios, primarily affecting the availability and integrity of the milking robot and its software. These scenarios involve a high likelihood of computer viruses or unauthorized access through remote control systems. On the other hand, suckler cow farms have no critical risks due to their lower reliance on technology, while pig farms face their highest scoring risk with a computer virus on the feeding system control computer. To impact food production on a national scale, threat actors are more likely to target elements of the supply chain rather than individual farms. Farm suppliers like Felleskøpet and Norsvin, data processors like Animalia, and market regulators like Nortura and Tine are potential targets due to their significant roles in Norwegian food production. Further research is needed to investigate the vulnerabilities and importance of these organizations for food production. Additionally, services like Landbrukets Dataflyt, which facilitate collective access to various agricultural software solutions and enable secure data sharing, should be studied for their potential cyber attack implications on the food supply chain.

In conclusion, safeguarding the nation's food production from cyber threats requires securing the supply chain and understanding vulnerabilities across various agricultural sectors. Future research should delve into these areas to develop effective strategies for protecting Norway's food production system.

References

1. Badia-Melis, R., Mishra, P., Ruiz-García, L.: Food traceability: new trends and recent advances. A review. Food Control **57**, 393–401 (2015)
2. Barreto, L., Amaral, A.: Smart farming: cyber security challenges. In: 2018 International Conference on Intelligent Systems (IS), pp. 870–876. IEEE (2018)
3. Chien, F., Anwar, A., Hsu, C.C., Sharif, A., Razzaq, A., Sinha, A.: The role of information and communication technology in encountering environmental degradation: proposing an SDG framework for the BRICS countries. Technol. Soc. **65**, 101587 (2021)
4. Ferrag, M.A., Shu, L., Friha, O., Yang, X.: Cyber security intrusion detection for agriculture 4.0: machine learning-based solutions, datasets, and future directions. IEEE/CAA J. Automatica Sinica **9**(3), 407–436 (2021)
5. Grgić, K., Žagar, D., Balen, J., Vlaović, J.: Internet of things in smart agriculture-possibilities and challenges. In: 2020 International Conference on Smart Systems and Technologies (SST), pp. 239–244. IEEE (2020)
6. Gupta, M., Abdelsalam, M., Khorsandroo, S., Mittal, S.: Security and privacy in smart farming: challenges and opportunities. IEEE Access **8**, 34564–34584 (2020)
7. International Organization for Standardization: Information security, cybersecurity and privacy protection—Guidance on managing information security risks. International Organization for Standardization, Vernier, Geneva, Switzerland, ISO/IEC 27005:2022(E) edn. (2022)
8. Kim, S.J., Lee, M.H.: Design and implementation of a malfunction detection system for livestock ventilation devices in smart poultry farms. Agriculture **12**(12), 2150 (2022)
9. Kjønås, K., Wangen, G.B.: A survey on cyber security research in the field of agriculture technology. In: IEEE International Symposium on Technology and Society (ISTAS). IEEE (2023)
10. Kjønås, K.: How cyber security incidents can affect Norwegian food production. Master's thesis, NTNU (2023)
11. Ladstein, T., Skoglund, T.: Utviklingen i norsk jordbruk 1950–2005. Technical report, Statistics Norway (2007)
12. Landbruksdirektoratet: Norsk landbruk - tall og fakta. https://www.landbruksdirektoratet.no/nb/norsk-landbruk-tall-og-fakta. Accessed 06 Feb 2023
13. Leedy, P.D., Ormrod, J.E.: Practical Research: Planning and Design, Global Edition, 6 edn. Pearson (2016)
14. Lovdata: Forskrift om hold av svin. https://lovdata.no/dokument/SF/forskrift/2003-02-18-175. Accessed 12 May 2023
15. Moysiadis, V., Sarigiannidis, P., Vitsas, V., Khelifi, A.: Smart farming in Europe. Comput. Sci. Rev. **39**, 100345 (2021)
16. NCSC, NFU: Cyber security for farmers: Practical tips on how to stay safe. Technical report, NCSC (2021)
17. Nikander, J., Manninen, O., Laajalahti, M.: Requirements for cybersecurity in agricultural communication networks. Comput. Electron. Agric. **179**, 105776 (2020)
18. Nvivo: About nvivo. https://help-nv.qsrinternational.com/20/win/Content/about-nvivo/about-nvivo.htm. Accessed 15 May 2023
19. Produsentregisteret: Velkommen til produsentregisteret. https://sak.prodreg.no/. Accessed 13 May 2023

20. Simonsen, H.: Konsekvensene ble mindre enn de kunne blitt. https://medlem.nortura.no/arkiv-2022/konsekvensene-ble-mindre-enn-de-kunne-blitt-article45593-18928.html
21. Statistics Norway: Fakta om jordbruk. https://www.ssb.no/jord-skog-jakt-og-fiskeri/faktaside/jordbruk. Accessed 06 Feb 2023
22. Taiwo, S., Vezi-Magigaba, M.: Human capital perspective of previous industrial revolutions: review in support of 4IR and its possible impacts. Multicult. Educ. **7**(8), 86–96 (2021)
23. Wang, T., Xu, X., Wang, C., Li, Z., Li, D.: From smart farming towards unmanned farms: a new mode of agricultural production. Agriculture **11**(2), 145 (2021)
24. Wangen, G., Hallstensen, C., Snekkenes, E.: A framework for estimating information security risk assessment method completeness: core unified risk framework, CURF. Int. J. Inf. Secur. **17**, 681–699 (2018)
25. Yazdinejad, A., et al.: A review on security of smart farming and precision agriculture: security aspects, attacks, threats and countermeasures. Appl. Sci. **11**(16), 7518 (2021)

Mean Value Analysis of Critical Attack Paths with Multiple Parameters

Rajendra Shivaji Patil[(✉)] [ID], Viktoria Fodor [ID], and Mathias Ekstedt [ID]

KTH Royal Institute of Technology, Stockholm, Sweden
{rpatil,vjfodor,mekstedt}@kth.se

Abstract. Graphical models like attack trees and attack graphs provide promising approaches to represent and analyze complex cyber infrastructures. One common analysis that graphical models are used for is to identify short, or other types of critical attack paths. In this paper, we consider attack graphs that are probabilistic, and the attack steps are characterized by multiple parameters, the probability of success, and the distribution of time to perform the attack step. We propose low-complexity solutions to find sets of critical paths according to flexible mean value-based utility functions. We demonstrate that the results are similar to the ones from Monte-Carlo simulations. Consequently, the utility function-based approach can substitute time-consuming simulations and can be a valuable component of dynamic defense strategies.

Keywords: Systems security · Graphical security modeling · Probabilistic attack graphs · Multiple criteria

1 Introduction

Cyber-infrastructures are becoming increasingly complex and assessing them for identifying the vulnerable parts is very difficult. Graphical models, like attack trees and attack graphs [1–3] provide a formalism that makes it possible to find sequences of exploits or attack steps that lead to successful attacks of valuable assets. This in turn helps to derive efficient defense strategies.

A common way of defining the vulnerable parts in an attack graph is to look for the critical paths, that is, attack paths that are likely to lead to a successful attack [2,4–7]. How potential attackers move in the attack graph is however nondeterministic, affected by the skills and resources of the attacker. Therefore attack graphs are often defined as probabilistic graphs, where the attack steps are characterized by random variables related to success probability, the time, cost or risk to perform the attack, or some other cost metric [4,6,8]. The goal of the analysis can then be to find attack paths that have the highest success probability and are likely to be completed in a short time, with low cost, or a combination of these. Such analysis is challenging even under a single parameter since the paths of the random realizations are correlated due to the overlapping path segments [9–11]. Therefore, the critical paths are found via Monte-Carlo

© The Author(s), under exclusive license to Springer Nature Switzerland AG 2024
L. Fritsch et al. (Eds.): NordSec 2023, LNCS 14324, pp. 126–143, 2024.
https://doi.org/10.1007/978-3-031-47748-5_8

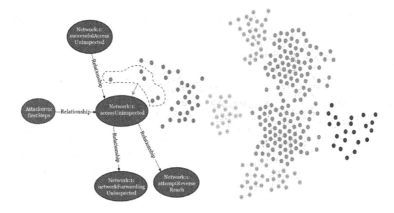

Fig. 1. A representative example of an attack graph according to [14].

simulations [12,13], or shortest paths in mean value sense are considered [6]. These methods are however either time-consuming or inaccurate.

In this paper, we define critical paths in a probabilistic attack graph through a *utility function* that combines the security parameters and approximates the Pareto boundary. This allows to weight parameters according to the goals of the security analysis. We define low-complexity algorithms to find a *set of critical paths* according to the utility function. We demonstrate that the results are reliable in the sense that they significantly overlap with those derived through Monte Carlo simulations. Since the proposed method provides critical paths quickly even for large infrastructures, it can help to evaluate alternative solutions for cyber-infrastructures or can be integrated with dynamic defense strategies.

Several forms of attack graphs are proposed in the literature [1–4]. We follow the framework of Meta Attack Language (MAL) [15]. Figure 1 shows a part of a representative example of a MAL attack graph designed using the domain-specific language coreLang [14]. The graph is generated by the MAL graph generator (mgg[1]) and considers a small IT infrastructure with a few local networks, web servers and operating systems. The goal of the attacker is to gain full access to the web server. While this is a small example, attack graphs can quickly grow in size to many thousands of nodes based on the expansion of a network of assets, their vulnerabilities, and their potential exploits.

In the attack graphs we consider, nodes are attack steps and the edges are logical conditions for being able to attempt an attack step. Attack steps are characterized by two probabilistic security parameters, the time-to-compromise (TTC), given by its distribution, and the probability that an attack step is performed successfully. A key property of these (and many other) attack graphs is that some of the nodes are so-called *AND* nodes, that require to be reached from all of the parents. This means that classical graph algorithms need to be modified to evaluate attack graphs.

---

[1] https://gitlab.com/gnebbia/mgg

The paper is organized as follows. Section 2 gives an overview of the related work, Sect. 3 describes the attack graph and the related metrics, Sect. 4 presents the algorithms developed to find critical paths, and Sect. 5 gives the numerical validation of the proposed approach. Section 6 concludes the paper.

2   Related Work

The problem of finding optimal paths in a graph is a classical part of operation research. In *probabilistic graphs* with a single edge parameter given by a probability distribution, the path costs (also called lengths) are random variables as well. In this case, one can be interested for example in the distribution of the shortest path lengths over all random realizations, or the probability that a given path is the shortest path. In [9] the shortest path and its probability distribution are identified by performing Monte-Carlo simulations. In [10] a branch-and-bound technique is combined with a K-shortest paths algorithm to find the shortest path in the probabilistic graph. Edge weights following exponential distribution are considered in [16] and the probability distribution of the shortest path is derived based on a Markov chain. These approaches focus on deriving probability distributions, which is a time-consuming process. Thus, other approaches propose analytic techniques based on a *utility function*. The utility function can be projected in such a way that it considers the edge weights as input and either maximizes or minimizes the outcome value of a utility. In [17] it is demonstrated that shortest-path solutions based on expected path cost do not account for cost variability, and a utility function based on the mean and variance of the path cost is proposed. The specific case of Gaussian weight distribution is considered in [11], again proposing a utility function that combines mean and variance. In [18] standard deviation is considered instead, leading to a more intuitive measure. However, it is also observed that the variance or standard deviation part in the shortest path problem is both nonlinear and non-additive, and this increases the computational complexity of finding the optimal path. In [19] a generalized utility function that is based on two functions, an increasing convex function, representing the mean and an increasing concave function representing the variance is presented. A new type of dominance (e-dominance) is introduced that follows Bellman's optimality principle.

For graphs where the edges are characterized by multiple, *deterministic* parameters, the optimal path problem becomes a multicriteria (or multiobjective) shortest path problem, and a variety of algorithms based on dynamic programming are proposed in [20–23] to determine the *Pareto optimal paths*. These algorithms perform dominance test for identifying the optimal paths. Other works address the multiobjective shortest path problem by treating some of the objectives as constraints. For example [24] considers three parameters, time, reliability, and flow capacity, sets two objectives as constraints, and uses dynamic programming to generate Pareto optimal paths. For *probabilistic* graphs with multiple stochastic parameters [25] proposes a flexible stochastic dominance test to trade off parameter importance. Finally, the multiobjective shortest path problem is turned into a utility maximization problem in [26], considering edge parameters that are positive and objective functions that are either of the "sum" type or of the "bottleneck" type.

Focusing on attack graphs, [4] and [8] consider deterministic, but conflicting parameters as cost, time, difficulty, and success probability. They define critical paths as paths on the Pareto boundary and derive these with the help of formal modeling. In [27] repeated attack step attempts with deterministic costs are considered, and polynomial algorithms are proposed to find the fastest attack path. Probabilistic attack graphs, with the TTC of the attack steps given by probability distributions, are considered in [6]. It defines the mean TTC as the security metric and finds critical paths by enumerating all paths, a solution that is suitable for small infrastructures. A similar model, but including also success probability is considered in [12], and the set of probabilistic shortest paths are found with Monte-Carlo simulation.

We advance previous works by proposing and validating *low complexity heuristics* to find the *set of k critical paths* in attack graph *containing AND nodes*, where attack steps are characterized by *two probabilistic parameters*, the success probability and the TTC distribution.

3   Scenario

3.1   Input Graph

We consider a probabilistic directed acyclic graph (DAG) $G = (V, E, T, S, V_A)$, where $V = \{v_1, v_2, \ldots, v_m\}$ is a set of nodes, $E = \{e_1, e_2, \ldots, e_n\}$ is a set of edges. A node represents an attack step, and an edge represents the logical condition for being able to perform an attack step. For an edge $e_i = (u, v)$, the parent node u represents the attack step that needs to be performed to attempt the step represented by node v. Furthermore, the edges of G are associated with two parameters S and T. $S = \{s_1, s_2, \ldots, s_n\}$ is a vector of success probabilities, giving the probability that the attack step represented by the child node is attempted and thus the attack continues in the given direction. Similarly, $T = \{T_1, T_2, \ldots, T_n\}$ is a vector of TTC distributions, where T_i is given by the probability density function $f_i(t)$ and represents the value of time to compromise of the child attack step of edge e_i. The attack step represented by node u may be reached from multiple directions and thus, a node may have multiple parents. The nodes may be of the type OR or AND. The node of type OR signifies that the attacker can reach the node when at least a single parent is compromised whereas to compromise an AND node, all its parents must be compromised. Accordingly, $V_A = \{a_1, a_2, \ldots, a_k\}$ is a set of AND nodes. All other nodes are OR nodes. In this work, we consider that the source or sources of the attack and the destination, that is the asset the attacker aims to reach are given.

3.2   Edge and Path Metrics

There are two kinds of metrics assigned to the edges: TTC and success probability. These metrics need to be combined with a utility function, to characterize the cost of an end-to-end attack path in a meaningful way. Our goal is to define the cost of a path in a way that tractable extensions of traditional shortest path algorithms can be used to find the critical paths.

Path Cost for Single Parameter: Let $\pi_i(v_s, v_t)$ be a simple path from v_s to v_t. Considering the additive weight w_i for an edge $e_i \in \prod(v_s, v_t)$, the path cost is the sum of edge weights and is defined as:

$$C(\pi(v_s, v_t)) = \sum_{e_i \in \pi(v_s, v_t)} w_i \qquad (1)$$

To calculate path costs to AND nodes, we follow the reasoning of [28]. We consider that the attacker has many resources and progresses on parallel paths through the attack graph. An AND node is discovered once it is reached through all its parents. To simplify the evaluation, we approximate the cost of reaching the AND node by the maximum of costs through all the parent nodes. That is, for the AND node a_i with p number of parents $v_1, v_2, ...v_p$, the path weight is the maximum path weight to reach all parent nodes plus the weight of the edge from the parent to the AND node:

$$C(\pi(v_s, a)) = \max_{i=1...p} (C(\pi(v_s, v_i)) + w_i). \qquad (2)$$

where w_i is the weight of the edge (v_i, a).

TTC values on a path are additive, and a path is critical if the path TCC value is low. Therefore the weight of an edge can be directly defined by the TTC value. Considering the success probabilities, two issues need to be addressed. First, critical paths are paths with the highest success probability, which leads to a maximization problem instead of a minimization one. Second, while TTC values are additive along an attack path, success probabilities should be multiplied. To handle these, we define the success probability-related weight as $w_i = \log(1/s_i)$.

Path Costs in a Mean Value Sense, with Multiple Parameters: We need a definition of path cost that i) can express the relative importance of the edge parameters, and ii) allows the use of low complexity shortest path algorithms. Therefore, we define the weight of an edge as the weighted combination of the two edge parameters. Such a definition allows us to approximate the Pareto efficient paths [4,8,20,29]. This leads us to the definition of path costs in the mean value sense:

$$w_i = \alpha E[T_i] + (1 - \alpha) \log_{10}(1/s_i), \qquad (3)$$

$$C(\pi(v_s, v_t)) = \alpha \sum_{e_i \in \pi(v_s, v_t)} E[T_i] + (1 - \alpha) \sum_{e_i \in \pi(v_s, v_t)} \log(1/s_i). \qquad (4)$$

Note, that the above definition gives back the average TTC path cost and the path success probability for $\alpha = 0$ and $\alpha = 1$ respectively.

Path Costs with Mean-Sigma Metric: Selecting shortest paths based on the mean value of the TTC is a common approach. However, this does not reflect that the path length distributions can have very different variances, and paths with high variance could often become the shortest ones in a random realization. To find paths that are shortest with high probability, comparing the lower percentiles of the end-to-end TTC distribution can be more reasonable. Considering that the sum of independent random variables converges to a normal distribution, we suggest the mean-sigma metric (approximately 15th-percentile) to compare the random path length [5,11]. Accordingly, the TTC weight of a single attack step is $E[T_i] - \sigma_i$, where σ_i is the standard deviation of $f_i(t)$.

As mean and variance (but not the standard deviation) values of independent random variables are additive, the TTC related cost component of any path segment $P(u, v)$ needs to be calculated as

$$\sum_{e_i \in \pi(u,v)} E[T_i] - \sqrt{\sum_{e_i \in \pi(u,v)} \sigma_i^2}. \tag{5}$$

Weighed with α, this can then be used in (4) instead of the first path cost term.

Path Cost and Path Frequency in Monte-Carlo Simulation: With the Monte-Carlo simulation, three cases can be covered. Both TTC and success probability are considered, if a random realization includes only the attack steps that are performed successfully according to the success probability s_i, and each attack step receives a TTC value selected randomly according to $T_i \sim f_i(t)$. Accordingly, the set of edges is $E' \subseteq E$, and $w_i = T_i$, $\forall i \in E'$. The cost of a path is then calculated as (1) and (2). By setting all $s_i = 1$, the single parameter scenario with only the TTC parameters is considered. Finally, if only the success probability is relevant, the most critical paths are the ones that exist in most of the random realizations, independently from their TTC value.

4   Algorithms to Find Critical Paths

To find the attack paths that are likely to be the shortest paths, and to compare the results gained from the analytic approaches and from Monte-Carlo simulations, the following algorithms are required, for graphs that contain AND nodes:

- Algorithm to find the set of *k-shortest paths*, that is, the k paths in the graph with the lowest cost, according to the mean and the mean-sigma values, and for different values of the weight α, and according to the TTC realizations in Monte-Carlos simulations;
- Algorithm to find the k paths that most often are possible paths under the random realizations of a graph in the Monte-Carlo simulation, when edges are removed according to s_i.

For these, we extend the classical Dijkstra and Yen's algorithms and an all-path enumeration algorithm to handle AND nodes in the attack graph.

4.1   Algorithm Descriptions

Dijkstra's Algorithm with AND Nodes: The extended Dijkstra's algorithm is given in Algorithm 1. The classical Dijkstra's algorithm is a known solution to find the shortest path in a graph [30]. It only considers graphs with nodes corresponding to OR attack steps, and it uses a 'min' function so that the cost

---

Algorithm 1: Dijkstra for graph with AND nodes

Input: $G = (V, E, W, S, V_A)$
Output: A shortest path, $par[V]$ parents of nodes;

```
1  Function Dijkstra_AND(G, v_s, v_t, α):
2  |   dist[v_i] ← ∞, the distance of v_i from v_s, ∀v_i ∈ V;
3  |   par[v_i] ← null, the parent of a node v_i, ∀v_i ∈ V;
4  |   npar[v_a] ← no. of parents of node v_a, ∀v_a ∈ V_A;
5  |   adj[v_i] ← adjacent nodes of node v_i, ∀v_i ∈ V;
6  |   Q, a priority queue ;
7  |   dist[v_s] ← 0 ;
8  |   Q ← Q.add(v_s, dist[v_s]);
9  |   while Q is not empty do
10 |   |   u ← node in Q with minimum dist[u];
11 |   |   Q ← Q.remove(u);
12 |   |   for v_i ∈ adj[u] do
13 |   |   |   cost_{u,v_i} ← (α × W_{uv_i}) + ((1-α) × (log(1/S_{uv_i})));
14 |   |   |   dist_new ← dist[u] + cost_{u,v_i};
15 |   |   |   if v_i ∈ V_A then
16 |   |   |   |   if dist_new > dist[v_i] * then
17 |   |   |   |   |   dist[v_i] ← dist_new;
18 |   |   |   |   |   par[v_i] ← u;
19 |   |   |   |   |   npar[v_i] ← npar[v_i] - 1;
20 |   |   |   |   |   if npar[v_i] = 0 then
21 |   |   |   |   |   |   Q ← Q.add(v_i, dist[v_i]);
22 |   |   |   |   |   end
23 |   |   |   |   end
24 |   |   |   end
25 |   |   |   else
26 |   |   |   |   if dist_new < dist[v_i] then
27 |   |   |   |   |   dist[v_i] ← dist_new;
28 |   |   |   |   |   par[v_i] ← u;
29 |   |   |   |   |   Q ← Q.add(v_i, dist[v_i]);
30 |   |   |   |   end
31 |   |   |   end
32 |   |   end
33 |   end
34 End Function
```

*In case of equal distance, paths with fewer edges are considered to be shorter.

to reach a given node is the minimum cost to reach it through any parent. The extended algorithm (Algorithm 1) handles AND nodes separately in lines 15–24, implementing (2). That is, it considers the shortest paths through each parent node and records the maximum of these costs. For example, consider a graph shown in Fig. 2 with node 7 as an AND node. The path cost to reach node 7 is 13.0 which is the maximum of costs to reach the node through node 4 or through node 5. The OR nodes are handled according to the classical algorithm, in lines 26–30.

In general, Dijkstra gives an approximate solution for the mean-sigma metric in (5), however, it gives exact results for several specific probability distributions, for example, for uniform, standard normal, or exponential distributions.

Yen's Algorithm with AND Nodes: The classical Yen's algorithm is a known solution to find the set of k shortest paths in a graph [31]. We summarize it briefly following Algorithm 2. Algorithm 2 already includes the handling of AND nodes, but of course graphs with OR nodes only are special cases. Yen's algorithm works in two parts. The first determines the first shortest path, and the second determines all other $k - 1$ shortest paths, by removing edges of already selected paths one by one, and repeatedly calling a shortest path algorithm. For example, in the graph shown in Fig. 2, we consider now all nodes to be OR nodes, set 0 as a source node and 9 as a destination node, and then run the classical Yen's algorithm. The first part computes the first shortest path as 0-2-5-8-9. The processing of the second part, lines 12–39 of Algorithm 2, which is equivalent to the second part of classical Yen's algorithm, is shown in Table 1 below, for the next four paths.

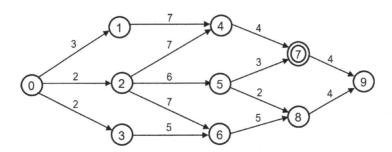

Fig. 2. A sample attack graph with AND node

Table 1. Processing of the second part of Yen's algorithm for k-1 paths

SN	spur Node	root Path	Removed edge	Removed node	spur Path	total Path	path Cost	B[]	k	A[k]	cost A[k]
1	–	–	–	–	–	–	–	–	1	0-2-5-8-9	14
2	0	0	0-2	–	0-3-6-8-9	0-3-6-8-9	16				
3	2	0-2	2-5	0	**2-4-7-9**	**0-2-4-7-9**	**17**	0-3-6-8-9,			
4	5	0-2-5	5-8	0, 2	5-7-9	0-2-5-7-9	15	0-2-4-7-9,			
5	8	0-2-5-8	8-9	0, 2, 5	null	null	–	0-2-5-7-9	2	0-2-5-7-9	15
6	0	0	0-2	–	0-3-6-8-9	0-3-6-8-9	16				
7	2	0-2	2-5	0	2-4-7-9	0-2-4-7-9	17				
8	5	0-2-5	5-8, 5-7	0, 2	null	null	–	0-2-4-7-9,			
9	7	0-2-5-7	8-9, 7-9	0, 2, 5	null	null	–	0-3-6-8-9	3	0-3-6-8-9	16
10	**0**	**0**	**0-2, 0-3**	–	**0-1-4-7-9**	**0-1-4-7-9**	**18**				
11	3	0-3	2-5, 3-6	0	null	null	–				
12	6	0-3-6	5-8, 5-7, 6-8	0, 3	null	null	–	0-2-4-7-9,			
13	8	0-3-6-8	8-9, 7-9	0, 3, 6	null	null	–	0-1-4-7-9	4	0-2-4-7-9	17
14	0	0	0-2, 0-3	–	0-1-4-7-9	0-1-4-7-9	18				
15	2	0-2	2-5, 3-6, 2-4	0	2-6-8-9	0-2-6-8-9	18				
16	4	0-2-4	5-8, 5-7,6-8, 4-7	0, 2	null	null	–	0-1-4-7-9,			
17	7	0-2-4-7	8-9, 7-9	0, 2, 4	null	null	–	0-2-6-8-9	5	0-1-4-7-9	18

The classical Yen's algorithm does not work for graphs with AND nodes directly. For example, consider a graph in Fig. 2 with AND node 7. The three shortest paths would be 0-2-5-8-9, 0-3-6-8-9, and then a path through the AND node. However, the path through the AND node is never detected, because edge 2–5 or 0–2 is removed in the iterations of Yen's algorithm (see row no. 3 and no. 10 in Table 1).

We extend Yen's algorithm to handle an arbitrary number of AND nodes, as presented in Algorithm 2. The approach is based on the understanding that a set of paths to an AND node can be represented by the highest-cost path through all the parents. In the first part of the extended Yen's algorithm, Algorithm 1 is utilized not only to find the shortest path but also to record the higher cost parent for each AND node, as shown in lines 1–3. In the second part, for each particular AND node, the algorithm keeps only edges from the selected parent and removes the edges from all other parents (lines 5–11). Thus, the second part receives the updated graph, can consider all nodes as OR nodes, and can employ the classical Dijkstra's algorithm (DA) to find the next $k-1$ shortest paths. Accordingly, as shown in Fig. 2, for the graph with 7 as the AND node, the extended algorithm first finds the first shortest paths as 0-2-5-8-9 of cost 14, selects the parent 4 of the AND node 7, and then removes the edge 5-7. In the second part, the extended algorithm takes the updated graph and finds the next two shortest paths as 0-3-6-8-9, 0-2-4-7-9 with costs 16 and 17 respectively, as intended.

All-Path Algorithm with AND Nodes: Typically, paths are enumerated in DAGs by using the classical All-path algorithm based on the recursive depth-

---

Algorithm 2: Yen's for graph with AND nodes

Input: $G = (V, E, W, S, V_A)$
Output: K shortest paths;

1 **Function** $Yen\_AND(G, v_s, v_t, \alpha, K)$**:**
2      $A[1], P[V_A] = Dijkstra\_AND(G, v_s, v_t, \alpha)$
3   where $A[1]$ stores the first shortest path, $P[V_A]$ stores the MAX parents of AND nodes;
4      $B = [] \;//$ stores tentative shortest paths;
5   **for** $v_i \in V$ **do**
6   **for** $v_j \in V_A$ **do**
7   **if** $edge(v_i, v_j) \in E$ *and* $v_i \neg P[V_A]$ **then**
8                  $E = E.remove(v_i, v_j)$;
9   **end**
10   **end**
11   **end**
12   **for** $k \leftarrow 2\ to\ K$ **do**
13   **for** $v_i \leftarrow 1\ to\ size(A[k-1]) - 1$ **do**
14              $E_y = E, V_y = V$;
15              $spurNode = A[k-1].node(v_i)$;
16              $rootPath = A[k-1].nodes(v_s, v_i)$;
17   **for** *each* $p \in A$ **do**
18   **if** $rootPath == p.nodes(v_s, v_i)$ **then**
19                      $E_y = E_y.remove(v_i, v_i + 1)$;
20   **end**
21   **end**
22   **for** $v_j \in rootPath$ **do**
23   **if** $v_j \neq spurNode$ **then**
24                      $V_y = V_y.remove(v_j)$;
25   **end**
26   **end**
27              $G = (V_y, E_y, W, S)$;
28              $spurPath = DA(G, spurNode, v_t, \alpha)$;
29              $totalPath = rootPath + spurPath$;
30   **if** $totalPath \neg B$ **then**
31                  $B = B.append(totalPath)$;
32   **end**
33   **end**
34          $B.sort(), A[k] = B[0], B.pop()$;
35   **end**
36 **End Function**

---

first search [32]. This algorithm only considers graphs with nodes corresponding to the OR type and computes all paths passing through such nodes.

To enumerate paths in graphs with AND nodes, we propose an approximate solution, through the modification of the classical All-path algorithm as given in Algorithm 3. It computes all paths between two nodes in a graph with the

---

Algorithm 3: All-path for graph with AND nodes

Input: $G = (V, E, V_A, v_s, v_t)$
Output: All paths;
1   $allpaths \leftarrow []$ // Initialize the set to store all paths;
2   **Function** $Allpath\_AND(G, v_s, v_t)$:
3     $path \leftarrow null$;
4     $path.add(v_s)$;
5     $visited[v_i] \leftarrow false, \forall v_i \in V$;
6     $AP(v_s, v_t, visited[V], path)$;
7   **return** $allpaths$;
8 **End Function**
9   $apath[v_i] \leftarrow \infty, \forall v_i \in V_A$;
10   $npar[v_i] \leftarrow n$, number of parents of v_i, $\forall v_i \in V_A$;
11 **Function** $AP(v_s, v_t, visited[V], lpath)$:
12   **if** $v_s = v_t$ **then**
13 | $allpaths.add(lpath)$;
14   **end**
15     $visited[v_s] \leftarrow true$;
16   **for** $v_i \in adjList[v_s]$ **do**
17   **if** $visited[v_i] \neq true$ **then**
18         $lpath.add(v_i)$;
19   **if** $v_i \in V_A$ **then**
20   **if** $lpath.size < apath[v_i].size$ **then**
21 | $apath[v_i] \leftarrow lpath$;
22   **end**
23           $npar[v_i] \leftarrow npar[v_i]$ - 1;
24   **if** $npar[v_i] = 0$ **then**
25             $AP(v_i, v_t, visited[V], apath[v_i])$;
26             $lpath.remove(v_i)$;
27   **end**
28   **else**
29 | $lpath.remove(v_i)$;
30   **end**
31   **end**
32   **else**
33           $AP(v_i, v_t, visited[V], lpath)$;
34           $lpath.remove(v_i)$;
35   **end**
36   **end**
37   **end**
38     $visited[v_s] = false$;
39 **End Function**

AND node. However, as in Yen's algorithm, for tractability, for each AND node only one path from one of the parents is kept. To ensure identical decisions for the several Monte-Carlo iterations, we characterize the paths with their length in a number of edges and record only the shortest path to the AND node (see lines 19–31). For example, as shown in Fig. 2, for the graph with AND node 7, the extended All-path algorithm finds that the parents 4 and 5 have equal path lengths (i.e. 2) and selects 4 as a single parent of node 7 since 4 appears first in the depth-first-search. It then finds all paths i.e. two paths as 0-1-4-7-9 and 0-2-4-7-9 passing through node 7, it does not count the path 0-2-5-7-9.

Algorithms 1, 2 and 3 calculate path costs, but do not record the shortest paths with the parallel branches through the AND nodes. These however can always be reconstructed by running Algorithms 1 on G.

4.2 Algorithm Complexities

The analytic approach applies the extended Yen's algorithm, Algorithm 2. It preserves the time complexity of the original algorithm, that is, $O(KV(E + V \log V))$ [31,33]. The simulation based evaluation needs Algorithm 1 or 3 in each simulation run, with complexities $O((V + E) \log V)$ [34] and $O(V * E)$ [35] respectively. While these algorithms have lower complexity than Yen's algorithm, experience shows that for graphs $V \approx 100$, 10,000 simulation runs need to be performed. Even if this number increases slowly with V, the runtime of the analytic solution remains significantly lower than that of the simulations.

4.3 Validation of the Analytic Approach

Our objective is to validate that the mean-value or mean-sigma based k-shortest path sufficiently overlaps with the set of shortest paths found by Monte-Carlo simulation. Therefore, we employ the extended Yen's k-shortest path algorithm (Algorithm 2), for various α values. We compare the lists of paths with three versions of Monte-Carlo simulations, with a high number of I iterations:

> *i) Monte-Carlo Simulation with only TTC values only:* In each iteration, the complete graph G is considered, with random realization of the TTC values. $Dijkstra\_AND$ algorithm (Algorithm 1) computes the shortest path.
>
> *ii) Monte-Carlo Simulation with success probabilities only:* In each iteration, edges are removed randomly from G, according to S. In the graph with remaining edges, the $Allpath\_AND$ algorithm (Algorithm 3) enumerates all paths.
>
> *iii) Monte-Carlo simulation with TTC values and success probabilities:* In each iteration, edges are removed according to S, and then the steps of (i) are followed.

For each of the cases, paths with AND nodes are considered to be identical, if the same AND nodes are visited, in the same order.

5 Numerical Evaluation

We generate a random graph with 100 nodes, 200 edges, and 10 randomly selected AND nodes. We perform 25 experiments over this graph. In each experiment, for each edge e_i, a random value $T_i \sim U[0,1]$ is generated, and then

$U[0, T_i]$ is assigned as the TTC distribution. Similarly, the success probability $s_i \in [0, 1]$ is selected from a truncated, negatively skewed normal distribution $N[\mu, \sigma^2]$, with $\mu \in [0.7, 0.8]$, $\sigma^2 \in [0.03, 0.04]$ and skewness $\in [-1, -0.5]$. With these parameters in the graph, first, analytic evaluation is performed considering the utility function (4) and (5), for each α value in the range $[0, 1]$. Second, three types of Monte-Carlo simulations are performed with 10000 iterations, as described in Sect. 4.3. Finally, the path hit is calculated as the number of matching paths in the $k = 10$ shortest paths of the analytic evaluation and 10 most popular paths of Monte-Carlo simulation. The figures show the average and the standard deviation of path hits (i.e. SD path hits) over the 25 experiments for each α value. A low value of SD path hits means that the path hits across all experiments are close to the average for the corresponding α value.

The path hits when the Monte-Carlo simulations consider the TTC values only are shown in Figs. 3 and 4. Path hits with the mean-sigma utility are slightly higher for all α values, showing that the mean-sigma utility has slightly better capability to capture the paths that does not have the lowest mean TTC but end up as the shortest path due to high variance. As expected, the average hit is highest for $\alpha = 1$, since in this case even the analytic evaluation with (3) considers the TTC values only. The path hit value is around 9 out of 10 in this case. The average hits decrease significantly with decreasing α, showing that indeed, the edge success probability changes the set of critical paths considerably. Similarly, Figs. 5 and 6 show the results when only the success probabilities are considered in the simulations, with the highest hits at $\alpha = 0$ as expected.

Finally, both edge parameters, the TTC value, and the success probability are considered both in the Monte-Carlo simulations and in the analytic evaluation, and the results are shown in Figs. 7 and 8. Remember, in Monte-Carlo simulations, edges are removed according to the success probabilities, and then the shortest paths are found according to the TTC realizations. The best hit value, at around $\alpha = 0.3$, is comparable to the ones of the extreme cases in the previous figures, with a value at around 8.3 out of 10. Also, the SD path hits value is low i.e. 0.94 at $\alpha = 0.3$. Similar results are observed for the top 25 and 50 paths. This means that the utility function successfully reflects the combined effect of the two parameters.

The results demonstrate that the proposed utility function-based analysis can substitute simulations when both, or only one of the security parameters are of importance. By tuning the α value it also allows to define the set of critical paths when success probability and TTC have different importance, an evaluation that is hard to do with simulations only.

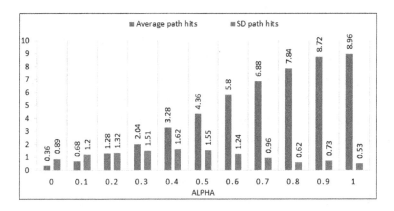

Fig. 3. Mean value path hits for Monte-Carlo simulations with TTC values only.

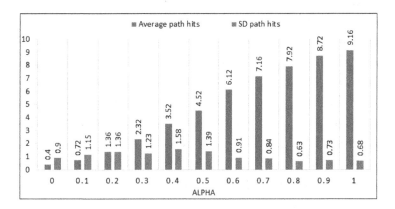

Fig. 4. Mean-sigma path hits for Monte-Carlo simulations with TTC values only.

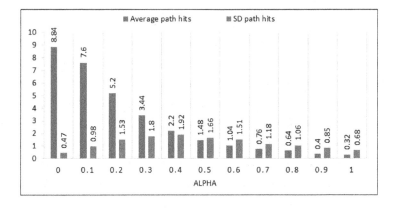

Fig. 5. Mean value path hits for Monte-Carlo simulations with success probabilities only.

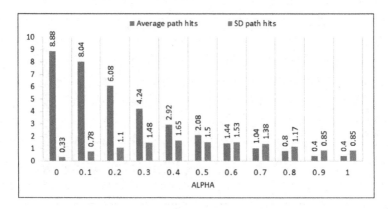

Fig. 6. Mean-sigma path hits for Monte-Carlo simulations with success probabilities only.

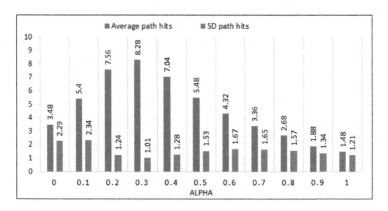

Fig. 7. Mean value path hits for Monte-Carlo simulations with both TTC values and success probabilities.

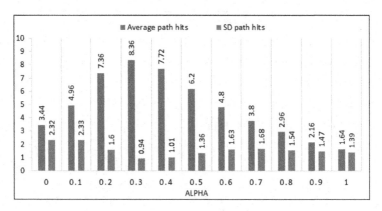

Fig. 8. Mean-sigma path hits for Monte-Carlo simulations with both TTC values and success probabilities.

6   Conclusions

This paper addresses the problem of identifying attack paths in cyber-infra-structures through which attackers can reach a valuable target in a short time with high probability. We claim that a set of these paths can be found via low-complexity shortest-path algorithms. For this, we define a utility function that incorporates both time-to-compromise and success probability, and extend known polynomial time graph algorithms to find approximate solutions to the resulting utility minimization problem. Through the Monte-Carlo simulation-based analysis, we demonstrate that the analytical methods with mean and mean-sigma value-based utilities reflect the approximate attacker behavior, and can identify the set of critical attack paths. This allows the security analysis of large infrastructures and opens the way to incorporating these algorithms in dynamic attack strategies.

Acknowledgment. This work was supported by the Swedish Governmental Agency for Innovation Systems (Vinnova).

References

1. Ammann, P., Wijesekera, D., Kaushik, S.: Scalable, graph-based network vulnerability analysis. In: 9th ACM Conference on Computer and Communications Security, pp. 217–224 (2002)
2. Li, W., Vaughn, R.B.: Cluster security research involving the modeling of network exploitations using exploitation graphs. In: 6th IEEE International Symposium on Cluster Computing and the Grid, vol. 2, p. 26 (2006)
3. Sheyner, O., Haines, J., Jha, S., Lippmann, R., Wing, J.M.: Automated generation and analysis of attack graphs. In: IEEE Symposium on Security & Privacy, pp. 273–284 (2002)
4. Fila, B., Widel, W.: Efficient attack-defense tree analysis using pareto attribute domains. In: 32nd IEEE Computer Security Foundations Symposium, pp. 200–215 (2019)
5. Idika, N., Bhargava, B.: Extending attack graph-based security metrics and aggregating their application. IEEE Trans. Dependable Secure Comput. **9**(1), 75–85 (2010)
6. Leversage, D.J., Byres, E.J.: Estimating a system's mean time-to-compromise. IEEE Secur. Priv. **6**(1), 52–60 (2008)
7. Ramos, A., Lazar, M., Holanda Filho, R., Rodrigues, J.J.: Model-based quantitative network security metrics: a survey. IEEE Commun. Surv. Tutor. **19**(4), 2704–2734 (2017)
8. Aslanyan, Z., Nielson, F.: Pareto efficient solutions of attack-defence trees. In: Focardi, R., Myers, A. (eds.) POST 2015. LNCS, vol. 9036, pp. 95–114. Springer, Heidelberg (2015). https://doi.org/10.1007/978-3-662-46666-7_6
9. Frank, H.: Shortest paths in probabilistic graphs. Oper. Res. **17**(4), 583–599 (1969)
10. Hall, R.W.: The fastest path through a network with random time-dependent travel times. Transp. Sci. **20**(3), 182–188 (1986)

11. Rasteiro, D., Anjo, A.: Optimal paths in probabilistic networks. J. Math. Sci. **120**(1), 974–987 (2004)
12. Xiong, W., Hacks, S., Lagerstrom, R.: A method for assigning probability distributions in attack simulation languages. Complex Syst. Inform. Model. Q. **151**(26), 55–77 (2021)
13. Van Slyke, R.M.: Monte Carlo methods and the pert problem. Oper. Res. **11**(5), 839–860 (1963)
14. Katsikeas, S., et al.: An attack simulation language for the IT domain. In: Eades III, H., Gadyatskaya, O. (eds.) GraMSec 2020. LNCS, vol. 12419, pp. 67–86. Springer, Cham (2020). https://doi.org/10.1007/978-3-030-62230-5_4
15. Wideł, W., Hacks, S., Ekstedt, M., Johnson, P., Lagerström, R.: The meta attack language - a formal description. Comput. Secur. **130**, 1–12 (2023)
16. Kulkarni, V.G.: Shortest paths in networks with exponentially distributed arc lengths. Networks **16**(3), 255–274 (1986)
17. Sen, S., Pillai, R., Joshi, S., Rathi, A.K.: A mean-variance model for route guidance in advanced traveler information systems. Transp. Sci. **35**(1), 37–49 (2001)
18. Khani, A., Boyles, S.D.: An exact algorithm for the mean-standard deviation shortest path problem. Transp. Res. Part B: Methodol. **81**, 252–266 (2015)
19. Hutson, K.R., Shier, D.R.: Extended dominance and a stochastic shortest path problem. Comput. Oper. Res. **36**(2), 584–596 (2009)
20. Martins, E.Q.V.: On a multicriteria shortest path problem. Eur. J. Oper. Res. **16**(2), 236–245 (1984)
21. Hartley, R.: Vector optimal routing by dynamic programming. Math. Multi Objective Optim. 215–224 (1985)
22. Warburton, A.: Approximation of pareto optima in multiple-objective, shortest-path problems. Oper. Res. **35**(1), 70–79 (1987)
23. Tung, C.T., Chew, K.L.: A multicriteria pareto-optimal path algorithm. Eur. J. Oper. Res. **62**(2), 203–209 (1992)
24. Sancho, N.: A new type of multi-objective routing problem. Eng. Optim. **14**(2), 115–119 (1988)
25. Wijeratne, A.B., Turnquist, M.A., Mirchandani, P.B.: Multiobjective routing of hazardous materials in stochastic networks. Eur. J. Oper. Res. **65**(1), 33–43 (1993)
26. Gandibleux, X., Beugnies, F., Randriamasy, S.: Martins' algorithm revisited for multi-objective shortest path problems with a maxmin cost function. 4OR **4**(1), 47–59 (2006)
27. Sarraute, C., Richarte, G., Lucangeli Obes, J.: An algorithm to find optimal attack paths in nondeterministic scenarios. In: 4th ACM Workshop on Security and Artificial Intelligence, pp. 71–80 (2011)
28. Johnson, P., Lagerstrom, R., Ekstedt, M.: A meta language for threat modeling and attack simulations. In: 13th ACM International Conference on Availability, Reliability and Security, pp. 1–8 (2018)
29. Steuer, R.: Multiple Criteria Optimization: Theory, Computation, and Application. WILEY Series in Probability and Mathematical Statistics. Wiley, Hoboken (1986)
30. Dijkstra, E.W.: A note on two problems in connexion with graphs. Numer. Math. **1**(1), 269–271 (1959)
31. Yen, J.Y.: Finding the k shortest loopless paths in a network. Manage. Sci. **17**(11), 712–716 (1971)
32. Tarjan, R.: Depth-first search and linear graph algorithms. SIAM J. Comput. **1**(2), 146–160 (1972)

33. Al Zoobi, A., Coudert, D., Nisse, N.: Space and time trade-off for the k shortest simple paths problem. In: 18th International Symposium on Experimental Algorithms, vol. 160, pp. 1–13 (2020)
34. Barbehenn, M.: A note on the complexity of Dijkstra's algorithm for graphs with weighted vertices. IEEE Trans. Comput. **47**(2), 263 (1998)
35. Rubin, F.: Enumerating all simple paths in a graph. IEEE Trans. Circ. Syst. **25**(8), 641–642 (1978)

RAMBO: Leaking Secrets from Air-Gap Computers by Spelling Covert Radio Signals from Computer RAM

Mordechai Guri[(✉)]

Department of Software and Information Systems Engineering,
Ben-Gurion University of the Negev, Be'er Sheva, Israel
gurim@post.bgu.ac.il

Abstract. Air-gapped systems are physically separated from external networks, including the Internet. This isolation is achieved by keeping the air-gap computers disconnected from wired or wireless networks, preventing direct or remote communication with other devices or networks. Air-gap measures may be used in sensitive environments where security and isolation are critical to prevent private and confidential information leakage.

In this paper, we present an attack allowing adversaries to leak information from air-gapped computers. We show that malware on a compromised computer can generate radio signals from memory buses (RAM). Using software-generated radio signals, malware can encode sensitive information such as files, images, keylogging, biometric information, and encryption keys. With software-defined radio (SDR) hardware, and a simple off-the-shelf antenna, an attacker can intercept transmitted raw radio signals from a distance. The signals can then be decoded and translated back into binary information. We discuss the design and implementation and present related work and evaluation results. This paper presents fast modification methods to leak data from air-gapped computers at 1000 bits per second. Finally, we propose countermeasures to mitigate this out-of-band air-gap threat.

Keywords: Air-gap · Radio · Electromagnetic · Covert Channels · Exfiltration · RAM · Memory

1 Introduction

Today's regulations, such as GDPR (General Data Protection Regulation), outline strict rules and principles for how organizations should collect, store, and share personal data. It grants individuals certain rights, such as the right to access their data, the right to be forgotten (i.e., to have their data erased), the right to data portability, and more. Organizations that handle personal data

---

Air-gap research page: http://www.covertchannels.com.

L. Fritsch et al. (Eds.): NordSec 2023, LNCS 14324, pp. 144–161, 2024.
https://doi.org/10.1007/978-3-031-47748-5_9

must follow certain practices to ensure privacy and security. They need explicit consent from individuals before processing their data. They need to implement strong data protection measures and report data breaches within a specific timeframe [1].

When sensitive data such as personal or confidential information is involved, the collection, processing, and storage of the information may be done in networks disconnected from the Internet. This security measure is known as an 'air gap.' Air-gap isolation protects information from cyberattacks, and online risks, including phishing emails, social engineering, and compromised websites [2].

1.1   Air-Gap Isolation

Enforcing an air gap in a computing or networking environment involves physically and logically isolating a system, network, or device from external networks or communication channels. This can be done by disconnecting network cables, disabling wireless interfaces, and disallowing USB connections. In addition, it must be ensured that the isolated system has no direct link to any external communication infrastructure [3].

1.2   Air-Gap Attacks

Despite air-gapped networks being considered highly secure, there have been incidents demonstrating that air-gapped networks are not immune to breaches. Stuxnet is one of the most famous air-gap malware [4]. Discovered in 2010, Stuxnet was a highly sophisticated worm that targeted industrial control systems (ICS), particularly those used in nuclear facilities. It exploited zero-day vulnerabilities and used several methods, including infected USB drives, to jump the air gap and spread it across isolated networks. The Agent.BTZ worm [5] was another type of air gap computer worm with advanced capabilities and a targeted type. It was specifically designed to spread through removable media, such as USB flash drives, and infiltrate computer networks, including highly secure or air-gapped. According to reports, the worm affected the U.S. Department of Defense classified networks. Notably more than twenty-five reported malware in the past targeted highly secured and air-gapped networks [6], including USBStealer, Agent.BTZ [5], Stuxnet [4], Fanny, MiniFlame, Flame, Gauss, ProjectSauron, EZCheese, Emotional Simian, USB Thief, USBFerry, Retro, and Ramsay.

1.3   The RAMBO Attack

In order to exfiltrate information from an infected air-gapped computer, attackers use special communication channels known as air-gap covert channels. There are several types of covert channels studied in the past twenty years [7,8]. These attacks leak data through electromagnetic emission [9–11], optical signals [12], acoustic noise [13,14], thermal changes [15], and even physical vibrations [16].

In this paper, we show how malware can manipulate RAM to generate radio signals at clock frequencies. These signals are modified and encoded in a particular encoding allowing them to be received from a distance away. The attacker can encode sensitive information (keylogging, documents, images, biometric information, etc.) and exfiltrate it via these radio signals. An attacker with appropriate hardware can receive the electromagnetic signals, demodulate and decode the data, and retrieve the exfiltrated information.

This paper is organized as follows. The attack model is first described in Sect. 2. Section 3 provides a review of related work. Section 4 describes the design and implementation of a transmitter and receiver, including modulation and encoding. The analysis and evaluation results are presented in Sect. 5. Section 6 provides a list of countermeasures, and we conclude in Sect. 7.

2   Attack Model

Attacks on air-gapped networks involve multi-phase strategies to breach isolated systems by delivering specialized malware through physical media or insider agents, initiating malware execution, propagating within the network, exfiltrating data using covert channels or compromised removable media, establishing remote command and control, evading detection, and covering tracks. In the context of the RAMBO attack, the adversary must infect the air-gap network in the initial phase. This can be done via a variety of attack vectors [2,6,17,18].

An attacker could plant malware on a USB drive and physically introduce it into an air-gapped network. An unsuspecting insider or employee might connect the USB drive to a computer within the isolated network, unknowingly activating the malware and allowing it to propagate and exfiltrate data through the same USB drive or via covert channels. An insider with access to the air-gapped network might intentionally introduce malware or provide unauthorized access to external parties. This could involve transferring sensitive data to personal devices or using covert communication methods like steganography to hide data within innocent-looking files. An attacker could also compromise hardware components or software updates during the supply chain process. Once these components are installed within the air-gapped network, hidden malware might activate and communicate with external parties. Note that APTs (Advanced Persistent Threats) in the past targeted highly secured and air-gapped networks, including USBStealer, Agent.BTZ [5], Stuxnet, Fanny, MiniFlame, Flame, Gauss, ProjectSauron, EZCheese, Emotional Simian, USB Thief, USBFerry, Brutal Kangaroo, Retro, PlugX, and Ramsay [6]. More recently, in August 2023, researchers at Kaspersky discovered another new malware and attributed it to the cyber-espionage group APT31, which targets air-gapped and isolated networks via infected USB drives [19].

In the second phase of the attack, the attacker collects information, e.g., keylogging, files, passwords, biometric data, and so on, and exfiltrate it via the air-gap covert channel. In our case, the malware utilizes electromagnetic emissions from the RAM to modulate the information and transmit it outward. A remote attacker with a radio receiver and antenna can receive the information, demodulate it, and decode it into its original binary or textual representation. The attack scenario is illustrated in Fig. 1. The RAMBO malware within the infected air-gapped workstation (A) transmits sensitive images (Optimus Prime) using covert electromagnetic radiation from the RAM. A remote attacker intercepts the information and decodes the data.

Fig. 1. Attack demonstration. An air-gap workstation processes a secret image (Optimus Prime). The RAMBO covert channel attack transmits the image via electromagnetic waves. A remote attacker intercepts the information and recovers the secret image.

3   Related Work

Air-gap covert channels refer to a type of covert communication method that transfers information between two physically isolated systems or networks that are not directly connected through wired or wireless means. In the security research domain, air-gap covert channels are rooted in the idea that even systems disconnected from external networks might still communicate through unintended or concealed means. While the air gap is intended to prevent unauthorized data transfer, various techniques have been explored to bypass this isolation and create hidden communication channels. The main types of air-gap covert channels are acoustic, optical, thermal, and electromagnetic. In this paper, RAMBO covert channels are categorized as electromagnetic covert channels. In acoustic covert channels, systems might use ultrasonic sound waves inaudible to humans to transmit data between air-gapped devices. Specialized software or malware can encode data into sound signals picked up by a microphone on the receiving device [20,21]. Previous work shows that attacks can exploit CPU and GPU fans [13,14], Hard-disk drives (HDD) [22], CD/DVD noise [23], and power-supply sound characteristics [24] to modulate information over an air gap. Data can be

encoded and transmitted using light signals, such as rapidly flashing LED lights
or screen brightness changes [25]. The receiving device might use a camera or
light sensor to detect and decode signals. Previous work showed that attackers could exploit keyboards [12], routers [26], hard-disk drives (HDD) [27], and
screen LEDs [25] to modulate information over air gaps for long distances. In
these cases, the receiver is a sensor or a camera. Attackers can transmit information by causing minor temperature fluctuations imperceptible to human senses
but detectable by sensitive thermal sensors. E.g., the BitWhistper attack [15],
presented by Guri et al., shows that the CPU can generate thermal signals
that nearby computers can sense to transfer data over air gaps. Electromagnetic
emissions, often unintended byproducts of computational activities, can be modulated to encode data. These emissions can then be captured and interpreted
by a receiver equipped with appropriate sensors. For example, malware might
exploit electromagnetic emissions of a computer's central processing unit (CPU)
to create a covert communication channel. Previous works focused on radio frequency covert channels including EMLoRa [11], AirHopper [10], GSMem [9],
Air-Fi [28], SATAn [29], and Lantenna [30].

4   Transmission and Reception

This section presents the implementation of the transmitter and receiver and the
signal generation, data modulation, demodulation, and encoding and decoding
schemes.

The RAM bus operates electrical lines or pathways that connect the CPU
to memory modules. These pathways transfer data, instructions, and addresses
between the CPU and RAM. The RAM bus includes various components [31].

- **Data Bus.** This is the portion of the RAM bus responsible for carrying
  the actual data being read from or written to memory. The data bus width
  determines the amount of data transferred simultaneously. For example, a
  64-bit data bus can transfer 64 bits (8 bytes) of data in one operation.
- **Address Bus.** The address bus carries memory addresses that indicate the
  specific location in memory from which the CPU wants to read or write
  data. The address bus width determines the maximum amount of memory
  the CPU can access directly. For instance, a 32-bit address bus can address
  up to 4 gigabytes of memory.
- **Control Lines.** These lines carry control signals coordinating data transfer timing and sequencing. Control lines handle reading, writing, activating
  memory chips, and signaling when data is ready.

When data is transferred through a RAM bus, it involves rapid voltage and
current changes, mainly in the Data bus. These voltage transitions create electromagnetic fields, which can radiate electromagnetic energy through electromagnetic interference (EMI) or radio frequency interference (RFI). The frequency
range of electromagnetic emanation from the RAM bus mainly depends on its
specific clock speed, measured in megahertz (MHz) or gigahertz (GHz). This

clock dictates how quickly data can be transferred between the CPU and memory. The emanation levels are influenced by other bus characteristics, including its data width, clock speed, and overall architecture. Faster RAM buses (e.g., DDR4 and DDR5) with wider data paths can lead to quicker data transfers with increased emissions.

4.1 Signal Generation

As explained above, when data is read from or written to memory, electrical currents flow through the RAM chips and the associated traces on the printed circuit board (PCB). These electrical currents generate electromagnetic fields as a byproduct, which radiates EM energy. To create an EM covert channel, the transmitter needs to modulate memory access patterns in a way that corresponds to binary data. For instance, they could alter the timing or frequency of memory access operations to encode information. The sender and receiver must establish rules that define how memory access patterns translate to binary values. For example, a reading or writing array to the physical memory for a specific timing interval might represent a '0' while another interval represents a '1'. The receiver detects and decodes the EM emissions caused by the modulated memory activity. This could involve sensitive radio frequency (RF) receivers or electromagnetic field sensors.

4.2 Modulation

Algorithm 1 shows the signal generation with OOK (On-Off Keying) modulation, a basic form of digital modulation used in communication systems to transmit digital data over a carrier wave. In our case, the OOK modulation involves turning the carrier wave on and off to represent binary data, where the presence of the carrier wave generated by memory activity corresponds to one binary state ("1"). The absence of the electromagnetic carrier wave (thread `sleep()`) corresponds to the other binary state ("0"). Note that to maintain the activity in the RAM buses, we used the MOVNTI instruction [32], which stands for Move Non-Temporal Integer. It performs a non-temporal store of integer data from a source operand to a destination memory location. This instruction is primarily associated with optimizing memory operations for certain types of data transfers, particularly in cases where the data is not to be reused immediately. Note that for the beginning of the transmission, we used the preamble sequence of `10101010`, allowing the receiver to be synched with the transmitter (Fig. 2).

Algorithm 1 modulateOOK (bits, bitTimeMillis, frameSizeBits)

1: $bitEndTime \leftarrow getCurrentTimeMillis()$
2: $frameStart \leftarrow 0$
3: **while** frameStart < (len(bits) - frameSizeBits) **do**
4:     $frameBits \leftarrow [1, 0, 1, 0, 1, 0, 1, 0]$
5:     $frameBits.append(bits[frameStart : frameStart + frameSizeBits])$
6:     $frameStart + = frameSizeBits$
7:     $frameBits.append(calcPartity(frameBits))$
8:     **for** bit in $frameBits$ **do**
9:         $bitEndTime \leftarrow bitEndTime + bitTimeMillis$
10:        **if** $bit == 1$ **then**
11:            **while** $getCurrentTimeMillis() < bitEndTime$ **do**
12:                $movnti(memoryAddress, value)$
13:            **end while**
14:        **else**
15:            $sleep(bitEndTime - getCurrentTimeMillis())$
16:        **end if**
17:    **end for**
18: **end while**

Fig. 2. The RAMBO attack signal generation with OOK modulation

---

Algorithm 2 modulateManchester (bits, bitTimeMillis, frameSizeBits)

1: $bitEndTime \leftarrow getCurrentTimeMillis()$
2: $frameStart \leftarrow 0$
3: **while** frameStart < (len(bits) - frameSizeBits) **do**
4:     $frameBits \leftarrow [1, 0, 1, 0, 1, 0, 1, 0]$
5:     $frameBits.append(bits[frameStart : frameStart + frameSizeBits])$
6:     $frameStart + = frameSizeBits$
7:     $frameBits.append(calcPartity(frameBits))$
8:     **for** bit in $frameBits$ **do**
9:         **if** $bit == 1$ **then**
10:            $bitEndTime \leftarrow bitEndTime + bitTimeMillis/2$
11:            **while** $getCurrentTimeMillis() < bitEndTime$ **do**
12:                $movnti(memoryAddress, value)$
13:            **end while**
14:            $bitEndTime \leftarrow bitEndTime + bitTimeMillis/2$
15:            $sleep(bitEndTime - getCurrentTimeMillis())$
16:        **else**
17:            $bitEndTime \leftarrow bitEndTime + bitTimeMillis/2$
18:            $sleep(bitEndTime - getCurrentTimeMillis())$
19:            $bitEndTime \leftarrow bitEndTime + bitTimeMillis/2$
20:            **while** $getCurrentTimeMillis() < bitEndTime$ **do**
21:                $movnti(memoryAddress, value)$
22:            **end while**
23:        **end if**
24:    **end for**
25: **end while**

Fig. 3. The transmission with Manchester encoding

4.3   Manchester Encoding

For the fast transmission, we used the Manchester encoding. In this encoding, each bit of the binary data is represented by a transition or change in signal level within a fixed period. Manchester encoding ensures a consistent number of signal transitions, making it useful for clock synchronization and error detection. The outline of our transmitter with Manchester encoding is presented in Algorithm 2 (Fig. 3).

4.4 Demodulation and Framing

We encode the data with a frame consisting of an alternating sequence of eight alternating bits that represents the frame's beginning. Our demodulator is presented in Algorithm 3. Figure 5 shows the spectrogram and waveform of the word 'DATA' (0x44 0x41 0x54 0x41) transmitted in the Manchester encoding (top) and OOK modulation (bottom). Our analysis shows that the Manchester encoding is more relevant for the requirements of the RAMBO covert channel due to two main reasons; (1) the encoding aids in clock synchronization between the sender and receiver, and (2) the frequent transitions make it easier to detect errors caused by signal loss, interference, or distortion. However, it's important to note that Manchester encoding doubles the required bandwidth compared to direct binary encoding (e.g., the OOK), as each bit requires two signal transitions within the bit interval. This increased bandwidth requirement can be a drawback in some scenarios, especially for high-speed data transmission (Fig. 4).

Algorithm 3 demodulate(sampleRate, frameSizeBits, bitTime, windowSize, signalRelativeFreq)

1: $windowsPerBit \leftarrow sampleRate/1e6 * bitTime/windowSize$
2:
3: **while** $True$ **do**
4:    $enabled \leftarrow False$
5:    $bitCounter \leftarrow 0$
6:    $bits \leftarrow []$
7:    **while** $len(bits) < frameSizeBits + 1$ **do**
8:       $windows.append(getNextWindows(windowSize))$
9:       **for** $window$ in $windows$ **do**
10:          $spectrum = welch(window, windowSize)$
11:          $sample \leftarrow spectrum[signalRelativeFreq]$
12:          $samples.append(sample)$
13:       **end for**
14:       **if** not $enabled$ **then**
15:          $thresh, enabled \leftarrow detectEnable(samples, windowsPerBit)$
16:       **end if**
17:       **while** enabled and len(samples) >= windowsPerBit **do**
18:          $bit \leftarrow samplesToBit(samples, windowsPerBit, thresh)$
19:          $bits.append(bit)$
20:          **if** len(bits) == frameSizeBits+1 **then**
21:             $outputFrame(bits[:-1])$
22:             **if** bits[-1] != calcPartity(bits[:-1]) **then**
23:                $logParityError()$
24:             **end if**
25:          **end if**
26:       **end while**
27:    **end while**
28: **end while**

Fig. 4. The demodulation algorithm

5 Evaluation

In this section, we present the evaluation of the covert channels. We tested three types of workstations. The PCs were all Intel i7 3.6 GHz CPUs and 16 GB

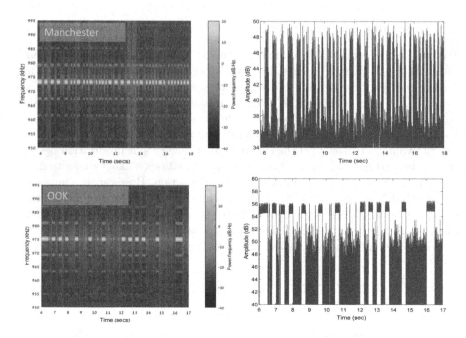

Fig. 5. The signal of the word 'DATA' (0x44 0x41 0x54 0x41) in Manchester encoding (top) and OOK modulation (bottom).

of 2.133–2.400 GHz RAM. The PC ran Linux Ubuntu 18.04.6 LTS 64-bit. For the reception, we used the software-defined radio (SDR) Ettus B210, which is a specific model of the Universal Software Radio Peripheral (USRP) developed by Ettus Research, National Instruments (6). The B210 offers a wide range of capabilities for researchers, engineers, and enthusiasts working in wireless communication, radio frequency (RF) research, and signal processing. It covers a frequency range from 70 MHz to 6 GHz and supports sample rates of up to 61.44 MS/s (mega-samples per second). The USRP was connected to a small form factor NUC computer with 16 GB RAM running the C demodulator. It also ran MathWorks Matlab for signal processing and spectrogram visualization.

5.1   Signal to Noise (SNR)

We evaluated the SNR levels at distances of 100–700 cm. Table 1 lists the average SNR levels. The SNR levels ranged from 38 dB–8 dB, which reflects the effective distance the covert channel can operate in this setup. Note that the SNR is also affected by the bit times. Figure 7 shows the thee different SNR with $t = 250$ ms (A), $t = 100$ ms (B), and $t = 50$ ms (C). As can be seen, the SNR is significantly affected by the bit time, with a differentiation of an average 7 dB between speeds with a shifting of 50 bit/sec (Fig. 6).

Fig. 6. Ettus B210 Universal Software Radio Peripheral (USRP).

Table 1. The average SNR levels in a range of 50–700 cm

	d = 50 cm	d = 100 cm	d = 200 cm	d = 300 cm	d = 400 cm	d = 500 cm	d = 600 cm	d = 700 cm
Average	38 dB	30 dB	27 dB	22 dB	17 dB	15 dB	12 dB	8 dB

5.2 Bitrates

We evaluated the three speeds' effective bit rates and corresponding bit-error rates. Tables 4, 3, and 2 shows the bit error rate (BER) values for $t = 10$ ms, $t = 5$ ms, $t = 1$ ms, respectively. With a slow transmission rate ($t = 10$ ms), A transmission is maintained at a distance of 700 cm away. With medium transmission rate ($t = 5$ ms), A transmitted is maintained at a distance of 450 cm away and BER of 3%–4%. With a fast transmission rate ($t = 1$ ms), a transmission is maintained at a distance of 300 cm away and BER of 2%–4%.

5.3 Data Exfiltration

Table 5 presents the time it takes to exfiltrate various types of information for three timing parameters (t). Keylogging can be exfiltrated in real-time with 16 bits per key (Unicode). A 4096-bit RSA encryption key can be exfiltrated at 41.96 s at a low speed and 4.096 bits at a high speed. Biometric information, small files (.jpg), and small documents (.txt and .docx) require 400 s at the low speed to a few seconds at the fast speeds. This indicates that the RAMBO covert channel can be used to leak relatively brief information over a short period.

Fig. 7. SNR with $t = 250$ ms (A), $t = 100$ ms (B), and $t = 50$ ms (C)

Table 2. Transmission with $t = 10$

	d = 50 cm	d = 100 cm	d = 200 cm	d = 300 cm	d = 400 cm	d = 500 cm	d = 600 cm	d = 700 cm
PC-1	0%	0%	0%	0%	0%	0%	0%	0%
PC-2	0%	0%	0%	0%	0%	0%	0%	0%
PC-3	0%	0%	0%	0%	0%	0%	0%	0%

Table 3. Transmission with t=5

	d = 50 cm	d = 100 cm	d = 200 cm	d = 300 cm	d = 400 cm	d = 450 cm
PC-1	0%	0%	0%	1%	2%	4%
PC-2	0%	0%	0%	0%	2%	3%
PC-3	0%	0%	0%	0%	3%	–

Table 4. Transmission with $t = 1$

	d = 50 cm	d = 100 cm	d = 200 cm	d = 300 cm
PC-1	0%	0%	0%	4%
PC-2	0%	0%	0%	3%
PC-3	0%	0%	0%	2%

Table 5. Exfiltration time of various types of information with RAMBO covert channel

Information	Size	t = 10 ms	t = 5 ms	t = 1 ms
Keylogging	16 bits (per key)	realtime	realtime	realtime
4096 bit RSA key	4096 bits	41.96 s	20.48 s	4.096 s
Biometric information	10000 bits	100 s	50 s	10 s
Password	128 bits	1.28 s	0.64 s	0.128 s
Small image (.jpg)	25000 bits	250 s	125 s	25 s
A textual document (.txt, .docx)	40000 bits	400 s	200 s	40 s

5.4 Faraday Shielding

It is possible to block electromagnetic radiation from the computer using a specialized metal chassis built as a Faraday cage. The attenuation of a Faraday cage, which measures how effectively it blocks electromagnetic radiation, depends on various factors, including the frequency of the radiation, the conductivity of the cage material, and the thickness of the cage walls. The attenuation (A) of electromagnetic radiation by a conductive material like a Faraday cage can be approximated using Eq. 1. The attenuation factors are listed in Table 6.

$$A = 10 \cdot \log_{10}\left(\frac{1}{1 + \left(\frac{\sigma d}{\mu f}\right)^2}\right) \tag{1}$$

Table 6. The computer chassis attenuation factors

Factor	Effect
A	The attenuation in decibels (dB)
σ	The conductivity of the material (siemens per meter, S/m)
d	The thickness of the material (meters)
μ	The permeability of the material (henries per meter, H/m)
f	the frequency of the electromagnetic radiation (hertz, Hz)

We analyzed and measured the effect of the Faraday chassis on the RAMBO covert channel using copper foil. This has electric field high Shielding properties (above 100 dB) and magnetic fields. The copper standard width is 1 mm effectively blocks the EMR from the transmitting workstation. However, as noted in the following section, this solution is costly and can not be deployed widely. Another option is to use a Faraday room which is typically constructed using metal that can conduct electric currents. The primary purpose of a Faraday room is to create an electromagnetically isolated environment, which means that electromagnetic fields from external sources are significantly reduced or prevented from entering the enclosed space. Faraday enclosures are presented in Fig. 8 with a PC-sized Faraday enclosure (A), general size Faraday enclosure (B), and a Faraday room (C).

5.5 Virtualization

We evaluated the effectiveness of the covert channel when the transmitting code operates from within a virtual machine (VM). For the evaluation, we used VMWare workstation 16.2.4 running Linux Ubuntu 18.04.6 LTS 64-bit on host and guest machines. Our test shows that the low BER of below 1% was kept even when the code ran with a VM. However, it is essential to note that a massive workload in the host OS or memory activity in another guest OS might interrupt the signal generation conducted by the compromised virtual machine.

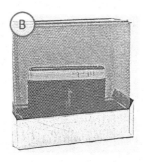
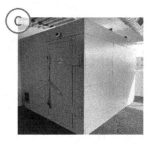

Fig. 8. The PC sized Faraday enclosure (A), general size Faraday enclosure (B), and a Faraday room (C).

5.6   Higher Bit-Rates

We tested the high bit rates of 5000 bps and above. Our evaluation shows that it is possible to demodulate the signal with mostly above 5% BER, rendering this speed less effective. The main reason is the low SNR levels the fast signal generation yielded. Figure 9 shows the waveform of the alternating short signal generated with 10000 bps. As depicted, the SNR is low (below 5%) and causes high BER levels during the modulation.

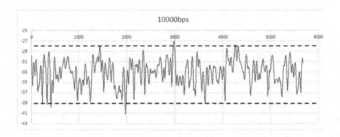

Fig. 9. The transmission with 10000 bps.

5.7   Frequency Ranges

The electromagnetic emission from DDR RAM and other digital components can span a wide frequency range, including fundamental frequencies, subharmonics, and spurious missions. The central frequencies are the direct clock frequencies and their harmonics. For example, with DDR RAM operating at a clock frequency of 1.6 GHz (corresponding to DDR4-3200), we can observe emissions around 1.6 GHz, 3.2 GHz, and 4.8 GHz (3rd harmonic). It is important to note that DDR RAM modules emit frequencies that are not direct harmonics but are related to the clock frequency more indirectly; these can include subharmonics and other spurious emissions. We don't use these frequencies for the RAMBO covert channel. Our tests show that some systems use spread spectrum clocking to spread electromagnetic emissions across a broader range of frequencies. This technique can help reduce the concentration of emissions at specific frequencies, making it less likely to carry the modulated information.

6   Countermeasures

Several defensive and protective countermeasures can be taken to defend against the proposed covert channel.

- **Zone restrictions.** The red-black separation concept involves creating a clear boundary or barrier between "red" and "black" components or environments to prevent unauthorized transfer of information from one domain to the other. This separation can be achieved through physical, logical, and procedural measures. In practice, defenders often use separate networks, hardware, and physical access controls to keep red and black systems physically separate from each other. There are several NATO and American standards, such as SDIP-27, AMSG, NSTISSAM, and ZONES, that mandate the segregation of areas that deal with the radiated electromagnetic, magnetic, optical, and acoustic energy of devices [33]. In this approach, radio receiver devices are eliminated from air-gapped computers or kept outside a specified radius of several meters away. The red-black separation concept may be applied in various domains, including military, intelligence, critical infrastructure, and organizations dealing with susceptible information [33]. In the context of the RAMBO attack, it can mitigate the risk of RAM leakage and unauthorized access by creating a clear separation between the two security domains.

- **Host intrusion detection systems (HIDS).** In this approach, we monitor the operating system's physical or virtual memory operations and detect suspicious operations. Such anomalies could be a process that abnormally reads and writes to memory regions. These are three different layers on which an intrusion detection system can operate. In this kernel-level approach, a driver/module is installed at the kernel level and continuously monitors the page access operations. Our experiment shows that all monitoring approaches imply high false positive rates. The main reason is that memory operations are always incurred by hundreds of threads in the OS, including the kernel level. Monitoring the analysis of these operations creates runtime overhead and leads to a high rate of false alarms.

- **Hypervisor-level memory access monitoring.** Because the hypervisor operates at a lower level of system control, it has visibility into the memory access patterns of the virtual machines it manages. This visibility allows the hypervisor to monitor memory access [34]. Technically, the hypervisor manages the virtual-to-physical memory mapping for each VM through memory page tables. An Extended Page Table (EPT) is a virtualization technology used in modern processors to enhance the performance of virtual machines (VMs) in a virtualized environment. EPT is specific to Intel processors and is equivalent to AMD's Nested Page Tables (NPT). By monitoring and controlling these page tables, the hypervisor can keep track of memory access patterns and perform memory isolation. Note that this approach was proposed by previous work to detect shellcode injection attacks and other types of vulnerability exploits. However, as the HIDS solution, it may lead to a high rate of false positives.

- **External radio monitoring.** Dedicated spectrum analyzers are specialized hardware devices designed to scan and analyze the radio frequency spectrum. They provide detailed information about signal strengths, frequency utilization, and interference sources. Spectrum monitoring refers to analyzing and observing the radio frequency (RF) spectrum used by wireless networks, e.g., those using the Wi-Fi standard. This monitoring helps understand the wireless communication environment's usage, interference, and overall health. It involves scanning and analyzing the different frequency channels within the RF spectrum to detect signals, identify sources of interference, and optimize the performance of wireless networks. In the context of a RAMBO attack, spectrum analyzers can provide visibility of the RF spectrum, showing signal strength across different frequency bands and detecting unintended transmission and covert channels.

- **Internal RAM jamming.** Another option is to interrupt the covert channel by applying random memory operations. Such jamming can be implemented as a user or kernel thread randomly interfering with memory and performing read-write operations. This approach has the main disadvantage of interfering with legitimate memory activities, resulting in significant overhead. In addition, internal jammer threads can be manipulated, bypassed, or terminated by malware with sufficient privileges running on a compromised computer.
- **External Electromagnetic jamming.** It is possible to defend against the covert channel using radio jammers, also known as signal jammers or RF (radio frequency) jammers. These devices are designed to interfere with or disrupt wireless communications by emitting radio frequency signals on the required frequencies used by the targeted communication systems. The goal of a radio jammer is to create a jamming signal that overwhelms and interferes with legitimate signals, rendering the communication systems ineffective or unreliable within the jamming area [35]. In the case of a RAMBO attack, the whole spectrum of DDR should be jammed. However, this approach requires dedicated external hardware transceivers and antennas, which are maintained in a secure area, which tend to pose another security threat.
- **Radio reduction/blocking Faraday enclosures.** A PC Faraday enclosure, also known as a Faraday cage or Faraday enclosure, is a shielded enclosure designed to block external electromagnetic fields and electromagnetic radiation from entering or leaving the enclosed space [36]. This shielding helps protect sensitive electronic devices and equipment from electromagnetic interference (EMI) and prevents emitted electromagnetic radiation from leaking out and potentially interfering with other devices or systems. The Faraday enclosures will limit the leakage of radio frequencies of the RAMBO attack. However, the solution is costly and not applied on a broad scale.

Table 7 lists the countermeasures and their limitations.

Table 7. Defensive countermeasures

Solution	Drawbacks
Zone restrictions (red-black separation)	Cost and space limitation
Host intrusion detection systems (user/kernel)	High rates of false positive
External electromagnetic spectrum monitoring	High rates of false positive
Internal RAM operation jamming	Disruption of the RAM functionality and overhead
External radio jamming of RAM frequencies	Radio interference, high cost, and power consumption
Radio reduction/blocking Faraday enclosures	Cost and maintenance

7   Conclusion

We present an air gap covert channel attack that allows attackers to exfiltrate sensitive data from isolated computers. We show that malicious code in the infected computers can manipulate memory operations and generate radio signals from the memory buses. By precisely controlling the memory-related instructions, arbitrary information can be encoded and modulated on the electromagnetic wave. An attacker with a software-defined radio (SDR) can receive the information, demodulate it, and decide. We showed that this method could be used to exfiltrate arbitrary types of information, such as keystroke logging, files, images, biometric data, etc. We presented architecture and implementation, provided evaluation results, and discussed preventive countermeasures. With this method, attackers can leak data from highly isolated, air-gapped computers to a nearby receiver at a bit rate of hundreds bits per second.

References

1. Albrecht, J.P.: How the GDPR will change the world. Eur. Data Prot. L. Rev. **2**, 287 (2016)
2. Guri, M., Elovici, Y.: Bridgeware: the air-gap malware. Commun. ACM **61**(4), 74–82 (2018)
3. Guri, M.: Usbculprit: USB-borne air-gap malware. In: European Interdisciplinary Cybersecurity Conference, pp. 7–13 (2021)
4. Chen, T.M., Abu-Nimeh, S.: Lessons from stuxnet. Computer **44**(4), 91–93 (2011)
5. Gostev, A.: Agent. btz: a source of inspiration? SecureList **12**(3) (2014)
6. Dorais-Joncas, A., Munõz, F.: Jumping the air gap (2021)
7. Cabaj, K., Caviglione, L., Mazurczyk, W., Wendzel, S., Woodward, A., Zander, S.: The new threats of information hiding: the road ahead. IT Prof. **20**(3), 31–39 (2018)
8. Caviglione, L.: Trends and challenges in network covert channels countermeasures. Appl. Sci. **11**(4), 1641 (2021)
9. Guri, M., Kachlon, A., Hasson, O., Kedma, G., Mirsky, Y., Elovici, Y.: GSMem: data exfiltration from air-gapped computers over GSM frequencies. In: USENIX Security Symposium, pp. 849–864 (2015)
10. Guri, M., Kedma, G., Kachlon, A., Elovici, Y.: Airhopper: bridging the air-gap between isolated networks and mobile phones using radio frequencies. In: Malicious and Unwanted Software: The Americas (MALWARE), 2014 9th International Conference on, pp. 58–67. IEEE (2014)
11. Shen, C., Liu, T., Huang, J., Tan, R.: When LoRa meets EMR: electromagnetic covert channels can be super resilient. In: 2021 IEEE Symposium on Security and Privacy (SP), pp. 1304–1317. IEEE (2021)
12. Guri, M., Zadov, B., Bykhovsky, D., Elovici, Y.: Ctrl-alt-led: leaking data from air-gapped computers via keyboard leds. In: 2019 IEEE 43rd Annual Computer Software and Applications Conference (COMPSAC), vol. 1, pp. 801–810. IEEE (2019)
13. Guri, M., Solewicz, Y., Elovici, Y.: Fansmitter: acoustic data exfiltration from air-gapped computers via fans noise. Comput. Secur. 101721 (2020)

14. Guri, M.: GPU-FAN: leaking sensitive data from air-gapped machines via covert noise from GPU fans. In: Reiser, H.P., Kyas, M. (eds.) Secure IT Systems. NordSec 2022. LNCS, vol. 13700, pp. 194–211. Springer, Cham (2022). https://doi.org/10.1007/978-3-031-22295-5_11
15. Guri, M., Monitz, M., Mirski, Y., Elovici, Y.: Bitwhisper: covert signaling channel between air-gapped computers using thermal manipulations. In: Computer Security Foundations Symposium (CSF), 2015 IEEE 28th, pp. 276–289. IEEE (2015)
16. Guri, M.: Exfiltrating data from air-gapped computers via vibrations. Futur. Gener. Comput. Syst. **122**, 69–81 (2021)
17. Air gapped networks: A false sense of security? - sentinelone. https://www.sentinelone.com/blog/air-gapped-networks-a-false-sense-of-security/. Accessed 14 July 2023
18. Beating the air-gap: How attackers can gain access to supposedly isolated systems — energy central. https://energycentral.com/c/iu/beating-air-gap-how-attackers-can-gain-access-supposedly-isolated-systems. Accessed 05 Apr 2023
19. Kaspersky uncovers malware for targeted data exfiltration from air-gapped environments — kaspersky. https://usa.kaspersky.com/about/press-releases/2023_kaspersky-uncovers-malware-for-targeted-data-exfiltration-from-air-gapped-environments. Accessed 20 Aug 2023
20. Deshotels, L.: Inaudible sound as a covert channel in mobile devices. In: WOOT (2014)
21. de Gortari Briseno, J., Singh, A.D., Srivastava, M.: Inkfiltration: using inkjet printers for acoustic data exfiltration from air-gapped networks. ACM Trans. Priv. Secur. **25**(2), 1–26 (2022)
22. Guri, M., Solewicz, Y., Daidakulov, A., Elovici, Y.: Acoustic data exfiltration from speakerless air-gapped computers via covert hard-drive noise diskfiltration. In: Foley, S.N., Gollmann, D., Snekkenes, E. (eds.) ESORICS 2017. LNCS, vol. 10493, pp. 98–115. Springer, Cham (2017). https://doi.org/10.1007/978-3-319-66399-9_6
23. Guri, M.: CD-LEAK: leaking secrets from audioless air-gapped computers using covert acoustic signals from CD/DVD drives. In: 2020 IEEE 44th Annual Computers, Software, and Applications Conference (COMPSAC), pp. 808–816. IEEE (2020)
24. Guri, M.: Power-supplay: leaking sensitive data from air-gapped, audio-gapped systems by turning the power supplies into speakers. IEEE Trans. Dependable Secure Comput. (2021)
25. Guri, M., Bykhovsky, D., Elovici, Y.: Brightness: leaking sensitive data from air-gapped workstations via screen brightness. In: 2019 12th CMI Conference on Cybersecurity and Privacy (CMI), pp. 1–6. IEEE (2019)
26. Guri, M., Zadov, B., Daidakulov, A., Elovici, Y.: xLED: covert data exfiltration from air-gapped networks via switch and router leds. In: 2018 16th Annual Conference on Privacy, Security and Trust (PST), pp. 1–12. IEEE (2018)
27. Guri, M., Zadov, B., Elovici, Y.: LED-it-GO: leaking (a lot of) data from air-gapped computers via the (small) hard drive LED. In: Polychronakis, M., Meier, M. (eds.) DIMVA 2017. LNCS, vol. 10327, pp. 161–184. Springer, Cham (2017). https://doi.org/10.1007/978-3-319-60876-1_8
28. Guri, M.: AIR-FI: leaking data from air-gapped computers using Wi-Fi frequencies. IEEE Trans. Dependable Secure Comput. (2022)
29. Guri, M.: SATAn: air-gap exfiltration attack via radio signals from SATA cables. In: 2022 19th Annual International Conference on Privacy, Security & Trust (PST), pp. 1–10. IEEE (2022)

30. Guri, M.: Lantenna: exfiltrating data from air-gapped networks via ethernet cables emission. In: 2021 IEEE 45th Annual Computers, Software, and Applications Conference (COMPSAC), pp. 745–754. IEEE (2021)

31. Romo, J.: DDR memories comparison and overview. Beyond Bits, p. 70

32. Movnti - store doubleword using non-temporal hint. https://www.felixcloutier.com/x86/movnti. Accessed 20 Aug 2023

33. https://cryptome.org Nstissam tempest/2-95 (2000). https://cryptome.org/tempest-2-95.htm. Accessed 01 Jan 2023

34. Tang, W., Mi, Z.: Secure and efficient in-hypervisor memory introspection using nested virtualization. In: 2018 IEEE Symposium on Service-Oriented System Engineering (SOSE), pp. 186–191. IEEE (2018)

35. Kasturi, G.S., Jain, A., Singh, J.: Detection and classification of radio frequency jamming attacks using machine learning. J. Wirel. Mob. Netw. Ubiquitous Comput. Dependable Appl. **11**(4), 49–62 (2020)

36. Chapman, S.J., Hewett, D.P., Trefethen, L.N.: Mathematics of the faraday cage. Siam Rev. **57**(3), 398–417 (2015)

Legal Considerations on Gray Zone Operations – From a Norwegian Perspective

Lars Berg[1,2], Kirsi Helkala[3(✉)], and André Årnes[2,4]

[1] Telenor, Fornebu, Norway
lars.c.n.berg@ntnu.no
[2] Norwegian University of Science and Technology, Trondheim, Norway
andrearn@ntnu.no
[3] Norwegian Defence University College/Norwegian Defence Cyber Academy, Trondheim, Norway
khelkala@mil.no
[4] White Label Consultancy, Oslo, Norway

Abstract. Threats in the digital domain is one of the, if not the most significant risks facing the individual, societies, and nation states worldwide. We are raising the question of whether the legal regulation of the digitally connected worldwide network is adequate to meet the challenges of harmful behavior to critical infrastructure. The general assumption among technical and security experts, as well as in the ongoing public debate, is that it is not. We look into the status of the current Nordic legislation, identify the main challenges, and point out future work.

Keywords: Cyber security · Cyber operation · Civilian actors · Law

1 Introduction

Military law is divided into three time-based phases: peace, conflict, and war. However, this division reflects a political state of affairs among nations and does not necessarily apply to conflict levels in the cyber domain. The definition of "peace time" is not equivalent in the physical domain and cyber domains, as there are ongoing attacks in cyber domain every day. Therefore, we argue that in the cyber domain there is no officially declared "peace-time" as such, only conflict and war. Conflict in the physical domain is among known persons, groups, or states. This again is not so clear in the cyber domain, as attribution may prove a difficult, time-consuming, and often futile task. Furthermore, the possibility of sanctioning unlawful or unwanted behavior in the cyber domain seems limited to non-existent. Areas in the cyber domain where the rules of law otherwise applicable are unclear, in conflict, not defined or unenforced, are often referred to as grey zones [1].

International Law, International Humanitarian Law and other existing supranational treaties or agreements neither advocates nor prohibits, grey zone cyber operations. It all seems to boil down to questions about who, what, how, when, and with what consequences – with the good advice of not doing too harmful things. In turn, should one get caught, the legal repercussions are ineffective and far from tangible.

L. Fritsch et al. (Eds.): NordSec 2023, LNCS 14324, pp. 162–181, 2024.
https://doi.org/10.1007/978-3-031-47748-5_10

The war in Ukraine has shown that public sectors takes part in the conflict with little to no concern for the previous common understanding of international law and carry out cyberattacks as a continuation of their policy with other means [2, 3]. The Ukrainian conflict has also shown that both private companies and civilians are also present on the cyber battlefield [2, 4]. Hybrid combatants present a challenge in international military law, as those actively partaking in a conflict are lawful targets for military operations, but civilians are not, as a rule of thumb. Of course, the IT armies of Russia and Ukraine are not the only actors in the Ukraine theatre of war. There are other groups of people involved that either will help one of the sides or try to gain something for themselves (hacktivists, cybercriminals, and nation-state groups) [2, 5]. This means that there are several actors with different motives simultaneously on the cyber battlefield. It is not clear, according to international law, which actors are lawful combatants/targets, which actors may be given rights to use active defensive methods or even offensive methods, and which actors are to be considered unlawful combatants, e.g., criminals.

Furthermore, the intentions and limitations set by international military and humanitarian law of war have not been followed. Civilian objects and critical infrastructure have been targeted with kinetical attacks as well as cyberattacks [2, 6–8]. An example of cyber-attacks includes the hacking of ViaSat's satellite communication causing modems not to function in Ukraine as well as causing wind farms disruption in central Europe [6, 7]. Malware, with the purpose of making data and systems unavailable, was specifically targeted at several Ukrainian organizations [9] as well as used in emails addressing the Ukraine-Russia conflict in general [5, 10].

We have also seen that the owners of critical infrastructure are within their full legal right to defend their infrastructure, customers, and business – to some extent. Through numerous examples, we have seen that passive defensive measures such as the digital equivalents of locking doors, using warnings, or calling the police, will in reality take far too long time with less than meagre results. Some [11] have argued for tipping the offensive/defensive balance by strengthening the attackee's rights to use active defensive measures (stopping the attack by cause harm to the attacker or the attacker's equipment used in the attack). But as the rules of law in cyberspace are not as clear and enforceable as in the kinetic world, the attackee is presented with legal conundrums.

The infrastructure in which the cyber attacks are carried out are privately owned and the military's role in privately owned infrastructure is inherently difficult. The ethical and legal dilemmas arising when nation states and their contractors launches "defensive and offensive operations" of a military and/or political nature when no war has been declared are abundant and for the most part unresolved. There are no international institutions enforcing international rules nor imposes sanctions on unwanted harmful behavior in cyberspace. It is assumed that the United Nations Charter applies in Cyberspace [12], but no international treaties nor agreement exist on the interpretation and implementation from the kinetical world into the digital world, as exemplified by the international stalemate and never-ending discussions on whether a cyber-attack can constitute an armed attack in accordance with UN art 51 cfr art 2(4) [13], as USA, China and Russia have reserved the right to "respond appropriately". What we have are recommendations from approximately 500 researchers [14] and rulings from the International Court of Justice (ICJ) before the age of cyber attacks. Apart from this, we have some statements from leaders of states and NATO. But these are all questions on when a state lawfully can wage war (jus ad bello). Regulations on lawful behaviour in war (jus in bello) are even more scarce in Cyberspace.

In this article, we look at the Nordic law and rules, and will seek to understand how "grey zone" cyberoperations are thought to be handled. We specially focus on Norwegian actors within the existing Norwegian legislation, regulations, and frameworks. In addition, we identify some key questions that need to be resolved in order to develop the legislation that will be applicable to the future cyber landscape with its plentiful and resourceful actors.

The structure of this paper is as follows. Methodology is briefly explained in Sect. 2. Section 3 gives some examples of related work. Section 4 contains the laws that are related to the cyber domain itself or use of cyber domain. The Norwegian case is presented in Sect. 5. What this all means is discussed in Sect. 6, Sect. 7 presents ideas for the future work and Sect. 8 concludes the paper. Citations to the laws and court documents are presented as footnotes, other sources are found in the references.

2 Methodology

As this paper's primary information sources are laws, regulation and court documents and secondary sources are analyses carried by others, we use both document and content analysis [15, 16] to obtain the results. We have looked at which current laws have direct applicability to cybersecurity in Nordic countries that have their own military: Finland, Sweden, Denmark, and Norway. Further, we have looked at how carrying out cyberoperations in Norway is regulated based on the doctrines and policies that describe and regulate today's situation in Norway.

Content analysis as Krippendorf [17] puts it, is answering questions concerning the context of texts. In our case, we focus on the questions that arouse when the text did not provide with a straightforward or satisfying answer. When reading the documentation, especially the regulative documentation, we have focused on concepts and issues that either are not clear or which are only partly define the situation and leave the room for various interpretations.

3 Related Work

ENISA concludes in its Threat Landscape 2022 "that state actors will likely adopt the structure and setup of the IT Army of Ukraine as a blueprint for non-state participation in future conflicts" [2, 4, 18]. The use of or participation of multi-billion ICT companies, as for example Amazon, Cloudflare, Google, and Microsoft [6, 19], is another issue that needs to be taken into planning the defense against future conflicts. Not only the largest commercial technology and cybersecurity companies have their role in conflicts, but other public and private resources could also be mobilized in conflicts or wars if national or international legislation allow [19].

Work has been done to look at what could be private actors' roles in cyber operations, as well as where the challenges of including private actor lies. For example, Lachow

[20] found that U.S. military cyber contractors play critical roles in supporting offensive cyberoperations, both in reconnaissance and mission support, and called for more public debate on the roles of cyber contractors' in military operations. Smeets [21] studied the benefits and risks of organizational integration of offensive cyber capabilities, finding both positive, such as better knowledge transfer and reduced mission overlap, and negative aspects, such as cost ineffectiveness. Pattison [22] looked at the ethical side of Active Cyber Defense (ACD) services offered by private military and security companies. He argued for a moderately restrictive approach, meaning that private firms can carry out defensive measures but should not perform offensive ones. Broeders [23] analyzed several reports and publications on ACD by Washington DC based commissions and think tanks, finding many of them propose legalizing forms of ACD pushing beyond the current American law. However, the authors point out that the reports focuses on domestic security (and political) problems but fails to address international security problems, which using ACD could also bring about.

A newer example of a state mapping its own capabilities comes from Finland [24]. Finland's Ministry of the Interior and the Ministry of Defence set up a project to assess the operating conditions of the authorities in ensuring national cyber security, combating cybercrime, and conducting cyber defense. The project concluded that the authorities' operating conditions are not adequate to effectively prepare for the most serious cyber threats or to combat them. The report proposes development and legislative changes in seven areas: defining a strategic target state of cyber security, cooperation and official processes, situational awareness, information exchange, influencing and countermeasures, information gathering, and protection of public authority networks.

We have no studies on private actors' legal status and role in cyber operations in Nordic countries.

4 Nordic Cyberlaw Perspective

In this section we summarize the essential laws that are related to cybersecurity in the Nordic countries. The EU has enacted regulations relevant for cyber security, that appliy, or will apply, in the near future, to all the four Nordic Countries, as Sweden, Denmark and Finland are members of EU and Norway through the EEA agreement pending national incorporation.

- EU Cybersecurity Act[1] and Digital Markets Act[2]
- The EU General Data Protection Regulation (GDPR)[3]. Although all countries have the same regulation (GDPR), the countries have supplemented GDPR in national law and national authorities' activities and interpretation relating to GDPR may vary. For example, in Denmark the authority is stricter (active and has stated its view clearly) than in other countries, which increases the risk of authority intervention in Denmark.
- The Network and Information Security2 (NIS2) Directive[4] on measures for a high common level of cybersecurity in net and information systems.

---

[1] https://eur-lex.europa.eu/eli/reg/2019/881/oj.

[2] http://data.europa.eu/eli/reg/2022/1925/oj.

[3] https://eur-lex.europa.eu/legal-content/EN/TXT/?uri=CELEX:32016R0679.

[4] https://eur-lex.europa.eu/eli/dir/2022/2555/oj.

- The Digital Operational Resilience Act[5] (DORA) Regulation for the finance sector has been approved and will be put into effect from January 2025.
- Proposed Directive on adapting non contractual civil liability rules to AI[6]
- International humanitarian and military law

4.1 Cyberlaws in Finland

There is no specific legislation on cybercrime or cybersecurity. Some of the essential Applicable Laws regarding cybersecurity are:

a) The GDPR is supplemented by the Finnish Data Protection Act (1050/2018)[7]
b) Finnish Act on Electronic Communications Services (917/2014)[8]
c) The Finnish Act on the Protection of Privacy in Working Life (759/2004)[9]

However, the Criminal Code of Finland contains several provisions that cover cybercrime (in its different forms) with its own provisions after adding a new chapter (Chapter 38) that includes the criminalization of acts that violate secrecy or secrecy of communications, and which also covers unlawful access to an information system. Section 12 especially regulates that the provisions on corporate criminal liability apply to a violation of the secrecy of communications, an aggravated violation of the secrecy of communications, interference with communications, aggravated interference with communications, unlawful access to an information system, interference with an information system, and aggravated interference with an information system.

In Finland the need and possibility for a general data security law has been recently assessed. It was concluded in 2018 that the data security requirements should still be kept in sector-specific laws. The Finnish privacy legislation is exceptionally strict compared with many other countries, including other EU member states, and grants the users of information communication systems very extensive rights [25]. The right to private communication and the protection of privacy in relation to the employees' private information are absolute and based on fundamental rights. Therefore, even when investigating cybercrimes and cyberattacks an employer may not access its employees' email accounts or personal files. The only possibility for the employer to access private information without the employees' consent is when such information has been processed by the police as a part of a criminal investigation.

For any commercially operating entity, there are general security obligations included even in the Companies Act and other local Finnish laws such as: Limited Liability Companies Act; Trade Register Act; Accounting Act; Accounting Decree; Auditing Act; Act on Prevention of Money Laundering and Terrorism; International Financial Reporting Standards; Tax Procedure Act; Securities Markets Act; EU Market Abuse Regulation.

---

[5] https://eur-lex.europa.eu/legal-content/EN/TXT/?uri=CELEX%3A32022R2554.

[6] https://commission.europa.eu/business-economy-euro/doing-business-eu/contract-rules/digital-contracts/liability-rules-artificial-intelligence_en.

[7] https://www.finlex.fi/fi/laki/alkup/2018/20181050.

[8] https://finlex.fi/fi/laki/ajantasa/2014/20140917.

[9] https://finlex.fi/fi/laki/ajantasa/2004/20040759.

In September 2015 the Ministry of Transport and Communications appointed a development group to prepare Finland's Information Security Strategy, which was published in April 2016[10]. Also, in April 2016 the Finnish Ministry of Justice and the Finnish Ministry of the Interior published a working group's report on a proposal for legislation on intelligence activities that would give law enforcement agencies more extensive access to data to increase the level of security[11,12]. The legislative process is in progress and new laws are to be expected soon.

4.2   Cyberlaws in Sweden

There is no specific legislation on cybercrime or cybersecurity, rather it extends over several areas of Swedish law:

a) GDPR is supplemented by the Swedish Data Protection Act[13].
b) Personal data processing by governmental authorities responsible for crime prevention, investigation and prosecution is regulated by Swedish Act on Processing of Personal Data Relating to Criminal Offences[14].
c) Criminal offences, including cybercrimes such as breaches of data security, are subject to the Swedish Criminal Code[15].
d) Copyright infringement is regulated by the Swedish Copyright Act[16].
e) Decoding activities regarding radio and TV are criminalized and regulated by the Swedish Act on Decoding[17].
f) Acts of terrorism, including cyber-attacks, are regulated by the Swedish Act on Criminal Responsibility for Terrorist Offences[18].
g) Providers of electronic communication services and electronic communication networks are subject to the Swedish Act on Electronic Communication[19].

---

[10] https://julkaisut.valtioneuvosto.fi/handle/10024/164793.

[11] https://fra.europa.eu/sites/default/files/fra_uploads/finland-study-data-surveillance-ii-legal-update-fi.pdf.

[12] https://intermin.fi/en/national-security/civilian-intelligence.

[13] https://www.government.se/government-policy/the-constitution-of-sweden-and-personal-privacy/act-containing-supplementary-provisions-to-the-eu-sfs-2018218-general-data-protection-regulation/.

[14] https://www.riksdagen.se/sv/dokument-och-lagar/dokument/svensk-forfattningssamling/brottsdatalag-20181177_sfs-2018-1177/.

[15] www.government.se/contentassets/7a2dcae0787e465e9a2431554b5eab03/the-swedish-criminal-code.pdf.

[16] https://lagen.nu/1960:729.

[17] www.mprt.se/globalassets/dokument/lagar-och-regler/the-swedish-radio-and-television-act.pdf.

[18] https://perma.cc/GUK7-BZFR.

[19] https://www.riksdagen.se/sv/dokument-och-lagar/dokument/svensk-forfattningssamling/lag-2022482-om-elektronisk-kommunikation_sfs-2022-482/.

h) Certain providers of "essential services" – mostly infrastructure – and digital services, are subject to the EU Directive on Security of Network and Information Systems (NIS), which has been implemented through the Act on Information Security Regarding Providers of Critical Infrastructure and Digital Services (NIS Act)[20].

i) Act on Payment Services regulates payment services provided in Sweden[21].

j) The disclosure of trade secrets is prohibited under the Swedish Trade Secrets Act[22].

k) Further, certain operations and activities deemed important to Swedish national security are regulated by the Swedish Protective Security Act[23].

4.3 Cyberlaws in Denmark

There is no one specific cybersecurity law as such in Denmark. Rather, the legal landscape is made up by several laws promoting cybersecurity.

a) The Danish Network and Information Security Act no. 1567 of 15.12.2015[24] and later changes[25] implements the Directive (EU) 2018/1972 of the European Parliament and of the Council of 11 December 2018 establishing the European Electronic Communications Code and sets requirements to minimum standards of security. These requirements have been detailed out by the Danish Centre for Cybersecurity (the national IT Security authority) in their regulation 'Information and Security Order'[26] under which a provider of public electronic communications networks or services is responsible for information security in its network based on a documented risk management process. A provider must identify any possible cybersecurity risks and using this risk assessment, implement proper measures to ensure the accessibility, integrity and confidentiality of its networks and services.

b) The main legislation concerning processing of personal data is the GDPR and the Danish supplementary act, the Data Protection Act (in force from 23 May 2018). In addition to the GDPR, the Data Protection Act and national practice implement certain derogations concerning the processing of personal data, especially in respect of processing of personal data within the employment sector and the processing of national registration numbers. The Act on Processing Personal Data that implemented Directive 95/46 EC came into force in 2002. But even though the Danish data protection regulation is 20 years old, not much attention was paid to data protection in Denmark until the GDPR was passed in 2016. The term 'data protection' was basically unheard of in the general Danish population and in most companies before

---

[20] https://www.riksdagen.se/sv/dokument-och-lagar/dokument/svensk-forfattningssamling/lag-20181174-om-informationssakerhet-for_sfs-2018-1174/.

[21] https://www.riksdagen.se/sv/dokument-och-lagar/dokument/svensk-forfattningssamling/lag-2010751-om-betaltjanster_sfs-2010-751/.

[22] https://www.riksdagen.se/sv/dokument-och-lagar/dokument/svensk-forfattningssamling/lag-2018558-om-foretagshemligheter_sfs-2018-558/.

[23] https://www.government.se/contentassets/7d1bd1801f8d46a69ded4cd2a30bb6fe/protective-security-act-2018-585.pdf.

[24] https://www.offentlighedsportalen.dk/dokument/219573.

[25] https://www.retsinformation.dk/eli/lta/2021/153#id5aafd591-62c0-4b56-8167-4f117d6dddfd.

[26] https://www.retsinformation.dk/eli/lta/2016/567.

2017–2018. Thus, the GDPR has been the dominant topic in recent years in terms of compliance. Since the implementation of the GDPR, Danish companies have continuously invested substantial resources in data protection compliance, mainly for commercial and legal risk management reasons.

4.4 Cyberlaws in Norway

There is no general applicable law especially dedicated to cybersecurity in Norway. The relevant Applicable Laws that regulate cybersecurity are fragmented and often sector specific. Some of the essential Applicable Laws regarding cybersecurity are:

a) GDPR is supplemented by The Norwegian Personal Data Act of 15 June 2018[27].
b) On May 5th 2023 The Norwegian government (Regjeringen) proposed to the parliament (Stortinget) an act on Digital Security [26] and asked for consent to the approval of two decisions in the EEA committee on the incorporation of the NIS1 directive, the associated implementing regulation and the cyber security regulation into the EEA agreement[28]. The incorporation of the NIS2[29] is not clear.
c) The National Security Act of 1 June 2018[30] aims, inter alia, to prevent, detect and counteract activities threatening national sovereignty, including regulations on information security.
d) The Electronic Communications Act of 4 July 2003[31] and the Electronic Communications Regulation of 16 February 2004[32] aim to give secure and modern communication services to the public.
e) The Energy Act of 29 June 1990[33] and the Power Supply Preparedness Regulation of 7 December 2012[34] aim to secure power supply and include regulations on information security and safety measures for control systems.
f) The Regulation on the Use of Information and Communication Technology of 21 May 2003[35] (ICT Regulation) within the financial services regulates, inter alia, the use and security of ICT systems in that sector, which has to be harmonized with DORA[36] in 2025.

4.5 Short Summary about the Nordic Cyberlaws

There is no specific legislation on cybercrime or cybersecurity in any of the Nordic countries. Rather, the legal landscape is made up of several laws promoting cybersecurity.

---

[27] https://lovdata.no/dokument/NL/lov/2018-06-15-38.

[28] https://www.regjeringen.no/no/dokumenter/prop.-109-ls-20222023/id2975558/.

[29] https://eur-lex.europa.eu/eli/dir/2022/2555/oj.

[30] https://lovdata.no/dokument/NL/lov/2018-06-01-24.

[31] https://lovdata.no/dokument/NL/lov/2003-07-04-83.

[32] https://lovdata.no/dokument/SF/forskrift/2004-02-16-401.

[33] https://lovdata.no/dokument/NL/lov/1990-06-29-50.

[34] https://webfileservice.nve.no/API/PublishedFiles/Download/5690526d-60af-4cd5-b7fc-51c 87cb66f48/202119965/3425769.

[35] https://www.finanstilsynet.no/globalassets/laws-and-regulations/regulations/regulations-on-use-of-ict.pdf.

[36] https://eur-lex.europa.eu/legal-content/EN/TXT/?uri=CELEX%3A32022R2554.

The relevant applicable laws that regulate cybersecurity are fragmented and often sector specific. The laws tend to be vague and discretionary, setting minimum standards and providing good advice. The proposed NIS2 EU regulation has a risk-based approach, leaving it up to the responsible entity to make a best effort judgement based on cost/benefit evaluations with the threat of fines should compliance or evaluations prove inadequate.

The current legislation and regulations are focused on the attackee, e.g., the victim, and its obligation to secure infrastructure, customers, and its activities. This illustrates the political realism in cyberspace; the EU does not have the political and economic power to attribute and hold the major actors in cyberspace accountable; USA, Russia, and China. Some of the members may even have benefits from the grey zones in cyber, ref GCHQs Operation Socialist in 2006–13 [27] and German Bundesnachrichtendienst surveillance of a.o. The White House 1998–2006 [28].

Post the world wars, legal focus has been on preventing the devastating consequences for societies and individuals by limiting if, when and how to go to war and how warfare should be conducted, with the expressive ambition that war to avoided. Policymakers also need to also have the attackers and their methods, objectives, and motivations in mind; who are they, what do they do, why do they do the things they do and how do they do it. Today it is not clear what a cyber defender may or may not do if and when under attack. For example, what possibly is illegal to do in the physical world or within the borders of own country, may not be unlawful in the digitally connected worldwide network.

5   A Deeper Look at the Norwegian Case

In the following, we will look into how the complex threats and legal landscape affect those who launches or are responsible for managing cyber attacks.

5.1   Complex Threats

Complex threats is a term for strategies of competition and confrontation below the threshold of direct armed conflict, which can combine diplomatic, informational, military, economic, financial, intelligence and legal means to achieve strategic objectives [29]. Complex threats can occur in grey areas of security policy, where the purpose is to create discord and destabilization. The use of instruments can be widely distributed and combine open and covert methods. The use of policy instruments may target specific activities or situations, or be oriented more long-term towards creating doubt, undermining trust, and thereby weakening our democratic values.

Norway is facing a heightened threat and risk picture and is challenged by states with security policy ambitions that do not correspond to Norwegian national security interests. Increased willingness to confront non-Western states, Russian use of military force and energy as weaponry are examples of this. The invasion of Ukraine has created lasting changes in relations between Russia and Western countries. Increased globalization, rivalry between the superpowers and constant changes in the security situation greatly affect the national threat picture and present us with security challenges. The increased strategic importance of the High North and Norway's role as an energy supplier makes

Norway particularly vulnerable to intelligence and sabotage activities and other undesirable activity [30]. In addition, climate change affects national security over time. Climate change is disrupting people's lives and damaging certain sectors of the economy, may exacerbate existing stressors, contributing to poverty, environmental degradation, and political instability, providing enabling environments for terrorist activity. For example, the impacts of climate change on key economic sectors, such as agriculture and water, can have profound effects on food security, posing threats to overall stability. Extreme weather events are also affecting energy production and delivery facilities, causing supply disruptions of varying lengths and magnitudes and affecting other infrastructure that depends on energy supply. The increasing risk of flooding affects human safety and health, property, infrastructure, economies, and ecology in many basins across Norway, the Nordics and the EU [31]. Furthermore, it is assumed that the annual budgetary room for maneuver will be reduced in the coming decades compared with preceding decades.

Traditional lines between peace, crisis, and armed conflict have become less clear. State actors such as Russia and China engage in activities that may initially be lawful activities to further their own strategic objectives [30], for instance by fundingg political parties or campaign organizations and other foreign interference [32, 33]. This appears to be part of the normal picture, but at the same time the activity can harm Norwegian national security. Nation states must consider that some states attempt to influence political decisions, opinion formation and the debate in their country. The diplomatic, informational, military, economic, financial, intelligence and legal instruments of individual states may, individually or in combination, constitute complex threats directed against Norway. In recent years, threats related to foreign investment and acquisitions that can be used to gain insight into and access to technology and resources of strategic importance have become more apparent.

Assets of importance to national security are increasingly managed and processed in cyberspace. Digitalization and technology development lead to increased efficiency and renewal, but at the same time introduce new vulnerabilities, dependencies, and concentration risks. This can be exploited by a threat actor. The rapid pace of development and changes in the security situation make it increasingly demanding for businesses to maintain a proper level of security throughout the crisis span.

5.2 The Military Point of View

NATO's cyberspace operation doctrine divides cyberspace operations into two types [34]: defensive cyberspace operation (DCO) and offensive cyberspace operation (OCO). DCO defined as "Defensive actions in or through cyberspace to preserve friendly freedom of action in cyberspace" and OCO as "Actions in or through cyberspace that project power to create effects which achieve military objectives." The actual actions are not specified in the doctrine, only the actions' effects.

Effects such as securing against compromise of confidentiality, integrity and availability of own communication and infrastructure systems, CIS, isolating the communication between adversaries and affected systems, containing the spread of the malicious activity, neutralizing malicious activity permanently from own CIS, and recovering quickly from the effects of malicious activity (network resilience) are thought to be effect of DCOs [35]. Similarly, OCOs have effects [35] such as manipulating the integrity of an adversary's CIS, exfiltrating the information of adversaries' networks, degrading an asset of an adversary to a level below its normal performance, disrupting an asset of an adversary for an extended period, or destroying an asset of the adversary.

Cyberspace Operation Centre is the primary point if coordination of NATO's COs, and one of their tasks is to facilitate the integration of Sovereign Cyber Effects Provided Voluntarily by Allies (SCEPVA) into alliance operation and missions [34]. However, the contributing nation will have command and control over groups providing SCEPVA. But the question arises, can SCEPVAs also include civilians?

Norway, as part of NATO, follows the cyberspace operation doctrine [34] via Norwegian joint military doctrine (Forsvarets fellesoperative doktrine) [36]. Norwegian doctrine states that, the Norwegian Intelligence Service (which is a Norwegian military intelligence agency under the Chief of Defence and the Ministry of Defence) has overall coordinating authority for military-related cyber operations [36]. This is to ensure that military DCO do not conflict with OCO or other intelligence activities. Further, there is a separation of which military units can conduct OCOs and DOCs. As NATOs doctrine, the Norwegian doctrine [36] does not specifically define DCOs and OCOs.

There is not as clear separation between our own and our adversaries CIS in the cyber domain as in the physical world, and the lines between civilian and military infrastructure are blurred. The Norwegian defense forces, as well as other allies, are depending on civilian infrastructure as well as civilian contractors. Therefore NATO's cyberspace operation doctrine [34] says that "Enhancing information sharing and mutual assistance in preventing, mitigating, and recovering from attacks in or through cyberspace is important. This requires civil-military interaction, which can be facilitated by CIMIC. A positive result from CIMIC is enhanced support to COs through maintaining freedom of access to cyberspace and capacity building."

The Norwegian Defence Commission Report [37] describes a challenging security environment and proposes a significant increase in defense spending and recommends as the third major measure an overall strengthening of the defense capability by developing a consistently larger defense with greater depth with closer links to the rest of a program of "Totalforsvaret" [38] (i.e. "Total Defence"), with strong public and private involvement and with several joint solutions in a Nordic and Allied framework.

Whereas Cyberspace Operation Doctrine is military related, Cyber Defence Pledge [39] also includes governmental, civilian and private sectors. NATO's Industry Cyber Partnership [40] is to provide platforms to exchange information, threat trends and best practices so that partners would be better be able to prevent and respond to cyberattacks.

In summary, NATO's cyberspace operation doctrine, Cyber Defence Pledge, and Industry Cyber Partnership are all including the civilian sector, but the civilian's status and role in cyber operations are legally unclear.

Even more complicated is the distinction between active and passive cyber operations, at a glance the difference seems to be obvious, but on applying cyber weapons there seem to be little to no difference between active and passive measures, as most weapons may be used both to attack and to protect.

5.3 Cyber Attacks on Non-military Objects; You are on Your Own

The lessons learned, not only from the Ukraine war but others, is that availability of communication channels are very important assets to protect. Most of the communication networks are civilian owned. Hence there are (at least) three parties responsible for digital communication in Norway; the Military, the Police, and the owners of the digital communication networks. For now, we leave out coordinating authorities and owners of the equipment and software solutions that are integrated in, connected to and in sum constitutes the worldwide network as well as the users and customers. Their role and responsibilities warrant separate focus and research.

The rules of law set the parameters for civilian and military activities in times of peace, conflict, and war. The purpose and mandates for the armed forces (Green) vs the policing authorities (Blue) is important to understand. Blue investigates crimes with the purpose of securing evidence and bringing criminals to justice before a court of law. Green addresses and manage threats to the sovereignty and security of the nation state. Blue ensures public order and safety, applying force only when appropriate and in accordance with the principle of proportionality. Green defends the nation state and applies force necessary to ensure the survival and safety of the state from other states and external threats. Blue's mandate takes precedence in peace, Green's in crises and war.

The National Framework for Handling ICT Security Incidents [41] describes how the incidents targeted non-military objects should be handled. The civilian cyber incident management involves coordination with the Norwegian Intelligence Service, the Norwegian National Security Authority and the Norwegian Police Security Service. The framework states [41] that the intelligence service has national level responsibility peace, crisis and armed conflict for uncovering foreign threats and generating intelligence on foreign threat actors in cyberspace, as well as responsibility for OCOs against foreign targets. It also states that the police have a monopoly on the use of force in Norway and the exclusive right to use force against citizens, also when incidents take place in digital space or by digital methods. The police can also take measures to prevent and stop criminal offences. Under investigations, the police have the authority to implement measures to obtain information and to prevent new criminal offences. However, neither the Intelligent Service, the National Security Authority, nor the Police will handle ICT incidents for enterprises. The owner of the enterprise, in the private or public sector, always holds the responsibility for handling ICT security incidents [41].

The framework [41] acknowledges three phases in incident management ": 1) stop the incident, limit the extent of damage and restore safe condition; 2) secure technical leads and make seizures and/or arrests in connection with investigations, and/or 3) implement offensive countermeasures." However, the framework only covers the first phase as it belongs to the civilian actors.

The framework [41] expects that businesses can establish the capability and capacity to handle ICT security incidents by themselves or have access to that capability and capacity by using a commercial third party; privately owned enterprises are on their own. The Norwegian National Security Authority has provided a list of approved service providers. The legal status of these third-party security service providers is unclear.

As per the above, private business's role in relation to cyber attacks is for the most part undefined. They should cover the point 1) ") stop the incident, limit the extent of damage and restore safe condition" but the question is how are they to do this? On one hand is the question of which cybersecurity guidance to follow and on the other is which alternatives they have to handle the incidents as they should both limit the damage as well as keep the services available.

The best practice landscape on cybersecurity is complex and difficult to navigate. Best Practices for managing cyber-attacks are found in several sources. Requirements and standards are also – directly or indirectly – to be found in general or sector-specific regulations. Standards and guidelines are offered by government of nation-states, for instance the US General Services Administration, which promotes management best practices and efficient government operations through the development of governmentwide policies, offers the National Institute of Standards and Technology (NIST) Cybersecurity Framework (CSF) [42] for Improving Critical Infrastructure Cybersecurity (NIST Cybersecurity Framework) and organizes basic cybersecurity activities at their highest level. Branches and niches within tech and other industries offer guidelines within their domains, e.g., GSMA provides security guidelines and advice on telecom, network, and IOT for network operators, i.e., its members. The ISO/IEC 27001 is the world's best-known standard for information security management systems (ISMS) and their requirements. Additional best practices in data protection and cyber resilience are covered by more than a dozen standards in the ISO/IEC 27000 family. The ambition is to enable organizations of all sectors and sizes to manage the security of assets such as financial information, intellectual property, employee data, and information entrusted to third parties. Most larger companies have developed their own policies and best practices, tailormade for their own situation, needs and experiences.

These requirements, policies, and guidelines cover a wide range of recommended actions to be taken, from Do Nothing to Retaliate. In considering response alternatives for private actors and the civilian sector have, one should not only study the theoretical possibilities but investigate possibilities within real business world boundaries. Internet Service Provider, ISP, or Network Infrastructure Operators, NIO, are bounded by contracts, agreed SLAs (defines the level of service you expect from a vendor, laying out the metrics by which ser-vice is measured, as well as remedies or penalties), permits, licenses, network agreements, etc. The ISP needs to consider what could happen before cutting off traffic from a specific IP address or network, as it may choke or hinder alarms to a hospital or other innocent communication as an unwanted side effect, leaving the ISP vulnerable to law-suits resulting from breaches of contracts or actions taken from governmental bodies. Therefore, ISP and NIO have to consider effects that an attack is causing on them and their customers as well as effects that response would cause.

6 Discussion - So What Does This Mean?

With a few certain starting points, we point out some of the major legal challenges in the gray zone; attribution, accountability, right to self-defense and use of automated responses and artificial intelligence.

6.1 Is It a Crime?

Getting clear on the basics; Yes, cyber attacks on others is a crime in Norway [43, 44].

Laws and legal rules are inextricably linked to states and states' sovereignty. This is recognized in international law which assigns the state exclusive monopoly over and responsibility for its territory and inhabitants and simultaneously rejects other states having supranational jurisdiction over the sovereign state. In Norway, this is stated in the Constitution, which nevertheless and under certain conditions can give the legal rules of other regional bodies effect also in Norway and towards Norwegian citizens.

For cyberspace, this means, firstly, that Norwegian law will apply to acts committed by Norwegians with effect in another country's territory, as well as to acts committed abroad with effect in Norway. In terms of criminal law, this follows from the Penal Code, chapter 21, cf. §7. A cyber attack will be punishable according to one of the descriptions of the offense in chapter 21 and because "the effect has occurred or been intentionally caused" in Norway according to Sect. 7, the act will be covered by the Criminal Code, cf. Sect. 4. This has been established in several decisions[37]. The same will to a large extent apply to other countries' laws, depending on how these countries have chosen to apply their rules. Since the laws vary between countries, it will vary what is permitted or prohibited, what can be punished, what penalties apply and whether/how legal rules can be enforced, and violations sanctioned. In this sense the rules of law in cyberspace have a fragmentary character.

6.2 The Legal Conundrum

No country is alone in facing the cyber security threat, for many the most significant one. In 2018 The US Secretary of Homeland Security [45] highlighted the seriousness of this challenge when noted that; "… cyber-attacks in terms of their breadth and scope of possible consequences now exceed the risk of physical attacks." Technological advances continue to outpace legal developments. While intelligence officials have suggested the most serious cyber attacks comes from "nation states", existing international legal frameworks fail to provide timely or effective legal remedies.

One of the most significant hurdles is the problem of attribution. For a nation state to be held responsible under international law for a particular act, that act must be attributable to that state. In the case of cyber attacks, however, states do not generally operate through formal state bodies. Instead, they tend to use "non-state actors" who are less visible, more removed and offer plausible deniability. This creates problems of both factual and legal attribution.

The factual problem is that it is often extremely difficult to accurately identify the origin of a cyber attack. The lack of boundaries and anonymity that are characteristic of cyberspace make it hard for states to identify exactly who is responsible for a specific cyber attack. Perpetrators are becoming increasingly effective at masking their true

---

[37] The Norwegian Supreme Court's ruling in Rt. 2003/1770 where a Swedish citizen was charged with fraud committed abroad but also with Norwegian victims. Whereas in Rt.2004/1619 the opposite was the case, when two Norwegian citizens were convicted for data breaches in several hundred of servers located outside of Norway.

identities and locations. They may even deliberately make it look as though innocent third parties are responsible for an attack.

The legal problem of attribution arises from the fact that international law does not generally hold states responsible for the actions of non-state actors. Responsibility will only be attributed if the state either acknowledges and adopts the conduct of the non-state actor as its own, or the state directs or controls the non-state actor. The former is unlikely given the lengths that states go to mask their involvement in cyber attacks in the first place. The latter is also unlikely, given the high threshold set by international law to establish the required direction or control. The International Court of Justice has held that a state must be shown to have had "effective control" over each specific act for which attribution is sought[38]. Simply providing financial aid or equipment to support a cyber attack, or even providing a safe haven base for individual hackers, would likely not be enough to meet the "effective control" test. Given these problems, it is highly unlikely that a state will ever be held publicly accountable under the existing legal framework. It is one thing for politicians and intelligence officials to privately suggest a certain state to be blamed for cyber attacks, but it is a long way to meet the high threshold required to establish state's responsibility under international law.

Even if legal attribution could be established, that does not solve the legal complexities. International law has few mechanisms that allow a state to respond effectively to a cyber attack once it has occurred. Even though there are Grey Zones where Green and Blue meets and the line between who does what gets blurry, the legislation organizing and governing lawful military and civilian activities is colored by from these fundamental differences in purposes and mandates. In choosing the legal level and toolset appropriate for Cyberspace, the decision makers need to take into consideration how important the digital infrastructure is for society; a playground for commercial interests or critical infrastructure for the survival for the state.

6.3 Is Counterattack Justified Against a State Sponsored Cyber Attack?

A state is allowed to use force in self-defense – but only in response to an armed attack[39]. The key questions then are whether a cyber attack amounts to a "use of force", whether hacking attributable to a state amount to an "armed attack", and if a cyber attack violates "territorial integrity". Traditionally, international law has answered these questions with reference to acts of physical violence – conventional military strikes. It's likely that a large-scale cyber attack against a state that has physical consequences within its territory may be characterized as a "use of force" and may violate "territorial integrity" under the charter. For instance, attacks that turn self-driving cars into weapons, knock out nuclear stations or paralyze the power grid might reach this threshold. An armed attack in this context refers to only the gravest use of force. It is highly unlikely that acts of cyber espionage focused primarily on gathering intelligence or data will be characterized as an armed attack under this definition.

But what if the attack is designed to sow confusion or generate internal discord, such as in the case of Russian hacking of the US election in 2016 [46]? Or attacks directed

---

[38] https://www.icj-cij.org/files/case-related/70/070-19860627-JUD-01-00-EN.pdf.

[39] https://www.un.org/en/about-us/un-charter/chapter-7.

beyond a particular country? Currently, these questions are not settled. Similarly, it's not certain that even large-scale hacking would rise to the level of an "armed attack". Based on the Nicaragua case, if a cyber attack has sufficient "scale and effects" it may amount to an armed attack. More importantly, if the attacks are attributable to a state (in this case the Islamic Revolutionary Guard[40]) – or are within its overall or effective control or direction – the armed attack would give rise to the right to self-defense. However, this may be difficult to establish in practice, as there may not be sufficient evidence connecting the hacker to the state to show control, and hence attribution.

Similarly, while countermeasures (a broad category of temporary, reversible measures designed to induce a state to cease its wrongful conduct) are allowed under international law in certain circumstances, the conditions imposed makes them of limited use in the context of cyber attacks. For example, in all but the most urgent circumstances, an injured state must notify the responsible state of the decision to take countermeasures and offer to negotiate with them before any countermeasures are taken. Such procedural requirements are simply impractical when responding to cyber attacks, given their potential speed and reach.

The permissible self-defense responses to cyber attacks under international law are not clear.

6.4   Automated Responses and Artificial Intelligence

Software is becoming better at detecting abnormalities and vulnerabilities in the system. The sheer amount of data to be monitored for such detection is already far beyond human abilities, and the speed at which things happen limits what humans can do. Therefore, it is only to be expected that cybersecurity experts are looking for ways to automate this process and make it more efficient. For the same reasons, and since detection is only the first step in countering an intrusion, software developers are also looking for ways for programs to take measures against intrusions autonomously.

The automated response may be triggered and targeted in numerous ways. For instance, an attackee subjected to a distributed denial-of-service (DDoS) operation against one of its systems, may take down a command and control server of a botnet or the whole botnet, thus stopping the DDoS attack. Alternatively, it could respond by destroying a server to which cyber espionage malware is sending data extracted from the attackee's system. In our context an even more critical example is a counterstrike against a system that seems to be the source of a cyber operation against critical infrastructure. In this case, the attackee may be entitled to take countermeasures against the origin conducting this operation, either assuming there is attribution or acting under the plea of necessity. It is not clear if and to what extent there exists a right to self-defense in cyberspace. And, even if we assume that there is a legal right to respond by taking destructive action against the assumed source of the incoming operation (which takes time to determine), there is a risk of exceeding the legal limitations of the response. It is not clear if and to what extent the limitations to self-defense – e.g., necessity, proportionality, attribution and containment of effects – applies in the cyber domain. As cyber attacks may be launched and completed in a blink of an eye, literally, the response may

---

[40] https://www.icj-cij.org/files/case-related/70/070-19860627-JUD-01-00-EN.pdf.

be preprogrammed and automated, as there is no time to determine the source of the incoming operation before response has to be launched. This again raises the question of whether it is legally acceptable that a decision and response be made without "human touch". As the predictability of autonomous systems is one of the main challenges, any cyber capability autonomously executing such measures risks causing unforeseen effects. Unforeseen consequences may be due to malfunction of the system caused by a technical failure or use in new or unknown situations and territory, the program disobeying the operator (especially relevant in AI-based systems) or external manipulation. This raises the question of whether unforeseen effects are acceptable, to what extent and who if anyone should be held responsible for them.

7 Future Work

The current Norwegian and NATO cyberspace operation doctrine [34] and National Framework for Handling ICT Security Incidents [41] allows military DCO and OCO or other intelligence activity, as ordered by appropriate military and political authority coordinated by The Norwegian Intelligence Service (E-tjenesten). It is the purpose, method and consequences that decides at what level the decision to launch an operation needs to be made. No reservations are made for ownership of targeted infrastructure.

Even though we may launch cyber operations, leaders in the cyber battlefield needs to consider can we. The question here is whether we can successfully perform the operation technically speaking and achieve the desired end result. Thus, the relevant question is not if Norway can launch cyber operations, but whether we should. The answer to this question is complex and highly debated. In our future research we will present the arguments as they have been presented in the ongoing discussion.

As mentioned, the legal status of the hybrid combatants in cyber warfare is not clear. A better understanding and regulation of private companies and civilians present on the cyber battlefield, is needed. Making all employees of for instance Microsoft, Google, HP, IBM, Lenovo, Tesla, Apple, Samsung, Huawei and other tech companies, or their suppliers, lawful targets because of local or regional war, warrants further research.

A better understanding of the civilian defender of critical infrastructure (the attackee), and if, when, who and how infrastructure critical to society may be protected and defended, is needed. A challenge is that there is no common understanding as to what defensive and offensive cyber operations are. Furthermore, there seems to be no distinction between cyber operations and other intelligence activity. We argue that there is a fundamental difference between activities and operations in equipment and networks you own yourself and equipment and networks owned by others. Further it seems logical to distinguish between the different types of activities. A possible model could be Passive investigation/Active Investigation/Active Investigation+/Active (Counter) Measures. In our future research, we will explore this model further.

One should focus on the impact on society, critical national functions, and the nation state, and raise the question of whether there exists a rule of proportionality in cyberspace similar to the rules of international humanitarian law on the conduct of hostilities for military operations, prohibiting attacks which may be expected to cause incidental loss of civilian life, injury to civilians, damage to civilian objects or a combination thereof, which would be excessive in relation to the concrete and direct military advantage anticipated. If so, one should study what key steps and elements that "belligerents" must take to give effect to the rule, with a particular focus on one side of proportionality assessments – the expected incidental harm.

Special attention should be given to the effects of automation and use of AI in cyber security, as both the need for timely and cost-efficient response requires state-of-the-art technical solutions to assess and launch countermeasures within milliseconds. Use of automated cyber weapons and AI warrants separate focus and research.

8 Conclusion

According to national laws hacking, data intrusions, data theft, digital extortion and other cyberattacks are illegal. This has done little to prevent or mitigate the rising tide of cybercrime. There is no specific legislation on cybercrime or cybersecurity in any of the Nordic countries. Rather, the legal landscape is made up by several laws promoting cybersecurity. The relevant applicable laws that regulate cybersecurity are fragmented and often sector specific, as well as they tend to be vague and discretionary, setting little more than minimum standards and provide good advice.

As seen, the technological advances continue to outpace legal developments and the existing international law framework fails to provide timely or effective legal remedies. International law does little to alleviate these legal challenges as attribution of incidents seems an insurmountable mountain to climb and should a nation through its contractors be called out, there is no efficient organization nor regulation to ensure accountability.

In order for legislators and policymakers to come up with practicable and acceptable national and international ways of managing and sanctioning unlawful or unwanted behavior in the cyber domain both the attackees and the attackers need to be understood; who are they, what do they do, why do they do the things they do and how do they do them. Much work, studies, and research need to be done.

In addition to addressing the problem of attribution and accountability, the legal status of hybrid combatants, contractors and "non-state actors" in cyber warfare needs to be addressed. The threshold set in the ICJ ruling of 1986[41] should be looked into in light of technological development and dawn of the digital age.

In our opinion, addressing and resolving the issues in "the grey zones", will clarify the problems of cyber attacks and the development of future adequate and efficient national and international legislation, regulation, and policymaking, as "all" the problems come clearly to light at once. Only by truly understanding the problems of cyber attacks and resolving these using a scientifically and fact-based approach, can we have the possibility to protect individuals, societies and nation states from unwanted and harmful behavior affecting critical infrastructure nationally, regionally and worldwide.

References

1. Corn, G.P.: Cyber national security: navigating gray-zone challenges in and through cyberspace. In: Williams, W.S., Ford, C.M. (eds.) Complex Battlespaces: The Law of Armed Conflict and the Dynamics of Modern Warfare. Oxford Academic (2019)

---

[41] https://www.icj-cij.org/files/case-related/70/070-19860627-JUD-01-00-EN.pdf.

2. ENISA: Threat Landscape 2022 (2022)
3. https://www.cfr.org/cyber-operations/ukrainian-it-army
4. Soesanto, S.: The IT Army of Ukraine - Structure, Tasking, and Ecosystem. Center for Security Studies (CSS), ETH Zürich (2022)
5. Cisco Talos: Threat advisory: Cybercriminals compromise users with malware disguised as pro-Ukraine cyber tools. Talos Intelligence, vol. 2023. Talos (2022)
6. Bateman, J.: Russia's Wartime Cyber Operations in Ukraine: Military Impacts, Influences, and Implications. Carnegie (2022)
7. Sheahan, M., Steitz, C., Rinke, A.: Satellite outage knocks out thousands of Enercon's wind turbines. Reuters. Reuters (2022)
8. Microsoft: An overview of Russia's cyberattack activity in Ukraine (2022)
9. https://www.microsoft.com/en-us/security/blog/2022/01/15/destructive-malware-targeting-ukrainian-organizations/
10. Bîzgă, A.: Bitdefender Labs Sees Increased Malicious and Scam Activity Exploiting the War in Ukraine. Bitdefender (2022)
11. Sklerov, M.J.: Solving the dilemma of state response to cyberattacks: a justification for the use of active defenses against states who neglect their duty to prevent. Mil. Law Rev. **201**, 1–85 (2009)
12. Utenriksdepartementet: Internasjonal cyberstrategi for Norge (2017)
13. Fjellvikås, S.B.: Grensene for en stats selvforsvarsrett etter FN-pakten artikkel 51 ved digitale angrep fra en annen stat. Det juridiske fakultet, vol. Master. University of Oslo (2018)
14. Schmitt, M.N.: Tallinn Manual 2.0 on the International Law Applicable to Cyber Operations. Cambridge University Press (2017)
15. Indeed. https://www.indeed.com/career-advice/career-development/document-analysis#:~: text=What%20is%20document%20analysis%3F,upon%20the%20information%20they% 20provide
16. Columbia University Mailman School of Public Health. https://www.publichealth.columbia. edu/research/population-health-methods/content-analysis
17. Krippendorff, K.: Content Analysis - An Introduction to Its Methodology. SAGE (2013)
18. Kaminska, M., Shires, J., Smeets, M.: Cyber Operations During the 2022 Russian invasion of Ukraine: Lessons Learned (so far). European Cyber Conflict Research Initiative (2022)
19. Beecroft, N.: Evaluating the International Support to Ukrainian Cyber Defense. Carnegie (2022)
20. Lachow, I.: The Private Sector Role in Offensive Cyber Operations: Benefits, Issues and Challenges. SSRN (2016)
21. Smeets, M.: Integrating offensive cyber capabilities: meaning, dilemmas, and assessment. Def. Stud. **18**, 395–410 (2018)
22. Pattison, J.: From defence to offence: the ethics of private cybersecurity. Eur. J. Int. Secur. **5**, 233–254 (2020)
23. Broeders, D.: Private active cyber defense and (international) cyber security—pushing the line? J. Cybersecur. **7** (2021)
24. Kyberselvityshankkeen työryhmä: Valtioneuvoston julkaisuja 2023:31. Selvitys viranomaisten toimintaedellytyksistä kyberturvallisuudessa. Valtioneuvosto (2023)
25. Lång, J., Haavikko, T.: Data Security and Cybercrime in Finland. Lexology (2019)
26. Justis- og beredskapsdepartementet: Norge får sin første lov om digital sikkerhet (2023)
27. Spiegel: Britain's GCHQ Hacked Belgian Telecoms Firm. Spiegel International (2013)
28. Baumgärtner, V.M., Knobbe, M., Schindler, J.: German Intelligence Also Snooped on White House. Spiegel International (2017)
29. Justis- og beredskapsdepartementet: Meld. St. 9 (2022–2023): Nasjonal kontroll og digital motstandskraft for å ivareta nasjonal sikkerhet—Så åpent som mulig, så sikkert som nødvendig (2022)

30. Etterretningstjenesten: Fokus 2023 Trusselvurdering (2023)
31. White House: Findings from Select Federal Reports: The National Security Implications of a Changing Climate. The White House (2015)
32. Jones, K.: Legal loopholes and the risk of foreign interference (2023)
33. Committee on Foreign Relations: Putin's Asymmetric Assault on Democracy in Russia and Europe: Implications for U.S. National Security. Senate Committee Print (2018)
34. Ministry of Defence: Allied Joint Publication-3.20, Allied Joint Doctrine for Cyberspace Operations. In: NATO (ed.) (2020)
35. Helkala, K., Cook, J., Lucas, G., Pasquale, F., Reichberg, G., Syse, H.: AI in cyber operations: ethical and legal considerations for end-users. In: Sipola, T., Kokkonen, T., Karjalainen, M. (eds.) Artificial Intelligence and Cybersecurity, pp. 185–206. Springer, Cham (2023). https://doi.org/10.1007/978-3-031-15030-2_9
36. Forsvaret: Forsvarets fellesoperative doktrine (2019)
37. Forsvarsdepartementet: NOU 2023:14 Forsvaskomisjonen av 2021 - Forsvar for fred og frihet (2023)
38. Forsvardepartementet, Justis- og beredskapsdepartementet: Støtte og samarbeid - En beskrivelse av totalforsvaret i dag (2015)
39. NATO: Cyber Defence Pledge (2016)
40. Brent, L.: NATO's role in cyberspace. NATO Review (2019)
41. Nasjonal sikkerhetsmyndighet: Rammeverk for håndtering av IKT-hendelser (2017)
42. National Institute of Standards and Technology: Framework for Improving Critical Infrastructure Cybersecurity Version 1.1 (2018)
43. Sunde, I.M.: Cyber crime law. In: Årnes, A. (ed.) Digital Forensics. Wiley (2017)
44. Sunde, I.M.: Cyber investigation law. In: Årnes, A. (ed.) Cyber Investigations. Wiley (2022)
45. https://www.dhs.gov/news/2018/09/05/secretary-nielsen-remarks-rethinking-homeland-security-age-disruption
46. https://www.fbi.gov/wanted/cyber/russian-interference-in-2016-u-s-elections

Aspects of Trust

Mobile App Distribution Transparency (MADT): Design and Evaluation of a System to Mitigate Necessary Trust in Mobile App Distribution Systems

Mario Lins[1]([✉]) [iD], René Mayrhofer[1] [iD], Michael Roland[1] [iD], and Alastair R. Beresford[2] [iD]

[1] Johannes Kepler University Linz, Altenberger Straße 69, 4040 Linz, Austria
{lins,rm,roland}@ins.jku.at
[2] Department of Computer Science and Technology, University of Cambridge, Cambridge CB3 0FD, UK
arb33@cam.ac.uk

Abstract. Current mobile app distribution systems use (asymmetric) digital signatures to ensure integrity and authenticity for their apps. However, there are realistic threat models under which trust in such signatures is compromised. One example is an unconsciously leaked signing key that allows an attacker to distribute malicious updates to an existing app; other examples are intentional key sharing as well as insider attacks. Recent app store policy changes like Google Play Signing (and other similar OEM and free app stores like F-Droid) are a practically relevant case of intentional key sharing: such distribution systems take over key handling and create app signatures themselves, breaking up the previous end-to-end verifiable trust from developer to end-user device. This paper addresses these threats by proposing a system design that incorporates transparency logs and end-to-end verification in mobile app distribution systems to make unauthorized distribution attempts transparent and thus detectable. We analyzed the relevant security considerations with regard to our threat model as well as the security implications in the case where an attacker is able to compromise our proposed system. Finally, we implemented an open-source prototype extending F-Droid, which demonstrates practicability, feasibility, and performance of our proposed system.

Keywords: Mobile app distribution · Transparency logs · Supply-chain security · Verifiable trust · Digital signatures

1 Introduction

Supply-chain attacks are popular, omnipresent, and effective as evidenced by recent reports about significant attacks and events such as NotPetya, XcodeGhost, or the SolarWind attack [5,13]. Due to their potential severity

© The Author(s), under exclusive license to Springer Nature Switzerland AG 2024
L. Fritsch et al. (Eds.): NordSec 2023, LNCS 14324, pp. 185–203, 2024.
https://doi.org/10.1007/978-3-031-47748-5_11

and automatic distribution to thousands or even millions of trusting users [5], state actors such as China or Russia are actively invested in exploiting software supply chains [13].

According to the MITRE ATT&CK® knowledge base [27], supply chains can be compromised in several ways, like manipulating the software update/distribution mechanisms, replacing legitimate software with modified versions, or selling modified/counterfeit products to legitimate distributors. These examples often involve compromising existing trust anchors like signing keys or certificates [13].

We focused our research on supply chain security of mobile app distribution systems which rely on certain trust anchors, like digital signatures. As these signatures are an integral component in well-known mobile app distributions systems such as Google Play or F-Droid, there is often no alternative but to trust them completely. Although, digital signatures are used to ensure the integrity and authenticity of apps, we have identified certain threats in current mobile app distribution systems that could lead to significant security concerns for a user or the developer of the respective app. These include leaked signing keys that may be used by unauthorized entities, malicious distributors, insider attacks or even attempts to distribute different app versions to specific users.

This paper introduces a novel concept, built on transparency logs, to improve verifiability and discoverability of potential attacks related to digital signatures, with a particular focus on mobile app distribution systems. We concentrate on the digital app signature since it is a key part of ecosystem security.

2   Preliminaries

2.1   App Signing Process

Google Play Store provides an integrated feature, called Play App Signing [12], that manages and protects the private key used for signing the APK file[1]. This approach requires that the private key is managed by Google's Key Management Service and thus it needs to be stored on Google's infrastructure. For Android apps published before August 2021, the Play App Signing approach is optional and developers can still manage app signing keys themselves. However, for newly published apps, the Play App Signing approach is mandatory. This particular policy adaption by Google results in a centralized trust anchor that has to be trusted by both the user and the developer (more details in Sect. 3.2).

F-Droid [9] is an alternative distribution system for free and open source Android apps. If a developer wants to sign an APK file, F-Droid provides two possible procedures for that. One approach is to publish two APK versions where one is signed by the developer and the other one is signed by the F-Droid repository (with a key held by F-Droid, comparable to Google Play Signing in this case). This is especially useful for distributing updates for apps that have been

---

[1] As developer identities are not directly verified by most Android app distribution systems, authenticity of signing keys is typically only guaranteed in the Trust-on-First-Use (TOFU) model.

installed via different distribution channels (e.g. Play Store) and for apps available through F-Droid. This approach requires including the signature of the developer into the corresponding metadata description of the particular app and that the app is still reproducible by F-Droid. The other approach requires the developer to provide a reference to the signed APK file. If F-Droid is able to reproduce the APK file in a way that it matches the referenced one, F-Droid publishes the signed APK of the developer directly without signing it again with the F-Droid repository key.

2.2 Verifiable Logs

A verifiable log [8,15,16] is a data structure that is based on an append-only ledger that is cryptographically secure. The Merkle tree is a popular example where it is not possible to retroactively insert, delete, or modify any record. One of the main advantages of this data structure is that these properties are auditable, either publicly or at least by its consumers (e.g. when hosted in an internal network). The data stored in a verifiable log is application-specific and is not defined by the log itself. A verifiable log is stored on one or preferably multiple servers that are accessible by clients, which may not necessarily be trusted. Clients do not have to trust the log server as the data structure allows verification of the proper behavior of the log itself.

Merkle Trees. We base our design on a verifiable log using a binary Merkle tree [20] to allow efficient auditing and to provide tamper protection due to its append-only property. The Merkle tree consists of leafs and nodes, with the top node called *root node*. The leaves represent data that are managed by the tree. Values are attached to internal nodes and are calculated as a cryptographic hash function (e.g. SHA-256) of their children, recursively, until a value of the root node is reached. Trees do not need to be balanced and therefore can store an arbitrary amount of data.

Inclusion Proofs. An *inclusion proof* allows one party to prove to another that a particular leaf exists in a Merkle tree. This proof can be constructed efficiently, as it only requires the so-called Merkle Audit Path [11,15,16] which represents the shortest path from the respective leaf to the root node hash of the tree. The remaining leaves and nodes are not needed for this calculation. This approach means that the calculated root node hash is compared to the expected root node hash. If these hashes are equal, we have proven the particular leaf is part of the tree[2]. The left tree in Fig. 1 highlights the path that is required for such an inclusion proof for *Record 2*. The required components for the calculation

---

[2] We consider a particular tree to be fully represented by its root hash, which can in turn be contained within an updated or larger tree with a different root hash. Within the scope of inclusion proofs we thus use the terms 'tree' and 'root hash' interchangeably wrt. the provided security guarantee.

are marked in red. Below is a step-by-step description of validating an inclusion proof for the example given in Fig. 1.

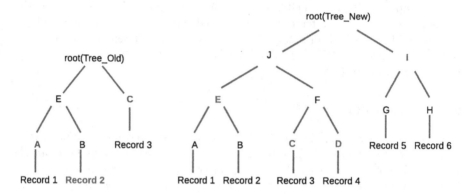

Fig. 1. Merkle Tree proofs (Color figure online)

Given an ordered list of node hashes A and C, the inclusion proof can be verified as followed:

1. Calculate the leaf hash of *Record 2*: B = SHA-256(0x00 || *Record 2*), where 0x00 is used as a prefix for leaf hashes and 0x01 for nodes to provide second preimage resistance [16].
2. Calculate the node hash E = SHA-256(0x01 || A || B).
3. Calculate the root node hash root = SHA-256(0x01 || E || C).
4. Compare the calculated root hash with the claimed root node hash.
5. The inclusion proof is valid if the hashes are equal.

Consistency Proofs. A consistency proof [16] can be used to verify if the append-only property of the Merkle tree is valid. The append-only property ensures that it is not possible to insert, modify, or delete a leaf or node in the tree retroactively. Therefore, the consistency proof validates if a previously generated version of the tree is part of the current tree that may have been extended by new entries.

Assuming two Merkle trees, Tree_Old and Tree_New as shown in Fig. 1, where Tree_Old is a previous version of Tree_New, a consistency proof provides an ordered list of node hashes in order to perform a verification whether the entries of Tree_Old is still equal to the corresponding entries in Tree_New or not. Given the root node hash of Tree_Old, a root node hash of Tree_New, and the corresponding consistency proof [E, C, D, I], the verification of that proof can be calculated as followed:

1. Calculate the resulting node hash: X = SHA-256(0x01 || E || C).
2. Verify that X is equal to root hash of Tree_Old.

3. Calculate $F =$ SHA-256(0x01 || C || D).
4. Calculate $J =$ SHA-256(0x01 || E || F).
5. Calculate root node hash of Tree_New: $Y =$ SHA-256(0x01 || J || I).
6. Compare the calculated root node hash Y with the claimed root node hash.
7. The consistency proof is valid if the hashes are equal.

2.3   Split-View Attack

A relevant attack on such verifiable logs that also applies to the design proposal of this paper is called split-view attack [18,24]. A log subject to such an attack would be able to present different log representations to its clients while still maintaining the append-only property given by the Merkle tree. This means that all operations performed by a client on a specific log (e.g. inclusion and consistency proofs) seem valid, yet receiving different data than seen by other clients. However, once a log carries out a split-view attack, it must consistently maintain different views for each subgroup of clients since doing otherwise is detectable. A security evaluation and suggestions to counter this kind of attack are given in Sect. 5.1.

2.4   Personality

The term *personality* is used by Google Trillian [6] and describes the application-specific interface to access a log server. The main responsibilities of a personality are defining and validating the application-specific data model, optionally providing access control and in case the personality and the log is maintained by different parties, providing auditable information for external verifiers.

2.5   Monitor, Auditor and Witness

One of the main advantages of a verifiable log is that it enables interested parties to detect misconduct up to even malicious behavior regarding certain log entries. It is possible to set up monitors, auditors or witnesses that periodically verify the behavior of the log or notify subscribers in case of suspicious behavior. A monitor may store previous copies of the verifiable log in order to verify the consistency between a new and previous versions. An auditor typically verifies the consistency of only a subset of the log by performing inclusion proofs. A witness [18,26] on the other hand is an independent entity that observes one or more log systems to prevent split-view attacks. Log auditors can thus have more confidence that a log system is truly and globally consistent if multiple independent witnesses have a consensus about the specific state (checkpoint) of the log. The witness cosigns a checkpoint after verifying that an evolution of a previously signed checkpoint is consistent with it. In case the log or the witness are new, the witness uses the trust-on-first-use approach.

3 Threat Model

The focus of our threat model is to identify potential security impacts with regard to the authenticity and integrity of APK files that are distributed by a mobile app distributor (e.g. Google Play, F-Droid). The most important security control that is used to ensure authenticity and integrity are digital signatures. Therefore, most of our threats[3] address scenarios where the signature is compromised or even used by malicious actors. As there are different parties involved in mobile app distribution systems, we first define potential stakeholders.

3.1 Stakeholders

Developer: The developer wants to distribute an app via a mobile app distribution system. From the developer's perspective, it is important that unauthorized entities cannot manipulate the app or even publish app updates on their behalf.

User: The user primarily wants to use the app and may want to verify the authenticity and integrity of the app to be sure that it has not been manipulated.

Distributor: The distributor wants to distribute apps to its users using secure infrastructure. Furthermore, the distributor wants to provide its users with security by incorporating controls such as digital signatures to prevent repository spoofing or malicious app updates[4].

A stakeholder may also take over more than one role, like a developer who is also hosting a distribution system.

3.2 Threats

Threat 1: Signing key is leaked and used by an unauthorized party. The most relevant threat that is addressed by the proposed system is that an unauthorized party uses the app signing key to distribute malicious updates. If the holder of the signing key is not aware that the key has leaked, they may not recognize that it is used by an unauthorized party. This is also relevant even in case that the holder of the signing key monitors certain distribution channels, directly as these could also be untrustworthy or even malicious.

Threat 2: Unauthorized usage of the signing key due to compulsory outsourcing. As mentioned in Sect. 2.1, the current Google Play policies enforce the developer to store the signing key on Google's infrastructure so that the developer is not in control of the signing key anymore and comparable app distributors have similar policies. This restriction requires full trust in this external storage and that no unauthorized entity can access the security relevant signing

---

[3] Most of the threats that we have identified can also be found elsewhere [2,3,17,19, 23].

[4] Payment and IP protection mechanisms are already addressed in existing systems and considered out of scope of the threat model in this paper.

key(s). In that particular case, the developer or the user cannot verify if the signing key has been compromised.

Threat 3: Deliberate use of the signing key. The key holder, who may be an outsourced storage provider, may for example be forced to sign the corresponding app update by the respective judicative or due to economic interests. The developer would not have a possibility to detect that the outsourced key has been abused. Reports of government interventions in the mobile world reinforce the associated potential threat. In 2021, the New York Times [22] reported the removal of tens of thousands of apps from Chinese app stores.

Threat 4: A user may get another version of an app than other users. If the signing key is compromised, a user cannot ensure to have the same version of the app as all other users have. A distributor could provide a tampered version only to a subset of users. This threat may also be interesting in terms of censorship, enforced by state actors like the Internet censorship regime of Iran [1]. How can a user be sure to receive the same version in, e.g., the USA and in Iran without any geographical differences? However, distributing different app versions is also done by the app developers themselves, as a recent study [14] revealed 596 apps with geographical differences that may expose a certain security and privacy risk for users in those countries.

4 Architecture of the Verifiable System Design

This section introduces the components used to design our novel concept. To evaluate and to verify the viability of the proposed system, we have implemented a proof-of-concept prototype. Specific implementation parts have been set up by using or adapting available open source components, including F-Droid for distributing Android apps and Google Trillian for the transparency log backend. The first subsection details the individual phases with regards to the previously defined stakeholders. The second subsection lists the involved system components from a more software-centered approach.

4.1 Phases

The proposed system design includes three main phases based on the intended usages of the defined stakeholders: distribution, verification, and monitoring phase. Figure 2 provides an overview about the phases including the relevant stakeholders and tasks.

Distribution Phase: The distribution phase begins as soon as the developer has finished the implementation of the app. At this point, the *developer* wants to distribute the app to its *users* by using the respective infrastructure of the *distributor*. First, the *developer* uploads the app or the source code of the app to the store provided by the *distributor*. Additionally, the *developer* may want to sign the app or allow the *distributor* to sign the final package.

At this point, our system proposal extends the workflow by extracting relevant app metadata that is going to be published and to create a respective log

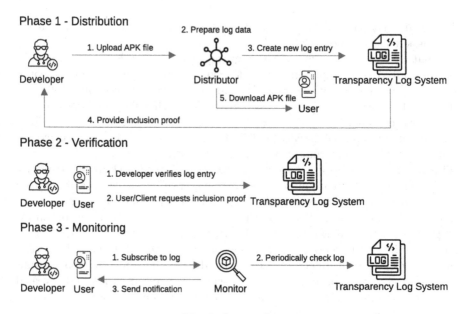

Fig. 2. System flow

entry via the dedicated transparency log system. This step is performed by the *distributor*. As soon as the log entry has been successfully added to the log, the *distributor* can release the app to its *users*.

Verification Phase: Once the app is available through the channel of the distributor, client-side verification can be conducted. Verification can be done by several entities: the developer, the user, and potentially also by existing witnesses. The developer may want to verify if the app has been logged properly. This can be done by requesting an inclusion proof of the log. If the inclusion proof verifies the developer can be sure that the distributor has properly logged the uploaded APK file. Automatic verification on the user side is done by the client of the distribution system (e.g. F-Droid client). The client downloads the requested app, calculates the expected logging information, and requests the corresponding inclusion proof from the personality. If the expected information and the logged information match, there will be no warnings shown to the user. If it does not match, the app can still be installed, but the user will receive a warning. As our transparency log system is publicly available, a user always has the possibility to verify the log entry manually even without trusting the client of the distributor.

Monitoring Phase: The monitoring phase may start after the app has been published and verified by the developer. The developer can subscribe to notifications from a monitoring instance that observes the transparency log for new entries based on the application ID and the version that the developer is interested in (e.g. `com.example.sampleapp:v1.0`). When the monitor detects a new log entry with the given namespace, it notifies all subscribers. In case the developer has not published a new update, someone else is trying to publish one.

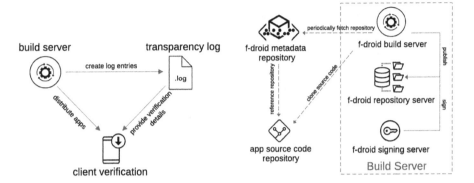

Fig. 3. System overview   Fig. 4. Build server

4.2   System Components

This section details the involved system components from a more technical point of view including the prototype implementation. Figure 3 illustrates the three main components and their interactions.

Build Server. The build server part includes the relevant components to build, publish (sign) and deploy the given app. The individual tasks of such a build server are to fetch and build the source code, to verify it's reproducibility and to sign and publish the APK to the distribution server. Our prototype implementation is built around F-Droid. The F-Droid build server includes the build environment, a dedicated F-Droid repository, and a signing server as illustrated in Fig. 4. There were no changes needed for the F-Droid repository and signing component. Although, for being used in a production environment, we would recommend to request an inclusion proof before making the APK file available to users.

Prototype Implementation: The most relevant changes for our prototype implementation were done in the build server component itself. During the publishing process, the build server signs the APK file and publishes it to the repository. At this point the prototype implementation adds additional steps to the workflow before the signed APK file is finally deployed to the remote web server where it is available for all users:

1. Extract relevant APK metadata (see Sect. 4.2).
2. Select the proper tree ID for the specific repository.

3. Create a JSON object compliant to the personality data.
4. Request an authentication token from the personality.
5. Send tree ID and JSON object to the personality to create new log entry.

Transparency Log. The transparency log system consists of three components as described below.

1. *Log Server:* The core element of our transparency log system is the log server that manages one or multiple Merkle trees including the associated function-alities like performing inclusion or consistency proofs. The log server implementation is based on Google Trillian and did not require any adaptions to work with the system as it is designed to be application-independent.
2. *Database:* The database is used to persist the Merkle tree. Our implementation uses a MySQL database.
3. *Personality:* The personality is the application-specific interface in front of the log server. The personality defines and validates the data structure that is used to store the leaf content in the transparency log. Additionally, it exposes an interface to its users to interact with the transparency log. Our prototype implementation does not allow everyone to create new log entries. There-fore, special endpoints of the personality can only be access when properly authenticated and authorized for them.

Prototype Implementation: Our prototype implementation includes a dedicated personality, developed as a REST service by using the .NET core framework. By using our build pipeline we are able to build a docker image including a configurable personality instance. The Google Trillian implementation of the log server provides the required *.proto files to interact with the log server via gRPC. The personality is responsible for defining the data structure that is stored within the Merkle tree and for potential data validation tasks. Furthermore, it also performs proper conversion from the C# object to the byte array that is finally stored in the transparency log. An essential implementation detail that we had to take care of was to use the proper hashing algorithm and dedicated prefixes depending on the type of the tree element (e.g. 0x00 for leaf and 0x01 for node elements), cf. RFC 9162 [16]. To prevent unauthorized write access on the log, we have introduced two roles and implemented a token-based authentication scheme. We are using an admin role responsible for managing trees (e.g. creating a new tree or deleting an existing one) and a build-server role that is authorized to create new log entries. Our docker image is parameterized to allow inclusion of pre-defined credentials for both roles. If the F-Droid build server, e.g., wants to create new log entries, it has to provide the correct credentials to the personality first. If the credentials are valid, the personality provides the F-Droid build server an authentication token that can be used to create new entries in the log.

Data Structure. The data structure of the records stored in the verifiable log includes the following information that is required to uniquely identify the package as well as to verify its integrity:

- *applicationId:* The unique APK file package name.
- *version:* The version number of the app release.
- *apkHash:* A cryptographic hash of the APK file to verify its integrity.

Client Verification. This component is responsible for verifying that apps are downloaded from a distributor were properly logged. This involves several steps as listed below:

1. The client downloads the APK file, but does not start the installation.
2. The verification library gets relevant metadata (application ID, version, and hash value) of the APK file.
3. An inclusion proof is requested by sending a specifically crafted data object including the metadata to the personality.
4. In case there is an inclusion proof available, the verification library calculates the expected root hash locally.
5. The locally calculated root hash is compared with the claimed root hash of the log server.
6. If the root hashes are equal and therefore the inclusion proof is valid, the client installs the app without further notice.
7. In case the inclusion proof is not valid, the user is notified, but can continue to install the app.

Prototype Implementation: We have implemented a dedicated Android library to perform the end-to-end verification of the distributed APK file to verify whether it is properly logged or not. One of the main functionalities that are currently implemented is the end-to-end verification by validating an inclusion proof that is provided by the personality. Besides the verification part, the prototype implementation handles all other kinds of communication to the personality (e.g. requesting available tree IDs). The library has been developed in Java and is publicly available. One main reason why we have decided to do the implementation in a dedicated Android library is that interested parties can easily use it in a separate app or even integrate it into the official clients of the mobile app distributors (e.g. within the official F-Droid client app).

5   Evaluation

5.1   Security Evaluation

This section evaluates our proposed system design to determine whether the identified threats, listed in Sect. 3.2 can be successfully mitigated. Furthermore, the security implications are analyzed in case an attacker is able to compromise one or multiple of the newly added components.

Threat Mitigation. Our system design makes any distribution attempt though (or by) a distributor transparent and thus verifiable. In particular, the client verifies the log entry before installing an app and therefore it is not possible to distribute an app without creating a new entry in the append-only and tamper-proofed logging system. As this entry includes the package string, the version, and the hash of the APK file, any interested party can verify if this aligns with the corresponding log entry and that it is the same APK version that everyone else has (Threat 4). A developer or an app distributor who monitors the log would receive a notification (Threats 1, 2, 3) as soon as the log entry of the particular app is created so that unauthorized distribution attempts can be detected. Our system design also enables independent and verifiable monitoring instances and thus does not rely on trustworthiness of a distributor. Therefore, we can also avoid falsified or missing information (e.g. suppression of publication attempts) compared to monitor specific distribution channels, directly (Threat 1).

Security Implications. An attacker who is able to compromise one or multiple of our newly added components could also have a major security impact with regards to authenticity and integrity of the mobile distribution system. Therefore, we also evaluate the security of our approach including the newly added components[5]. The following paragraphs describe the results of our evaluation.

Malicious Distributor Bypasses the Logging System. If a compromised distributor tries to bypass or manipulate the log entry, it avoids creating a new log entry so that a manipulated APK version could be distributed because it cannot be verified. In that case, the client would detect that for this particular APK the log entry is missing and notify the user about this security incident, who can decide how to proceed.

Malicious Distributor Creates a Manipulated Log Entry. As a client would detect the absence of expected log entries, a malicious distributor may try to create a manipulated log entry. To provide a valid log entry that matches a manipulated APK file, the distributor needs to calculate the hash value of the manipulated version and write the new hash value to the log. A client that verifies the manipulated APK file, calculates the hash of it and verifies the respective log entry. The verification would be successful as a log entry is present and the hash values match. However, this manipulation attempt may be detected by monitors. The developer of the app, for example, may have registered the APK name space on a monitor that observes the log. The monitor would recognize that there is a new log entry for a particular APK file so the developer (as subscriber) will be notified. The developer could then easily compare the real hash value of the original version with the hash value of the log entry and would detect the manipulation

---

[5] Note that global passive adversaries may learn which apps are installed by clients by monitoring transmitted inclusion proofs, leaf log entries, and/or the embedded APK metadata. However, as there are many other ways to learn the same information under our threat model, we consider this as out of scope and not a reason for keeping such data confidential.

attempt. Further steps to be taken in that particular case are out of scope for this paper.

Malicious Client Bypasses the Log Verification. An attacker may be successful in tricking the victim into installing a manipulated version of the distribution client that bypasses the logging verification to allow an attacker to distribute malicious APK files via the distribution channel. Besides the fact that an attacker who is able to trick a victim into installing a malicious client could also install other malicious APK files the same way, there are two efficient countermeasures in place: First, the client app could also be logged in the transparency log so that the client can manually perform an inclusion proof. Second, the user could use a dedicated app that performs the necessary calculations and communication to the personality.

Malicious Log Server. A log operator may try to manipulate a log entry while maintaining the same root hash. In this scenario the log operator may only manipulate a single leaf, but keeps the root node hash the same so that the cryptographic proofs for the remaining entries are still valid. This attack scenario can be mitigated by running full audits on the Merkle tree. A full audit recalculates the root node hash from the available leaf values. If the full audit results in a root node hash that does not match the claimed one, the suspicious behavior can be detected. From a component point-of-view, a full audit could be performed by monitors.

Unauthorized Write Access to the Log Server. The transparency log should be publicly readable by design to allow every interested party to verify log entries. However, when it comes to write permissions, it is essential to consciously decide who is allowed to write to the log. In case arbitrary parties are allowed to write to the log, it is still possible to verify the entries. However, data that has been written to the log can never be removed again due to its append-only property. In regard to the design proposal, it is suggested to only allow authenticated distribution systems to write to such logs.

Split-View Attack by a Malicious Log Server. A split-view attack can be mitigated by using witnesses. The log server is independent of the specific application and thus any witness system could be used. However, to make use of the advantages of the consensus of witnesses, the client would need to verify them in addition to inclusion proofs. This functionality is currently not implemented in the prototype.

Orthogonally to the use of witnesses, split-view attacks can be mitigated by querying the personality and log server, e.g. via Tor [28] circuits, as this would make providing consistent split views unrealistic.

Malicious Personality. A personality is not necessarily hosted in the same trust zone or operated by the same operator as the log server. Therefore, an external auditor may also want to audit the personality to verify its behavior. The personality can prove correct behavior by additionally monitoring the log server and thus persisting the signed tree heads. If it changes retroactively, the personality can detect that.

5.2 Performance Evaluation

To evaluate the performance of our transparency log system, we used the metadata of all publicly available APK files in the official F-Droid repository and created the corresponding log entries in our system. To perform that evaluation, we wrote a Python script that first fetches the current F-Droid index file[6] of the official repository. The second step is to parse the index file in order to prepare the proper log format required by our personality. Next, the script requests an access token for the buildserver user and starts to send the POST requests to create the new log entries.

For our performance measurements we used a computer with an Intel i7-1185G7 @ 3.00 GHz CPU and 32 GB of RAM for fetching the current F-Droid index file of the official repository, to prepare the log entries and to send the POST requests to our transparency log backend. Our transparency log backend, including the personality and the log itself, is deployed on a virtual machine with 2 cores and 2 GB RAM (Host CPU: Intel E5-2620 v3 @ 2.40 GHz). For the client side end-to-end verification we used an Android emulator running API level 31 with 1536 MB RAM.

There are 9705 APK files in the official F-Droid repository. It took less than 47 min to create our log, less than 30 ms on average per APK. The log database required 8 MB of disk storage. Inclusion proofs consist of 14 hashes (825 B) for the first leaf and of 7 hashes (510 B) for the last leaf. Consistency proofs similarly ranged from 14 hashes (821 B) to 8 hashes (533 B). An end-to-end verification with our Android library of the first leaf that requires the maximum amount of intermediate node hashes in that particular tree took 296 ms.

6 Open Research Questions

We have introduced a novel concept to mitigate necessary trust in mobile app distribution systems, especially with focus on digital signatures on APK files. Our current approach includes mitigation techniques, but does not get rid of trust anchors completely. Therefore, we are looking for a solution to remove such trust anchors completely by extending our transparency log system in a way that still meets the same security requirements (e.g. integrity and authenticity checks) as digital signatures. Another open research question exists around third-party libraries in apps. More precisely, we plan to enhance our transparency log system so that it can also detect outdated or compromised third party libraries even in obfuscated APK files.

7 Related Work

7.1 Certificate Transparency

Certificate Transparency (CT) [10] is a process that is part of the web's public key infrastructure. Its main purpose is to detect unauthorized or even maliciously

---

[6] https://f-droid.org/repo/index-v2.json (accessed: 2023-02-07).

issued TLS certificates for websites by making them transparent and verifiable. Whenever a certificate authority (CA) issues a new certificate, a new entry gets recorded in one of the approved verifiable logs. These logs can be checked for suspicious behavior by independent monitors. As these logs are publicly auditable, interested parties are able to create such a monitor. In that case the browser is one of the possible auditors to verify if the particular certificate is part of the verifiable log.

Difference: Both, CT and our proposed system are based on Merkle trees. Therefore, we can use the same underlying Google Trillian implementation to handle the tree structure. However, data stored within the tree is application-specific as CT needs to store TLS certificate information and our system deals with information about mobile apps. The most relevant difference is the end-to-end verification. In the CT ecosystem, the browser is responsible for verifying if the certificate is properly logged by checking the signed certificate timestamp (SCT), e.g., the X.509v3 certificate extension [21]. Our proposal, on the other hand, does not need additional information, like an SCT on the client side as the end-to-end verification is directly performed with the transparency log system. At this point we do not rely on digital signatures as our end-to-end verification implementation crafts the expected log entry at the beginning of the verification stage and directly verifies if a corresponding log entry is available or not.

7.2   Binary Transparency in F-Droid

F-Droid has already incorporated a module [25] that logs the signed app index metadata files in append-only storage. These files contain information about the available APKs of a specific F-Droid repository so that every update or change also requires a change on the related file. To fulfill the requirement of append-only storage, F-Droid uses a git repository that it claims is tamper proof. This approach allows interested parties to verify if a specific binary was published by the expected publishing entity as only an authorized party is allowed to push to the respective git repository. As of the time of writing this paper, this feature is activated for the Guardian Project repository.

Difference: A git repository is a content-addressable filesystem [4] that is based on a Merkle tree—the same data structure we use in our approach and prototype implementation. If a new or updated file is stored in a git repository, git calculates the SHA-1 hash based on the file's content (called a *blob* object) and stores this information in an internal object database. A blob does not store the filename itself. Instead, we store the names of files in a *tree* object; tree objects may contain tree objects. This approach is analogous to the Unix file system, where a blob object would correspond to the data associated with a file object, while a tree corresponds to the entries found in a directory object.

The logging approach by F-Droid stores the app index metadata file in a specific git repository that is responsible for version control. This approach is not scalable as metadata of all the available apps in the F-Droid ecosystem is stored in one single file. Furthermore, the information required to carry out the verification task is not directly managed by the tree structure, because it is just stored in a file, and thus the verification does not benefit from optimizations of a tree structure like efficient searching. Consequently, if an entity wants to verify if a specific value is part of the tree, the whole file must be downloaded by the client. This file is also larger than necessary for verification since it contains information that is not relevant for the verification task at all (e.g. the applied license). While such an approach may work reasonably well for F-Droid, this approach would not scale to the distribution scale seen in larger markets. In contrast, our approach is scalable since we use Merkle trees directly and make efficient use of communication and computation effort through the direct provision of consistency proofs over time with snapshots. We do not require the use of a full data structure at once.

7.3 Blockchain

Blockchains are built around a distributed public ledger that provides similar properties to our approach, including an append-only data structure, tamper resistance, and transparent verification. The ledger contains blocks that consist of a hash of the previous block, a timestamp, and the transaction data.

The problems tackled by using a blockchain are orthogonal with regards to authentication, integrity, and non-repudiation [7] that can be addressed by using digital signatures. A digital signature can prove that signed data has not been tampered with afterwards and that it is signed by an entity that possesses the respective signing key. However, for example, the time of signing requires trust in the signing party that is essential for financial transactions or legal contracts. To address this trust dependency, a blockchain uses a distributed trust mechanism, where interested parties can store a list of transactions and thus are able to verify that they have not been tampered with.

Difference: From a security point of view, blockchains fulfill requirements like tamper protection as well. However, their verification procedure is not scalable[7]. For a full end-to-end verification, a blockchain based approach requires the clients to download the whole chain whereas the transparency log approach only requires the hashes of the audit path ($log(n)$) and ideally checkpoints signed by independent witnesses.

8 Conclusion

Current mobile app distribution systems use digital signatures to ensure integrity and authenticity of their apps. However, as shown in this paper, there are realistic threats which may compromise digital signatures. For example, it is currently

---

[7] In terms of efficiency comparison, we are not even assuming proof-of-work consensus algorithms, but permissioned ledgers comparable to the authentication of submitters performed by the personality.

impossible to detect unauthorized usage of signing keys. A more general perspective on this kind of problem is how to compliment or enhance the trust placed on digital signatures in mobile app distribution systems.

This paper introduces a novel concept to mitigate threats found in mobile app distribution systems by making any distribution attempt transparent and thus verifiable. Additionally, a prototype has been implemented to prove the practicability and feasibility of the design proposal, including a detailed security evaluation of the newly added components as well its performance. Our evaluation shows that an attacker would have to compromise all the involved system components and security controls to successfully distribute a malicious APK file without detection. While the proposed system focuses on mobile app distribution systems, it can also be applied in other scenarios where digital signatures are used and may not be trustworthy.

Acknowledgment. This work has been carried out within the scope of Digidow, the Christian Doppler Laboratory for Private Digital Authentication in the Physical World and has partially been supported by the LIT Secure and Correct Systems Lab. We gratefully acknowledge financial support by the Austrian Federal Ministry of Labour and Economy, the National Foundation for Research, Technology and Development, the Christian Doppler Research Association, 3 Banken IT GmbH, ekey biometric systems GmbH, Kepler Universitätsklinikum GmbH, NXP Semiconductors Austria GmbH & Co KG, Österreichische Staatsdruckerei GmbH, and the State of Upper Austria.

A   Availability

Our prototype implementation consists of the following component repositories and is publicly available.

- **F-Droid server:** The relevant source code segments have been extracted from the fork of the official F-Droid server code. Source Code: `https://github.com/mobilesec/fdroidserver_transparencyextension`
- **Personality:** The personality project contains the code for the application-specific interface between the client library, the F-Droid server, and the Google Trillian logging infrastructure. Source Code: `https://github.com/mobilesec/mobiletransparency-personality`
- **Android library:** The Android library project contains the code for the end-to-end verification of APK files. Source Code: `https://github.com/mobilesec/mobiletransparency-androidlibrary`
- **Evaluation setup:** Contains the test script, configuration file and reference data of our performance evaluation. Source Code: `https://github.com/mobilesec/mobiletransparency-data`

We also provide a running personality with this version of the codebase along with a transparency log running the unmodified Google Trillian case (from `https://github.com/google/trillian`) that has been pre-filled with APK metadata from the index of the official F-Droid repository as well as some of our test apps using the Android library for verification. It is available through a Tor Onion service at `http://madt16agno7zze41166y1xmb41km b72attwfhcmfbspyx35v4e6ut5ad.onion/Log/ListTrees`.

References

1. Aryan, S., Aryan, H., Halderman, J.A.: Internet censorship in Iran: a first look. In: 3rd USENIX Workshop on Free and Open Communications on the Internet (FOCI 2013), Washington, DC, USA. USENIX Association (2013). https://www.usenix. org/conference/foci13/workshop-program/presentation/aryan
2. Barrera, D., McCarney, D., Clark, J., van Oorschot, P.C.: Baton: certificate agility for android's decentralized signing infrastructure. In: WiSec 2014: Proceedings of the 2014 ACM Conference on Security and Privacy in Wireless & Mobile Networks, Oxford, United Kingdom, pp. 1–12. ACM (2014). https://doi.org/10.1145/ 2627393.2627397
3. Basin, D., Cremers, C., Kim, T.H.J., Perrig, A., Sasse, R., Szalachowski, P.: ARPKI: attack resilient public-key infrastructure. In: CCS 2014: Proceedings of the 2014 ACM SIGSAC Conference on Computer and Communications Security, Scottsdale, AZ, USA, pp. 382–393. ACM (2014). https://doi.org/10.1145/2660267. 2660298
4. Chacon, S., Straub, B.: Pro Git, 2nd edn. Apress, Berkeley (2022). https://git-scm.com/book/en/v2
5. Coufalìková, A., Klaban, I., Šlajs, T.: Complex strategy against supply chain attacks. In: 2021 International Conference on Military Technologies (ICMT), Brno, Czech Republic, pp. 1–5. IEEE (2021). https://doi.org/10.1109/ICMT52455.2021. 9502768
6. Cutter, A., Drysdale, D.: Trillian Personalities (2022). https://github.com/google/ trillian/blob/05001d1876f9340e42ba8b839c94e1b79246207b/docs/Personalities. md
7. Di Pierro, M.: What is the blockchain? Comput. Sci. Eng. **19**(5), 92–95 (2017). https://doi.org/10.1109/MCSE.2017.3421554
8. Eijdenberg, A., Laurie, B., Cutter, A.: Verifiable data structures (2015). https:// github.com/google/trillian/blob/30160804ab5203cde4412fe26f55a4149112bd92/ docs/papers/VerifiableDataStructures.pdf
9. F-Droid: Docs - F-Droid - Free and Open Source Android App Repository (2023). https://f-droid.org/docs/. Accessed 23 Jan 2023
10. Google: Certificate Transparency (2023). https://certificate.transparency.dev/. Accessed 23 Jan 2023
11. Google: How Log Proofs Work - Certificate Transparency (2023). https://sites. google.com/site/certificatetransparency/log-proofs-work. Accessed 23 Jan 2023
12. Google: Use Play App Signing - Play Console Help (2023). https://support.google. com/googleplay/android-developer/answer/9842756. Accessed 12 Jan 2023
13. Herr, T., Loomis, W., Scott, S., Lee, J., Schroeder, E.: Breaking Trust - Shades of Crisis Across an Insecure Software Supply Chain (2021). https://www.usenix.org/ conference/enigma2021/presentation/herr
14. Kumar, R., Virkud, A., Raman, R.S., Prakash, A., Ensafi, R.: A large-scale investigation into geodifferences in mobile apps. In: Proceedings of the 31st USENIX Security Symposium (USENIX Security 2022), Boston, MA, USA, pp. 1203–1220. USENIX Association (2022). www.usenix.org/conference/usenixsecurity22/ presentation/kumar

15. Laurie, B., Langley, A., Kasper, E.: RFC 6962: Certificate Transparency (2013). https://doi.org/10.17487/RFC6962
16. Laurie, B., Messeri, E., Stradling, R.: RFC 9162: Certificate Transparency Version 2.0 (2021). https://doi.org/10.17487/RFC9162
17. Mayrhofer, R., Stoep, J.V., Brubaker, C., Kralevich, N.: The Android platform security model. ACM Trans. Priv. Secur. **24**(3), 1–35 (2021). https://doi.org/10.1145/3448609
18. Meiklejohn, S., et al.: Think global, act local: gossip and client audits in verifiable data structures. Computing Research Repository (CoRR) (2020). arXiv:2011.04551. https://doi.org/10.48550/ARXIV.2011.04551
19. Melara, M.S., Blankstein, A., Bonneau, J., Felten, E.W., Freedman, M.J.: CONIKS: bringing key transparency to end users. In: Proceedings of the 24th USENIX Security Symposium (USENIX Security 2015), Washington, DC, USA, pp. 383–398. USENIX Association (2015). https://www.usenix.org/conference/usenixsecurity15/technical-sessions/presentation/melara
20. Merkle, R.C.: A digital signature based on a conventional encryption function. In: Pomerance, C. (ed.) CRYPTO 1987. LNCS, vol. 293, pp. 369–378. Springer, Heidelberg (1988). https://doi.org/10.1007/3-540-48184-2_32
21. Mozilla: Certificate Transparency (2023). https://developer.mozilla.org/en-US/docs/Web/Security/Certificate_Transparency. Accessed 23 Jan 2023
22. Nicas, J., Zhong, R., Wakabayashi, D.: Censorship, surveillance and profits: a hard bargain for Apple in China. The New York Times (2021). https://www.nytimes.com/2021/05/17/technology/apple-china-censorship-data.html. Accessed 23 Jan 2023
23. Nikitin, K., et al.: CHAINIAC: proactive software-update transparency via collectively signed skipchains and verified builds. In: Proceedings of the 26th USENIX Security Symposium (USENIX Security 2017), Vancouver, BC, Canada, pp. 1271–1287. USENIX Association (2017). www.usenix.org/conference/usenixsecurity17/technical-sessions/presentation/nikitin
24. Nordberg, L., Gillmor, D.K., Ritter, T.: Gossiping in CT. Internet-Draft draft-ietf-trans-gossip-05, Internet Engineering Task Force (2018). https://datatracker.ietf.org/doc/draft-ietf-trans-gossip/05/. Work in Progress
25. Steiner, H.C.: Binary Transparency Log for https://guardianproject.info/fdroid (2023). https://github.com/guardianproject/binary_transparency_log. Accessed 23 Jan 2023
26. Syta, E., et al.: Keeping authorities "honest or bust" with decentralized witness cosigning. In: 2016 IEEE Symposium on Security and Privacy (SP), San Jose, CA, USA, pp. 526–545. IEEE (2016). https://doi.org/10.1109/SP.2016.38
27. The MITRE Corporation: Supply Chain Compromise (2023). https://attack.mitre.org/techniques/T1195/. Accessed 23 Jan 2023
28. The Tor Project: Tor Project - Anonymity Online (2023). https://www.torproject.org/. Accessed 07 Feb 2023

DIPSAUCE: Efficient Private Stream Aggregation Without Trusted Parties

Joakim Brorsson$^{(\boxtimes)}$ and Martin Gunnarsson

Lund University, Lund, Sweden
{joakim.brorsson,martin.gunnarsson}@eit.lth.se

Abstract. Private Stream Aggregation (PSA) schemes are efficient protocols for distributed data analytics. In a PSA scheme, a set of data producers can encrypt data for a central party so that it learns the sum of all encrypted values, but nothing about each individual value. Thus, a trusted aggregator is avoided. However, all known PSA schemes still require a trusted party for key generation. In this paper we propose the first PSA scheme that does not rely on a trusted party. We argue its security against static and mobile malicious adversaries, and show its efficiency by implementing both our scheme and the previous state-of-the-art on realistic IoT devices, and compare their performance. Our security and efficiency evaluations show that it is indeed possible to construct an efficient PSA scheme without a trusted central party. Surprisingly, our results also show that, as side effect, our method for distributing the setup procedure also makes the encryption procedure *more efficient* than the state of the art PSA schemes which rely on trusted parties.

Keywords: Private Stream Aggregation · IoT · Privacy

1 Introduction

Internet of Things (IoT) data analytics enable central parties to learn statistics derived from device data. This data is often privacy sensitive, and thus systems must be designed with privacy in mind. Consider for example the concept of smart metering [24] where a central party calculates the sum of readings of household electricity meters in real-time. Disclosing individual readings in real-time reveals a surprisingly high amount of privacy sensitive data about a household [31]. Thus an untrusted central party should not have access to individual data readings. There exist works studying how to centrally derive statistics without revealing individual data points for the case of smart meters [22,25,28]. We are however interested in developing general techniques for IoT data analytics.

Supported by the Wallenberg AI, Autonomous Systems and Software Program (WASP) funded by the Knut and Alice Wallenberg Foundation.
Supported by grant RIT17-0032 from the Swedish Foundation for Strategic Research.

L. Fritsch et al. (Eds.): NordSec 2023, LNCS 14324, pp. 204–222, 2024.
https://doi.org/10.1007/978-3-031-47748-5_12

A known technique for data analytics is *Functional Encryption* (FE) [8], where knowledge of a *functional decryption key* allows function evaluation on encrypted data. For IoT data analytics on privacy sensitive data, the FE subclass of (Decentralized) Multi Client Functional Encryption ((D)MCFE) is particularly interesting, since it defines FE for multiple parties contributing encrypted data for a centralized evaluator. However, IoT devices are often *constrained* [9], *i.e.* they have low computational power and memory, operate over low throughput lossy networks or are battery powered. Even the most efficient DMCFE schemes [2,17,18], which evaluate inner products of encrypted data, are too costly for constrained environments since they rely on bilinear parings or have ciphertext sizes proportional to the number of data producers.

When the evaluated function is specifically a *sum*, one can instead consider Secure Aggregation (SA) [7] and Private Stream Aggregation (PSA) [35].

SA schemes, which are proposed in the context of federated learning, compute the plaintext sum of a set of encrypted vectors, with a focus on *robustness* against frequent client drop-outs (*e.g.* 6–10% drop-outs per summation [6]). The robustness is achieved by introducing *multiple rounds of client interaction and computation* per summation, making SA schemes unfit for constrained devices.

PSA schemes have instead been suggested for IoT data analytics applications which involve constrained devices. PSA schemes also compute the plaintext sum of encrypted values, but instead focus on *efficiency*. As such, they use efficient primitives and avoid client interaction. However, to the best of our knowledge, all known PSA schemes rely upon a *trusted party* during the setup procedure, which includes key generation [3,5,14,20,21,23,27,35–37,39].

We argue that since the purpose of a PSA scheme is to allow an untrusted party to derive statistics without learning anything about individual data points, relying on a trusted party is not in line with the goals of PSA. Such a design erodes trust in a privacy enhancing technology and is particularly engraving for PSA schemes, since their purpose is to avoid a central party with access to individual data. We therefore propose DIPSAUCE, a PSA scheme which does not rely on trusted parties, and which is suitable for constrained devices.

1.1   Contributions

In this paper we (1) introduce a definition for *distributed setup* PSA and its corresponding security model, (2) present DIPSAUCE, the first PSA scheme which does not rely on a trusted party, (3) prove this scheme secure under static corruptions, (4) describe modifications for security under mobile corruptions, (5) demonstrate its efficiency by implementing it on realistic, off-the-shelf devices advertised as being suitable for *e.g.* smart-metering. Since no other PSA scheme is evaluated on realistic devices, we also (6) implement two state-of-the-art PSA schemes [21,39] on the same devices and compare the performance to our scheme. All code and raw data are made publicly available [12,13].

Looking ahead, DIPSAUCE shows a speedup of 78× and 49× respectively compared with the suggestions for a distributed setup in KH-PRF-PSA [21] and

LaSS-PSA [39] for 10000 parties. For the encryption procedure our results show a speedup of 22× compared to KH-PRF-PSA and 50× compared to LaSS-PSA.

1.2   Our Techniques

It is known how to distribute the setup procedure between all n parties (see Sect. 1.3 for details). This is however too costly for constrained devices. Our key innovation is a mechanism which reduces the number of key agreements to $k <<$ n, while still tolerating a high degree $(>> k)$ of corruptions among the parties, and without introducing network overhead. We do this by leveraging a k-*regular graph* of order n where each vertex represents a party in the system. The graph is randomly permuted, and each party is assigned a committee, consisting of the parties represented by its k neighbouring vertices in the randomly permuted graph. Each party then engages in non-interactive pairwise key exchange, *but only has to do so for its committee of the k random neighbours.*

By using a random permutation of a k-regular graph, we guarantee a random committee of the correct size for each user. This further enables us to let the *graph structure* (but not the random permutation of it) be known in advance and stored locally with the parties. Each party can then, instead of expensively obtaining a large random graph over the network, locally derive a random permutation of the graph defined by a single shared randomness seed from an external distributed randomness beacon service [16,19], This results in minimal network overhead which enables a distributed setup on constrained devices.

1.3   Related Work

The current state-of-the-art for PSA schemes are the KH-PRF-PSA [21] and LaSS-PSA [39] schemes. While TERSE [36] measures faster encryption times, these results are not directly comparable with KH-PRF-PSA and LaSS-PSA since they are based on precomputations and only measure the "on-line" time. Similar precomputations can be done for LaSS-PSA and KH-PRF-PSA as well, and the resulting "on-line" stages then consists of a single modular addition, while the TERSE "on-line" stage uses more complex operations. A direct comparison is therefore needed before it can challenge the state-of-the-art.

Notably, both KH-PRF-PSA and LaSS-PSA briefly discuss how to avoid a trusted party by using a distributed setup. Both works propose to adopt the methods of the DMCFE scheme by Chotard et al. [18], where centrally generated keys are replaced with pairwise agreed upon keys between all n parties. These methods are secure under *adaptive corruptions*. However, neither KH-PRF-PSA nor LaSS-PSA have any formal protocol description, security evaluation or efficiency evaluation of the proposal for a distributed setup. As we show in Sect. 4, these methods are too inefficient for constrained environments.

We also note that the approach of securing a distributed setup by pairwise user key agreement is present in SA schemes [7], and that Bell et al. [4] propose a version of the technique which lessens the CPU load by establishing smaller random committees. However, in contrast to our non-interactively generated random permutation of a k-regular graph, Bell et al. resort to users *interactively generating a directed random graph* over the network to provide security against static malicious adversaries. Therefore, their approach does not transfer to PSA schemes, which need to work with constrained network resources. Bell et al. do also propose a version with non-interactive graph generation, but which can only achieve security against a *semi-honest static* adversary.

Let us summarize. State-of-the-art PSA schemes [21,39] sketch distributed setup procedures for PSA schemes, which are possible to prove secure under *adaptive* corruptions, but which are infeasibly inefficient due to high CPU overhead. The state-of-the-art SA scheme [7] also provides a distributed setup, proved secure under *static malicious* corruptions, but which is infeasible for constrained devices due to high network overhead.

Related Concurrent Work. Concurrently to our work, the FLAMINGO SA scheme [29] has proposed to rely on a similar mechanism for non-interactively establishing small random committees. Let us elaborate on the differences between DIPSAUCE and FLAMINGO. DIPSAUCE is a PSA scheme focused on efficiency and suitable for constrained devices. FLAMINGO is an SA scheme focused on dropout resilience and not suitable for constrained devices. Both works rely on a novel strategy where a randomness beacon is used to non-interactively construct a graph with small random committees of neighbours. FLAMINGO establishes a graph by joining 2 of the n vertices with an edge if a random value is below a threshold. DIPSAUCE establishes a graph by permuting a k-regular graph based on a random input. In FLAMINGO, the number of neighbours to a vertex is probabilistic, while in DIPSAUCE each vertex always has k neighbours, which allows a simpler security proof. Our work first appeared on ePrint at the 17:th of February 2023 and [29] later appeared on the 4:th of March 2023. Although we published our work first, to the best of the author's knowledge both works were developed unaware of each other.

2 Preliminaries

Notation: $\lambda \in \mathbb{N}$ denotes the computational security parameter which controls the security level of cryptographic components. A specific party in a scheme is denoted $\mathcal{P}_i$. We use the notation $\vec{a}[i]$ to denote the i'th element of the vector $\vec{a}$. We use $[n]$ as a short hand notation for $\{1, \ldots, n\}$. Let $\mathsf{Perm}(n)$ be the lexicographically ordered set of permutations of $[n]$. We denote the k:th permutation of this set as $\mathsf{Perm}_k(n)$. For any permutation of $[n]$, $\rho_k = \mathsf{Perm}_k(n)$, we denote the value of i:th element in ρ_k as $\rho_k(i)$. We denote a graph as $G = (V, E)$, where V is the set of vertices in the graph and E the set of edges. The set of neighbouring vertices of $v_i \in V$ is denoted $N(v_i)$, and $\vec{J}_i$ denotes the set of all indices of vertices in $N(v_i)$. We denote the floor function of x, *i.e.* the greatest integer less than or equal to x, as $\lfloor x \rfloor$. As a shorthand we sometimes write $(-1)^{(i<j)}$. In this notation $(i < j)$ is the boolean function so that $(-1)^{(i<j)} = (-1)$ when $i < j$ and $(-1)^{(i<j)} = 1$ when $i > j$. The function is undefined for $i = j$.

Private Stream Aggregation: We here give an informal definition of *standard* PSA. A formal definition is available in the full version of this paper [11]. Our notion of *distributed setup* PSA is given in Sect. 3.

In a Private Stream Aggregation scheme PSA = (Setup, Enc, Aggr) an aggregator can learn the sum of the inputs $\{m_1, \ldots, m_n\}$, from a set of parties $\{\mathcal{P}_1, \ldots, \mathcal{P}_n\}$ without learning the individual inputs. The Setup procedure is executed by a trusted party and generates an encryption key for each party, and the aggregation key for the aggregator. The Enc procedure is executed by party $\mathcal{P}_i$, and encrypts input m_i. Then, the aggregator can execute Aggr which outputs the sum of all user inputs. Informally, a PSA scheme is *correct* if the output of Aggr will always be equal to the sum of the inputs, and *secure* if nothing but the sum of the inputs of *honest* users is learned by an adversary.

k-Regular Graphs: A k-regular graph is a graph in which each vertex has exactly k neighbours. It is well known how to efficiently generate regular graphs [30].

Distributed Randomness Beacons: In a Distributed Randomness Beacon (DRB) protocol [16], a set of entropy providers jointly compute *publicly verifiable randomness*. The beacon function, $r = \text{Beacon}(t)$, returns an m-bit near-uniformly random value r at each epoch e. Any party can obtain and verify this randomness, *i.e.* also external parties not part of the randomness generation.

Informally, a secure DRB should be *unpredictable*, *i.e.* the advantage for an adversary predicting r before the epoch e begins should be negligible, *unbiased*, *i.e.* r must be statistically close to an m-bit uniformly random string, and *live*, *i.e.* the probability of no output during each epoch should be negligible. These properties should hold also when a fraction of the entropy providers are corrupt.

Non-interactive Key Exchange: A NIKE scheme, defined in Definition 1, is correct if $\Pr[\text{SharedKey}(\text{pp}, \text{pk}_i, \text{sk}_j) = \text{SharedKey}(\text{pp}, \text{pk}_j, \text{sk}_i)] = 1$. A NIKE scheme is secure against a computationally bounded adversary given $(\text{pp}, \text{pk}_i, \text{pk}_j)$ if it cannot distinguish the output of $\text{SharedKey}(\text{pp}, \text{pk}_i, \text{sk}_j)$ from a random string of the same length. We refer to [18] for a full definition of the security game.

Definition 1 (NIKE). *A Non-Interactive Key Exchange scheme establishes a shared key between two parties and consists of the following algorithms:*
Setup(λ): *On input a security parameter λ, output public parameters* pp.
KeyGen(pp): *On input the public parameters* pp, *output a keypair* $(\text{pk}_i, \text{sk}_i)$.
SharedKey(pp, pk_i, sk_j): *On input the public parameters* pp, *a public key* pk_i *and secret key* sk_j, *deterministically output a shared key* K.

Pseudo-Random Functions: Let $\mathcal{F}$ denote a family of efficiently-computable functions $F_k : X \to Y$ indexed by $k \in K$. The family $\mathcal{F}$ is said to be a (t, ϵ) strong PRF if for every $k \in K$, no adversary $\mathcal{A}$ running in time t can distinguish F_k from a random function $f : X \to Y$. We will denote such a function F_k as PRF_k. Further, $\mathcal{F}$ is *additively* key-homomorphic if $\forall F_{k_i}, F_{k_j} \in \mathcal{F}$, the condition $F_{k_i}(x) + F_{k_j}(x) = F_{k_i+k_j}(x)$ holds. We denote such a function as KH-PRF_k.

Sum-of-PRFs: The sum-of-PRFs technique, first introduced in [15], allows parties $\{\mathcal{P}_1, \ldots, \mathcal{P}_n\}$ to derive the sum of their inputs $\{m_1, \ldots, m_n\}$ without revealing the individual m_i:s from honest users. An adversary who corrupts the aggregator and $m < n - 2$ parties can then only learn the *sum* of the inputs of the honest users. The technique assumes that each pair of users, $\mathcal{P}_i, \mathcal{P}_j$ has a shared secret $K_{i,j}$. To mask its message m_i, $\mathcal{P}_i$ derives $c_i \leftarrow m_i + \sum_{j \in [n] \setminus \{i\}} (-1)^{i<j} \cdot \mathsf{PRF}_{K_{i,j}}(x)$ (note the $(-1)^{i<j}$ notation). Then, the sum of all m_i can be calculated as $\sum_{i=1}^{n} c_i = \sum_{i=1}^{n} m_i$. Summing any set smaller than n of c_i containing at least 2 ciphertexts from honest users will result in a random output.

3   DIPSAUCE

As we show in Sect. 4, the suggestions for distributing the setup in state-of-the-art PSA schemes [21,39] are too inefficient for use on constrained devices. To address this, we now present our protocol for DIstributed setup PSA for Use in Constrained Environments (DIPSAUCE). It takes inspiration from the LaSS-PSA scheme [39, Section 4], but crucially differs by not relying on a trusted party.

Approach: The suggestions for distributing the setup procedures of LaSS-PSA and KH-PRF-PSA use the sum-of-PRFs technique, which works by each party evaluating a PRF once for each party in its *committee*. This committee consists of *all other parties*, and thus its size is $n - 1$. In these schemes, a party is secure against an *adaptive* adversary which corrupts up to $n - 2$ of the committee parties (but not the targeted party itself). While this is a very strong security guarantee, the resulting protocol is rendered too inefficient for practical use (see Sect. 4). The main bottleneck for this inefficiency is the committee size.

Simply shrinking the committee size would make the protocol more efficient, but simultaneously lower the corruption tolerance, sacrificing security. How then to shrink the committee size without also lowering the corruption tolerance? A key insight is that a *static* or *mobile* adversary cannot target devices in a committee for corruption (within an epoch) if it cannot predict what devices constitutes the committee. Using an unpredictable committee of size $k << n$ we can create a more efficient construction, secure in the presence of a *static* or a *mobile* adversary capable of corrupting up to t devices, where $k < t < n$.

The technical novelty of our protocol lays in how it uses a k-regular graph and a randomness beacon to non-interactively and efficiently establish unpredictable committees. The protocol defines each committee using the output of an external distributed public randomness beacon. However, an efficient protocol cannot directly use the beacon output to determine the committees. Sampling n committees of size k and sending this data to the devices would mean sending $\mathcal{O}(nk)$ group elements to each device, which is not feasible for constrained devices or networks. Instead, we first let each device be represented as a vertex in a k-regular graph which is part of the system configuration. Then, a *single* output of the beacon is used to determine a pseudorandom permutation of this graph. The committee of each party is then determined by the k neighbours in the randomly permuted graph. This committee is then used in a *threshold sum-of-PRFs* where each party evaluates a PRF for only k other parties.

Aggregation Output: In line with previous PSA schemes, we consider a definition for PSA which outputs the sum of all plaintexts to the aggregator, *i.e.* we do not strive to achieve differential privacy. In contrast to existing definitions of PSA, no secret key is needed to aggregate the sum of plaintexts. This is a more general definition. If it is a desired system property to allow only one specific party to aggregate, then this property can be obtained by sending the ciphertexts over an encrypted channel to the aggregator, or by including the aggregator among the encrypting parties and letting it encrypt zero without publishing the ciphertext.

3.1   Syntax and Security Model

Assumptions: We assume that all parties have access to a distributed randomness beacon and a Public Key Infrastructure (PKI) assumed to behave correctly, *e.g.* not accepting duplicate keys and verifying knowledge of private keys, etc. While such a PKI is a standard assumption, we note that it is possible to *distributively audit* a PKI for correct behaviour [26]. We also assume that each vertex in G has been assigned an index.

Corruptions: We consider an adversary $\mathcal{A}$ capable of corrupting any party $\mathcal{P}_i$, up to a threshold of t parties. Once a party is corrupt, $\mathcal{A}$ takes control of the execution of that party, meaning that it controls the actions and learns the internal state throughout the execution. The set of corrupt parties is denoted $\mathcal{C}$.

Definition 2 (Distributed Setup Private Stream Aggregation). *A Distributed Setup Private Stream Aggregation (DS-PSA) scheme over $\mathbb{Z}_R$, where $R \in \mathbb{N}$, is defined for a set of parties $\mathcal{P} = \{\mathcal{P}_1, \ldots, \mathcal{P}_n\}$ and a special party called the evaluator $\mathcal{E}$, and consists of the following procedures:*

- Setup$(\lambda, conf)$: *On input a security parameter λ and optional configuration parameters $conf$, the procedure outputs the system parameters* pp.
- KeyGen(pp, i) *On input the system parameters* pp *and the users index in the system, i, output an encryption key* ek_i.
- Enc(pp, ek_i, m_i, l): *On input the system parameters* pp*, an encryption key ek_i, a message m_i and a label l, output an encryption c_i of m_i under* ek_i.
- Aggr$(pp, \{c_i\}_{i \in [n]}, l)$: *On input the system parameters* pp*, a set of n ciphertexts $\{c_i\}_{i \in [n]}$ and a label l, output the sum of all plaintexts, M* (mod R)*.*

Note that, as is often the case in PSA, our scheme returns the sum of the encrypted values modulo R, where R is a system parameter.

We say that a Distributed Setup PSA scheme is *correct* if for all pp $\leftarrow$ Setup$(\lambda, conf)$, m_i, l, $\{ek_i \leftarrow$ KeyGen$(pp, i)\}_{i \in [n]}$, we have:

$$\Pr\left[\mathsf{Aggr}\left(\{\mathsf{Enc}(pp, ek_i, m_i, l)\}_{i \in [n]}\right) = \sum_{i=1}^{n} m_i\right] = 1$$

A DS-PSA scheme is secure if an adversary has a negligible probability of winning the game for Aggregator Obliviousness (AO) in Definition 3.

$$
\begin{array}{|l|}
\hline
\\
\mathsf{AO}_b(\lambda, n, conf, \mathcal{A}) \\
\\
L \leftarrow \emptyset \\
\mathcal{C} \leftarrow \mathcal{A}, s.t. |\mathcal{C}| \leq t \\
\mathsf{pp} \leftarrow \mathsf{Setup}(\lambda, conf) \\
\textbf{for } i \text{ where } \mathcal{P}_i \in \mathcal{P} \setminus \mathcal{C} \textbf{ do} \\
\quad \mathsf{ek}_i \leftarrow \mathsf{KeyGen}(\mathsf{pp}, i) \\
\textbf{end for} \\
\gamma \leftarrow \mathcal{A}^{\mathsf{QEnc, QLeftRight}} \\
\textbf{return } \gamma \overset{?}{=} b \\
\\
\hline
\end{array}
$$

Fig. 1. The AO experiment defining security for a distributed setup PSA scheme.

Definition 3 (Aggregator Obliviousness (AO)). *Security is defined via the game of Aggregator Obliviousness* $\mathsf{AO}_b(\lambda, n, \mathcal{A})$, $b \in \{0, 1\}$ *in Fig. 1.* $\mathcal{A}$ *denotes the adversary with access to the following oracles:*

- QEnc(i, m_i, l^*): *Given a user index* i, *a message* m_i *and a label* l^*, *if* $(i, l^*) \notin L$ *and* $\mathcal{P}_i \notin \mathcal{C}$ *then it lets* $L \leftarrow L \cup \{(i, l^*)\}$ *and returns* $c_i = \mathsf{Enc}(\mathsf{ek}_i, m_i, l^*)$.
- QLeftRight$(\mathcal{U}, \{m_i^0\}_{i \in \mathcal{U}}, \{m_i^1\}_{i \in \mathcal{U}}, l^*)$: *Given a set* $\mathcal{U}$ *of user indices, two sets* $\{m_i^0\}_{i \in \mathcal{U}}$ *and* $\{m_i^1\}_{i \in \mathcal{U}}$, *and a label* l^*, *it checks if* $\forall i \in \mathcal{U} : (i, l^*) \notin L$ *and* $\{\mathcal{P}_i\}_{i \in \mathcal{U}} \cap \mathcal{C} = \emptyset$ *and no previous calls has been made to* QLeftRight. *If further* $\{\mathcal{P}_i\}_{i \in \mathcal{U}} \cup \mathcal{C} = \{\mathcal{P}_i\}_{i \in [n]}$ *it also checks if* $\sum_{i \in \mathcal{U}} m_i^0 = \sum_{i \in \mathcal{U}} m_i^1$. *If all checks return true, it lets* $L \leftarrow L \cup \{(i, l^*)\}_{i \in \mathcal{U}}$ *and returns* $\{c_i\}_{i \in \mathcal{U}}$, *where* $c_i = \mathsf{Enc}(\mathsf{ek}_i, m_i^b, l^*)$.

At the end of the game, $\mathcal{A}$ *outputs a guess,* γ, *of whether* b *equals 0 or 1.*

Static corruptions is modeled by the adversary picking the set $\mathcal{C}$ of at most t corrupt parties at the start of the game. We model *encrypt-once* security, i.e. restricting each party to only encrypt a single message per label (which is the natural usage of the scheme), by both QEnc and QLeftRight maintaining the set L, where they store which label has been used for each user and ignoring any requests which reuse labels. Further, since any party has the ability to aggregate in Definition 2, the QLeftRight enforces that $\sum_{i \in \mathcal{U}} m_i^0 = \sum_{i \in \mathcal{U}} m_i^1$ when all honest users are part of the QLeftRight call. This prevents $\mathcal{A}$ from trivially winning the game by receiving a ciphertext for each honest user and then checking whether the output of Aggr contains $\{m_i^0\}_{i \in \mathcal{U}}$ or $\{m_i^1\}_{i \in \mathcal{U}}$.

This AO-game is similar to the AO-games for LaSS-PSA and KH-PRF-PSA. The main differences are the modeling of corruptions as full party takeovers rather than a key leaking oracle, and the lack of a dedicated aggregator key.

Protocol 1 – DIPSAUCE

Setup($\lambda, conf = \{n, k, time, R\}$):

1: Generate a k-regular graph $G = (V, E)$ where $|G| = n$
2: npp $\leftarrow$ NIKE.Setup(λ)
3: **return** pp $= \{$npp$, n, k, G, time, R\}$

KeyGen(pp, i):

1: $(\mathsf{pk}_i, \mathsf{sk}_i) \leftarrow$ NIKE.KeyGen(npp)
2: Post $(\mathcal{P}_i, \mathsf{pk}_i)$ to the PKI
3: $r \leftarrow$ Beacon($time$)
4: $\rho \leftarrow$ Perm$_r(n)$
5: Let $\vec{J}_i$ be the vector s.t $\forall \vec{J}_i[\ell] = j : v_j \in N(v_{\rho(i)})$, (i.e. the indices of $\mathcal{P}_i$:s neighbors in the permuted graph)
6: **for** $\ell \in \{1, \ldots, k\}$ **do**
7:    $\ell' = \vec{J}_i[\ell]$
8:    Wait until the PKI returns an entry $\mathsf{pk}_{\ell'}$ for $\mathcal{P}_{\ell'}$
9:    $\vec{K}_i[\ell'] \leftarrow$ NIKE.SharedKey($\mathsf{pk}_{\ell'}, \mathsf{sk}_i$)
10: **end for**
11: **return** $\mathsf{ek}_i = (\vec{K}_i, \vec{J}_i)$

Enc(pp, $\mathsf{ek}_i = (\vec{K}_i, \vec{J}_i), m_i, l$):

1: $t_i \leftarrow \sum_{\ell=1}^{k}(-1)^{i < \vec{J}_i[\ell]} \cdot \mathsf{PRF}_{\vec{K}_i[\ell]}(l)$
2: **return** $c_i = (t_i + m_i) \pmod{R}$

Aggr(pp, $\{c_i\}_{i \in [n]}$):

1: **return** $M = \sum_{i \in n} c_i \pmod{R}$

3.2   Construction

The protocol is defined in Protocol 1. It is run with n parties, assigned indexes from 1 to n in an arbitrary fashion (e.g. based on network addresses).

First, the Setup procedure must be executed, and the public parameters distributed to each party. Then, each party can compute its encryption key ek_i in the KeyGen procedure. To do this, party $\mathcal{P}_i$ first generates a keypair and posts the public key to a PKI (line 1–2). It then permutes the k-regular graph based on random beacon output and defines its committee as all parties $\mathcal{P}_j$ where the j:th vertex is a neighbour to the i:th vertex in G (line 3–5). Then, it computes a shared key for each committee member and outputs the PSA encryption key, consisting of the indexes and shared keys for the committee members (line 6–11).

To encrypt a message, $\mathcal{P}_i$ executes the Enc procedure, which outputs the message masked with the value t_i. t_i is computed as a sum-of-PRFs for the i:th committee. In more detail, for each $\mathcal{P}_j$ in the committee, compute the output of the PRF indexed by the shared key between $\mathcal{P}_i$ and $\mathcal{P}_j$, on input the current label. If $i < j$, the output of the PRF is subtracted from the sum. Otherwise it is added. Thus, each time $\mathcal{P}_i$ adds a random value to its masking value, its neighbour $\mathcal{P}_j$, will subtract *the same value* from its masking value.

The Aggr procedure computes the sum of all plaintexts by summing all ciphertexts. This will only work if all ciphertexts are included, otherwise, the masking values will not cancel out.

Correctness: Let us now prove correctness. By definition:

$$\text{DIPSAUCE.Aggr}\left(\{c_i\}_{i \in n}\right) = \sum_{i \in n} c_i = \sum_{i \in n} m_i + \sum_{i \in n} t_i.$$

Since G is k-regular and there exists a one-to-one mapping (bijection) between every vertex v_i and its neighbour set $N(v_i)$, there exist unique indices $i_1, \ldots, i_k$ with $i_j \neq i$ for $j = 1 \ldots, k$, such that $i \in \vec{J}_{i_j}$ for $j = 1, \ldots, k$.

Let i' denote any one of the indices i_j. Since NIKE is correct – that is, since NIKE.SharedKey$(\text{pk}_i, \text{sk}_{i'}) = $ NIKE.SharedKey$(\text{pk}_{i'}, \text{sk}_i)$, we also have:

$$\forall K_i[\ell] : \exists K_{i'}[\ell'] \text{ s.t. } K_i[\ell] = K_{i'}[\ell']$$

Thus DIPSAUCE is correct if NIKE is correct and G is k-regular, since then all $K_i[\ell]$ cancels out during aggregation s.t. $\sum_{i \in n} t_i = 0$.

3.3   Security Analysis

We use a similar proof strategy as LaSS-PSA, originating from Abdalla et al. [1], where we form a hybrid argument from a series of games, where each game changes the definition of the QLeftRight-oracle. Table 1 illustrates the strategy.

The first game, G_0, corresponds to the AO_0-game where QLeftRight queries are answered with the encryption of m_i^0. The last game, G_3, corresponds to the AO_1-game where QLeftRight queries are answered with the encryption of m_i^1. Thus, if the security of the transitions between the games hold, the adversary cannot tell the AO_0-game from the AO_1-game. The transition from G_0 to G_1 consists of adding a *perfect* secret sharing (denoted PSS in Table 1) of zero to the threshold-sum-of-PRFs, so that all t_i are perfectly random without destroying the correctness of the scheme. This transition is justified if the threshold sum-of-PRFs produces t_i so that it is indistinguishable from randomness. Next, consider the transition from G_1 to G_2, where c_i now encrypts m_i^1 instead of m_i^0. This transition is justified since t_i is now perfectly random, and thus an adversary cannot distinguish whether c_i is an encryption of m_i^0 or m_i^1. Finally, the transition from G_2 to G_3 consists of undoing the change made in G_1 (with the same security argument). We arrive at the following theorem.

Theorem 1. DIPSAUCE *is* AO*-secure if* t_i *is indistinguishable from randomness for a computationally bounded adversary except with a negligible advantage.*

Proving the Threshold Sum-of-PRFs Technique. We now prove that t_i is indistinguishable from randomness to a static malicious adversary.

Table 1. Strategy for proving AO-Security. A box marks the change in each game.

Game	Definition of QLeftRight-oracle	Argument
G_0	$t_i \leftarrow \sum_{\ell=1}^{k}(-1)^{i<\vec{J}_i[\ell]} \cdot \mathsf{PRF}_{\vec{K}_i[\ell]}(l)$ $c_i \leftarrow m_i^0 + t_i$	
G_1	$\boxed{t_i' \leftarrow \sum_{\ell=1}^{k}(-1)^{i<\vec{J}_i[\ell]} \cdot \mathsf{PRF}_{\vec{K}_i[\ell]}(l)}$ $\boxed{t_i \leftarrow t_i' + \mathsf{PSS}(0, i, n - |\mathcal{C}|)}$ $c_i \leftarrow m_i^0 + t_i$	t_i indisting. from rand.
G_2	$t_i' \leftarrow \sum_{\ell=1}^{k}(-1)^{i<\vec{J}_i[\ell]} \cdot \mathsf{PRF}_{\vec{K}_i[\ell]}(l)$ $t_i \leftarrow t_i' + \mathsf{PSS}(0, i, n - |\mathcal{C}|)$ $c_i \leftarrow \boxed{m_i^1} + t_i$	one-time-pad info. theo. secure
G_3	$\boxed{t_i \leftarrow \sum_{\ell=1}^{k}(-1)^{i<\vec{J}_i[\ell]} \cdot \mathsf{PRF}_{\vec{K}_i[\ell]}(l)}$ $c_i \leftarrow m_i^1 + t_i$	t_i indisting. from rand.

Proof Outline: We first formalize the security of our building blocks NIKE and sum-of-PRFs in the context of our scheme in Lemmas 1 and 2. Intuitively Lemma 1 states that all NIKE derived keys are private to the negotiating parties, and Lemma 2 states that the sum-of-PRF output, t_i, is secret to an adversary which corrupts all but one out of the parties in a sum-of-PRFs committee. We then, in Theorem 2, consider the DIPSAUCE method, with k-sized committees randomly selected from a population of n parties with a threshold t of corrupt parties. Finally, we conclude with Theorem 3 which formalizes the indistinguishably of t_i as a consequence of the previous theorem and lemmas.

Proof Details: First, we restate the security of NIKE in the context of our scheme, *i.e.* that NIKE keys derived for honest committee members do not leak anything to the adversary. As a consequence of the security of NIKE, Lemma 1 is true.

Lemma 1 (Pseudo-Random Shared Keys). DIPSAUCE.KeyGen *outputs encryption keys* $\mathsf{ek}_i = (\vec{K}_i, \vec{J}_i)$ *s.t each key* $\vec{K}_i[\ell]$ *is indistinguishable from randomness to a computationally bounded adversary when* $\mathcal{P}_i$ *and the committee counterparty* $\mathcal{P}_{\vec{J}[\ell]}$ *(whose index is defined in* $\vec{J}[\ell]$*) are both honest.*

We also restate the security of the sum-of-PRFs technique in our setting. If a key $\vec{K}_i[\ell]$ is (pseudo)-random (*i.e.* when $\mathcal{P}_{\vec{J}[\ell]}$ is honest), the output of $\mathsf{PRF}_{\vec{K}_i[\ell]}(l)$ is also (pseudo)-random. Then since t_i is the sum of all such values, a single honest $\mathcal{P}_j$ renders t_i (pseudo)-random. Thus, an adversary must corrupt all k parties in the committee to learn anything about t_i. We get Lemma 2.

Lemma 2 (Sum-of-PRFs). *An adversary given l and up to $k - 1$ entries in* $\vec{K}_i$ *has a negligible advantage in distinguishing* $t_i = \sum_{\ell=1}^{k}(-1)^{i<\vec{J}_i[\ell]} \cdot \mathsf{PRF}_{\vec{K}_i[\ell]}(l)$ *from randomness.*

By relying on just Lemma 2, security can only hold against an adversary corrupting up to $t = k - 1$ parties. We therefore transfer from the standard sum-of-PRFs technique to our threshold version. Theorem 2 states that for a random committee, an adversary corrupting up to t parties has a negligible chance to corrupt *all* k committee members of a user with these t corruptions.

In the proof, we first argue that the permutation of the graph is pseudorandom. Then, as a stepping stone, we consider the advantage of an adversary guessing the committee of a *specific* party. Intuitively, if each committee is random, a static adversary's best strategy is to randomly guess the k users in the committee. Finally we put an upper bound on the advantage when attempting to guess the committee of *any* honest user, and fully prove the security of the scheme, by considering an adversary which attempts to learn *any* t_i.

Theorem 2 (Incorruptible Committee). DIPSAUCE.KeyGen *outputs* $\mathsf{ek}_i = (\cdot, \vec{J}_i)$ *s.t a static adversary allowed to corrupt up to t parties, $k < t < n$, has a negligible probability in guessing $\vec{J}'$ s.t. $|\vec{J}'| = k$ and $\forall j \in \vec{J}' : j \in \vec{J}_i$, for some i.*

Proof. **Graph Pseudorandomness:** The permutation ρ is determined by the output r of the randomness beacon. Since r is thus *unbiased* and *unpredictable* to a static $\mathcal{A}$, it cannot predict anything about ρ except with the negligible advantage Adv_{beacon}. Then, since $|G| = |\rho|$, $\mathcal{A}$ has a negligible advantage in determining which $\mathcal{P}_i$ is associated with which $v_j \in G$.

Incorruptability of Specific Committees: Consider the number of possible k-sized committees and the number of k-sized committees an adversary can form from t random corruptions. The number of unordered sets of size k within the n parties is $\binom{n}{k}$. An adversary allowed to corrupt up to t out of n parties can form $\binom{t}{k}$ sets of k corrupt parties. Thus, the probability of obtaining a *specific* k-sized committee of a specific party when corrupting t out of n parties is $\frac{\binom{t}{k}}{\binom{n}{k}}$.

Incorruptability of Any Committee: An upper bound on the capability to corrupt *all* members in the committee of *any* honest party for a static adversary allowed to corrupt up to t out of n parties can thus be calculated as $n \cdot \frac{\binom{t}{k}}{\binom{n}{k}}$.

Synthesis: In conclusion, the advantage to corrupt all committee members of some party is at most $Adv_{beacon} + n \cdot \frac{\binom{t}{k}}{\binom{n}{k}}$, which is negligible for realistic values of n, t, k (see Appendix A for a discussion on the values of n, t, k).

Since a static adversary cannot corrupt all nodes in a committee (Theorem 2), and the sum-of-PRFs technique is secure when at least one committee member is honest (Lemma 2), t_i is indistinguishable from randomness.

Theorem 3 (t_i Indistinguishability). *In DIPSAUCE.Enc, each t_i is indistinguishable from randomness to a static adversary allowed to corrupt up to t parties except with a negligible advantage.*

3.4 Security Against a Mobile Adversary

Let us sketch a version of DIPSAUCE which is secure against a *mobile* adversary.

Modelling Mobile Security. We model mobile security according to Ostrovsky and Yung [32], allowing corruptions and uncorruptions as follows.

Epochs: Time is divided into consecutive *epochs* indexed by a counter.

Corruptions: A mobile adversary is allowed to corrupt any party $\mathcal{P}_i$. The adversary must make its selection of corrupt parties *before* an epoch is started, but will gain no information from the corrupt parties *until* that epoch is started. An adversary can additionally *uncorrupt* (leave) a corrupted party. When doing so, the adversary retains all knowledge of secrets learned from that party, but has no further control and learns no further secrets. The total number of corrupt parties at the start of an epoch can never exceed t. In this model all parties can be corrupt during some stage of the protocol execution, but the adversary learns secrets from at most t parties during each epoch.

Mobile Security with a PKI. We can trivially achieve mobile security by discarding all secrets and re-executing the Setup and KeyGen procedures at the start of an epoch. Since the Setup and KeyGen procedures are efficient in DIPSAUCE, this modification is feasible in practice. There is a caveat to this though. For brevity we have so far omitted how the PKI trust relation is achieved, *i.e.* how the PKI verifies that a public key actually belongs to the claimed identity. However, when secrets are deleted at the end of an epoch, any secret related to the trust relation with the PKI will also be destroyed. This is necessary to prevent a mobile adversary from using this secret to impersonate previously corrupt parties. How then to maintain a relation with the PKI in between epoch changes?

Ostrovsy and Yung describes two methods of maintaining such trust relations. In the first method, the device is assumed to be able to store a secret key that cannot be learned by an adversary corrupting the device. This can be realized using a Trusted Platform Module (TPM) [38] or trusted execution techniques that provide secure storage [33].

The second method consists of updating keys by generating a new key-pair and posting the new public key signed with the previous secret key. While an adversary can also post a new key signed with the previous key, the system will notice that two such public keys have been published and thus consider the device compromised. This assumes that the adversary cannot suppress messages.

We can thus obtain mobile security for DIPSAUCE as follows. Divide the execution of the protocol into a *setup* phase comprised of the Setup and KeyGen procedures, and an *operational* phase comprised of any number of Enc and Aggr procedures. When an epoch ends, each party erases all secrets except the PKI relation secret and then enters the setup phase once the next epoch begins. In this phase, it awaits the system parameters output from the Setup procedure.

It then calls the KeyGen procedure (using one of the PKI relation maintaining methods described above) to generate new secrets. This concludes the setup phase, and initiates the operational phase. We arrive at the following.

Theorem 4 (Informal). *Let there be a scheme so that the PKI will not accept more than one $(\mathcal{P}_i, pk_i)$ for each $\mathcal{P}_i$. Further, let there be at least one fresh output from the randomness beacon every epoch. Then the above transformation of* DIPSAUCE *is secure against a mobile adversary, corrupting up to t parties.*

4   Experimental Evaluation

In this section we evaluate the performance of DIPSAUCE by implementing it on realistic hardware and measuring its performance. The current state-of-the-art schemes KH-PRF-PSA and LaSS-PSA were only evaluated on Intel i5 CPUs in [21, 39], giving little insight into how these schemes perform on realistic hardware. For a fair comparison, we have therefore also implemented these schemes and their suggestions for distributing the setup on the same realistic hardware. The code and raw data from our experiments are available at [12] and [13].

4.1   Scenario and Experiments

Scenario: n *Clients* measure a statistic, *e.g.* power, and wants to send the sum of the measurements to a *Server*, without revealing individual measurements.

Setup: We have implemented the protocols on CC1352 devices with ARM Cortex M4 processors, utilizing their hardware acceleration of AES, ECC and SHA256. These devices can be considered "mid-range" constrained devices, as they are classified as C3 devices in [10], and are advertised as being suitable for smartmetering. Further details on CC1325 is given in the full version of this paper [11].

Experiments: We evaluate the client side efficiency of LaSS-PSA, KH-PRF-PSA and DIPSAUCE by measuring the execution time of the Enc and Setup + KeyGen procedures. For Enc, time is measured from the start of the procedure until the ciphertext is ready to be transmitted. No network overhead is measured for Enc, since all schemes return ciphertexts as random numbers in $\mathbb{Z}_R$ and thus have equivalent network overhead. For Setup+KeyGen, time is measured from the start of the process, including the time needed to transfer data, such as keys, over the network. In the experiments in [21,39], the number of clients (*i.e.* n) tested are groups of 1000 to 10000 clients in even increments of 1000. Our tests are done for $n = 1024, 2025, 3025, 4096, 5041, 6084, 7056, 8100, 9025$ and 10000. These sizes are selected to be comparable with previous work, while remaining compatible with requirements in our specific implementation of the DIPSAUCE protocol, which has additional requirements on the group sizes as explained in Sect. 4.2. Each experiment was repeated 10 times for each group size. Our results are the average of these runs.

4.2   Implementations

DIPSAUCE. We have implemented the graph G as a rook's graph. As a consequence all n must be square numbers and $k = 2\sqrt{n-1}$. We remark that this is an implementation property, and that regular graphs for other k, n can be efficiently generated [30]. The KeyGen procedure is straightforwardly implemented according to Protocol 1, using a Python based PKI with a CoAP [34] interface, instantiating Beacon as the Drand service [19], and instantiating NIKE as ECDH on the P-256 curve. The Enc instantiates the PRF using AES-128. Both AES-128 and ECDH P-256 utilizes the hardware acceleration of the CC1352 platform.

KH-PRF-PSA and **LaSS-PSA.** We here give details on security parameters, chosen instantiations of primitives, and hardware acceleration. For all details on these schemes and our implementations, see the full version of this paper [11].

KH-PRF-PSA: We have implemented the KH-PRF-PSA scheme in [21, Sec. 4] and their proposal for a distributed setup in [21, Sec. 5.1]. The implementation uses security parameters $\lambda = 2096$, $q = 2^{128}$ and $p = 2^{85}$. In [21], KH-PRF-PSA uses a hash based KH-PRF, instantiated as SHA3-512. For a fair comparison, we however select a more efficient hash function, SHA256, which is hardware accelerated on the CC1352 platform.

LaSS-PSA: We have implemented the LaSS-PSA scheme in [39, Sec. 4] and the proposal for a distributed setup in [39, Sec. 7]. The implementation uses security parameter $\lambda = 128$. We here implement the version which instantiates the PRF using AES-128, since its the most efficient instantiation in the measurements of [39], and is hardware accelerated on the CC1352 platform.

4.3   Results

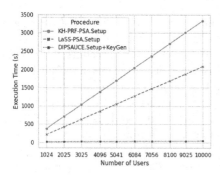

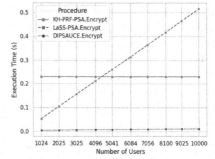

Fig. 2. Setup/KeyGen execution time.

Fig. 3. Encryption execution time.

Setup and KeyGen. Our evaluation shows that DIPSAUCE significantly out-performs the distributed setups proposed in KH-PRF-PSA and LaSS-PSA in terms of execution time for the setup (and keygen) procedure. We show the execution times in Fig. 2. The slope of the graph indicates that DIPSAUCE will have the shortest execution time for all number of users in the system. The execution time of DIPSAUCE grows with the number of users at rate of 3.2 ms per user, a lower rate than KH-PRF-PSA which grows with 330 ms per user and LaSS-PSA which grows with 210 ms per user. This is due to DIPSAUCE only generating $k = 2\sqrt{n-1}$ NIKE shared secrets for n users, rather than n derived secrets as in LaSS-PSA, and LaSS-PSA in turn, being more efficient than KH-PRF-PSA. Compared to LaSS-PSA, DIPSAUCE shows a speedup of 66x.

Encrypt. Our evaluation of the Enc procedures shows that DIPSAUCE outper-form KH-PRF-PSA and LaSS-PSA for all measured number of users in the sys-tem. We show the measured execution times of the encrypt procedure in Fig. 3. LaSS-PSA and DIPSAUCE have execution times linear in the number of users. The execution time of the Enc procedure grows with 0.052 ms per user for LaSS-PSA and with 0.00075 ms per user for DIPSAUCE. The speedup per user of DIPSAUCE compared to LaSS-PSA is 69x.

KH-PRF-PSA shows a constant execution time of 230 ms for any number of users in the system. Thus, it will outperform DIPSAUCE for large numbers of users. Extrapolating from the measured times, this occurs when $n \approx 300000$.

5   Conclusion

In this paper we have showed state-of-the-art PSA schemes and their proposals for a distributed setup, and found them practically infeasible due to computa-tional complexity which grows with the number of users. To address this, we have provided a formal definition of PSA with a distributed setup, suggested a new PSA scheme adhering to this definition, proved it secure and implemented it on realistic hardware. We found its performance sufficient to be deployed in practice. Let us further elaborate on the following discussion point.

Client Failures. In a secure PSA scheme, nothing is learned by the aggregator unless all ciphertexts are included in an aggregation. Therefore, a dropped mes-sage from an honest client will prevent the aggregator from learning anything. We note that there is a general *non-interactive* mitigation to this practical prob-lem [14] for dealing with client errors, which is applicable to *all* PSA schemes including ours. This however increases computational and network costs. Since the setup in DIPSAUCE is efficient, another alternative to deal with client fail-ures can be to exclude failing clients from the protocol and re-execute the setup, if the failures are fairly infrequent.

Acknowledgements. We would like to thank Paul Stankovski Wagner, Elena Pagnin and Christian Gehrmann for valuable discussions of this work.

Appendix

A   Adversary Advantage

The adversary advantage (excluding the potential advantage resulting from the beacon) is calculated as $n \cdot \frac{\binom{t}{k}}{\binom{n}{k}}$ in Theorem 2. Table 2 shows this advantage for realistic n, t and k, where $t = n/2$ and $k = 2\sqrt{n} - 2$) in a rook's graph which is the k-regular graph which was used in our implementation.

Table 2. Adversary advantage in DIPSAUCE with a rook's graph given by $n \cdot \frac{\binom{t}{k}}{\binom{n}{k}}$ for different values of n and a corruption ratio of 0.5.

n	k	t	Advantage
1024	62	512	2^{-55}
2025	88	1012	2^{-78}
3025	108	1512	2^{-99}
4096	126	2048	2^{-117}
5041	140	2520	2^{-131}
6084	154	3042	2^{-144}
7056	166	3528	2^{-156}
8100	178	4050	2^{-168}
9025	188	4512	2^{-178}
10000	198	5000	2^{-188}

References

1. Abdalla, M., Benhamouda, F., Gay, R.: From single-input to multi-client inner-product functional encryption. In: Galbraith, S.D., Moriai, S. (eds.) ASIACRYPT 2019. LNCS, vol. 11923, pp. 552–582. Springer, Cham (2019). https://doi.org/10.1007/978-3-030-34618-8_19
2. Abdalla, M., Benhamouda, F., Kohlweiss, M., Waldner, H.: Decentralizing inner-product functional encryption. In: Lin, D., Sako, K. (eds.) PKC 2019. LNCS, vol. 11443, pp. 128–157. Springer, Cham (2019). https://doi.org/10.1007/978-3-030-17259-6_5
3. Becker, D., Guajardo, J., Zimmermann, K.H.: Revisiting private stream aggregation: lattice-based PSA. In: NDSS. Internet Society, Reston (2018)
4. Bell, J.H., Bonawitz, K.A., Gascón, A., Lepoint, T., Raykova, M.: Secure single-server aggregation with (poly) logarithmic overhead. In: Proceedings of the 2020 ACM SIGSAC Conference on Computer and Communications Security, pp. 1253–1269 (2020)

5. Benhamouda, F., Joye, M., Libert, B.: A new framework for privacy-preserving aggregation of time-series data. ACM Trans. Inf. Syst. Secur. (TISSEC) **18**(3), 1–21 (2016)

6. Bonawitz, K., et al.: Towards federated learning at scale: system design. In: Proceedings of Machine Learning and Systems, vol. 1, pp. 374–388 (2019)

7. Bonawitz, K., et al.: Practical secure aggregation for privacy-preserving machine learning. In: Proceedings of the 2017 ACM SIGSAC Conference on Computer and Communications Security, pp. 1175–1191 (2017)

8. Boneh, D., Sahai, A., Waters, B.: Functional encryption: definitions and challenges. In: Ishai, Y. (ed.) TCC 2011. LNCS, vol. 6597, pp. 253–273. Springer, Heidelberg (2011). https://doi.org/10.1007/978-3-642-19571-6_16

9. Bormann, C., Ersue, M., Keranen, A.: Terminology for constrained-node networks. RFC 7228, RFC Editor (2014). http://www.rfc-editor.org/rfc/rfc7228.txt

10. Bormann, C., Ersue, M., Keränen, A., Gomez, C.: Terminology for Constrained-Node Networks. Internet-Draft draft-ietf-lwig-7228bis-00. Internet Engineering Task Force (2022). https://datatracker.ietf.org/doc/draft-ietf-lwig-7228bis/00/. Work in Progress

11. Brorsson, J., Gunnarsson, M.: DIPSAUCE: efficient private stream aggregation without trusted parties. Cryptology ePrint Archive, Paper 2023/214 (2023). https://eprint.iacr.org/2023/214

12. Brorsson, J., Gunnarsson, M.: Protocol and experiments (2023). https://github.com/Gunzter/DIPSAUCE-contiki-ng

13. Brorsson, J., Gunnarsson, M.: Results and corresponding raw data (2023). https://github.com/Gunzter/practical_psa_results

14. Chan, T.-H.H., Shi, E., Song, D.: Privacy-preserving stream aggregation with fault tolerance. In: Keromytis, A.D. (ed.) FC 2012. LNCS, vol. 7397, pp. 200–214. Springer, Heidelberg (2012). https://doi.org/10.1007/978-3-642-32946-3_15

15. Chase, M., Chow, S.S.: Improving privacy and security in multi-authority attribute-based encryption. In: Proceedings of the 16th ACM Conference on Computer and Communications Security, pp. 121–130. ACM, New York (2009)

16. Choi, K., Manoj, A., Bonneau, J.: SoK: distributed randomness beacons. Cryptology ePrint Archive, Paper 2023/728 (2023). https://eprint.iacr.org/2023/728

17. Chotard, J., Dufour Sans, E., Gay, R., Phan, D.H., Pointcheval, D.: Decentralized multi-client functional encryption for inner product. In: Peyrin, T., Galbraith, S. (eds.) ASIACRYPT 2018. LNCS, vol. 11273, pp. 703–732. Springer, Cham (2018). https://doi.org/10.1007/978-3-030-03329-3_24

18. Chotard, J., Dufour-Sans, E., Gay, R., Phan, D.H., Pointcheval, D.: Dynamic decentralized functional encryption. In: Micciancio, D., Ristenpart, T. (eds.) CRYPTO 2020. LNCS, vol. 12170, pp. 747–775. Springer, Cham (2020). https://doi.org/10.1007/978-3-030-56784-2_25

19. Drand: Drand - a distributed randomness beacon daemon (2022). https://github.com/drand/drand

20. Emura, K.: Privacy-preserving aggregation of time-series data with public verifiability from simple assumptions. In: Pieprzyk, J., Suriadi, S. (eds.) ACISP 2017. LNCS, vol. 10343, pp. 193–213. Springer, Cham (2017). https://doi.org/10.1007/978-3-319-59870-3_11

21. Ernst, J., Koch, A.: Private stream aggregation with labels in the standard model. Proc. Priv. Enhancing Technol. **2021**(4), 117–138 (2021)

22. Gope, P., Sikdar, B.: Lightweight and privacy-friendly spatial data aggregation for secure power supply and demand management in smart grids. IEEE Trans. Inf. Forensics Secur. **14**(6), 1554–1566 (2018)

23. Joye, M., Libert, B.: A scalable scheme for privacy-preserving aggregation of time-series data. In: Sadeghi, A.-R. (ed.) FC 2013. LNCS, vol. 7859, pp. 111–125. Springer, Heidelberg (2013). https://doi.org/10.1007/978-3-642-39884-1_10

24. Kabalci, Y.: A survey on smart metering and smart grid communication. Renew. Sustain. Energy Rev. **57**, 302–318 (2016)

25. Kursawe, K., Danezis, G., Kohlweiss, M.: Privacy-friendly aggregation for the smart-grid. In: Fischer-Hübner, S., Hopper, N. (eds.) PETS 2011. LNCS, vol. 6794, pp. 175–191. Springer, Heidelberg (2011). https://doi.org/10.1007/978-3-642-22263-4_10

26. Laurie, B.: Certificate transparency. Commun. ACM **57**(10), 40–46 (2014)

27. Leontiadis, I., Elkhiyaoui, K., Molva, R.: Private and dynamic time-series data aggregation with trust relaxation. In: Gritzalis, D., Kiayias, A., Askoxylakis, I. (eds.) CANS 2014. LNCS, vol. 8813, pp. 305–320. Springer, Cham (2014). https://doi.org/10.1007/978-3-319-12280-9_20

28. Lyu, L., Nandakumar, K., Rubinstein, B., Jin, J., Bedo, J., Palaniswami, M.: PPFA: privacy preserving fog-enabled aggregation in smart grid. IEEE Trans. Ind. Inf. **14**(8), 3733–3744 (2018)

29. Ma, Y., Woods, J., Angel, S., Polychroniadou, A., Rabin, T.: Flamingo: multi-round single-server secure aggregation with applications to private federated learning. In: 2023 IEEE Symposium on Security and Privacy (SP), pp. 477–496. IEEE Computer Society (2023)

30. Meringer, M.: Fast generation of regular graphs and construction of cages. J. Graph Theory **30**(2), 137–146 (1999)

31. Molina-Markham, A., Shenoy, P., Fu, K., Cecchet, E., Irwin, D.: Private memoirs of a smart meter. In: Proceedings of the 2nd ACM Workshop on Embedded Sensing Systems for Energy-Efficiency in Building, pp. 61–66. ACM, New York (2010)

32. Ostrovsky, R., Yung, M.: How to withstand mobile virus attacks. In: Proceedings of the Tenth Annual ACM Symposium on Principles of Distributed Computing, pp. 51–59. ACM, New York (1991)

33. Pinto, S., Santos, N.: Demystifying arm trustzone: a comprehensive survey. ACM Comput. Surv. (CSUR) **51**(6), 1–36 (2019)

34. Shelby, Z., Hartke, K., Bormann, C.: The constrained application protocol (CoAP). RFC 7252 (2014). https://doi.org/10.17487/RFC7252. https://www.rfc-editor.org/info/rfc7252

35. Shi, E., Hubert Chan, T.H., Rieffel, E., Chow, R., Song, D.: Privacy-preserving aggregation of time-series data. In: Network and Distributed System Security Symposium, NDSS 2011, p. 17 (2011)

36. Takeshita, J., Carmichael, Z., Karl, R., Jung, T.: TERSE: tiny encryptions and really speedy execution for post-quantum private stream aggregation. In: Li, F., Liang, K., Lin, Z., Katsikas, S.K. (eds.) SecureComm 2022. LNICST, vol. 462, pp. 331–352. Springer, Cham (2023). https://doi.org/10.1007/978-3-031-25538-0_18

37. Takeshita, J., Karl, R., Gong, T., Jung, T.: SLAP: simple lattice-based private stream aggregation protocol. Cryptology ePrint Archive, Paper 2020/1611 (2020). https://eprint.iacr.org/2020/1611

38. TCG: TCG TPM specification version 1.2 - part 1 design principles. Technical report, TCG, Beaverton, OR, United States (2011)

39. Waldner, H., Marc, T., Stopar, M., Abdalla, M.: Private stream aggregation from labeled secret sharing schemes. Cryptology ePrint Archive, Paper 2021/081 (2021). https://eprint.iacr.org/2021/081

What is Your Information Worth?
A Systematic Analysis of the Endowment
Effect of Different Data Types

Vera Schmitt[1,2]([✉]) [ID], Daniel Sivizaca Conde[1], Premtim Sahitaj[1,2],
and Sebastian Möller[1,2]

[1] Quality and Usability Lab, Technische Universität Berlin, Berlin, Germany
[2] Speech and Language Technology Lab, German Research Center for Artificial
Intelligence, Kaiserslautern, Germany
vera.schmitt@tu-berlin.de

Abstract. Various smartphone and web applications use personal information to estimate the user's behaviour among others for targeted advertising and improvement of personalized applications. Often applications and web services offer only two choices, either accept their privacy policies or not use the services. Hereby, the general scenario is to *pay* applications and web services with personal data. As privacy policies are lengthy to read and not comprehensible, most users accept the terms and conditions without the awareness of potential consequences. Thus, most users are unaware of continuously being tracked by many applications installed on their smart devices or accept sharing personal data in exchange for using applications and services online. Therefore, this study attempts to shed some light on the willingness to pay for data protection when offered this option in a continuous data-sharing scenario, and the willingness to accept when offered the option to sell personal data to two different data requestors. The study (N = 500) is conducted via crowdsourcing and examines the monetary valuation of users with respect to different data-sharing scenarios and different data types to allow for a more fine-grained analysis of user preferences. Moreover, different influencing factors such as privacy concerns, awareness and intended behaviour are examined in relation to the user's monetary valuation. The results show significant differences between willingness to pay and accept for ten different data types and the two sharing scenarios contributing to further empirical evidence for the *endowment effect*. However, the sharing scenarios seem to have not a big influence on willingness to pay but showed significant differences in willingness to accept. Furthermore, the privacy influencing factors seem to negatively correlate with willingness to pay and positively correlate with willingness to accept.

Keywords: Economics of privacy · usable privacy · privacy literacy · privacy awareness · privacy concern

L. Fritsch et al. (Eds.): NordSec 2023, LNCS 14324, pp. 223–242, 2024.
https://doi.org/10.1007/978-3-031-47748-5_13

1   Introduction

Numerous business models rely on ongoing data collection to generate profits through the use of personal information. Companies like Google and Facebook compel users to continually provide data as a condition of using their services, allowing them to make money by using targeted profiling and advertising [16, 37]. Moreover, an increasing number of companies and organizations participate in the trade of users' personal information, frequently operating in uncertain legal territory when managing the profits resulting from such transactions [36]. Instances of improper management and exploitation of personal information have raised awareness among governments regarding the need to establish regulatory frameworks to safeguard personal data online. The European Union's General Data Protection Directive (GDPR) and the California Consumer Privacy Act (CCPA) are such examples [40], standardizing data privacy laws and increasing people's control over personal data. Whereas the industry sector has assigned monetary values to personal data by using it for various businesses ranging from social media and advertising to improving personalized products. However, the monetary valuation from a user perspective is still an underexplored research domain. For examining the monetary valuation of certain goods from users' perspective the measures Willingness to Pay (WTP) for a certain good and the Willingness to Accept (WTA) money in exchange for the same good [2] is used. In the context of privacy, the users are confronted with an abstract concept of privacy. It is difficult to assess short- and long-term benefits and risks, as the consequences of continuous data sharing remain most often opaque for the users [35]. Previous research has started to consider different sharing contexts when examining the WTP and WTA constructs. However, not much research has been done examining the WTP and WTA valuation for different data types by considering the ambiguity of data-sharing scenarios [28,37,40]. Therefore, this research will take (1) the sharing context and (2) different data types into account to allow for a more fine-grained examination of user monetary valuation of their data.

The following crowdsourcing study is based on the valuation of two different sharing scenarios and ten different data types to allow for a closer examination of users' preferences. Furthermore, various influencing factors, such as privacy concerns, privacy literacy and privacy awareness, are examined. Additionally, different privacy nudges are designed to examine what effect additional information about information collection on smartphones have on privacy concern, privacy awareness and WTP and WTA. Moreover, a detailed analysis is presented to create further evidence for the *endowment effect* in the context of sharing different data types in a continuous data-sharing scenario.

Thus, this study aims to examine the following research questions:

RQ1: Is it possible to explore the *endowment effect* across varying data formats and sharing scenarios?
RQ2: Is there a positive correlation between privacy-influencing factors and higher values for WTP and WTA?

RQ3: Can the use of framing effects, such as privacy nudges, lead to an increase in privacy awareness, WTP, and WTA?

In sum, the contributions of this work are the following: (1) collecting more granular evidence to contribute to the ongoing discussion of the *endowment effect* and *privacy paradox*, (2) the examination of the influence of various privacy influencing factors on the monetary valuation of different data types in different sharing contexts, and (3) provide further empirical evidence for the monetary valuation of privacy in different sharing contexts considering the theory of *contextual integrity*. This paper is organized as follows: first, an overview of related work is given in Sect. 2. In Sect. 3, the methodological background and the study workflow are introduced, and in Sect. 4, the results of the user study are presented. Furthermore, Sect. 5 discusses the limitations of the experiment, and finally, in Sect. 5, we conclude this paper and indicate future research directions.

2 Related Work

Numerous business strategies rely on the continuous collection of data as a means to generate profits from individuals' personal information. Big tech companies, such as Google and Facebook require users to continuously share personal information in exchange for their services, and generate profit from targeted advertising and profiling strategies [16,37]. Moreover, a growing number of businesses and organizations collect, and trade user's personal information. Repeatably, the data collection processes operate in ambiguous legal areas [30,32] while managing the assets obtained from trading personal data [36]. Instances of misuse of personal data have sparked the development of legal frameworks, especially in the European Union, such as the General Data Protection Regulation (GDPR), Data Governance Act (DGA), and Data Act (DA), to safeguard the handling of data shared online [15,40]. The aim of these regulations is to enhance oversight of personal information shared online, but they often lead to complex rules and settings that may not be well-suited to individual users' requirements. Nonetheless, users often demonstrate limited abilities to judge when assessing the advantages and disadvantages of data trading situations, and they may agree to long-term privacy risks in exchange for immediate gains [1]. A primary question regarding privacy regulations and configurations revolves around whether users prioritize and value their privacy [40].

Often, such research inquiries are assessed by examining the importance users attach to their privacy, typically determined through their Willingness to Pay (WTP) for data protection or their Willingness to Accept (WTA) monetary compensation in exchange for their data [2,5,19]. WTP and WTA are the primary metrics used to assess how much users value various goods, and as a result, they have been employed in the field of privacy research [3,8,28,29,31]. Furthermore, numerous earlier investigations have pointed out that the value individuals place on privacy, as determined by their WTA, is significantly higher than their WTP [28,37,40]. This is described as the *endowment effect* and is a well-known phenomenon that offers a potential explanation for the phenomenon of *loss aversion*. *Loss aversion* is a key characteristic of the *prospect theory* [17]. *Prospect theory* describes the tendency of overvaluating possessions. This phenomenon has been observed in numerous empirical studies [2,26,29,33,40]. These studies consistently reveal that participants tend to attribute significantly higher values to WTA in contrast to WTP. While utilizing WTP and WTA metrics to measure the monetary value for products where the impact on the individual's life and risks and benefits can be assessed is straightforward, applying WTP and WTA to scenarios where the effects remain vague and uncertain is considerably less reliable [35,40]. However, the use of WTP and WTA measures still yields valuable insights into which types of data are more sensitive to users and which data types users are typically more inclined to pay for in order to secure better protection [28]. The primary focus of previous research was on the examination of WTA [26,28]. Thus, one contribution of this research is to provide further empirical evidence on the comparison of WTP and WTA and their association to other privacy constructs. Additional methods have demonstrated promising results when assessing WTP and WTA by employing methods of contingent valuation surveys within a concrete data-sharing situation [28]. When assessing the monetary worth of various data types, the focus has predominantly been on examining location information [26,29,39]. Notably, there have been significant differences in monetary values between WTP WTA, as well as variations across different types of locations. Also, other data types have been empirically examined, but mainly for WTA [28]. Moreover, the association with other privacy constructs, such as privacy literacy and privacy behaviour is still an underexplored research field. The Protection Motivation Theory (PMT) [9] serves as one of the primary theoretical frameworks examining behavioural choices in the data-sharing context. It is derived from the Protection Behavior Theory (PBT) and centres on the protective element of privacy behaviour. PMT posits that individuals are inclined to safeguard themselves against a perceived threat when they believe that the threat is applicable to them, which is known as *threat appraisal*. Additionally, a *coping appraisal* is conducted, wherein individuals evaluate their ability to effectively protect themselves using the available methods (*self-efficacy* and *response efficacy*). If both the threat and coping appraisal are high, motivation to adopt protective behaviour is also high [9,12]. According to the PMT, there is a significant relationship between concern for privacy and protective behaviours, as demonstrated by previous research [7,12]. Furthermore, Furthermore, privacy literacy has been examined in relation to privacy concerns and behaviour and also WTP and WTA, showing positive correlations, especially with WTA [26]. Also, privacy nudges [38] have been examined in relation to privacy awareness, privacy literacy, concern and behaviour [4,18,27]. However, not much research has been done on the influence of privacy nudges in the context of monetary valuation of privacy for different data types and sharing contexts [6]. Thus the different influencing factors will be examined in relation to the monetary quantification of privacy in this study. In the following section, the methodological approach will be described more closely.

3   Methodology

In the following the methodological approach to measure WTP and WTA, the influencing factors and the study design are explained.

3.1   WTP and WTA

Previous studies have demonstrated the effectiveness of discrete choice surveys in assessing WTP and WTA [2,19,28,33,40]. However, WTA has received more attention from the scientific community compared to WTP. The question of how to set an upper limit for monetary values is a significant concern when using discrete choice surveys to evaluate WTP and WTA. Previous studies, as noted by Winegar and Sunstein [40], have raised questions about the appropriateness of not setting an upper limit, as it often leads to unreasonably high values for WTA. On the other hand, WTP seems to be less influenced by the upper limit, regardless of whether it is set or not. To avoid unrealistically high values for WTA in discrete choice surveys, the average WTA values from previous studies [2,19,28,33,40] have been used as a guide to determine a reasonable upper limit for WTA and WTP. An indirect price assessment questionnaire was constructed to assess an ideal price range rather than directly asking participants for an ideal price evaluation [21]. To determine the ideal price range, an indirect price assessment questionnaire was developed, which asked participants to provide both a lower and an upper limit of what they were willing to pay in exchange for their data. By analyzing the upper and lower bounds, the optimal price point could be calculated [20]. Previous research has shown that users may not be able to make a well-informed assessment of the value of their data, making it difficult to calculate the appropriate price. To simplify this process, creating realistic scenarios for data trading has been found to be effective [25,26]. Thus, two different sharing scenarios were created with two well-known data requestors: (1) **Apple:** private data requestor asking for the personal information to mainly use it for improving their services and applications, and (2) **Google:** private data requestor asking for the personal information for selling it to third parties, personalized advertising and improving their services. The data requestors and differences in processing and handling personal related data have been explained to the participants. Furthermore, ten different data types (including the category of all information) have been included in the study design to allow for a more fine-grained analysis of WTP and WTA. The categories have been defined based on previous research [2,28,40]. Within the study, the order of the data types and the sharing scenarios are randomized. Also, the order of WTP or WTA-related questions is randomized.

3.2   Influencing Factors

Further measures are integrated into the experiment to assess the correlation of WTP and WTA values with different dimensions of privacy concern, privacy literacy, privacy awareness, and demographic information. To assess the relation of monetary values with the participants' privacy concerns, the Mobile Users Information Privacy Concern (MUIPC) model was adapted from Xu et al. [41] and extended with further dimensions of the Internet Users' Information Privacy Concern (IUIPC) [22,34]. Overall, three dimensions consisting of ten items were used to measure various aspects of privacy concerns. (1) Control over personal information, (2) awareness about data protection, (3) data collection practices. All questions are answered on a 7-point Likert Scale ranging from 1 (strongly disagree) to 7 (strongly agree). To measure the relation of intended privacy behaviour on WTP and WTA, two dimensions of intended privacy behaviour have been extracted from previous research [7,9,12], namely (1) privacy protection behaviour, measured with ten items and *self-efficacy*, measured with four items. The questions are answered on a 7-point Likert Scale ranging from 1 (strongly disagree) to 7 (strongly agree). Furthermore, privacy literacy is measured by using the *Online Privacy Literacy Scale* (OPLIS) [23] consisting of twenty items covering four dimensions: (1) Knowledge about institutional practices, (2) knowledge about technical aspects of data protection, (3) knowledge about protection strategies, and (4) knowledge about institutional regulations. The number of right answers is summed up over all four dimensions to create the privacy literacy score, where overall, 20 points can be achieved when answering all questions correctly. To assess privacy awareness, different privacy nudges have been designed based on two commonly used apps accessing sensitive information regularly (Google Maps and Amazon Shopping). The permission requests of these apps have been examined over one week following the approach of [14,24]. The permission requests of both apps have been analysed, grouped into different data categories and visualized for the user study. Hereby, *information* and *visualization* framing effects have been used to nudge participants and measure the influence of presented information on the user's privacy awareness and concern. For the experiment, two different nudge types have been designed (1) a plain nudge, not containing any signal colours to emphasise potential dangerous permissions, and (2) a nudge containing signal colours [red, green] to highlight potential dangerous permissions and further information about the necessity of the information requested by the app.

Privacy awareness is hereby measured by five dimensions withdrawn from previous research [10]: (1) perceived sensitivity of personal information, (2) perceived surveillance, (3) perceived intrusion, (4) perceived control over personal information, (5) perceived secondary use of personal information. The questions are answered on a 7-point Likert Scale ranging from 1 (strongly disagree) to 7 (strongly agree).

3.3 Experimental Setup

The experiment was divided into four smaller experiments due to time constraints. Running the study by asking for all the different influencing factors would have increased the length of the study drastically. Thus, in Fig. 1 the workflow of the first three studies is shown, as the studies follow a similar structure. The only difference is the influencing factor included in the respective survey.

Hereby, study 2 (N = 100) included privacy literacy, and study 3 (N = 100) intended privacy behaviour. Throughout all three studies (N = 300) the WTP and WTA experimental part and the privacy concern survey are the same[1].

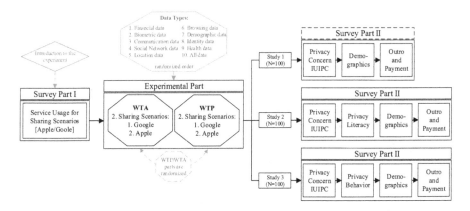

Fig. 1. Workflow of surveys covering WTP/WTA, privacy concern, privacy literacy, and privacy behaviour. This workflow includes three experiments: (1) examining WTP and WTA and privacy concern; (2) examining WTP and WTA and privacy literacy; and (3) examining WTP and WTA and privacy behaviour.

To examine the influence of privacy nudges on WTP, WTA and privacy awareness, another study version (N = 200) has been designed, shown in Fig. 2. Here, the WTP and WTA part and privacy concern questionnaire are the same as in the other study versions, but the privacy nudges and privacy awareness questionnaires are included. This study part is further divided into a control group (N = 100) receiving the plain privacy nudges and an experimental group (N = 100) receiving the colourful nudges and further information on the consequences of data sharing[2].

3.4 Ethical Considerations

The experiment was thoughtfully planned to safeguard the privacy of participants. A distinct personal identifier was generated at the beginning of the study, and only the participants had the ability to regenerate it. As a result, the entire experimental process relied solely on anonymized data about the participants, making it impossible to identify any individuals. The ethics committee of Faculty IV at Technische Universität Berlin granted approval for the experiment without any additional concerns or requirements to address.

---

[1] The HTML files of the experiments and privacy nudges are available open source in the following GitHub repository: https://github.com/veraschmitt/MonVal_Experiment.git.

[2] An example of the nudges for Google Maps can be found in the Appendix A.

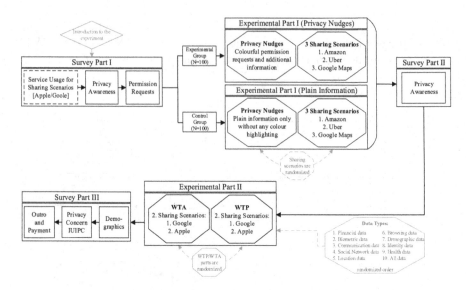

Fig. 2. Workflow of experiment 4 including the privacy nudges and privacy awareness questionnaire. Experiment 4 is split into two experiments with 100 participants each. In the control group privacy nudges are used containing limited information and following a simple design. In the experimental group different framing effects are integrated to examine their influence on privacy awareness.

4   Results

Overall, 500 participants participated in the four studies where 51% of the participants were female, 42% had a university degree, 78% were employees, and 15% stated that they are currently practising in IT-related domains. After a Shapiro Wilk test for all variables in the dataset, no normal distribution is present, and therefore we have to rely on non-parametric tests for the following analysis.

4.1   WTP and WTA Comparison

WTP and WTA for Different Data Types. WTP and WTA is measured in all four studies similarly, thus the WTP and WTA analysis is based on 500 participants. The analysis of the *endowment effect* can also be shown in this study. In Table 1, the different data types are displayed with the respective WTP and WTA values, as well as the results from the Wilcoxon signed-rank test (applying the Benjamini-Hochberg *p-value* correction to avoid α cumulation errors) indicating significant differences between WTP and WTA, indicating that for all data types the *endowment effect* can be observed.

Furthermore, the range is also included in the Table 1 displaying the differences between WTP and WTA is also displayed in Fig. 3. *Financial* and *Health* data are among the highest valued data types which is in line with the findings from [28] for similar data types but only evaluated for WTA. Interestingly, the

Table 1. Differences between WTP and WTA Overall.

Data Type	WTP €	WTA €	Range €	F	p
Financial	6.35	15.77	9.42	5524.5	<.001
Biometric	5.88	13.04	7.16	14545	<.001
Location	5.51	15.31	9.80	4692	<.001
Social Media	6.29	13.58	7.30	13955.5	<.001
Communication	5.61	15.80	7.79	10066.5	<.001
Web Traffic	6.27	15.87	9.60	5285.5	<.001
Demographics	6.12	14.28	8.17	7925.5	<.001
Identity	5.93	15.64	9.71	3885.5	<.001
Health	6.14	14.02	7.88	9137	<.001
All	7.11	14.95	7.85	8080	<.001

All data category is only slightly above the highest WTP values and even below the highest rated WTA category, indicating the sum of WTP and WTA over all data types cannot be taken as a basis for analysing the overall WTP and WTA and needs to appear as a separate category, as implemented in this study.

In addition, in Fig. 4, 5, and 6 the significant differences among the different data types for the respective WTP, WTA and Range analysis are displayed. After running a Kruskal-Wallis Test (with Dunn post-hoc analysis) the data type *All* and *Communication* show significant differences in comparison with all the other data types. Also *Location* significantly differs with most of the other data types. However, the other seven data type seem to be very similar, indicating that the differentiation of data types for WTP might be not so relevant as for WTA. In Fig. 5 the significant differences can be found for more data types where the differentiation might be more useful.

WTP and WTA for Sharing Scenarios. When comparing the monetary valuation for different sharing scenarios with the Wilcoxon signed-rank test (applying the Benjamini-Hochberg *p-value* correction to avoid α accumulation errors), for WTP only two data types have significant differences when comparing Google with the Apple scenario as summarised in Table 2.

Here the mean values are only slightly higher for Apple, indicating that participants would pay significantly more for the protection of their *Biometric* and *Location* data to Apple than to Google.

When comparing WTA for both scenarios (see Table 3, all data types show significant differences. When comparing the means for all data types participants request more money from Apple than from Google in exchange for their data. Overall, from the assessment of the difference between WTP and WTA, it can be observed that when an upper limit is set, the *endowment effect* can be minimized compared to the findings of [40].

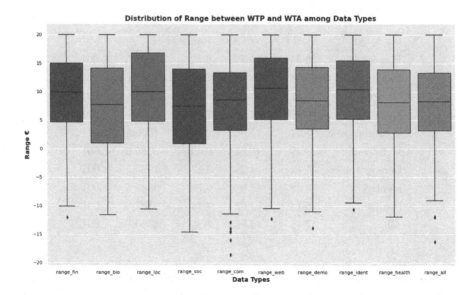

Fig. 3. Distribution of the range (WTA - WTP) among the data types (fin = financial data, bio = biometric data; loc = location information; com = communication data; web = web traffic data; demo = demographic information; ident = personal identity; health = health data; all = mean over all data categories)

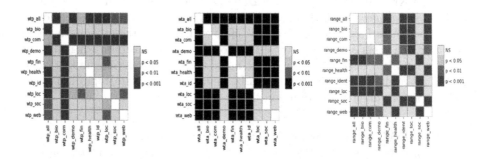

Fig. 4. Significant differences of data types in WTP.

Fig. 5. Significant differences of data types in WTA.

Fig. 6. Significant differences of data types for the range between WTP and WTA.

Table 2. Differences between WTP Google and WTP Apple.

Data Type	WTP G €	WTP A €	F	p
Biometric	6.03	6.66	24661.5	<.001
Location	5.17	5.47	26517.0	<.001

Table 3. Differences between WTA Google and WTA Apple.

Data Type	WTA G €	WTA A €	F	p
Financial	15.59	15.97	4582.5	<.001
Biometric	15.43	15.71	5794	<.001
Location	12.87	13.19	7716	<.001
Social Media	13.11	13.56	7559.5	<.001
Communication	15.14	15.51	5408.5	<.001
Web Traffic	13.52	13.90	7260.5	<.001
Demographics	13.45	13.74	8660.5	<.001
Identity	15.41	15.77	6154.5	<.001
Health	15.69	15.92	5276	<.001
All	17.72	17.83	3539.5	.02

4.2 Influencing Factors

Reliability Analysis of Influencing Factors. The reliability of the privacy constructs needs to be assessed to determine the internal consistency of the constructs. The Cronbach's α coefficient is a statistical tool used to assess the internal consistency or reliability of a group of survey questions. The Cronbach's α coefficient is expressed on a standardized scale of 0 to 1, with higher values indicating greater agreement among the survey items. Therefore, Cronbach's α can be used to quantify the level of agreement among the questions and ensure that they are measuring the intended characteristic effectively [11]. Hair et al. [13] suggest that Cronbach's α coefficient of $\geq.70$ is widely accepted as an adequate level of reliability, but values as low as $\geq.60$ could be considered acceptable in the context of exploratory research. In Table 4 Cronbach's α is displayed for each construct. All privacy dimensions yield acceptable or good (and in two cases excellent) α values, except for one dimension of privacy concern, perceived control (PC1: Control). Removing single items did not result in an improved Cronbach's α, but a Cronbach's α of .64 is still acceptable for exploratory research, and will therefore, be taken into consideration for further analysis. All other constructs can be integrated into the analysis with their respective items, yielding sufficient internal consistency.

Privacy Concern. For the analysis of the association of *Privacy Concern* and WTP and WTA, the responses of only 500 participants can be taken into account as the *Privacy Concern* questionnaire was integrated in all four studies.

Table 4. Reliability Analysis of Influencing Factors.

Influencing Factor	Cronbachs α	Conf. Interval	Reliability
PB: Prot. Beh	0.80	0.74, 0.86	good
PB: Self Efficacy	0.75	0.75, 0.87	acceptable
PC: Overall	0.89	0.87, 0.90	good
PC1: Control	0.64	0.58, 0.69	poor
PC2: Awareness	0.78	0.74, 0.81	acceptable
PC3: Collection	0.85	0.82, 0.87	good
AW: Overall	0.88	0.86, 0.89	good
AW1: Perc. Sensit	0.83	0.79, 0.85	good
AW2: Perc. Surv	0.90	0.88, 0.91	excellent
AW3: Perc. Intr	0.82	0.79, 0.85	good
AW4: Per. Contr	0.79	0.75, 0.81	acceptable
AW5: Second. Use	0.91	0.89, 0.92	excellent

In Fig. 7 the association of *Privacy Concern* shows only small negative correlations (after running Spearmans correlation analysis), whereas in Fig. 8 positive moderate correlations can be seen between *Privacy Concern* and WTA, indicating the more concern participants are the more money they demand in exchange for their personal data.

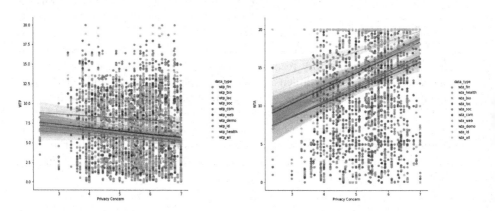

Fig. 7. Correlation between WTP and Privacy Concern displaying all Data Types.

Fig. 8. Correlation between WTA and Privacy Concern displaying all Data Types.

Privacy Behaviour. For the analysis of the association of privacy behaviour and WTP and WTA, the responses of only 100 participants can be taken into account as the privacy behaviour questionnaire was only integrated in study 2.

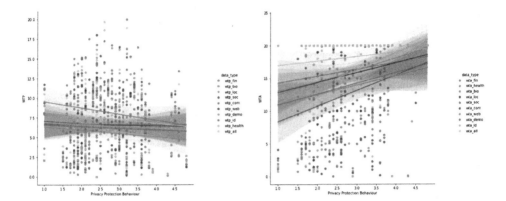

Fig. 9. Correlation between WTP and Privacy Protection Behavior displaying all Data Types.

Fig. 10. Correlation between WTA and Privacy Protection Behavior displaying all Data Types.

In Fig. 9 the association of *privacy Protection Behavior* shows only small negative correlations (after running Spearmans correlation analysis), whereas for the data types *Location Communication* the correlations are more negative but still weak. In comparison to In Fig. 10 we see only positive correlations between *Privacy Protection Behavior* and WTA, showing mostly moderate positive correlations. The differences between WTP and WTA are interesting to examine as we assumed that with higher *privacy Protection Behavior* WTP would also increase, where the opposite is shown. For WTA the correlations are examined as expected, indicating with higher *Privacy Protection Behavior* participants also demand more money in exchange for their different data types.

Privacy Literacy. For the analysis of the association of privacy literacy and WTP and WTA, the responses of only 100 participants can be taken into account as the privacy literacy questionnaire was only integrated into study 3. Similar effects can be observed when comparing *Privacy Literacy* with WTP and TWA. In Fig. 11 the correlations can be observed between *Privacy Literacy* and WTP, where for most data types only a very weak positive correlation can be examined. When comparing it with Fig. 12, again mostly positive moderate correlations can be observed between *Privacy Literacy* and WTA, indicating, with higher *Privacy Literacy* participants demand more money in exchange for their personal data.

Privacy Awareness. To evaluate the influence of the privacy nudges the privacy awareness questionnaire has been asked before and after the nudges have

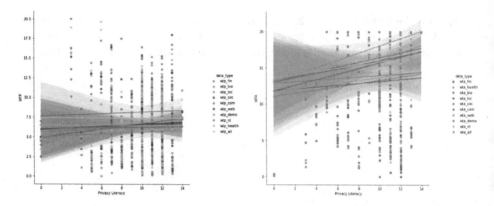

Fig. 11. Correlation between WTP and Privacy Literacy displaying all Data Types.

Fig. 12. Correlation between WTA and Privacy Literacy displaying all Data Types.

been presented. When evaluating the different privacy awareness dimensions for the general influence of privacy nudges without taking the type of nudge into consideration, we can observe a significant difference only for two privacy awareness dimensions (*Perceived Surveillance* an *Perceived Intrusion*), indicating that the nudges do not have a great effect on privacy awareness (see Table 5).

Table 5. Privacy Awareness Before and After the Privacy Nudges.

Awareness Dim.	Mean B	Mean A	F	p
Perc. Surveillance	4.96	5.2	2738.5	.003
Perc. Intrusion	4.94	5.13	2689.5	<.001

However, no significant differences were found for the comparison of the privacy awareness dimensions before the privacy nudges were shown between the experimental and control group, and only the overall privacy awareness score showed significant differences after running a Mann-Whitney U Test (U statistics 4154, $p = .038$, Benjamini Hochberg corrected p-values). Interestingly, the control group had a slightly increased overall awareness (mean = 4.79) in comparison to the experimental group (mean = 4.63).

5   Discussion and Conclusion

In this study, the monetary evaluation of different data types has been examined by applying a discrete choice survey for the evaluation of WTP and WTA. Different privacy constructs have been examined to measure their influence on WTP and WTA. The results of the WTP and WTA comparison types show significant differences for all data types, adding more empirical evidence to the observation of the *endowment effect* [2,28,40]. However, the unreasonable evaluation of WTA examined by [40] could be lowered by introducing an upper limit in the discrete choice survey. The two different sharing scenarios only yielded significant differences for WTA, where participants were requesting more money from Apple in exchange for all their data types in comparison to Google. For WTP significant differences could only be found for two data types, where participants are willing to pay more for their protection to Apple than to Google. Overall, our findings regarding the WTP and WTA comparison validate the ongoing discussion of the *endowment effect* and *loss aversion* when comparing WTP and WTA. The analysis of the privacy concern, literacy, behaviour and awareness with the WTP and WTA assessment did not show the expected results. The correlation analysis sometimes shows counter-intuitive associations between WTP and WTA, whereas the association with WTA is always positively correlated and for WTP negative or not correlated. This indicates that WTA is a more reliable measure for monetary valuation as it is more in line with previous findings of [2,28,40].

Overall, the research questions can be answered as follows:

RQ1: Is it possible to explore the *endowment effect* across varying data formats and sharing scenarios? Significant differences has been detected between WTP and WTA for all different data types, thus the *endowment effect* can be examined. However, only for WTA the sharing scenario showed significant differences among all data types, but only for two data types for WTP.

RQ2: Is there a positive correlation between privacy-influencing factors and higher values for WTP and WTA? Moderate positive correlations can only be observed between all influencing factors and WTA, but not for WTP. Interestingly, WTP shows a moderate or weak negative correlation with privacy concerns, privacy behaviour and privacy literacy. This might indicate, that WTP and WTA need to be examined separately from each other and do not measure the same construct.

RQ3: Can the use of framing effects, such as privacy nudges, lead to an increase in privacy awareness, WTP, and WTA? The privacy nudges did not increase privacy awareness after the nudges had been presented. Only two dimensions of privacy awareness slightly increased for the overall privacy awareness evaluation. The type of nudge did not result in significant differences in the privacy awareness dimensions between the experimental and control groups after the nudge had been presented, indicating that the privacy nudges did not have an influence on privacy awareness.

Finally, the study can confirm effects observed in previous studies in relation to the *endowment effect* and *loss aversion* between WTP and WTA and can also confirm previous findings of the influence of privacy concern on WTA [26]. Overall, when dealing with everyday products, it is typically reasonable to assume that the value of known goods can be measured reliably. However, in the domain of data privacy, this assumption becomes vague. Due to information gaps and cognitive biases, both WTP and WTA metrics are unlikely to serve as reliable indicators of the individual valuation of data privacy [40]. Hence, on their own, the monetary estimates cannot reveal the true net worth of privacy, or monetary value individuals attach to different types of personal information. For future research, the design of the privacy nudges needs to be improved in order to make them more meaningful and expressive.

Appendix

A   Privacy Nudges, Demographics and Relation to Influencing Factors

See Figs. 13, 14, 15, 16, 17, 18 and 19.

Fig. 13. Example of the privacy nudges used in the control group (nudge on the left side) and the experimental group (information nudge and visual nudge on the right side).

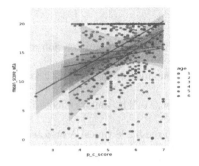

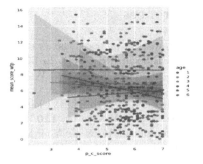

Fig. 14. Correlation between WTA and Privacy Concern with Age Categories.

Fig. 15. Correlation between WTP and Privacy Concern with Age Categories.

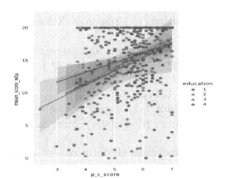

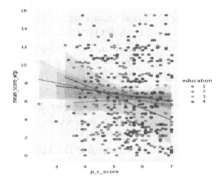

Fig. 16. Correlation between WTA and Privacy Concern with Education Categories.

Fig. 17. Correlation between WTP and Privacy Concern with Education Categories.

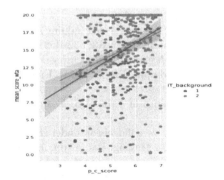

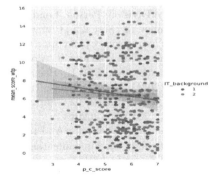

Fig. 18. Correlation between WTA and Privacy Concern with IT Background.

Fig. 19. Correlation between WTP and Privacy Concern with IT Background.

References

1. Acquisti, A., Grossklags, J.: Privacy and rationality in individual decision making. IEEE Secur. Priv. **3**(1), 26–33 (2005)
2. Acquisti, A., Taylor, C., Wagman, L.: The economics of privacy. J. Econ. Lit. **54**(2), 442–92 (2016)
3. Allcott, H., Braghieri, L., Eichmeyer, S., Gentzkow, M.: The welfare effects of social media. Am. Econ. Rev. **110**(3), 629–76 (2020)
4. Almuhimedi, H., et al.: Your location has been shared 5,398 times! A field study on mobile app privacy nudging. In: Proceedings of the 33rd Annual ACM Conference on Human Factors in Computing Systems, pp. 787–796 (2015)
5. Athey, S., Catalini, C., Tucker, C.: The digital privacy paradox: small money, small costs, small talk. Technical report, National Bureau of Economic Research (2017)
6. Barth, S., de Jong, M.D., Junger, M., Hartel, P.H., Roppelt, J.C.: Putting the privacy paradox to the test: online privacy and security behaviors among users with technical knowledge, privacy awareness, and financial resources. Telematics Inform. **41**, 55–69 (2019)
7. Baruh, L., Secinti, E., Cemalcilar, Z.: Online privacy concerns and privacy management: a meta-analytical review. J. Commun. **67**(1), 26–53 (2017)
8. Bizon, W., Poszewiecki, A.: The willingness to trade privacy in the context of WTA and WTP. Int. J. Trade Econ. Finance **7**(4), 121–124 (2016)
9. Boerman, S.C., Kruikemeier, S., Zuiderveen Borgesius, F.J.: Exploring motivations for online privacy protection behavior: insights from panel data. Commun. Res. **48**(7), 953–977 (2021)
10. Correia, J., Compeau, D.: Information privacy awareness (IPA): a review of the use, definition and measurement of IPA (2017)
11. Cronbach, L.J.: Coefficient alpha and the internal structure of tests. Psychometrika **16**(3), 297–334 (1951). https://doi.org/10.1007/BF02310555
12. Fleming, P., Bayliss, A.P., Edwards, S.G., Seger, C.R.: The role of personal data value, culture and self-construal in online privacy behaviour. PLoS ONE **16**(7), e0253568 (2021)
13. Hair, J., Black, W., Babin, B., Anderson, R.: Multivariate Data Analysis: Pearson College Division. Person, London (2010)
14. Hatamian, M., Serna, J., Rannenberg, K.: Revealing the unrevealed: mining smartphone users privacy perception on app markets. Comput. Secur. **83**, 332–353 (2019)
15. Hatamian, M., Wairimu, S., Momen, N., Fritsch, L.: A privacy and security analysis of early-deployed COVID-19 contact tracing Android apps. Empir. Softw. Eng. **26**, 1–51 (2021). https://doi.org/10.1007/s10664-020-09934-4
16. Jones, C.I., Tonetti, C.: Nonrivalry and the economics of data. Am. Econ. Rev. **110**(9), 2819–58 (2020)
17. Kahneman, D., Tversky, A.: Prospect theory: an analysis of decision under risk. In: Handbook of the Fundamentals of Financial Decision Making: Part I, pp. 99–127. World Scientific (2013)
18. Kroll, T., Stieglitz, S.: Digital nudging and privacy: improving decisions about self-disclosure in social networks. Behav. Inf. Technol. **40**(1), 1–19 (2021)
19. Li, X.B., Liu, X., Motiwalla, L.: Valuing personal data with privacy consideration. Decis. Sci. **52**(2), 393–426 (2021)
20. Lieberman, M.: Pricing research: a new take on the Van Westendorp model. Quirk's Mark. Res. Rev. **2**, 1–5 (2015)

21. Lipovetsky, S., Magnan, S., Zanetti-Polzi, A.: Pricing models in marketing research (2011)
22. Malhotra, N.K., Kim, S.S., Agarwal, J.: Internet users' information privacy concerns (IUIPC): the construct, the scale, and a causal model. Inf. Syst. Res. **15**(4), 336–355 (2004)
23. Masur, P.K., Teutsch, D., Trepte, S.: Entwicklung und validierung der online-privatheitskompetenzskala (OPLIS). Diagnostica **63**, 256–268 (2017)
24. Momen, N., Hatamian, M., Fritsch, L.: Did app privacy improve after the GDPR? IEEE Secur. Priv. **17**(6), 10–20 (2019)
25. Poikela, M., Kaiser, F.: 'it is a topic that confuses me'-privacy perceptions in usage of location-based applications. In: European Workshop on Usable Security (EuroUSEC) (2016)
26. Poikela, M., Toch, E.: Understanding the valuation of location privacy: a crowdsourcing-based approach. In: Proceedings of the 50th Hawaii International Conference on System Sciences (2017)
27. Pötzsch, S.: Privacy awareness: a means to solve the privacy paradox? In: Matyáš, V., Fischer-Hübner, S., Cvrček, D., Švenda, P. (eds.) Privacy and Identity 2008. IAICT, vol. 298, pp. 226–236. Springer, Heidelberg (2009). https://doi.org/10.1007/978-3-642-03315-5_17
28. Prince, J., Wallsten, S.: How much is privacy worth around the world and across platforms? In: TPRC48: The 48th Research Conference on Communication, Information and Internet Policy (2020)
29. Schmitt, V., Li, Z., Poikela, M., Spang, R.P., Möller, S.: What is your location privacy worth? Monetary valuation of different location types and privacy influencing factors. In: Proceedings of the 16th ACM Conference on Security and Privacy in Wireless and Mobile Networks, pp. 19–29 (2023)
30. Schmitt, V., Nicholson, J., Möller, S.: Is your surveillance camera app watching you? A privacy analysis. In: Arai, K. (ed.) SAI 2023. LNNS, vol. 739, pp. 1375–1393. Springer, Cham (2023)
31. Schmitt, V., Poikela, M., Möller, S.: Willingness to pay for the protection of different data types (2021)
32. Schmitt, V., Poikela, M., Möller, S.: Android permission manager, visual cues, and their effect on privacy awareness and privacy literacy. In: Proceedings of the 17th International Conference on Availability, Reliability and Security, ARES 2022. Association for Computing Machinery, New York (2022). https://doi.org/10.1145/3538969.3543790
33. Sindermann, C., Yang, H., Yang, S., Elhai, J.D., Montag, C.: Willingness to accept (WTA), willingness to pay (WTP), and the WTA/WTP disparity in Chinese social media platforms: descriptive statistics and associations with personality and social media use. Acta Physiol. (Oxf) **223**, 103462 (2022)
34. Smith, H.J., Milberg, S.J., Burke, S.J.: Information privacy: measuring individuals' concerns about organizational practices. MIS Q. **20**(2), 167–196 (1996)
35. Solove, D.J.: The myth of the privacy paradox. Geo. Wash. L. Rev. **89**, 1 (2021)
36. Spiekermann, S., Acquisti, A., Böhme, R., Hui, K.L.: The challenges of personal data markets and privacy. Electron. Markets **25**(2), 161–167 (2015). https://doi.org/10.1007/s12525-015-0191-0
37. Tang, Y., Wang, L.: How Chinese web users value their personal information: an empirical study on WeChat users. Psychol. Res. Behav. Manag. **14**, 987 (2021)
38. Thaler, R.H., Sunstein, C.R.: Nudge: The Final Edition. Yale University Press (2021)

39. Toch, E., et al.: Empirical models of privacy in location sharing. In: Proceedings of the 12th ACM International Conference on Ubiquitous Computing, pp. 129–138 (2010)
40. Winegar, A.G., Sunstein, C.R.: How much is data privacy worth? A preliminary investigation. J. Consum. Policy **42**(3), 425–440 (2019). https://doi.org/10.1007/s10603-019-09419-y
41. Xu, H., Gupta, S., Rosson, M.B., Carroll, J.M.: Measuring mobile users' concerns for information privacy (2012)

Defenses and Forensics

Towards Generic Malware Unpacking: A Comprehensive Study on the Unpacking Behavior of Malicious Run-Time Packers

Thorsten Jenke[✉], Elmar Padilla, and Lilli Bruckschen

Fraunhofer FKIE, Zanderstraße 5, 53177 Bonn, Germany
{thorsten.jenke,elmar.padilla,lilli.bruckschen}@fkie.fraunhofer.de

Abstract. The presence of packing techniques in malicious software remains a significant obstacle in malware analysis. Consequently, numerous research efforts have emerged with the objective of developing a generic methodology to unpack malware. However, these unpacking methodologies often rely on assumptions about the capabilities of packers. These assumptions include factors such as the origin of memory sources, code-writing techniques used to fulfill packing capabilities, the number of packing layers used, the persistence of code within memory, and the clear distinction between packer and malware code. In our paper, we aim to advance the state-of-the-art by addressing these underlying assumptions associated with malware unpacking. Based on these assumptions, we formulate five research questions to be addressed in a study on the packer capabilities found in a real-world Windows malware and clinical data set consisting of off-the-shelf packers. The answers deduced from our study demonstrate that the majority of common generic unpacking methodologies in the literature show significant blind spots, with the notable exception of the Renovo methodology and its derivatives.

1 Introduction

In 2022, 96,987,253 new distinct malware samples were identified [5]. Examining each one of them manually is very time-consuming, so an automated analysis system is desirable. This figure is inflated due to packers introducing polymorphism into malware and does not reflect the number of functionally unique samples [9,19]. According to the number of known unique malware families, this figure is likely between 454 [22] and 2908 [15]. Therefore, removing this polymorphism by unpacking the samples would significantly reduce the problem and is therefore desirable. With our work, we are aiming to aid the development of unpackers by addressing typical assumptions that are used in common implementations at the moment.

In order to tackle the packer problem, numerous unpackers have been developed. However, due to the high number of new samples every year, creating a specific unpacker for each of them or for each particular packer is not feasible. Therefore, the development of a generic unpacker that can handle a large

L. Fritsch et al. (Eds.): NordSec 2023, LNCS 14324, pp. 245–262, 2024.
https://doi.org/10.1007/978-3-031-47748-5_14

number of different samples is desirable. Current generic unpacking prototypes use a variety of assumptions to observe the sample's behavior, waiting for the unpacking to finish, and extracting the unpacked code once or multiple times in a loop [7,16,20,21,23,27,33]. This methodology leverages the fact that code has to be in its unpacked form in memory in order to get executed.

Therefore, the unpacker needs to identify the location of the written memory bytes and has to be aware of the sample's write operations. This leads to the first assumption that a generic unpacker needs to make: Should it limit itself to specific memory locations, e.g. only new allocations or sections that were created when the image was loaded, or should it invest more resources to not limit itself? The same is true for the type of memory writes the unpacker needs to look for. To make matters more complicated, malware authors can leverage multiple layers [11], or code waves, of packing [18,37] or overwrite previously written code [37]. Thus, general unpackers need to make the choice whether they want to invest resources to be aware of such processes or deem them to be nonsignificant. Lastly, it was shown [37] that there are types of samples for which the entire unpacked code is never in the memory all at once. This goes against the common assumption that there is a clear difference between malware and packer code.

The answers to those questions differ between different implementations of generic unpackers that are currently discussed in the literature. Furthermore, to our knowledge, there has so far been no study of the behavior of malware samples with packer functionality in the context of those assumptions. This is problematic as it limits the number of educated choices during development and increases the likelihood of blind spots. For example, a generic unpacker that searches for packing functions that can be separated from malicious functionality might be blind to samples that show interwoven behavior. However, if there is not a significant number of samples with interwoven behavior, searching for them would unnecessarily slow down the unpacker, potentially limiting its use cases.

In this paper, we aim to provide guidelines for developers of generic unpackers by creating a study about the behavior of malware with packer functionality in the context of the assumptions mentioned above. More formally, we want to answer the following research questions:

RQ1 Which sources are used by malware to obtain memory for unpacking?
RQ2 Which functions and/or techniques are used by malware to write malicious code?
RQ3 What is the ratio between malware whose entire code is available at the end of the execution and the remaining malware?
RQ4 How many unpacking stages are typically used?
RQ5 Is it feasible to differentiate between packing and malicious functionality?

To this end, we used 3714 samples from the real-life data set Malpedia [30] and 2931 samples of the off-the-shelf packer data set dataset-packed-pe [2] (Packed-PE) to conduct a study using our program to monitor the code and memory writes executed from malware samples. Malpedia is a manually curated data set striving to contain a representative of every version of every malware family without the polymorphism introduced by packers. Packed-PE strives to include samples of every available off-the-shelf packer. The results of the study and the ensuing answers to the research question are the contributions of this paper.

2 Related Work

In this section, we give an overview of the current knowledge of packer behavior and elate our research questions to the methods of common generic unpackers.

2.1 Packer Behavior Surveys

Muralidharan et al. [29] provide a comprehensive overview of malware packing in general. They elaborate on the different types of packers by enumerating different packing techniques, off-the-shelf packers, and their distribution in the wild. They also give an overview of different packer identification and detection techniques among other things.

There are also several programs to statically detect the packer used in the outer layer, such as PEiD [3] or Exeinfo PE by ASL [1]. They utilize different signature data bases to detect packers.

An extensive survey on the behavior of packers was conducted by Ugarte-Pedrero et al. [37]. They suggest that there are six types of packers. The first three types describe the topology of the unpacking layers. The first type is characterized through a singular tail jump, which is a transition between two unpacking layers without the second unpacking layer giving control back to the first layer. The second type describes packers with multiple tail jumps in a row, and the third type is more complex topologies. Types four and five are distinguished by the location of the 'malicious code'. They have used a series of metrics to distinguish between 'malicious code' and 'packer code'. Type six is a packer that encrypts and decrypts the packed code as needed.

2.2 Unpacking Heuristic

In the research of packers and unpackers, several different unpacking heuristics have been proposed.

One possible unpacking heuristic is called Hump-And-Dump [35]. It is based on the idea that unpacking utilizes big loops, and therefore the execution of big loops is a strong indicator for them. However, the malware might instead utilize functions like the LoadLibrary family of functions for unpacking, so no big loops are being executed by the malware.

Other heuristics are based on the assumption that API calls such as NtTerminateProcess or NtCreateUserProcess signal that the packing has concluded or that a new process is launched with the unpacked malware inside [27]. Though these API-traced heuristics can be circumvented by the malware [24].

The write-then-execute heuristic manifests the idea that code must be written in order to be executed and has already shown promising results [16, 23, 37]. It is a very generic principle and makes no assumptions about the properties of the malware.

2.3   Generic Unpacker Designs

During our literature survey, we found 9 different generic unpacking designs, each with different assumptions about packer behavior. These differences motivated the creation of this work. The unpackers are described below, with respect to their answers to our research questions, and summarized in Table 1.

Polyunpack [33] (2006) uses a mixture of static and dynamic analysis to find the original entry point (OEP). It is compatible with all possible memory locations (RQ.1) and write operations (RQ.2). It assumes that there is only one unpacking layer (RQ.3) without overwrites (RQ.4), as well as a clear divide between malware and packer code (RQ.5).

Omniunpack [27] (2007) observes executions and memory writes at page-level (RQ.1) granularity and determines the singular extraction point with a heuristic based on API calls and an AV scanner (RQ.2). Its methodology assumes that there are multiple transitions before the malware is unpacked (RQ.3). It is unaware of code overwrites (RQ4) and assumes a distinction between malware and packer code (RQ.5).

Renovo [23] (2007) uses emulation and shadow memory to determine the unpacking state of every byte in the system. It extracts modified bytes every time a written byte is executed and is therefore compatible with any memory location (RQ.1) and any write operation (RQ.2). It assumes multiple transitions (RQ.3) and malware overwrites during unpacking (RQ.4), as well as no clear distinction between the packer and malware functionality of a given sample (RQ.5). **Renovo** also represents **EtherUnpack** [16] (2008) and **Malwise** [9] (2012), as they are modified reimplementations of Renovo. **CoDisasm** [8] (2015) and **PinDemonium** [14] are also grouped under Renovo, since they use a very similar method based on PIN [26].

Eureka [34] (2008) uses different heuristics based on API calls and bigram analysis to unpack samples. It is compatible with any memory location, as it dumps the entire process image (RQ.1) and all possible write operations (RQ.2). It assumes multiple transitions (RQ.3), no overwrites (RQ.4), and a clear divide between malware and packer code (RQ.5).

Pandora's Bochs [7] (2008) uses introspection based on Bochs to perform unpacking. It assumes that the unpacked code is in the image section (RQ.1) and compatible with any kind of write operation (RQ.2). It also takes multiple transitions into account (RQ.3), as well as overwrites during execution (RQ.4), and sees malware and packer code as indistinguishable (RQ.5).

Coogan et al.'s unpacking methodology [12] (2009) extracts the unpacking method statically and executes it outside of its binary. It is compatible with any memory location (RQ.1), assumes only direct access to memory (RQ.2), only one transition (RQ.3), no overwrites (RQ.4), and a distinction between malware and packer code (RQ.5).

Jeong et al. [21] (2010) proposed an unpacking methodology that involves an entropy analysis to determine the state of the unpacking every time a basic block ends. It assumes that the malware unpacks in sections allocated during the loading of the image (RQ.1) with any kind of write operation (RQ.2). It further assumes that there is only one transition (RQ.3), no overwrites (RQ.4), and that malware and packer code are indistinguishable (RQ.5).

BinUnpack [11] (2018) uses function hooking to find the exact point, when the import address table (IAT) is constructed. They argue that the creation of a new IAT is the point when the malware is fully unpacked and the whole process is dumped. Their method is therefore compatible with any memory location (RQ.1) and write operations (RQ.2), assumes multiple transitions (RQ.3), no overwrites (RQ.4), and that malware and packer code cannot be distinguished (RQ.5). **BinUnpack** also represents **BareUnpack** [10] (2018) which employs a very similar methodology based on Microsoft Detours [28].

Roamer [20] (2019) observes changes in the memory maps of all processes and dumps new memory regions that meet certain criteria after a set timeout. It assumes that only new allocated memory regions are used (RQ.1), any memory writes (RQ.2), multiple transitions (RQ.3), no overwritten code (RQ.4), and no distinction between malware and packer code (RQ.5).

Table 1. This table presents the findings of our survey on what common unpackers assume about packing behavior. "Any" in the Memory location and Memory Writes columns means that they are able to work with any common techniques and functions used by malware to write code. "New Allocs" describes that the unpacker is only compatible with newly allocated sections. "Only Images" describes unpackers that focus on malware that conduct their unpacking purely within the sections of the loaded image. "Aware" in the Transitions column means that they are aware that there might be multiple transitions. "Unaware" means that it is assumed that there is only one transition. "Aware" in Overwrites means that the unpacker is not aware of whether code is overwritten or not. "Heuristic" describes that the unpacker is aware of overwrites but uses a heuristic to determine the number of transitions. The last column determines whether the unpacker assumes that malware and packer code are the same.

Generic Unpacker	RQ1	RQ2	RQ3	RQ4	RQ5
	Mem. Location	*Mem. Writes*	*Transitions*	*Overwrites*	*M.==P.*
Polyunpack [33]	Any	Any	Unaware	Unaware	No
Omniunpack [27]	Any	Unaware	Heuristic	Agnostic	No
Renovo [23]	Any	Any	Aware	Aware	Yes
Eureka [34]	Any	Any	Aware	Unaware	Yes
Pandora's Bochs [7]	Only Image	Any	Aware	Aware	No
Coogan [12]	Any	only direct	Unaware	Unaware	No
Jeong et al. [21]	Only Image	Any	Unaware	Unaware	No
BinUnpack [11]	Any	Any	Aware	Unaware	Yes
Roamer [20]	New Allocs	Any	Aware	Unaware	Yes

3   Unpacking Model

To answer the research questions, we first need a theoretical model for our findings. Since our study focuses on the exploration of unpacking behavior in malware, we have chosen write-then-execute as our unpacking heuristic. Using such an open heuristic introduces the potential for false positives. We have addressed the identification and mitigation of false positives in the implementation chapter.

At first we introduce the kinds of information that belong to our modified concept of code waves [18], which we call unpacking stages. This information helps establish connections among the unpacking stages, which describe the unpacking behavior conducted by a given sample. This theoretical base is implemented in a program to measure the unpacking behavior of malware, which is described in the subsequent chapter.

3.1   Unpacking Stages

We divide the execution of malware into instances of write-then-execute triggers. At the beginning of the execution, we start with an unpacking stage L and each instance of a write-then-execute introduces a new instance of L. Let L be a tuple of (I, E, W, A) with $I \in \mathbb{N}$ being the identifier of the unpacking stage, E being a set of executed basic blocks, W being a set of addresses w with $w \in \mathbb{N}$ that have been written to, and A being a set of called API functions. A basic block is a linear sequence of code without any control manipulation such as jumps, calls, etc. Every basic block $e \in E$ being a tuple (s, l, I) with $s, l, I \in \mathbb{N}$ being the start address and the length of the executed basic block and the identifier for the unpacking stage that was the last to manipulate at least one byte at an address within the range of the basic block. Every API call $a \in A$ being a tuple $(name, P, r)$ with $name$ being the name of the called function, $P \subset \mathbb{N}$ being the list of the in- and out-parameters with $r \in \mathbb{N}$ being the return value.

An instance of write-then-execute is triggered when an address b is executed with $b \in W$ of the current unpacking stage. As a result, a new empty unpacking layer is created with the basic block associated with b as its first executed basic block. Additionally, repeated execution of basic blocks belonging to previous unpacking stages attributes these blocks to the current unpacking stage. Thus, basic blocks can belong to more than one unpacking stage. Therefore, our definition of unpacking stages differs from the model of unpacking layers [37], because this model arranges its code waves in a graph and encodes the repeated execution of basic blocks as jumps between layers so that every basic block belongs to at most one unpacking layer.

3.2   Packer Tags

We have decided on using a tagging system instead of an exclusive category system. Exclusive category systems demand that there is a mapping from every sample to a single category. Given the abundance of diverse packers, attempting to map each one to a single category necessitates striking a balance between an overly broad classification and an excessively narrow classification. However, being too broad may group together unrelated packers, and being too narrow would result in an escalating number of categories. A tagging system can act like a non-exclusive category system.

A tag always describes the relationship between two unpacking stages. We define a tag as a triple (L_m, L_n, T), with L_m and L_n being unpacking stages and T being a type of tag with

$T \in \{Transition, Share\text{-}Code, Overwrite, Memory\text{-}Source, Memory\text{-}Writer\}$.

Note that L_m can be equal to L_n. The tags *Memory-Source* and *Memory-Writer* are further decorated by the function or technique used. Two unpacking stages that are completely unrelated do not get a tag assigned to them. The complete unpacking behavior of a specific sample can be accurately described by a set of the following tags.

Transition describes the transition from L_m to L_n. As mentioned above, this unpacking stage intuitively says that the 1st unpacking stage executes a byte it had previously written and, therefore, introduces the L_n.

Share-Code shows that the two unpacking stages L_m and L_n share unaltered code. This indicates a strong functional and programmatic relationship between the two unpacking stages.

Overwrite indicates that L_n has been partially or completely overwritten by a later or the same stage L_m. Multiple stages can overwrite the same stage. However, the initial stage is excluded from this, because the overwritten code from the initial stage can be replicated from the image file and, therefore, does not need to get unpacked. Therefore, it indicates whether all stages of the code are available at the end of the execution.

Memory-Source states the source of the memory in which the code of L_n resides. The source describes the way the handle to the writable memory has been obtained. However, this only describes that L_m gained the handle on a memory section that is used by either L_m or at a later stage to write and execute the code of L_n.

Memory-Writer describes the writing relationship between L_m and L_n. L_m has written the entirety or parts of L_n. For every *Memory-Writer* there exists only one *Memory-Source* but each *Memory-Source* may have multiple *Memory-Writes*.

4   Implementation

In this section, we describe the technical implementation of the model described in Sect. 3. The implementation is used to describe the unpacking capabilities of a given sample and is used for the study on the packer capabilities to answer the posed research questions.

As described in Sect. 3.1, the implementation needs to be able to record memory writes, executed code, and API calls. This requires insight into the execution of the malware. There are several ways of achieving this through static or dynamic analysis. While it is possible to use static analysis, not all code is available before and possibly during the unpacking process. Therefore, we have chosen an approach based on dynamic analysis.

The fastest way employs a debugger which steps through the program. However, not only do various methods exist to detect and circumvent a debugger, but also single stepping through a program or setting the correct breakpoints is very time-consuming. Introspection approaches are generally more covert and harder to detect than debuggers.

Therefore, we have chosen the emulation introspection framework PANDA [17] to implement our program using PyPanda [13] due to its popularity and stable API. PANDA is based on QEMU and directly ties into the execution of it.

4.1 Behavior Recording

As described in Sect. 3.1, we need to record the executed *basic blocks, written memory addresses*, and API calls. Executed *basic blocks* and *written memory addresses* are monitored through callbacks provided by PANDA. We decided to implement our system for the x86 Intel architecture, since we found that only 6.49% of the Windows executables uploaded to Malware Bazaar [4] from February 2020 until March 2023 are 64bit executables.

The callbacks for the *memory writes* and *basic blocks* each produce log lines containing the current process-id, thread-id, an indicator to which callback has produced the log line, and the current program counter. The log lines associated with the *memory writes* also contain the address of the write, the length of the written data, and the written data. The log lines produced by the *basic block* callbacks contain the base address and the size of the basic block.

We have found that the extensive use of callbacks is detrimental to the run time of the analysis. Since we want to achieve good performance for our program, we have chosen to implement several optimizations. First, we limit the recording to the processes of interest. To this end, we utilize the callback of PANDA which is executed every time the CR3 register changes. The CR3 register contains the current Address Space ID (ASID), which is an indicator of the currently active process. Therefore, callbacks are only activated when the ASID indicates that a process of interest is being executed. The PIDs of the processes of interest are gathered in a watch list. The original malware process is initially added to this list. Additional processes are deemed 'of interest' and their PIDs are added to the list if they are launched by the malware or a process injection is performed. PIDs are removed from the list when a process on that list terminates. An empty watch list ends the analysis rather than waiting for the timeout to expire.

Second, callbacks are deactivated when a big loop is being executed as an evasion technique, as described by Lita et al. [25]. To this end, a hash map is created containing a counter each for every written memory address and executed basic block counting the number of writes and executions. Anytime one of the counters reaches a certain threshold, the respective callback is deactivated. To determine whether we have left the big loop, we utilize the basic block translation callback by PANDA. This callback ties directly into the way QEMU [6], which

PANDA is based on, executes code. To emulate code, QEMU divides it into basic blocks and translates these into tiny code, which is a platform-independent code. Then this code is compiled and run directly on the host machine. To ensure efficiency, every basic block is translated once and stored in a lookup to limit the need for redundant translations. Therefore, the translation of basic blocks serves as an indicator that novel code has been executed, indicating that the big loop has been exited. So, the translation of code flushes the hash maps and reactivates deactivated callbacks.

For the last aspect, we record the API functions by utilizing PANDA's hooks2 framework. Deactivating Address Space Layout Randomization (ASLR) enables us to recognize called API functions by their addresses. Therefore, we created lookups of both addresses using APIScout [31] and function signatures for the API functions that are relevant for malware unpacking. From this information, a hook is created for each relevant function. These hooks read the input parameters of its function and create a second hook that breaks on the return address which is read from the stack. The second hook reads both the output parameters and the return value of the function, before removing itself. In case a function is called that has the potential to alter the memory map of the process, a list of all loaded modules with their names, base addresses, and sizes is also logged. With this, all important recordings for the unpacking stage L have been described.

Lastly, the analysis starts with the execution of the malware inside the emulated operating system and runs for a predetermined amount of time. When the operating system first switches context into the malware process, it is recognized by the name of the process and activates the callbacks. Also, the process' PID is added to the monitored watch list, as mentioned above.

4.2   Generating Unpacking Stages

To create an unpacking stage, the log file is first read line by line. Each write operation, executed basic block, and API call by the malware is attributed to the current unpacking stage. Since the unpacking stage should be limited to the actual malicious code and not include libraries, all write operations, executed blocks, and API calls performed by a library are discarded. The discarding is based on whether the program counter contained in that log line is within the range of a loaded library. However, the library might have been modified by the malware either on disc or in memory, in which case the operations are not discarded as long as they are within the modified ranges of the library. This not only allows us to distinguish the direct addressing of memory locations by malware from those by libraries but also to detect code caves [36]. Furthermore, this reduces false positives triggered by libraries due to the generic write-then-execute heuristic.

But there is also the possibility of libraries performing unpacking tasks on behalf of the malware, e.g. RTLDecompressBuffer. Therefore, we need to identify the functions that malware uses to unpack. To achieve this, a whitelist of functions has been iteratively generated by tagging every executed basic block with its associated memory location and source. When the source of a basic block could not be determined, the sample was manually debugged to identify the source of the memory for the untagged basic block. The function is added to the whitelist and it is then checked whether our system is able to attribute the source to the basic blocks. This ensures that the diverse methods that are at the disposal of malware are accounted for and that a warning is generated in case new methods are developed to quickly detect them. However, this method is not able to record unpacking behavior conducted using return oriented programming.

So whenever a new basic block is executed which has been previously written to by the same unpacking stage, a new unpacking stage is created. All subsequent memory writes, executions, and API calls are attributed to the new unpacking stage, as described in Sect. 3.1. In case the analysis involves more than one process, this approach is parallelized to accommodate each process. The result of this analysis is a sequence of unpacking stages.

4.3   Generating Packer Tags

The unpacking stages are organized in a list, and consecutive stages are tagged with a *Transition* tag. A nonempty intersection between the sets of executed blocks of two unpacking stages triggers a *Share-Code* tag. Analogously, a nonempty intersection between the sets of the write operation of a later stage and executed code of an earlier unpacking stage triggers an *Overwrite* tag. The *Memory-Writer* tag is triggered by a non-empty intersection between the sets of write operations of an earlier stage and executed code of a later unpacking stage. The *Memory-Source* tag is applied through the generation or usage of memory from an earlier unpacking stage in which the executed basic blocks of a later unpacking stage reside.

The result is a set of tags that describes the unpacking behavior of the malware.

4.4   Limitations

Our methodology assumes that the code is executed at the point where it has been written. Unfortunately, this is not the case with interpreted languages, for example, those that use a custom bytecode representation for their code. Some malware is written in .NET [30], which employs a byte code and JIT compilation. Therefore, our methodology is not compatible with .NET malware.

To utilize PyPanda for our experiments, we had to employ runtime optimizations, as mentioned above. These optimizations may lead to imprecise results, e.g., that certain memory writes are not recorded or that overlapping code between two unpacking layers is not fully recorded. For example, it may happen that a layer is overwritten by a previous one but when memory-write callbacks are deactivated, these overwrites are not recorded by the system. However, this imprecision does not have a major impact on the central statements of our results, since they only involve the quantity of overwritten and overlapping code between two unpacking stages and therefore have no influence on the binary nature of the *Overwrite* and *Share-Code* tags.

The general problems of sandboxing malware also apply, like the malware detecting that it is running inside PANDA and henceforth altering its behavior.

5   Study

In this section, we present our study using the implementation of Sect. 4 of the unpacking model described in Sect. 3. This study aims to gain a comprehensive understanding of the packer capabilities of malware by exploring the tags assigned to the samples. We begin by introducing our real-world data set, followed by a description of the experimental setup. Using this information, we answer the previously posed research questions and assess the unpacking methodologies on their generality.

5.1   Data Set

We desire two data sets, one consisting of a diverse set of in the wild malware and a clinical data set consisting of a diverse range of off-the-shelf packers. The in the wild data set needs to meet the prudent practices described by Rossow [32] and Plohmann [30]. It needs to encompass a wide array of different actors and families in order to have a realistic picture of the usage of off-the-shelf packers and particularly custom packers in the wild. In this way, we remedy the effect that most packer studies use data sets made up of well-known and documented packers, as mentioned in [29]. Therefore, we have chosen Malpedia [30]. It is a manually curated data set that aims for representativeness by covering as many malware families as possible while limiting itself to one unique version of an unpacked sample. To enhance reproducibility, Malpedia is organized in a GIT repository. The commit of our data set is `a272e8b71`. We used all 3714 32bit executable samples from Malpedia. A first investigation of the data revealed that 435 (11.71%) of the samples are composed using the .NET framework. Since our methodology is not compatible with such samples, we have decided to exclude them from the data set to not compromise the integrity of the results. Also, 382 (10.29%) of the samples have been removed due to not being able to run inside the VM or not finishing the analysis step. Furthermore, we have removed 48 (1.29%) of the samples because we were unable to fully describe the memory sources or writers. Therefore, the curated data set consists of 2897 samples. Our system was able to detect unpacking behavior in 1206 samples (41.63%).

In addition to Malpedia, we also desire a clinical data set comprised of off-the-shelf packers to compare it with. So, we can differentiate which behavior is replicable with goodware packed in off-the-shelf packers in a clinical setting and which can be observed in the wild. To this end, we have decided to use dataset-packed-pe [2] (short: Packed-PE) as the clinical data set. The commit used is `d64d90d`. We used 2931 samples from Packed-PE. Analogously to Malpedia, we removed 119 (4.06%) .NET samples, 254 (8.67%) broken runs, and 16 (0.55%)

not fully described samples from the data set. Lastly, we were able to detect unpacking behavior in 2001 (78.23%) samples.

5.2 Setup

We have used twelve instances of our tool simultaneously and have chosen a timeout of ten minutes. The virtual machines had 2 GB of RAM and the operating system was Windows 7 on i386 architecture. Although Windows 7 is relatively old and its user base has migrated to newer versions, Windows 7 still has very high compatibility with new and older malware.

5.3 Results

To present our findings, we first explore the *Memory-Source* tags.

Memory-Source: Our findings are presented in Table 2. Note that each technique and function is counted only once per sample rather than being counted across all unpacking stages. The most commonly used memory sources are image sections and memory sections allocated with VirtualAlloc. In Malpedia 797 and 794 samples exhibited this behavior respectively, while in Packed-PE there were 1699 and 456 samples.

Additionally, there are samples in Malpedia leveraging various heap functions. Allocating memory on the heap is a very common and safe way of allocating memory. However, some malware also use code caves, with 80 samples in Malpedia and 111 in Packed-PE. Also 63 samples in Malpedia utilize the stack, which has not been observed in the Packed-PE samples. Another notable technique is the usage of LoadLibrary functions. Here, the malware first writes or modifies a DLL file on the hard drive, before loading that DLL with LoadLibrary and, therefore, fulfilling the write-then-execute metric. It can also be seen that the number of different techniques is much less diverse, with only 7 different techniques in the off-the-shelf packers and 18 in Malpedia.

In conclusion, the answer to **RQ.1** is that malware uses all kinds of memory sources, with the image sections and the new sections of VirtualAlloc being the most prominent. Other possible techniques are rather rare, however, a true generic unpacker has to be compatible with all kinds of different memory sources. This shows that Roamer [20], Jeong et al. [21], and Pandora's Bochs [7] have blind spots in their methodology.

Memory-Writer: In this segment, we dive into the functions and techniques employed by malware to write code.

The results are presented in Table 3. In analogy to the above, the techniques are counted once for each sample. Directly accessing memory, with 1119 samples in Malpedia and 2001 samples in Packed-PE, emerges as the most popular method in our study. This means that no Windows function has been used to write the code. Therefore, directly accessing memory is very common for

Table 2. This table shows the sources used by samples from our datasets to gain access to a memory region.

Used Memory Source	Malpedia Samples [%]	Packed-PE Samples [%]
image	66.09	84.91
VirtualAlloc	65.84	22.79
NtMapViewOfSection	27.61	19.84
RtlAllocateHeap	8.79	0.40
NtAllocateVirtualMemory	8.13	0
codecave	6.63	5.55
VirtualAllocEx	5.64	0
stack	5.22	0
LoadLibraryExW	3.90	0
LocalAlloc	3.07	0
LoadLibraryExA	2.49	0
GlobalAlloc	2.40	0.10
HeapCreate	2.07	0.25
LoadLibraryA	1.58	0
malloc	0.58	0
LoadLibraryW	0.58	0
MapViewOfFile	0.41	0
VirtualAllocExNuma	0.08	0

all examined off-the-shelf packers in Packed-PE. It is worth mentioning that some compilers may translate memcpy into a loop that directly accesses memory. Additionally, memcpy is employed by 158 samples in Malpedia and 149 in Packed-PE. This is a significant decrease compared to the direct access to memory. The LoadLibrary usages are also reflected in *Memory-Writer*. The range of techniques employed by off-the-shelf packers is much more limited than in the preceding section, with only four techniques used across the entire Packed-PE data set and seven to ten used in Malpedia.

Our findings in response to **RQ.2** reveal that malware mostly relies on the direct addressing of memory locations when writing code, while the utilization of functions plays a minor role in comparison. However, there is still a significant amount of malware that utilizes API calls to write code. Therefore, unpacking methodologies have to be made aware of both possibilities, or they would be imprecise for a significant amount of samples. This shows that the methodology by Coogan et al. [12] has blind spots for malware using API functions.

Overwrite: In this section, we describe and elaborate on the phenomenon of malware overwriting itself.

Our results are displayed in Table 4. Our data shows that 23.38% in Malpedia and 28.79% in Packed-PE overwrite parts of their executed code during execution. These parts cannot be extracted from the code of the image file.

Table 3. This table shows the functions and techniques used by samples from our datasets to write data that is later executed. The "direct" stands for the direct access to memory.

Used Write Function/Technique	Malpedia Samples [%]	Packed-PE Samples [%]
direct	92.79	100.00
memcpy	13.10	7.45
LoadLibraryExW	3.90	0
LoadLibraryExA	2.49	0
memmove	2.16	0
WriteProcessMemory	1.99	0.10
RtlDecompressBuffer	1.82	0
LoadLibraryA	1.58	0
RtlMoveMemory	1.08	0.50
LoadLibraryW	0.58	0

Table 4. This table shows the amount of samples from our datasets, whose code is overwritten.

Code Overrides	Malpedia Samples [%]	Packed-PE Samples [%]
Yes	23.38	28.79
No	76.62	71.21

This discovery shows that unpacking schemes that unpack malware without taking overwrites into account generate imprecise results for a quarter of the samples, which answers **RQ.3**. This renders the methodologies that employ a singular extraction such as Omniunpack [27], Roamer [20], Eureka [34], BinUnpack [11], and the methodology of Jeong et al. [21] insufficiently generic.

Unpacking Stages: In this section, we investigate the number of unpacking stages utilized in malware. To this end, we present the absolute numerical values and a statistical analysis of the distribution of stages for a comprehensive overview.

In Table 5, it is evident 432 samples (35.82%) in Malpedia and 432 samples (35.82%) in Packed-PE comprise only two layers, making them the simplest group. However, the groups consisting of three and four layers contain 284 (23.55%) and 219 (18.16%) samples for Malpedia and 511 (25.54%) and 395 (19.74%) for Packed-PE. In particular, these groups are nearly equal in size to the group of samples with two layers. On average malware of Malpedia uses 9.15 unpacking stages with the median being at 3.0 and the maximum being at 3120 unpacking stages. Therefore, it is very similar to Packed-PE with a median of 3.0. However, there is no outlier at the maximum, since the average is very close to the median with 3.82, and the maximum is at 487.

The concept of having multiple code waves as described by Bonfante et al. [8] is an integral part of every methodology for a generic malware unpacker. Our answer to **RQ.4** reflects, as it does for **RQ.1** and **RQ.2**, that malware mostly adheres to a set of clear rules and that the unpacking stages are rather limited. However, more complex behavior can be observed in the wild and should therefore be considered. Therefore, Polyunpack [33], the methodology of Coogan et al. [12], and Eureka [34] have significant blind spots in their methodology.

Table 5. Number of unpacking stages per sample.

Number of Unpacking Stages	Malpedia Samples [%]	Packed-PE Samples [%]
2	35.82	44.88
3	23.55	25.54
4	18.16	19.74
5	10.03	0.40
6	5.06	0.30
7	1.16	0.30
8	0.83	0.25
9	0.66	5.80
10	0.50	0.15
11	0.08	0.15
12	0.08	0.10
13	0.17	0
≥ 15	3.90	2.40

Malicious and Unpacking Functionalities: In this section, we take a look at the connections and dependencies of the unpacking and malware functionality of the samples.

To properly evaluate this, we used the *Share-Code* tag, to identify whether malware functionalities are executed during an unpacker stage.

Our argument is that when malicious functionalities are executed during an unpacker stage, it signifies a functional dependency between them. Therefore, there is no clear distinction between the execution point of malicious functionalities and unpacker functionalities, and a distinction between the two is not feasible.

Our findings are displayed in Table 6. It shows that in 979 samples (81.18%) in Malpedia and 1818 samples (90.85%) in Packed-PE no malicious functionalities have been observed during the unpacking stages, while in 227 or 183 samples they were observed. This means that a significant part of our samples showed malicious functionalities during the unpacking stages.

260   T. Jenke et al.

Therefore, with respect to **RQ.5**, we contend that rigid differentiation between malicious and packer code is not a good generalization, as it does not align with the pursuit of research generalizability due to the significant portion of malware not being able to be described by it. Therefore, Omniunpack [27], Polyunpack [33], the methodologies by Coogan et al. [12] and Jeon et al. [21], and Pandora's Bochs [7] are not suitable as generic unpacking methodologies.

Table 6. This table shows the number of samples that displayed malicious functionalities during unpacking stages.

Malicious Functionalities During Unpacking Stages	Malpedia Samples [%]	Packed-PE Samples [%]
No	81.18	90.85
Yes	18.82	9.15

6 Conclusion

The goal of this paper is to push the state-of-the-art of understanding malware unpacking. To do so, we have identified five assumptions that generic unpackers make in order to be compatible with what they expect to be the behavior of the majority of samples. Based on these assumptions, we have posed five research questions to measure their relevancy and correctness and answered them in this study.

For this study, we have introduced five different tags that describe the interactions between two unpacking stages. When applied to a sample, these tags describe the unpacking behavior of that given sample. We have explored the different techniques and functions used by malware to acquire memory and write unpacked code. Furthermore, we have found that a considerable amount of in the wild samples (64.18%) employ more than one unpacking stage and only in three quarters of samples is the entire unpacked code available at the end of the execution. Lastly, we have shown that it is no longer feasible to differentiate between malware and packer code, as there is a significant portion of in the wild samples (18.82%) in which malicious and packer functionalities are so intertwined that a clear distinction has been made impossible.

We found that the unpacking scheme Renovo is the only one that is able to cope with the unpacking behaviors explored in our study. Therefore, we suggest that Renovo should be taken as a basis for future endeavors in generic malware unpacking. However, more research is still needed to address various evasion techniques, such as injection into benign processes used during the unpacking process, to develop a robust generic malware unpacking methodology.

Acknowledgments. We want to thank Sophie Jenke, Martin Lambertz, Daniel Plohmann, Mariia Rybalka, and Nils Weissgerber for their valuable feedback and discussions.

References

1. GitHub - ExeinfoASL/ASL: Free Windows Software—github.com. https://github.com/ExeinfoASL/ASL. Accessed 21 July 2023
2. GitHub - packing-box/dataset-packed-pe: Dataset of packed PE samples—github.com. https://github.com/packing-box/dataset-packed-pe. Accessed 28 July 2023
3. GitHub - packing-box/peid: Python implementation of the Packed Executable iDentifier (PEiD)—github.com. https://github.com/packing-box/peid. Accessed 21 July 2023
4. Malware Bazaar (2023). https://bazaar.abuse.ch/
5. AV-Test GmbH: Malware Statistics, tracking website by AV-Test. https://www.av-test.org/en/statistics/malware/
6. Bellard, F.: QEMU, a fast and portable dynamic translator. In: USENIX Annual Technical Conference, FREENIX Track, California, USA, vol. 41, p. 46 (2005)
7. Bohne, L., Holz, T.: Pandora's Bochs: automated malware unpacking. Master's thesis, RWTH Aachen University (2008)
8. Bonfante, G., Fernandez, J., Marion, J.Y., Rouxel, B., Sabatier, F., Thierry, A.: CoDisasm: medium scale concatic disassembly of self-modifying binaries with overlapping instructions. In: Proceedings of the 22nd ACM SIGSAC Conference on Computer and Communications Security, pp. 745–756. ACM (2015)
9. Cesare, S., Xiang, Y., Zhou, W.: Malwise—an effective and efficient classification system for packed and polymorphic malware. IEEE Trans. Comput. **62**(6), 1193–1206 (2012)
10. Cheng, B., Li, P.: BareUnpack: generic unpacking on the bare-metal operating system. IEICE Trans. Inf. Syst. **101**(12), 3083–3091 (2018)
11. Cheng, B., et al.: Towards paving the way for large-scale windows malware analysis: generic binary unpacking with orders-of-magnitude performance boost. In: Proceedings of the 2018 ACM SIGSAC Conference on Computer and Communications Security, pp. 395–411 (2018)
12. Coogan, K., Debray, S., Kaochar, T., Townsend, G.: Automatic static unpacking of malware binaries. In: 2009 16th Working Conference on Reverse Engineering, pp. 167–176. IEEE (2009)
13. Craig, L., Fasano, A., Ballo, T., Leek, T., Dolan-Gavitt, B., Robertson, W.: PyPANDA: taming the pandamonium of whole system dynamic analysis. In: NDSS Binary Analysis Research Workshop (2021)
14. D'ALESSIO, S., MARIANI, S.: PinDemonium: a DBI-based generic unpacker for windows executables (2016)
15. Plohmann, D., Enders, S.: Malpedia, general Statistics. https://malpedia.caad.fkie.fraunhofer.de/stats/general
16. Dinaburg, A., Royal, P., Sharif, M., Lee, W.: Ether: malware analysis via hardware virtualization extensions. In: Proceedings of the 15th ACM Conference on Computer and Communications Security, pp. 51–62. ACM (2008)
17. Dolan-Gavitt, B., Hodosh, J., Hulin, P., Leek, T., Whelan, R.: Repeatable reverse engineering with panda. In: Proceedings of the 5th Program Protection and Reverse Engineering Workshop, pp. 1–11 (2015)
18. Guizani, W., Marion, J.Y., Reynaud-Plantey, D.: Server-side dynamic code analysis. In: 2009 4th International Conference on Malicious and Unwanted Software (MALWARE), pp. 55–62. IEEE (2009)

19. Haq, I., Chica, S., Caballero, J., Jha, S.: Malware lineage in the wild. Comput. Secur. **78**, 347–363 (2018)
20. Jenke, T., Plohmann, D., Padilla, E.: RoAMer: the robust automated malware unpacker. In: 14th International Conference on Malicious and Unwanted Software (MALWARE), Nantucket, MA, USA, pp. 67–74 (2019)
21. Jeong, G., Choo, E., Lee, J., Bat-Erdene, M., Lee, H.: Generic unpacking using entropy analysis. In: 2010 5th International Conference on Malicious and Unwanted Software, pp. 98–105. IEEE (2010)
22. Joyce, R.J., Amlani, D., Nicholas, C., Raff, E.: MOTIF: a large malware reference dataset with ground truth family labels. arXiv preprint arXiv:2111.15031 (2021)
23. Kang, M.G., Poosankam, P., Yin, H.: Renovo: a hidden code extractor for packed executables. In: Proceedings of the 2007 ACM Workshop on Recurring Malcode, pp. 46–53. ACM (2007)
24. Kawakoya, Y., Shioji, E., Iwamura, M., Miyoshi, J.: API chaser: taint-assisted sandbox for evasive malware analysis. J. Inf. Process. **27**, 297–314 (2019)
25. Liță, C.V., Cosovan, D., Gavriluț, D.: Anti-emulation trends in modern packers: a survey on the evolution of anti-emulation techniques in UPA packers. J. Comput. Virol. Hacking Tech. **14**, 107–126 (2018)
26. Luk, C.K., et al.: Pin: building customized program analysis tools with dynamic instrumentation. ACM SIGPLAN Not. **40**(6), 190–200 (2005)
27. Martignoni, L., Christodorescu, M., Jha, S.: OmniUnpack: fast, generic, and safe unpacking of malware. In: 2007 Twenty-Third Annual Computer Security Applications Conference, ACSAC 2007, pp. 431–441. IEEE (2007)
28. Microsoft: Microsoft detours. https://github.com/microsoft/Detours. Accessed 02 May 2022
29. Muralidharan, T., Cohen, A., Gerson, N., Nissim, N.: File packing from the malware perspective: techniques, analysis approaches, and directions for enhancements. ACM Comput. Surv. **55**(5), 1–45 (2022)
30. Plohmann, D., Clauss, M., Enders, S., Padilla, E.: Malpedia: a collaborative effort to inventorize the malware landscape. In: Proceedings of the Botconf (2017)
31. Plohmann, D., Enders, S., Padilla, E.: ApiScout: robust windows API usage recovery for malware characterization and similarity analysis. J. Cybercrime Digit. Invest. **4**, 1–16 (2018). https://journal.cecyf.fr/ojs/index.php/cybin/issue/view/5
32. Rossow, C., et al.: Prudent practices for designing malware experiments: status quo and outlook. In: Proceedings of the 33rd IEEE Symposium on Security and Privacy (S&P), San Francisco, CA (2012)
33. Royal, P., Halpin, M., Dagon, D.: PolyUnpack: automating the hidden-code extraction of unpack-executing malware. In: ACSAC, pp. 289–300 (2006)
34. Sharif, M., Yegneswaran, V., Saidi, H., Porras, P., Lee, W.: Eureka: a framework for enabling static malware analysis. In: Jajodia, S., Lopez, J. (eds.) ESORICS 2008. LNCS, vol. 5283, pp. 481–500. Springer, Heidelberg (2008). https://doi.org/10.1007/978-3-540-88313-5_31
35. Sun, L.: Hump-and-dump: efficient generic unpacking using an ordered address execution histogram. In: 2008 2nd International Computer Anti-Virus Researchers Organization (CARO) Workshop (2008)
36. Szor, P.: The Art of Computer Virus Research and Defense: Art Comp Virus Res Defense _p1. Pearson Education, London (2005)
37. Ugarte-Pedrero, X., Balzarotti, D., Santos, I., Bringas, P.G.: SoK: deep packer inspection: a longitudinal study of the complexity of run-time packers. In: 2015 IEEE Symposium on Security and Privacy, pp. 659–673. IEEE (2015)

A Self-forming Community Approach for Intrusion Detection in Heterogeneous Networks

Philipp Eichhammer[1]([⊠])(iD) and Hans P. Reiser[1,2](iD)

[1] University of Passau, Passau, Germany
pe@sec.uni-passau.de, hansr@ru.is
[2] Reykjavik University, Reykjavik, Iceland

Abstract. Detecting intrusions in modern network infrastructures is challenging because of the growing size and, along with it, the increasing complexity of structure. While several approaches try to cope with those challenges, few address problems arising from heterogeneity and changes within those infrastructures.

We present a self-forming community approach that integrates federated learning (FL) with distributed intrusion detection systems based on anomaly detection. It autonomously separates the anomaly detection models into communities at runtime with the goal of mutual information exchange using FL techniques to improve detection accuracy. Community formation is realized via the introduction of a similarity score between each pair of models, indicating which models would profit from aggregation. Through a re-evaluation of the similarity score during runtime, changes in the deployed infrastructure can be considered, and the communities adapted. Our experiments show our approach reported no false alarms when evaluated with a real-world dataset and an intrusion detection rate of up to 97%.

Keywords: collaborative IDS · federated learning · anomaly detection

1 Introduction

Intrusion detection systems (IDSs) play an essential role in securing network infrastructures against attacks and unwanted access [2,6]. However, modern infrastructures have grown significantly in size, complexity, and heterogeneity. This evolution, particularly exemplified by the Internet of Things (IoT) and edge computing, renders conventional, standalone IDSs inadequate to manage the size and complexity. Collaborative intrusion detection systems (CIDSs) have emerged as a solution in which several *sensors* and one or multiple *analysis units* collaborate and distribute the workload [14]. In centralized CIDSs, all sensors forward data to a single central analysis unit, which creates a single point of failure (SPoF) and a bottleneck. In distributed CIDSs, multiple nodes perform a distributed analysis, mitigating the disadvantages of a centralized approach, but usually at the cost of reduced detection accuracy [14].

Cordero et al. [5] introduced the concept of community-based CIDSs. In their concept, the set of all IDS entities is split into subsets called communities. Within each community, a centralized community head performs the analysis of data from all sensors within that community. This concept provides scalability, and experiments demonstrated the performance with ensemble learning methods. However, the centralized structure inherits the disadvantages of SPoF and limits scalability within communities. Furthermore, the authors propose a randomized approach to community formation, which is simple but potentially leaves a significant gap for improvements. A similar approach improved upon anomaly detection accuracy by forming communities on the set of IoT devices across IoT gateways and incorporating federated learning (FL) strategies [9]. This concept utilizes the similarity of IoT devices, which is defined by an external analysis tool, to aggregate similar anomaly detection models. However, this analysis tool is only applicable to IoT devices and IoT infrastructures in general, so this approach works within the boundaries of fixed and predefined communities, without adaptivity toward other infrastructures.

With this paper, we focus on research questions that address the main issues of the state of the art of community-based CIDS:

1. *How to autonomously form communities in a way beneficial for detection accuracy?*
2. *How to adapt the communities to changes within the observed infrastructure during runtime?*

To address the above research questions, we propose a novel concept of self-forming communities within distributed CIDS, utilizing similarity relations among monitored entities gathered at runtime. The key idea is to form the communities in an iterative process from the ground up. This means grouping and aggregating initially trained anomaly detection models of single entities based on their similarity. The aggregation is implemented by the concept of FL, resulting in mutual information exchange, thus, potentially increasing model accuracy for the contained models. To realize our concept, we introduce a similarity measurement technique that allows the comparison of anomaly detection models with respect to their ability to correctly predict network traffic behavior. The reevaluation of similarity relations allows for models to change communities at runtime, eventually grouping with the optimal models and rearranging communities in case of changes to the infrastructure. With this approach, we are strengthening scalability, adaptivity, and practicality by performing autonomous community formation at runtime.

The remainder of the paper is structured as follows. In Sect. 2 we provide related work and background information for further comprehension of the paper, which we continue with introducing our approach in detail in Sect. 3, followed by our implementation and evaluation described in Sect. 4, before we summarize with future work in Sect. 5.

2   Background and Related Work

Despite collaborative intrusion detection and federated learning sharing similar ideas about distributing workload and locality-based computation, they differ in key aspects. Therefore, in this section, we introduce their concepts, describe their properties, and examine their respective advantages and drawbacks, while also discussing related work.

2.1   Collaborative Intrusion Detection

Collaborative Intrusion Detection Systems (CIDSs) were introduced as a solution to the requirements of intrusion detection within growing-size networks. The main concept behind this approach is the establishment of collaboration among individual monitoring entities e.g. IDSs or simple data collectors with the goal of retrieving a holistic view of the monitored environment and increased detection accuracy compared to traditional IDS deployments [14]. Collaboration, in this context, is realized as the different participants sending monitoring information, e.g. intrusion alarms or network data, to certain predefined participants for information aggregation and analysis. There are several approaches for CIDSs that differ in architecture, data dissemination, aggregation functions, etc. each with individual strengths and weaknesses.

In particular, centralized architectures, while usually yielding the best detection accuracy through holistic information at the central entity, suffer from implementing a single point of failure (SPoF) and weak scalability. Distributed CIDSs, on the other hand, provide the most versatility and scalability [5,14], hence we focus on this type of architecture. Here, the individual participants are distributed and communicate without a central entity. Furthermore, all collaborating entities usually perform both, data acquisition, meaning the collection of monitoring data, as well as, the analysis of this very data.

Communities. The concept of communities within distributed CIDSs was introduced as a solution to increase the detection accuracy of distributed CIDS compared to centralized implementations [5]. The main idea is to partition the set of IDS entities within a CIDS into subsets, so-called communities, providing a centralized architecture where ensemble learning methods can increase detection accuracy. For each community, one member is chosen as a so-called *community-head* with the task of solely performing intrusion detection analysis on data while the remaining members acquire this very same data. Through this separation of responsibilities, certain drawbacks, distributed architectures circumvented, are reintroduced, leading to SPoF and scalability issues within the communities. Our approach can be seen as an enhancement by the introduction of federated learning which provides an improvement in SPoF handling and increases scalability. Further, the in-community similarity goes hand in hand with a structured member selection, where the original realization implements random group assignments with the goal of fulfilling certain pre-defined community sizes or numbers of communities.

Another approach, focusing mainly on community creation in distributed CIDS is called SkipMon [15], a CIDS that dynamically configures communities based on the similarity of the alert data. Similarity is defined through bloom filters applied to alert data. Every client is spanning a matrix containing the similarity score to all other clients, which is used to form communities for more detailed alert data exchange, once the values are above a certain threshold. However, the authors utilized traditional signature-based IDS for evaluation purposes and focused solely on distributing alert information. This stands in opposition to our utilization of anomaly detection as the detection technique extending the detection horizon to zero-day attacks. Additionally, the communities also implement a centralized architecture being dependent on one central node for intrusion detection, whereas our implementation relies on a peer-to-peer infrastructure.

2.2   Federated Learning (FL)

The concept and term Federated Learning has been created in recent years [8] and resembles a research area in the world of machine learning with decentralization and distribution in mind. The key idea is to collaboratively train models on clients orchestrated by a central server while keeping the training data decentralized [1,7]. The realization of that concept operates in four consecutive steps forming a cycle. At first, all clients receive an initial model which they then autonomously train with their locally collected data. After a certain amount of time or training iterations, the now adopted model is sent, as the second step, to the central server. Having received a certain number of individual models, the central server aggregates those with the resulting model combining features of the individual ones. This new global model is then distributed to all clients closing the cycle, and the clients perform model training again. Figure 1 visualizes this process.

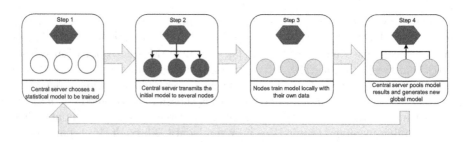

Fig. 1. The four cyclic steps of federated learning.

Through its conception, FL supports the preservation of privacy and does not assume that training data are identically distributed [8]. As an example that utilizes those features for an intrusion detection system within the IoT, Nguyen et al. [9] introduced DIoT, a federated self-learning anomaly detection module for the IoT. The authors feature an anomaly-based IDS built on recurrent neural networks (RNNs) and an automatic classification of IoT devices connected to each gateway. Each gateway trains a device-type-specific model for each device category and sends this data to a central aggregation server. They achieved a low false-positive value, but rely on an external device categorization service, hence, the classification only works for IoT devices. Furthermore, their concept of a central aggregation server might not be beneficial or even possible in certain complex and dynamic IoT infrastructures.

Considering peer-to-peer federated learning, the approach is to distribute the model aggregation to the clients, who are connected in a peer-to-peer fashion. The motive behind this is the fact, that each client can then aggregate its own global model adjusting the aggregation to suit its needs. Examples of such approaches are the works of Roy et al. [11] which first applied peer-to-peer federated learning and tested it with a medical application. The aggregation of personalized global models for clients can improve detection accuracy, however, those clients do not have control over the diversity of connected IoT-devices. Hence, our approach provides a more careful selection of models within the communities which, once aggregated, can increase the model accuracy of all participants more precisely.

On a different path of decentralizing federated learning, Briggs et al. [3] used the concept of hierarchical clustering within FL to distribute the learning process and improve the handling of independent and identically distributed (iid) data. This concept is also implemented by Saadat et al. [12] utilizing the approach of hierarchical clustering techniques. However, their approaches still require the use of a central server. A more related approach to ours is achieved by the work of Sun et al. [13], which are forming groups within federated learning for intrusion detection. They introduced segmented federated learning, separating FL participants into groups based on their contribution to the main model. Groups get formed, thus participants get separated, when they diverge regarding their contribution to the main model of their respective group. This results in a community generation based on model characteristics. However, there is no feature of rejoining members of different groups once they are separated. Furthermore, there is no onboarding procedure for new models to be assigned to the best possible group, which is a necessity in the case of highly dynamic infrastructures such as IoT.

To the best of our knowledge, our approach is the first to incorporate the concept of communities within a peer-to-peer federated learning infrastructure. Furthermore, we realize the community formation in an autonomous and dynamic manner, aiming for similarity of models, thus being infrastructure independent and reacting to changes within the deployed infrastructure.

3   Self-adaptive Community Formation

In this section, we define the goals that we want to achieve with our design, give a high-level overview of our basic concept, followed by an in-depth description of our automated approach to optimize community formation. Furthermore, we give an overview of our intrusion detection strategy.

3.1 Goals

Our design aims to provide a solution to the research questions outlined in the introduction, i.e., combine community-based CIDS with federated learning and automatically organize entities into communities. With our solution, we pursue the following goals:

- **G1 - High detection accuracy.** The focus on detection accuracy is twofold, with the number of false positives, the number of incorrectly reported incidents, to be as low as possible, while, simultaneously the number of true positives, the number of correctly reported incidents, as high as possible. Our goal is not to distract operators by reporting false alarms, but, at the same time, not to miss any intrusions in that process.
- **G2 - Preserve Privacy.** The preservation of privacy has gained in popularity in recent years. Especially within the field of intrusion detection, analyzing potentially sensible data, privacy protection is of growing interest to both industry and the research community. We focus on the privacy of network traffic data.
- **G3 - Adapt to changes.** Changes within infrastructures are inevitable, considering the vast amount of portable connected devices. Adaptability of defense mechanisms is therefore an important cornerstone in maintaining high defense accuracy while experiencing such changes.

3.2 Basic Concept

The underlying concept of our approach is based on the autonomous formation of communities containing similar anomaly detection models among a set of potentially heterogeneous models. Similarity is defined by our similarity measurement technique, which generates similarity scores indicating models best suited for building communities (see Sect. 3.3). The reason for forming these communities is the mutual information exchange of trained normal behavior information between models via aggregation. This enables the models to profit from each other's findings, potentially increasing detection accuracy. To realize our approach, our concept implements one anomaly detection model for each to-be-observed entity, in the sense that it is solely trained on the behavior of this entity's network traffic. This enables the models of those entities expressing similar network traffic behavior to be grouped into communities. Within these communities, model aggregation via the concept of federated learning is applied (see Sect. 3.4). As changes within the deployed infrastructure might occur, model training, model aggregation, community formation, and associated similarity score calculation are periodically reiterated.

This concept allows for the following advantages. First, to enable a potential increase in the anomaly detection accuracy of the grouped models, hence fulfilling goal **G1**. This is achieved by the application of federated learning, which works best if the aggregated models are trained on rather similar data [9]. Second, to preserve the privacy of the entities' network data. This is accomplished by only exchanging model information and not the network traffic data for both the model aggregation and the similarity score calculation, fulfilling goal **G2**. Third, by reevaluation of the similarity relations during runtime, we are able to adapt to changes in the deployed infrastructure and to achieve our goal **G3**.

The system model of our approach is visualized in Fig. 2 and consists of one or multiple gateways to which the to-be-observed entities are connected. Gateways are connected in a peer-to-peer fashion and contain IDS and management logic. The IDS is responsible for monitoring the network traffic using anomaly detection models, generating intrusion alerts where necessary, and communicating those to the corresponding actors. The management logic consists of community management, responsible for community formation and general model management, federated learning, responsible for model aggregation, and data management, which provides the data for the score calculation. Further, we decided to use Gated Recurrent Units (GRUs) for our anomaly detection models which utilize basic approaches of natural language processing for the representation and classification of network traffic (Sect. 3.5). GRUs represent an evolution and improved version of recurrent neural networks and do not require a labeled dataset.

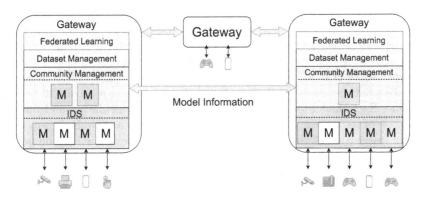

Fig. 2. A visual overview of our approach shown exemplary with three gateways containing the dataset and model management services and connected via a network. The different entities are connected to the gateways and the colors of the Models symbolize the communities those models belong to.

3.3   Community Formation

Unlike the original community-based concept [5], which randomly assigned their IDS nodes to communities, we purposely aggregate models to form communities that represent similar network traffic behavior, regardless of size or quantity constraints. Furthermore, our approach does not require external analysis tools and categorization of communities prior to runtime, as is the case with other concepts [9], due to working exclusively with data that can be acquired during runtime. This is enabled by our similarity measurement technique, which calculates and assigns similarity scores to each pair of models. This information is then used for forming communities of similar entities.

Similarity Score Calculation. The main idea is to define the similarity between two models as the accuracy of each model in the data of the other model. Accuracy means the ratio between the number of correctly predicted network packets and all tested network packets. Essentially, the models get cross-evaluated on each other's datasets with the goal of finding models trained on similar data. Following this approach, we implicitly make a connection between the similarity in the network behavior of the entities based on how their models are trained.

In detail, the similarity score $s_{i,j}$ of the model M_i in regards to model M_j is calculated utilizing the following equation:

$$s_{i,j} = \frac{|C^i_{M_j}|}{|D^i_{M_j}|} \tag{1}$$

$C^i_{M_j} \subseteq D^i_{M_j}$ represents the set of correctly classified datapoints of model M_i in the data set of model M_j and the set $D^i_{M_j}$ contains all the data points tested. This calculation happens between each pair of models and also across the individual gateways every time a model updates their datasets. The similarity score table, present at each gateway, is then filled and updated with the calculated values accordingly. The values are of the form $s_{i,j}$ where i indicates the row, hence the score of model i on the data of model j represented by the column. The tables between each gateway are synchronized to have a consistent table for everyone. Each model management is responsible for calculating and updating the values of its models. In Table 1 an example of such a table is shown.

The calculation of the similarity scores is always performed in the gateway where the data is collected. As a result, the models themselves are exchanged for this calculation, having the advantage of preserving the privacy of device-specific network traffic.

Table 1. The similarity table is present on every gateway. The values are read as the model M_x of the row is tested with the dataset D_y of the model y of the column and results in the corresponding similarity score.

	D_1	D_2	D_3
M_1	0,90	0,90	0,21
M_2	0,82	0,85	0,25
M_3	0,13	0,37	0,68

Formation. The formation of the communities is performed according to the compatibility of the models with other models or existing members, measured by the similarity score. Generally, when the mutual similarity score of two or more models is above a certain threshold, a community among them is formed. The same is true for models added to existing communities. In case a similarity score of a community member falls below the threshold or its value is higher with other models or communities, this member is leaving the community. In the special case, when there is one model with a similarity score above the threshold for several communities and models, the community or model for which the model has the highest score above the threshold wins. When forming or expanding a community, the mutual similarity scores of all participants must be above our threshold. This provides the assurance that the similarity is definitely above the threshold between all members. However, our threshold is dependent on the compared model's M_i own score $s_{i,i}$, thus a product between a limiting factor l and $s_{i,i}$. The following formula shows the requirements each model of a community C has to fulfill.

$$threshold_i = l \cdot s_{i,i} \tag{2}$$

$$M_i \in C \Rightarrow \forall j \in J, s_{i,j} \geq l \cdot s_{j,j} \wedge s_{j,i} \geq l \cdot s_{i,i} \tag{3}$$

With J being the set of indices of the models within the community C.

The reason for incorporating the own accuracy of the model into the threshold generation is to allow for communities of similar models to be formed since a score $s_{i,i}$ of a model M_i on its own dataset D_i might not be above a fixed value, e.g. 0,7, so the threshold of similar models have to be related to $s_{i,i}$.

The limiting factor l of the threshold is $l = 0,9$. In our evaluation, we discovered that this is the optimal value for forming communities with suitable similarity to improve the accuracy of the model (see Sect. 4).

Applying the described community formation to the exemplary similarity table shown in Table 1, models M_1 and M_2 would form a community since both similarity scores $s_{1,2} = 0,9 \geq l \cdot s_{2,2} = 0,9 \cdot 0,85$ (M_1 on D_2) and $s_{2,1} = 0,82 \geq l \cdot s_{1,1} = 0,9 \cdot 0,9$ (M_2 on D_1) are above the corresponding thresholds. Model M_3 would not be part of this community due to not exceeding the threshold for its corresponding similarity scores, e.g. $s_{3,1} = 0,1$.

Once a community is formed, one gateway, usually the one responsible for the most models within that community, acts as the community head, meaning it manages the FL process by instantiating an FL server where the models of that community are being transferred to, aggregated, and, finally, redistributed.

The dynamics within the community formation enable the best possible model combination in regard to similarity even in cases of changing behavior in the entities. This changing behavior can be evoked through firmware updates or the reallocation of new responsibilities to those entities. In addition, this approach also allows us, to a certain degree, to tolerate crash faults of community heads. In the case of a crashed community head, another gateway gets to be the head of that community; hence the model aggregation can still be performed.

However, this is only possible if the community is spread over at least two gateways and if there are at least two other models of other gateways involved.

Dataset Management. Prior to the community formation, the dataset management is tasked with, on the one hand, selecting relevant data snippets, which are characteristic for testing other models, and, on the other hand, storing and updating this information to a local database for the calculation of the similarity score. The data snippet for each model representing its network traffic consists of its training dataset. By doing so, we can evaluate the investigated model's similarity on the same data the compared model was trained on; hence, utilizing our similarity score, we can draw the conclusion of whether both models were trained on similar data. This happens without exposing that data itself to other gateways, but by exchanging the models themselves for similarity score calculation. After each model training phase, the updated training data gets merged with the old data and stored in the database.

3.4 Federated Learning

The concept of Federated Learning (FL) is utilized by our approach to aggregate individual models, which are found to be similar, to a general model. The goal is to improve the detection accuracy of the individual models by mutual information exchange about the learned network traffic behavior of the associated entities. By selectively aggregating similar models, we allow the model aggregation to best support the models to learn from each other's findings [9]. An aggregation across all heterogeneous models would potentially not be of benefit regarding mutual learning, hence we combined FL with our community formation strategy.

Each community is operating its own FL setup with the community head as the instance operating the model aggregation. The aggregation process is essentially the aggregation of the weights of the models to create a new general model, which in turn is then distributed to the IDSs as a replacement for the current models. The aggregation is performed as described in the work of McMahan et al. [8] through the so-called FedAvg algorithm averaging the values. Once the general model is built and distributed to the other model management services, a new round of individual model training is started.

3.5 Intrusion Detection

Anomaly detection is the core part of our intrusion detection, which we try to improve by realizing our community formation approach in combination with the concept of federated learning.

Anomaly Detection. The local monitoring performed by our approach is based on anomaly detection utilizing a certain form of Recurrent Neural Network (RNN) called Gated Recurrent Units (GRU) [4]. This machine learning algorithm can be seen as an improvement to the Long Short Term Memory (LSTM) algorithm

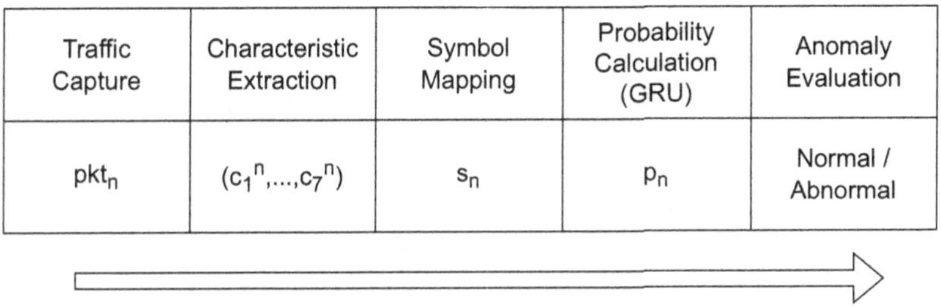

Traffic Capture	Characteristic Extraction	Symbol Mapping	Probability Calculation (GRU)	Anomaly Evaluation
pkt_n	$(c_1^n,...,c_7^n)$	s_n	p_n	Normal / Abnormal

Fig. 3. The utilization of GRU for anomaly-detection within network intrusion detection

regarding the ability to connect and detect the occurrence and order of certain events. These algorithms originate from the field of Natural Language Processing (NLP), where they are utilized for predicting word orders, e.g. to reason about the content of sentences. This feature can also be utilized for intrusion detection, particularly anomaly detection since benign network traffic is partly predictive and repetitive [9]. Utilizing this property enables the algorithm to link certain events in time, and thus can detect anomalous behavior when certain events fall out of the frame. This approach was originally introduced by Nguyen et al. [9], hence, for reasons of comparability, we adopted it almost identically, with an exception within the extracted data features (see below).

Functionality. The application of GRUs as an anomaly detection algorithm for network intrusion detection works as follows and is visualized in Fig. 3. First, seven characteristic features of the network packets are extracted that most efficiently represent a packet. Those features are listed in Table 2 and encompass the *packet length, direction, protocol,* etc. The next step is to translate the individual network packets into words of an alphabet. Thereby, the tuple of seven characteristic features is, depending on the values, mapped to a certain word in the alphabet chosen. After this symbol mapping, the actual GRU algorithm is used for predicting the probability of the symbol s_i representing $packet_i$, based on the last k previous packages with $k = 20$, after having trained the model first. Finally, a packet is seen as anomalous if its predicted probability p_i of appearance is below a certain threshold $p_i < \delta$ with $\delta = 10^{-2}$. However, to reduce the number of false positive alerts, an alert is only triggered for a set of consecutive packets $W = pkt_1, ..., pkt_w$ and the following is valid:

$$\frac{|\{pkt_i \in W | p_i < \delta\}|}{w} > \gamma \tag{4}$$

with $\gamma = 0.5$ and $w = |W|$.

The principle behind the utilization of GRU is to learn which symbols usually follow which other symbols. If then, once the model is trained, the symbol order is different, a possible anomaly is detected, and potentially an alarm is raised.

The stated values for the introduced variables, the size, and structure of the neural network, as well as the characteristic features, are all taken from related work [9]. Hence, we implemented the GRU with three hidden layers each containing 128 neurons. Only the use of all seven characteristic features for all models is an exception to the original approach in which different model types utilize a different number of those seven features. The reason for that is the required comparability for later aggregation of our models since we do not group them before but during execution.

Table 2. Those are the characteristic features extracted from a network packet most useful for describing such a packet. Additionally, the scope of the values of the individual features is shown.

Characteristic	Value
Protocol	encapsulated protocol types
Packet length	bin index of packet length
Direction	1 = incoming, 0 = outgoing
Local port type	bin index of port type
remote port type	bin index of port type
TCP flags	TCP flag values
IAT bin	bin index of packet inter-arrival time

Once an alert is generated by an IDS, this information is propagated to a central alert aggregation service for further analysis. This functionality of alert data exchange and information extraction from alerts is out of the scope of this paper.

4   Implementation and Evaluation

Our approach is implemented using the Python Programming Language[1] which enables us to use a machine learning library, called "Tensorflow[2]" combined with the federated learning framework "Flower[3]". Both are open-source libraries developed by Google and FlowerLabs, respectively. Tensorflow is providing state-of-the-art machine learning algorithms including Gated Recurrent Units (GRU), while Flower realizes the client-server interaction and model aggregation when federated learning is applied.

---

[1] https://www.python.org/.

[2] https://www.tensorflow.org/.

[3] https://flower.dev/.

4.1   Experimental Setup

The setup of our approach is similar to the concept shown in Sect. 3.2. For evaluation purposes, we focus on an IoT infrastructure setup, but our concept can be applied to a variety of different infrastructures. The reasons for deciding on an IoT infrastructure are the natural heterogeneity, size, and complexity of such networks. Our setup essentially encompasses two types of relevant entities, namely IoT devices and gateways. The remaining domains of the ISO reference IoT architecture are of little concern for this approach[4].

Each IoT gateway encompasses an IDS and management logic. IoT devices include a diverse set of appliances fit for different purposes with the commonality of being connected to one gateway via, in our case, IP-based communication. The gateways themselves, as is known from the IoT context, manage the connections to a fluctuating number of devices and, simultaneously, are connected to other gateways in a peer-to-peer fashion.

Dataset. For the evaluation of our approach, we settled on a dataset that provides a good balance between depicting current network traffic in IoT infrastructures and being representative for comparison to other works. This dataset was built by Nguyen et al. [9,10] and also used in their work for evaluation purposes. It provides network traffic data of a variety of different IoT devices implemented in different infrastructure scenarios. The key benefit of this dataset is the clear association of network traffic with single IoT devices, allowing us to realize our setup and gain insight into the community formation decisions taken autonomously. The content of the dataset includes both benign and attack data, where the attack data originates from the application of the Mirai attack onto IoT devices. This plays a part in contributing to its actuality, however, other attacks are currently not included in this dataset. In total there are 33 IoT devices; however, for only five of those devices, there is malicious network traffic available. Further, only 14 devices were deployed in a realistic smart home infrastructure, which our evaluation is mainly based on.

Evaluation Metrics. As suitable evaluation metrics to measure accuracy, we use the false positive rate (FPR) and the true positive rate (TPR). Thereby, FPR indicates the rate at which benign network traffic is incorrectly classified as anomalous, while TPR is the rate of correctly detected attacks as anomalies. Our intention is to achieve a low FPR causing fewer false intrusion alerts, while simultaneously maximizing the TPR to increase detection accuracy. To evaluate the FPR values, we performed a four-fold cross-validation on the training dataset, which means that we divided the data equally into four folds with three folds for training/validation and one fold for testing. As the testing data only contains benign data every generated alert is guaranteed to be a false alarm. The same four-fold cross-validation is performed when testing for TPR. For this rate, however, the attack data is used which contains malicious, as well as, benign traffic. Hence, a window of $w = 250$ (see Eq. 4) is considered a false negative when

---

[4] ISO/IEC 30141:2018.

less than half ($\gamma = 0,5$) of the packets are classified as anomalous, otherwise, it would be considered a true positive.

4.2   Results and Discussion

Our focus on evaluation encompasses in addition to the general accuracy of our approach, also an approach to determine the best limiting value l for the community formation thresholds, as well as an investigation on how well our formation can adapt to infrastructural changes.

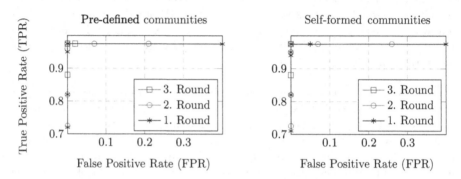

Fig. 4. Receiver Operating Characteristic (ROC) curve of FPR and TPR comparing the accuracy of our self-forming communities to the pre-defined communities of related work.

Accuracy. To evaluate the detection accuracy of our approach we measure the detection accuracy after model training and community formation rounds. Within each round, consisting of community formation and model training, the model training encompasses 17 epochs with a total of three training rounds. We chose those values to have a basis for comparison with the related work of Nguyen et al. [9]. In that notice, we evaluated our approach using the same data set that contains 14 IoT devices with attack data for five of them.

Looking at the Receiver Operating Characteristic (ROC) curve in Fig. 4, which compares our approach to the related work, we can see that our self-formed communities perform comparably well with respect to detection accuracy. While the true positive rate of our approach is slightly lower after the first round (deviation of up to 2%), the false positive rate of our approach is 0% where the related work is up to 2% after all rounds are executed. A possible reason for the lower TPR in the first rounds could be the fact, that our approach requires us to have at least one round to form the most beneficial communities, whereas the concept of pre-defined communities has this setup from the beginning.

Investigating community formation in this scenario, there were three communities formed after the first round (see Table 3). These match the pre-defined

Table 3. Showing the models of devices that were autonomously selected to participate in communities by our approach. Additionally, the rounds are given in which the communities existed.

Device	Community #	1. Round	2. Round	3. Round
D-LinkCamDCS930L	1	✗	✓	✓
D-LinkCamDCS932L				
EdimaxPlug1101W	2	✗	✓	✓
EdimaxPlug2101W				
iKettle2	3	✗	✓	✓
SmarterCoffee				
Lightify	4	✗	✗	✓
Hue Switch				

Table 4. Showing the communities formed when testing all 33 devices with our approach. Note only those communities of models are included in this table, that are not already listed in Table 3. However, all communities shown in both tables together were formed when testing all 33 devices. All of the communities of this table were formed after the first round and stayed in this constellation throughout the execution of our approach.

Communities (Each row is one community)				
D-LinkDoorSensor	D-LinkSensor	D-LinkSiren	D-LinkSwitch	D-LinkWaterSensor
TP-LinkPlugHS100	TP-LinkPlugHS110			
WeMoInsightSwitch	WeMoSwitch			
EdimaxCamIC3115	EdimaxCamIC3115			

communities of the related work, however, our approach also formed a community among two lighting-related devices seen in Table 3 in community number four. However, this community that formed after the second round did not have an effect on the FPR value of those models, since both models already had an FPR of 0%. Note that there is no attack data for those devices, so no TPR values could be collected. When performing our community formation on the models of all 33 devices, the formed communities result as shown in Tables 3 and 4. Those additional communities of Table 4 were formed after the first round and stayed as such throughout the remaining runtime.

The results of this evaluation show, that our approach is comparable to the accuracy of related approaches and that our autonomous community formation is comparable to other mechanisms that classify IoT devices.

Efficiency of Similarity Measure. The efficiency of community formation depends on a suitable threshold to be able to group the appropriate models and exclude the improper ones. As our threshold is dependent on the similarity score of the compared model on its own data (see Eq. 2), we have to determine the appropriate value for the limiting factor l.

We evaluated the best value for l by investigating the deviation between the similarity score of a model M_i ($s_{i,j}$) and the comparative value s_{jj} as of Eq. 1. For that, we performed our community formation on all 33 devices of the dataset which resulted in the communities shown in Tables 3 and 4. Focusing on the models of our formed communities which also correlate with the pre-defined communities of related work [9], we discovered that the deviation of the values to be compared is within 90% of $s_{j,j}$. Further, when we investigated the next possible community not formed by $l = 0.9$, we discovered that the value for l had to be dropped to 0.55, however, when executing model aggregation among those models there was no benefit in mutual information exchange regarding the FPR recognizable. This behavior can be subject to change when investigating with other datasets, however.

Adaption to Change. To evaluate how our community formation behaves under changes in the deployed infrastructure, we set up a scenario where IoT devices are exchanged. We were measuring the number of rounds it takes for our approach to adjust to those changes and how or if the accuracy is affected.

When testing with our accuracy evaluation setup where the formed communities are shown in Table 3, we changed the first device "D-LinkCamDCS930L" with the third "EdimaxPlug1101W". As a result, communities number 1 and 2 were immediately dissolved, and, within the same round, two new communities were formed between the D-Link cameras and Edimax plugs. Thereby, neither the models of the D-Link devices nor the models of the Edimax devices experienced deficits within their FPR or TPR. This can be explained by the fact that the transformation, dissolving one community and forming another one, happened within one round. As a consequence, there was no time the model aggregation was performed between two unsimilar models, hence compromising the detection accuracy of those. Similar tests encompassing all 33 devices showed the same behavior, which confirms our approach can adapt to changes within the infrastructure.

5   Summary and Future Work

Our approach exclusively utilizes available information on similarity during runtime to improve anomaly detection accuracy within heterogeneous infrastructures. The main idea is to autonomously aggregate models, representing entities with similar network behavior, to gain profit from each other's findings and improve detection accuracy. Furthermore, our concept is capable of adapting to changes within infrastructures and can be applied to a variety of infrastructures that express IP-based communication. The evaluation results show an equal if not superior detection accuracy of our approach compared to related work, without requiring data preparation through labeling.

Future work includes adapting our approach to analyze network flow data for a more accurate traceability of malicious network traffic, instead of only considering the sequential arrival of network packets. This enables a more precise classification of the relationships among network traffic, especially a more accurate distinction between benign and malicious traffic flows when reporting alerts. As a consequence, other machine learning mechanisms could be evaluated or might be necessary when analyzing network flow data.

References

1. Agrawal, S., et al.: Federated learning for intrusion detection system: concepts, challenges and future directions (2021)
2. Barry, B.I., Chan, H.A.: Intrusion detection systems. In: Handbook of Information and Communication Security, pp. 193–205. Springer, Heidelberg (2010). https://doi.org/10.1007/978-3-642-04117-4_10
3. Briggs, C., Fan, Z., Andras, P.: Federated learning with hierarchical clustering of local updates to improve training on non-IID data. In: 2020 International Joint Conference on Neural Networks (IJCNN), pp. 1–9 (2020). https://doi.org/10.1109/IJCNN48605.2020.9207469
4. Cho, K., van Merrienboer, B., Bahdanau, D., Bengio, Y.: On the properties of neural machine translation: encoder-decoder approaches (2014)
5. Cordero, C.G., Vasilomanolakis, E., Mühlhäuser, M., Fischer, M.: Community-based collaborative intrusion detection. In: Thuraisingham, B., Wang, X.F., Yegneswaran, V. (eds.) SecureComm 2015. LNICST, vol. 164, pp. 665–681. Springer, Cham (2015). https://doi.org/10.1007/978-3-319-28865-9_44
6. García-Teodoro, P., Díaz-Verdejo, J., Maciá-Fernández, G., Vázquez, E.: Anomaly-based network intrusion detection: techniques, systems and challenges. Comput. Secur. **28**(1), 18–28 (2009). https://doi.org/10.1016/j.cose.2008.08.003, https://www.sciencedirect.com/science/article/pii/S0167404808000692
7. Kairouz, P., et al.: Advances and open problems in federated learning (2021)
8. McMahan, B., Moore, E., Ramage, D., Hampson, S., Arcas, B.A.Y.: Communication-efficient learning of deep networks from decentralized data. In: Singh, A., Zhu, J. (eds.) Proceedings of the 20th International Conference on Artificial Intelligence and Statistics. Proceedings of Machine Learning Research, vol. 54, pp. 1273–1282. PMLR, 20–22 April 2017. https://proceedings.mlr.press/v54/mcmahan17a.html
9. Nguyen, T.D., Marchal, S., Miettinen, M., Fereidooni, H., Asokan, N., Sadeghi, A.R.: DIoT: a federated self-learning anomaly detection system for IoT. In: 2019 IEEE 39th International Conference on Distributed Computing Systems (ICDCS), pp. 756–767 (2019). https://doi.org/10.1109/ICDCS.2019.00080
10. Nguyen, T.D., et al.: FLAME: taming backdoors in federated learning. In: 31st USENIX Security Symposium (USENIX Security 22), pp. 1415–1432 (2022)
11. Roy, A.G., Siddiqui, S., Pölsterl, S., Navab, N., Wachinger, C.: Brain0: a peer-to-peer environment for decentralized federated learning. CoRR abs/1905.06731 (2019). http://arxiv.org/abs/1905.06731
12. Saadat, H., Aboumadi, A., Mohamed, A., Erbad, A., Guizani, M.: Hierarchical federated learning for collaborative IDS in IoT applications. In: 2021 10th Mediterranean Conference on Embedded Computing (MECO), pp. 1–6. IEEE, Budva, Montenegro (2021). https://doi.org/10.1109/MECO52532.2021.9460304, https://ieeexplore.ieee.org/document/9460304/
13. Sun, Y., Ochiai, H., Esaki, H.: Intrusion detection with segmented federated learning for large-scale multiple LANs. In: 2020 International Joint Conference on Neural Networks (IJCNN), pp. 1–8. IEEE, Glasgow, United

Kingdom (2020). https://doi.org/10.1109/IJCNN48605.2020.9207094, https://ieeexplore.ieee.org/document/9207094/

14. Vasilomanolakis, E., Karuppayah, S., Mühlhäuser, M., Fischer, M.: Taxonomy and survey of collaborative intrusion detection. ACM Comput. Surv. **47**(4), 1–33 (2015). https://doi.org/10.1145/2716260

15. Vasilomanolakis, E., Krügl, M., Cordero, C.G., Mühlhäuser, M., Fischer, M.: Skip-Mon: a locality-aware collaborative intrusion detection system. In: 2015 IEEE 34th International Performance Computing and Communications Conference (IPCCC), pp. 1–8 (2015). https://doi.org/10.1109/PCCC.2015.7410282

To Possess or Not to Possess - WhatsApp for Android Revisited with a Focus on Stickers

Samantha Klier$^{(\boxtimes)}$ and Harald Baier

Research Institute CODE, Universität der Bundeswehr München, Munich, Germany
{samantha.klier,harald.baier}@unibw.de
https://www.unibw.de/digfor

Abstract. WhatsApp stickers are a popular hybrid of images and emoticons that can contain user-created content. Stickers are mostly sent for legitimate reasons, but are also used to distribute illicit content such as Child Sexual Abuse Material (CSAM). As the process of creating stickers becomes easier for users from version to version, a digital forensic analysis is still lacking. Therefore, we present the first comprehensive digital forensic analysis of WhatsApp's sticker handling on Android, with a special focus on the legal context, i.e. the definition of possession of illicit content. Our analysis is based on 40 scenarios that reflect the full lifecycle of community-created stickers. We show how the distribution channel of a sticker found on a device can be reconstructed, partially even when its traces have been removed from WhatsApp and are not visible through WhatsApp's user interface. In addition, we show that Google Drive backups recover stickers, making device seizure dispensable; however, stickers can still be permanently deleted. Most importantly, we show that simply finding a sticker on a device is not sufficient to meet the requirements of the legal definition of possession. Therefore, prosecution for possession of a sticker requires additional evidence, which we provide.

Keywords: WhatsApp · sticker · possession · CSAM · digital forensics · Android

1 Introduction

WhatsApp by Meta is the most used messenger app globally [22] and the third most used Social Network [23]. In 2018 Meta introduced stickers to WhatsApp, which are a hybrid of images and emojis and were designed to "share your feelings in a way that you can't always express with words" in an "easy and fun" way [27]. Unlike emojis, stickers can be created by users based on any image, except for format restrictions. Back in 2018 sticker creation was complicated, as it involved the development of a dedicated sticker app [26]. Later, so-called sticker makers became popular, such as the "Sticker.ly - Sticker Maker" which has been downloaded more than 100 million times from Google's Play Store alone [24].

© The Author(s), under exclusive license to Springer Nature Switzerland AG 2024
L. Fritsch et al. (Eds.): NordSec 2023, LNCS 14324, pp. 281–303, 2024.
https://doi.org/10.1007/978-3-031-47748-5_16

Not surprisingly, stickers are used to distribute not only memes, but also illegal content such as CSAM [5,14] and Nazi propaganda [21]. Even worse, WhatsApp automatically saves every sticker received in a chat, hence users may have incriminating stickers on their devices without knowing or wanting to. This sounds absurd at first, but the German police reported that CSAM stickers were posted to a group chat of climate activists ("Fridays for Future") [2] placing all members of the group in the precarious position to have CSAM on their devices, which can have serious consequences for the device owner, such as jail sentences, if, for example, a sticker depicts CSAM, the possession of which is illegal in 140 countries [12].

Right now, WhatsApp is rolling out the ability to create stickers directly in WhatsApp [25,28] based on any common image format, making the creation and sending of personalized stickers even easier. Therefore, a digital forensic understanding of stickers is of increasing importance. With this paper, we contribute a comprehensive digital forensic analysis of WhatsApp's Sticker handling, with particular attention to the legal definition of possession.

Contributions and Organization of Paper. First off, we introduce stickers from a user perspective and concentrate on their peer-to-peer nature and find that stickers can be collected but are otherwise concealed from a user's perception, in contrast to other media types commonly shared per WhatsApp (Sect. 2).

Importantly, we highlight the legal prerequisites that must be met to assume that a sticker file is possessed by a user, namely control, knowledge, and intent, as these are the drivers of a digital forensic examination (Sect. 3). Furthermore, we analyze and compare existing research on WhatsApp to put our work in perspective (Sect. 4).

To examine the real evidential weight of artifacts, we design and evaluate 40 scenarios, which cover all possibilities a user has to interact with stickers. Our scenarios incorporate the areas of reception, interaction, removal, and backup (Sect. 5). Subsequently, we execute the scenarios on one physical and two emulated devices running Android 9, 10 and 13, as well as two different versions of WhatsApp, respectively. We base our evaluation on WhatsApp's directories in both the Android media and data partition, and reduce the data to eleven relevant artifacts.

Then, we present our fundamental results and, most importantly, reconstruct the communication from the stored sticker up to its origin (Sect. 6). Next, we identify the `msgstore.db` as the primary source for evidence of distribution, but find that the `stickers.db` and the `whatsapp.log` can be used to prove distribution if the data from the `msgstore.db` is not available (Sect. 7).

In contrast to distribution, proving possession is complex; therefore, we shed light on the aspect of control and knowledge (Sect. 8) and find that the mere existence of a sticker on a device is not sufficient to satisfy the legal requirements of possession. Consequently, we present artifacts that prove that a user had control over a file and knew it existed, namely the favorite and quoted messages in the `msgstore.db`, favorite stickers in the `stickers.db` and cached sticker files, which are only available when the user interacted with a sticker.

Coherently, we sum our findings per artifact in a conclusive table and find that without access to the data stored on the data partition there is no evidence that supports prosecution (Sect. 9) and finally conclude our paper (Sect. 10).

2 Sticker Foundations

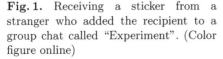

Fig. 1. Receiving a sticker from a stranger who added the recipient to a group chat called "Experiment". (Color figure online)

Fig. 2. The user sent the sticker they had just received, which is recorded in the recent sticker menu (red box).(Color figure online)

First of all, we now introduce the foundations of WhatsApp sticker handling with a focus on the user experience, while we dismiss the technical details mostly to Sect. 6.

2.1 Receiving and Sending Stickers

Any user can receive stickers in a chat, as you can see in Fig. 1 in the orange box. To use stickers, a user can collect previously received stickers by clicking and selecting "mark as favorite" or the star button which will add the sticker to the users favorites menu, which is shown at the bottom of Fig. 1, and is activated by clicking first on the sticker button (red box) and then on the star button (blue box). In this example, the user has not yet "favorited" any sticker.

Our user now "favorited" the received sticker and can subsequently redistribute it, as can be seen in Fig. 2. The recipient responded with the sticker they had just received. Another way to obtain stickers is to install official sticker packs, which are available by clicking on the plus button in the bottom right corner. However, these sticker packs are beyond the scope of this paper, as they are subject to Meta's Terms of Service, and are therefore unlikely to contain content of interest to Law Enforcement Agencies (LEAs). Nevertheless, any sent sticker is recorded by an entry in the recently used stickers menu (red box).

2.2   Stickers are Different

This means that stickers can be distributed in a peer-to-peer-like manner, can be collected by users, and hence "going viral" is part of their design. This is very different from the behavior of emojis and GIFs (available with the buttons to the left of the sticker button), which serve a similar purpose but cannot be collected because the available content is the same for every user and is exclusively provided by the respective platform.

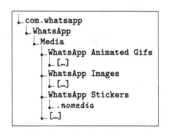

Fig. 3. Excerpt of data initially stored by WhatsApp in the user-accessible media partition.

However, just as GIFs, photos, and videos, stickers are stored locally on the device, but unlike these other media files, stickers are only partially affected by the settings for the automatic download of media files. By default the automatic download of media files is enabled but can be disabled in the settings, then, WhatsApp suggests that "no media" other than voice messages will be downloaded. This is misleading, as static stickers are downloaded nonetheless (see Sect. 8.1), therefore, a user can prohibit the download of any media file except for static stickers.

Every downloaded media file is stored in its dedicated directory in the user-accessible media partition, for which we show an excerpt in Fig. 3, and is presented to the user outside of WhatsApp's user interface, for example, in the device gallery, except for stickers. This is due to the fact that only the WhatsApp Stickers directory is marked with a .nomedia file, which signals Android's

Fig. 4. WhatsApp's can search for, e.g. images and videos across all chats, but not for stickers.

media scanner to ignore this directory and its content [7]. As a result, a user is never confronted with the fact that stickers are stored on their device, in contrast to other media files.

However, stickers are also hidden from the user's perception in WhatsApp's user interface. For example, a user can get an overview of all photos, videos, and GIFs from all chats, which is impossible for stickers, as shown in Fig. 4. Therefore, apart from used and collected stickers, a user is never confronted with stickers that are stored on its device beyond the chat in which a sticker was received.

3   A Special Emphasis on Possession

The differences shown in sticker handling in contrast to the handling of other media files are a problem in light of the legal definition of possession. For example, the civil codes of European countries explicitly define possession as having *actual control* and sometimes even require specific *intent* [4]. On the contrary, common law legislation does not provide a precise definition of possession, although the concepts applied are similar [4,11]. The aspect of possession of files has already been argued in court proceedings, for example, when the only CSAM files found were in the browser cache [11,16].

In proceedings based on CSAM found in a browser cache, some defendants have admitted that they intentionally viewed CSAM on the Internet, but argued that they were unaware of the existence of a browser cache and never intended to possess these images. Consequently, they claimed that they had no control over these files and therefore did not possess them [11,16]. Although some courts have accepted this reasoning, others have contended that cached files merely serve as evidence of past possession while intentionally viewed CSAM was possessed in the form of the image displayed [11].

Consequently, Howard [11] aptly distinguished the two approaches followed by the courts and named them *Present Possession* approach and *Evidence Of* approach. The *Present Possession* approach assumes that the cached files are the possessed files, which can be circumvented by technical ignorance, e.g., the existence of the browser cache was unknown to the defendant. On the contrary, the *Evidence Of* approach expects the cached files to be the witness of a crime and, hence, cannot be circumvented by technical ignorance. However, it is hard to prove that an artifact effectively testifies that a crime was committed. For example, Horsman [9,10] showed that the existence of a file in a browser cache does not prove that it was actually displayed on the screen, let alone viewed by the user, and therefore has little evidentiary value.

In the rest of this paper, we follow the *Evidence of* approach and concentrate solely on technical facts that prove a defendant's capability to control a sticker and knowledge of its existence, summing up to *actual control*, and avoid jumping to conclusions or making assessments, which is the duty of the judge and jury [3].

4   Related Work

So far, no light has been shed on WhatsApp's sticker handling, although some specific WhatsApp functionalities have been studied by the community, such as the call signaling messages [13] or the security of group chats [20].

However, back in 2014 Anglano [1] established with his work a thorough understanding of WhatsApp's artifacts, which included not just the extraction of information but also correlation from several artifacts to reconstruct, e.g. deleted messages, but also the temporal context. Anglano focused on SQLite databases that were stored in the /data/com.whatsapp/databases directory of the data partition. Anglano identified, for example, the msgstore.db to contain exchanged messages. But, for the reconstruction of deleted information and the temporal context, Anglano incorporated also the log file of WhatsApp (i.e. /data/com.whatsapp/files/Logs/whatsapp.log). Fortunately, these artifacts are still relevant in newer versions of WhatsApp, which we show i.a. in Sect. 6.2.

Although the focus of Anglano [1] was not on media sharing, the exchange of multimedia files was briefly examined on the example of an image. However, at the time of the study, WhatsApp did not automatically download received images; instead, only thumbnails were displayed. As a result, identifying instances of incriminating images on a device always implied that users had manually downloaded and retained them. Thus, the question of possession of incriminating images did not arise. In addition, the study could not include an analysis of stickers as they had not yet been introduced at the time.

Furthermore, significant transformations have occurred in the realm of backups since the publication of Anglano [1]. Today, WhatsApp's backup strategy is using Google Drive by default, while additionally creating encrypted local copies of some files which were studied by Anglano [1]. However, back in 2014, the backups were encrypted with a universal encryption key that was publicly known for all users, whereas today these backups are encrypted using AES-256 and employ a unique key stored in Android's protected data partition [6]. Therefore, we focus on Google Drive backups which were not studied before, and only remark the potential existence of local encrypted backups for some databases (see Table 2, artifacts with ID 3-5).

5   Research Approach

We aim to find which artifacts effectively prove that a user had actual control over a sticker or distributed a sticker, therefore, we study the complete life cycle of stickers collected from peers which results in 40 scenarios, we divide into the areas of (I) reception, (II) interaction, (III) removal, and (IV) backups, respectively in the context of one-on-one and group chats. We now give a brief overview of our scenarios, the execution of the scenarios and our evaluation methodology. For a detailed and atomic description of our experiments, please refer to Table 4 in Appendix A.

5.1   Scenarios

Generally, our scenarios are created with the idea of comparing the resulting artifacts against each other, to determine their meaningfulness. For example, in the reception area, we have the scenario RECEIVE-OFF-NODISPLAY (I.4) and its direct counterpart RECEIVE-OFF-DISPLAY (I.3). In Fig. 5, we show the flow

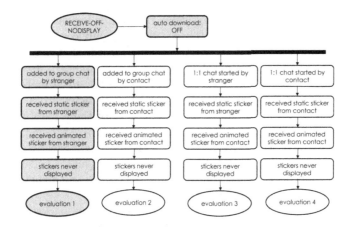

Fig. 5. Flow diagram of the `RECEIVE-OFF-NODISPLAY` scenario.

diagram of the scenario `RECEIVE-OFF-NODISPLAY` (I.4) which combines every possible characteristic of receiving a sticker, resulting in four subscenarios. The colored boxes highlight a subscenario that represents a case where a user disabled auto-download, was added to a group chat by a stranger, and received an animated and a static sticker that were never displayed. In contrast, the `RECEIVE-OFF-DISPLAY` scenario is identical except that the stickers were displayed because the user opened the chat after receiving them. These complementary scenarios allow us to determine whether there are artifacts that reliably indicate that a sticker was displayed.

5.2 Execution

In order to have a convenient full access to the file system, we use an emulated[1] Google Pixel 6 Pro smartphone, running Android 13, to execute each scenario. We installed and registered WhatsApp in version 2.23.7.76 with the official package installer[2]. Furthermore, we validate the results of the emulated device by executing key scenarios on a physical Samsung Galaxy S9+ (Android 9 with WhatsApp v2.22.23.84). To study whether different operating system versions and app versions have an impact on the artifacts, we executed some scenarios on an emulated Google Pixel 3a (Android 10 with WhatsApp v2.23.7.76). Please refer to Table 4 in the Appendix A for a detailed mapping of the devices to scenarios. We also provide the extracted data upon request with the assurance that the phone numbers and accounts involved will not be disclosed.

5.3 Evaluation

For our evaluation we consider artifacts stored in the WhatsApp directories in the media and the data partition, we acquired logically. Therefore, the recovery

---

[1] Using: Android Studio Electric Eel — 2022.1.1 Patch 2.
[2] https://www.whatsapp.com/android/?lang=en.

of deleted files, which requires a physical extraction, is beyond the scope of this work. Furthermore, we analyzed databases, by commonly connecting and querying them, therefore, we did not consider deleted records that may be recovered by analyzing their WAL files, which, however, is a discipline of its own [17–19].

Nevertheless, we acquired more data than is feasible for a manual analysis. For each scenario, more than 200 files have been extracted from WhatsApp's directories, including up to twelve databases. Two of these databases, namely wa.db and msgstore.db, which were already presented by Anglano [1], contained three tables in 2014, respectively. Now, wa.db and msgstore.db have 33 and 164 tables, respectively. Therefore, we applied a systematic and reproducible preprocessing step prior to the analysis phase to reduce and structure the data corpora to a manageable amount for review.

We identify relevant artifacts, by applying a recursive backward search, as proposed by Klier et al. [15], which starts from the known metadata of a file, and searches within artifacts for appearances of those metadata and consequently collects further metadata to search for, until no new metadata can be found. In this case, we start the search with the sticker's filename and its SHA-256 file hash in Base64 representation, based on the findings of Anglano [1]. The collected findings are saved to a JSON file, which allows a straightforward comparison of complementing scenarios and a starting point for an in-depth analysis.

Finally, in Table 1 and Table 2, we show all relevant artifacts we identified with our approach for sticker handling, including a self-assigned ID for further reference. Please note that square brackets are used to represent a naming scheme (for an example, see Sect. 6.1).

Table 1. Relevant artifacts of the media partition, located in /media/... (Android 9/10) or /media/Android/media/com.whatsapp/... (Android 13).

ID	Filename	Path	Type	Content
1	STK-[YYYYMMDD]-WA[NNNN].webp	WhatsApp/Media/WhatsApp Stickers/	WEBP	actual sticker file
2	[Base64].thumb.webp	WhatsApp/.StickerThumbs/	WEBP	animated sticker file preview

Table 2. Relevant artifacts of the data partition, for all Android versions located in /data/data/com.whatsapp/....

ID	Filename	Path	Type	Content
3	wa.db	databases/	SQLite	contact & profile records
4	msgstore.db	databases/	SQLite	communication records
5	stickers.db	databases/	SQLite	data for sticker menu
6	media.db	databases/	SQLite	media download records
7	whatsapp.log	files/Logs/	text file	main log of WhatsApp
8	whatsapp-[YYYY-MM-DD].log.gz	files/Logs/	GNU zip	former versions of log
9	[SHA256 in Base64].webp	files/Stickers/	WEBP	copy of sticker file
10	[SHA256 in Base64][RESOLUTION].0	cache/webp_static_cache/	PNG	preview of sticker
11	[SHA256 in Base64].tmp[RESOLUTION].0	cache/webp_static_cache/	PNG	preview of sticker

6   Fundamental Results

We will now explain our fundamental results before addressing the legal questions at hand in the subsequent sections. Most importantly, each downloaded sticker file (ID 1, in Table 1) is stored in the directory /WhatsApp/Media /WhatsApp Stickers which is either located in the root directory (Android 9/10) or in /Android/media/com.whatsapp (Android 13) of the media partition.

6.1   Sticker Files

The filenames of the sticker files adhere to the scheme: STK-[YYYYMMDD] -WA[NNNN].webp, whereas the date (YYYYMMDD) reflects the day of reception and is based on the device time,

Listing 6.1. The structure of a static sticker file with optional ICC profile and alpha channel information.

```
Chunk  |  Length | Offset | Payload (excerpt)
RIFF   |  21346  |     0  | WEBP
VP8X   |     10  |    12  | 8.......
ICCP   |    536  |    30  | .........0..mntrRGB XYZ ...
ALPH   |   7164  |   574  | .!.m.F....._8I.BD.'.I. ...o>
VP8    |  13218  |  7746  | p....*....>1..D"!..yu. ....
EXIF   |    374  | 20972  | II*.......AW..'.......{"sti
```

just like the file system timestamp. In addition, NNNN is a counter that starts at 0 and increments by 1 with each sticker received that day. However, each sticker, as identified by its SHA256 hash, is only saved once, regardless of the time it was received, how many times, or in which chats. However, this is only true when WhatsApp correctly references all stored stickers; for exceptions, see Sect. 8.1. Nevertheless, the filename reflects the circumstances of the very first time that sticker was received.

The stickers adhere to the WebP standard [8], which is a container format for media content and is based on the Resource Interchange File Format (RIFF). In Listing 6.1 we show the structure of a static sticker file. The VP8X chunk indicates which features are present in the given file, such as alpha channel information. Next, follow optional chunks for an ICC profile (indicated by ICCP) or the referenced alpha channel information (ALPH). Then, a VP8 chunk follows which contains the actual image data to be displayed. On the contrary, animated stickers contain an additional chunk with animation information (ANIM) and carry the media content in multiple frames (each indicated by ANMF). Afterwards, optional metadata follows, whereas each examined sticker file concludes with a chunk of Exif information (EXIF).

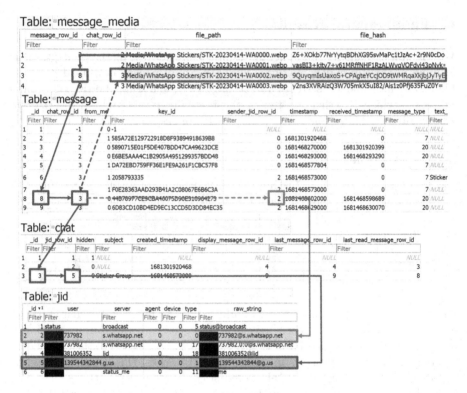

Fig. 6. Excerpts of `msgstore.db`, markings show the reconstruction of a sticker origin by the example of a group chat. (Color figure online)

6.2 Tracing the Sender

WhatsApp records communication in the `msgstore.db` (see ID 4 in Table 2), including receiving and sending of stickers. In Fig. 6 we trace a sticker, as identified by its file hash and file path (highlighted yellow) in the `message_media` table, back to the originating chat (red markings). First of all, the column `message_row_id` references an entry in the `message` table which, in turn references an entry in the `chat` table. The `chat` table is also referenced by the `message_media` table, hence, this is redundant information. The `chat` table, most importantly, references an entry in the `jid` table by a `jid_row_id`, which finally points to the chat in which the sticker was received, in this case, this is a group with the identifier ******139544342844.

In contrast, if the sticker had been received in a one-on-one chat, we would discover a user identifier and thus the sender. However, in this case we only identified a group. Now, to identify the concrete sender within the group, we need further information from the `message` table (blue markings), namely, the `sender_jid_row_id`, which again references the `jid` table. But this time the referenced entry contains the user identifier, which is actually the registered phone number (******737982), of the user who sent the sticker to the group, hence the sender is identified. In a one-on-one chat, the `sender_jid_row_id` is 0, hence, invalid.

Furthermore, if the user of the device under investigation is the sender of the sticker in question, the value of the `from_me` column in the `message` table would be 1 while the `chat_row_id` would identify the recipient, again either a specific user or a group.

6.3 Timestamps Set by WhatsApp

WhatsApp uses several timestamps in its databases, in the `whatsapp.log` and for its file names (see Sect. 6.1). We found that the timestamps in the `whatsapp.log` reflect the local device time without stating the local timezone used and are in human readable format (similar ISO 8601). Furthermore, we can confirm that timestamps which indicate by their name to come from the server, e.g. `receipt_server_timestamp`, indeed reflect the server time in our experiments. On the contrary, any other timestamp reflects the local device time in UTC+0, which is consistent with the findings of Anglano [1].

6.4 Hints to the Origin

Information of a stickers origin and creation may be found in the embedded metadata, for example, in the `EXIF` tag (see Listing 6.1).

Each of the stickers studied contained a JSON in its `EXIF` tag, an example is shown in Listing 6.2 which is not altered by distribution. The embedded information is partly used to retrieve more stickers from the same source, e.g. by the `sticker-pack-id` or to manage stickers within WhatsApp, e.g. the `emojis` key is used to organize stickers by mood. In this case, the `sticker-pack-publisher` and the `android-app-store-link` point to the sticker maker that was used to create the sticker. The `sticker-pack-name` was assigned by us, in contrast, the `sticker-pack-id` was assigned by the sticker maker app used. However, while every sticker has such an embedded JSON, the actual available information differs tremendously, depending on a sticker's origin.

Listing 6.2. Exif metadata of a sticker.

```
{"sticker-pack-id": "stickerwhatsapp.com.stickers.stickercontentprovider afylruu",
"sticker-pack-name": "RECEIVE",
"sticker-pack-publisher": "Sticker Make for Wha[sic]",
"android-app-store-link": "https://play.google.com/store/apps/details?id=stickerwhatsapp.com.
     ↪ stickers",
"emojis": [[...]]}
```

6.5 Google Drive Backups

A Google Drive backup restores sticker files that were referenced in a chat and stored on the device at the time of backup, as well as data from the `/data/com.whatsapp/` directory, including databases, log files, and even cache files. Therefore, all of our findings can be applied to data restored from a Google

Drive back up, as even the original filenames of the stickers are recovered, and
hence the filename still represents the circumstances of the very first reception
before the backup. This means that it is possible that the filename of a sticker
points to a date on which the device at hand was not yet in use. Consequently,
a device can contain evidence of crimes committed with another device.

7   Evidence for Distribution

The distribution of a sticker by the user of the device under investigation can be
proven with the `msgstore.db` database (ID 4, in Table 2), as shown in Sect. 6.2.
In summary, the complete communication, including the time of distribution and
the recipients, can be reconstructed, under the premise that the `message_media`
table has a record for the searched sticker. However, these records are only available if the respective message or chat have not been deleted after the distribution.
In this case, the distribution can be proven by resorting to WhatsApp's records
of recently used stickers (see Fig. 2).

The recently sent stickers are recorded in the `recent_stickers` table of the
`stickers.db` (artifact ID 5, in Table 2) in which a sticker can be identified by
its file hash, referred to as `plaintext_hash` here. Furthermore, the timestamp
of the last distribution is available in the `last_sticker_sent_ts` column, and
the `entry_weight` column is actually a counter for executed send operations.
However, a user can easily initiate the removal of these entries by deleting a
sticker from the recent stickers menu (see Fig. 2). Fortunately, every insertion
and removal from the `recent_stickers` table is recorded in `whatsapp.log`, as
shown in Listing 7.1. Therefore, while the recipients of a sticker remain unclear,
some distributions can be proven.

Listing 7.1. Excerpt of whatsapp.log that records the sending or forwarding of a
sticker.

```
2023-04-12 12:29:41.552 [...] RecentStickers/addEntry/adding entry:
    ↪ WeightedRecentStickerIdentifier{stickerIdentifier=RecentStickerIdentifier{fileHash='
    ↪ ELkg[...]', imageHash='sqrI[...]', sticker=Sticker{[...]}, weight=1.0}
[...]
2023-04-18 09:13:32.573 [...] RecentStickers/removeEntry/removing entry:
    ↪ RecentStickerIdentifier{fileHash='ELkg[...]', imageHash='sqrI[...]', sticker=Sticker
    ↪ {[...]}, lastStickerSentTs=1681302581878,[...]}
```

8   Evidence for Possession

While the evidence for distribution is unambiguous, the determination if a sticker
in the `WhatsApp Stickers` directory is possessed by a defendant is complex;
hence, we now discuss the aspects of control and knowledge of existence, identified as the main characteristics of possession in Sect. 3, in detail. While intention
is also an integral component in some jurisdictions and must be considered in a
prosecution, we will not discuss its aspects in this paper, as it is hardly technically.

8.1 Control

Cache Behavior. Although sticker files are stored in the media partition, they exhibit cache-like behavior. For example, stickers are automatically stored on the device upon receipt and are automatically deleted from the file system when they are no longer referenced in a chat. Additionally, a user has little option to affect this behavior. To be more precise, static stickers are downloaded even when the automatic media download has been disabled while the user cannot object to the automatic removal in any way, for example, when the sticker was part of a disappearing message. Consequently, sticker files are temporary and only reflect the state of the sticker within WhatsApp.

This is also reflected by the fact that stickers are downloaded and stored only once, regardless of how often they have been received. Therefore, storing the sticker files locally improves the user experience, e.g. due to offline displaying capabilities, reduced loading times and reduced data usage; hence, improve the apps performance which is the typical aim of caching. Furthermore, there is no indication that WhatsApp wants a user to handle sticker files, as they are treated differently than other media file types (see Sect. 2). To summarize, sticker files are temporary, improve the performance and are solely managed by WhatsApp, which is typical behavior for an application cache.

File System Access. Due to the full read and write privileges on the media partition, a user is capable to exercise full control over a sticker file in the file system once downloaded and before deleted. Most importantly, stickers deleted by the user in the file system are not automatically recovered by WhatsApp, not even when a backup is restored[3]. However, only technically skilled users can exercise this control over sticker files by manually browsing the file system with a file manager, as the respective storage area is not presented to the user, unlike, for example, the WhatsApp Images directory (see Sect. 2.2).

Control from WhatsApp. In turn, from within WhatsApp, every user can exercise three types of control over a sticker. First, a user can delete sticker files indirectly, yet reliably, from the WhatsApp Stickers directory[4] by any kind of removing operation offered, such as removing the received sticker from the chat, clearing the entire chat history, or blocking the contact. Second, a user is capable to redistribute stickers, as shown in Sect. 2. Third, users can control whether a sticker is added to their sticker menu by marking it as a favorite. These WhatsApp-specific options enable every user to control stickers to some extent.

---

[3] The deleted sticker in the respective chat is replaced by a button that allows the user to re-download a missing sticker.

[4] Under the condition that the sticker is not used in another chat.

Uninstalling and Migrating WhatsApp. In general, the files within the WhatsApp Stickers directory are in sync with the status of a sticker in WhatsApp. However, this linkage dissolves when WhatsApp is uninstalled on Android 9 and Android 10[5], while, the sticker files remain on the device. In this case, the only way a non-technically savvy user can exhibit control of a sticker diminishes. Even when WhatsApp is reinstalled and recovered from a backup the link to the stored sticker files is not recovered, in contrary, they are simply re-downloaded which leads unusually to several instances of identical stickers. The newly downloaded stickers again can be controlled from within WhatsApp, but not the old instances.

Although this effect appeared in our scenarios only on Android 9 and Android 10, sticker files on newer operating system may also be affected, as the device may have been upgraded from an older Android version which would migrate the sticker files to the newer operating system without restoring the ability to control these files.

Assessing Control for Prosecution. To sum up, although the sticker files are saved in a user-accessible storage area, there are arguments that contradict the assumption that the sticker files in the WhatsApp Stickers directory are under the control of the user. Therefore, the ascertainment that a sticker file is stored on a device is not sufficient and a digital forensic examination should bring those sticker files to light, which are accessible from within WhatsApp, and hence, evidently controllable by a user.

8.2   Knowledge of Existence

First of all, WhatsApp downloads sticker files to the WhatsApp Stickers directory, regardless of whether the chat has been opened by the user. Since the user is not confronted with sticker files in any other context, as shown in Sect. 2.2, an investigator cannot assume that a user knows that a sticker exists even when it is referenced in WhatsApp's user interface. Therefore, an examination must further verify the evidence of knowledge.

Distributing, Quoting and Starring. The best evidence for knowledge is the proof that a user actively engaged with a sticker, for example, by distributing, quoting, or starring. Therefore, the evidence of distribution that we presented in Sect. 7 can also be used to prove knowledge. However, stickers that were quoted, which is not a distribution, are handled slightly differently. To be more precise, they are recorded in message_quoted_media table of the msgstore.db instead of the message_media table while the rest of the communication can be reconstructed, as demonstrated in Sect. 7 and Fig. 6.

Additionally, the msgstore.db database (ID 4, in Table 2) records which sticker messages have been marked as favorites by setting the starred column

---

[5] WhatsApp on Android 13 asks the user if "keep app data" is desired. Irrespective of the users' choice on Android 13 the user stays in control of the sticker files.

of the `message` table to 1. Furthermore, the `stickers.db` database (ID 5, in Table 2) records favorite stickers in the `starred_stickers` table. Finally, every sticker that was sent, forwarded or marked as favorite is additionally stored in the `/data/com.whatsapp/files/verbStickers/` directory of the data partition, by the name of their file hash, e.g. `aOFxYpH-avyuN7RqWB+Zdz7Kd6DhyNWbc++cVy 7xeoE=.webp` (ID 9, in Table 2). This is not the case for stickers with which the user has not been interacting with; hence, this also proves that the user was aware of the existence of a sticker.

Manual Download. Furthermore, a manual download of a sticker is also strong evidence that a user must know of the existence of a sticker. Fortunately, WhatsApp logs media downloads with their respective settings in the `whatsapp.log` log file (artifact ID 7, in Table 2), as shown in Listing 8.1 for a manually downloaded sticker. A manual download is indicated by `autoDownload=0`, `mode=manual` and `MediaDownloadManager/` start manual download, consequently, automatically downloaded stickers are logged with `autoDownload=1`, `mode=auto` and `MediaDownloadManager/` queueDownload auto download. Therefore, the log records the actual mode that was used to download a sticker and not the state of the auto-download setting; hence, actually proves a manual download.

Listing 8.1. Excerpt of whatsapp.log that indicates an automatic download of a sticker as identified by its hash.

```
2023-04-18 11:41:02.691 [...] MediaDownload/initialized;mediaHash=fSxk[...] autoDownload=0
[...]
2023-04-18 11:41:02.694 [...] MediaDownloadManager/start manual download [...], message.
    ↪ mediaHash=fSxk[...]
[...]
2023-04-18 11:41:03.004 [...] MediaDownload/updateMessageAfterDownload/mediaHash=fSxk[...]
    ↪ url=https://157.240.223.60/[...]&mode=manual status=success
```

Evidence for Display. While the display of a sticker may indicate knowledge, it is rather weak evidence, as a user must not see everything that was displayed, e.g. when scrolling to the end of a conversation rapidly. However, the display can be proven, as WhatsApp creates thumbnails of stickers when displaying them in a chat or in the notification bar. These thumbnails are stored in the data partition in the `/data/com.whatsapp/cache/webp_static_cache` directory (ID 10 and 11 in Table 2). The thumbnail file name contains the resolution (i.e. 64x64px) and the SHA256 hash of the actual sticker encoded in Base64, e.g. $\backslash Z6 + XOkb77NrYytqBDhXG95svMaPc1tJzAc + 2r9NOcDo = .tmp\_64\_64.0$. The existence of a thumbnail with a resolution of 64x64px indicates that the sticker was shown in the notification bar whereas a thumbnail with a resolution of 438x438px was displayed in a chat.

9 Summary

We strongly advise that a prosecution should not be based exclusively on the existence of an incriminating sticker file in the WhatsApp Stickers directory, as this neither proves knowledge nor control. Therefore, in Table 3 we sum up our findings for each relevant artifact with respect to the evidence available under a given premise and, hence, open up the opportunity to prosecute stickers profoundly.

However, all artifacts that can prove distribution, knowledge, or control are stored in Android's data partition, which may not be acquirable in an investigation. This issue can at least partially be circumvented with a live examination, as the contents of the msgstore.db database and the stickers.db database, are reflected in WhatsApp's user interface.

Table 3. Summary of artifacts, incl. ID and evidence contained for Distribution, Knowledge and Control.

ID	Name	Premise	Evidence of...		
			Dis.	Knowl.	Cont.
1	STK-[YYYYMMDD]-WA[NNNN].webp	-	×	×	×
2	[Base64].thumb.webp	-	×	×	×
3	wa.db	-	×	×	×
4	msgstore.db: message_media	hash & path identical	×	×	✓
4	msgstore.db: message_media	hash & path identical, from_me=1	✓	✓	✓
4	msgstore.db: message_quoted_media	hash & path identical	×	✓	✓
4	msgstore.db: message	starred=1	×	✓	✓
5	stickers.db: recent_stickers	hash identical	✓	✓	✓
5	stickers.db: starred_stickers	hash identical	×	✓	✓
6	media.db	-	×	×	×
7	whatsapp.log	hash in RecentStickers/[add|remove]Entry	✓	✓	✓
8	whatsapp-[YYYY-MM-DD].log.gz	hash in RecentStickers/[add|remove]Entry	✓	✓	✓
9	[SHA256 in Base64].webp	hash in file name	×	✓	✓
10	[SHA256 in Base64].=.tmp_64_64.0	hash in file name	×	see Sect. 8.2	✓
10	[SHA256 in Base64]_438_438.0	hash in file name	×	see Sect. 8.2	✓

10   Conclusion

WhatsApp and stickers are a widespread and popular way to communicate. However, they can be used to distribute incriminated files and, hence, are in the focus of LEAs. Our study shows that a user can have stickers on its device without knowing or wanting to. For example, as a member of a innocuous group which is muted and rarely read a user has no option to prevent the unaware and automatic storage of a sticker on its device. Therefore, the mere existence of an incriminated sticker does not satisfy the prerequisites for possession. However, in such cases we show that deleting the sticker from the chat and from the file system is sufficient to effectively extirpate the incriminated content.

Furthermore, to hold offenders accountable, we identified evidence that proves distribution, knowledge, or control, even when the respective information has been removed from WhatsApp's user interface. However, our results show that a logical acquisition of an Android device is insufficient for prosecution in any case, whereas a live examination can be used in case access to the data partition is not available. On the other hand, we show that seizing a device is not effective to deny an offender access to the incriminated material as stickers can be immediately restored from a Google Drive backup, hence, the access to the backup must be prohibited, as well.

Overall, we showed that the concept of possession presents several intricate challenges that require careful examination during a digital investigation. While the possession of digital files when they are stored in an application's working directory has concerned courts for a long time, there is little digital forensic research on the topic, especially beyond browser caches. This is concerning, as smartphones and their apps are an important part of most peoples lives today, and, while it is the duty of the judge and the jury to evaluate if incriminated files are possessed, it is the duty of us to deliver the facts necessary to make the evaluation.

A   Detailed Description of Executed Scenarios

Table 4. Scenarios executed for this paper.

ID	scenarios	chat types	contact status	auto downl.	sticker types	devices	actions
I.1	RECEIVE-ON-DISPLAY	1:1, group	contact, stranger	ON	3rd-party, 1st-party anim.	(virt.) Pixel 6a Pro, (virt.) Pixel 3a, Galaxy S9+	sticker received, chat opened
I.2	RECEIVE-ON-NODISPLAY	1:1, group	contact, stranger	ON	3rd-party, 1st-party anim.	(virt.) Pixel 6a Pro, (virt.) Pixel 3a, Galaxy S9+	sticker received, chat unopened
I.3	RECEIVE-OFF-DISPLAY	1:1, group	contact, stranger	OFF	3rd-party, 1st-party anim.	(virt.) Pixel 6a Pro, (virt.) Pixel 3a	sticker received, chat opened
I.4	RECEIVE-OFF-NODISPLAY	1:1, group	contact, stranger	OFF	3rd-party, 1st-party anim.	(virt.) Pixel 6a Pro, (virt.) Pixel 3a	sticker received, chat unopened
I.5	RECEIVE-TWICE	1:1, group	contact, stranger	ON	3rd-party	(virt.) Pixel 3a, Galaxy S9+	same sticker received twice in one chat
I.6	RECEIVE-TWICE-CROSSCHAT	1:1, group	contact, stranger	ON	3rd-party	(virt.) Pixel 6a Pro	same sticker received in one group chat and in a 1:1 chat
I.7	MARK-AS-READ-NODISPLAY	1:1	contact, stranger	ON	3rd-party, 1st-party anim.	(virt.) Pixel 6a Pro	sticker received automatically, chat unopened, chat marked as read
I.8	MARK-AS-READ-DISPLAY	1:1	contact, stranger	ON	3rd-party, 1st-party anim.	(virt.) Pixel 6a Pro	sticker received automatically, chat unopened, chat marked as read, chat opened
I.9	WRONG-DEVICE-TIME	1:1	stranger	ON	3rd-party, 1st-party anim.	(virt.) Pixel 6a Pro	sticker received, system time set to past, sticker received, system time set to future, sticker received
II.1	INTERACT-REPLY	1:1, group	stranger	ON	3rd-party	(virt.) Pixel 6a Pro	reply to received sticker
II.2	INTERACT-FAVORITE	1:1, group	stranger	ON	3rd-party	(virt.) Pixel 3a, Galaxy S9+	mark received sticker as favorite

(continued)

Table 4. (*continued*)

ID	scenarios	chat types	contact status	auto downl.	sticker types	devices	actions
II.3	INTERACT-FORWARD	1:1, group	stranger	ON	3rd-party	(virt.) Pixel 3a, Galaxy S9+	forward received sticker
II.4	INTERACT-SEND	1:1, group	stranger	ON	3rd-party	(virt.) Pixel 3a, Galaxy S9+	mark received sticker as favorite (prerequ. for sending of received stickers) than sent by receiver, than sent again (repeat 5 times)
III.1	DELETE-FROM-CHAT	1:1, group	stranger	ON	3rd-party, 1st-party anim.	(virt.) Pixel 6a Pro, (virt.) Pixel 3a, Galaxy S9+	sticker received, sticker message deleted in chat
III.2	DELETE-CHAT	1:1, group	stranger	ON	3rd-party, 1st-party anim.	(virt.) Pixel 3a, Galaxy S9+	sticker received, complete chat deleted
III.3	CLEAR-CHAT	1:1, group	stranger	ON	3rd-party, 1st-party anim.	(virt.) Pixel 6a Pro	sticker received, chat cleared
III.4	DELETE-FROM-FS	1:1, group	stranger	ON	3rd-party, 1st-party anim.	(virt.) Pixel 6a Pro	sticker received, sticker deleted from file-system, +analysis of Google Drive BU (see IV.5)
III.5	DELETE-ONE-OF-TWO	1:1, group	stranger	ON	3rd-party	(virt.) Pixel 6a Pro	same sticker received twice in one chat, one of two sticker messages deleted
III.6	DEL-ONE-OF-TWO-CROSS	1:1, group	stranger	ON	3rd-party	(virt.) Pixel 6a Pro	same sticker received in one group chat and in one 1:1 chat, one of two sticker messages deleted
III.7	DELETE-BY-ADMIN	group	stranger	ON	3rd-party	(virt.) Pixel 3a, Galaxy S9+	sticker received, sticker deleted by admin for all group members

(*continued*)

Table 4. (*continued*)

III.8	DISAPPEARING	group	stranger	ON	3rd-party, 1st-party anim.	(virt.) Pixel 6a Pro	sticker sent to a group which messages will disappear after 24 hours
III.9	DISAPPEARING-AFTER	group	stranger	ON	3rd-party, 1st-party anim.	(virt.) Pixel 6a Pro	sticker sent to a group which messages disappeared after 24 hours
III.10	DELETE-REPLY-CHAT	1:1, group	stranger	ON	3rd-party	(virt.) Pixel 6a Pro	reply to received sticker, delete all traces of sticker from chat
III.11	DELETE-FAV-CHAT	1:1, group	stranger	ON	3rd-party	(virt.) Pixel 6a Pro	mark received sticker as favorite, delete all traces of sticker from chat
III.12	DELETE-FWD-CHAT	1:1, group	stranger	ON	3rd-party	(virt.) Pixel 6a Pro	forward received sticker, delete all traces of sticker from chat
III.13	DELETE-SEND-CHAT	1:1, group	stranger	ON	3rd-party	(virt.) Pixel 6a Pro	mark received sticker as favorite (prerequ. for sending of received stickers) than sent by receiver, delete all traces of sticker from chat
III.14	DELETE-FAV-MENU	1:1, group	stranger	ON	3rd-party	(virt.) Pixel 3a, Galaxy S9+	mark received sticker as favorite, delete from favorites menu
III.15	DELETE-FWD-MENU	1:1, group	stranger	ON	3rd-party	(virt.) Pixel 6a Pro	forward received sticker, delete from recent menu
III.16	DELETE-SEND-MENU	1:1, group	stranger	ON	3rd-party	(virt.) Pixel 3a, Galaxy S9+	mark received sticker as favorite (prerequ. for sending of received stickers) than sent by receiver, delete sticker from favorites and recent menu
III.17	DELETE-FAV-COMPLETE	1:1, group	stranger	ON	3rd-party	(virt.) Pixel 6a Pro	mark received sticker as favorite, delete all traces of sticker from chat and favorites menu
III.18	DELETE-FWD-COMPLETE	1:1, group	stranger	ON	3rd-party	(virt.) Pixel 6a Pro	forward received sticker, delete all traces of sticker from chat and recent menu

(continued)

Table 4. (*continued*)

III.19	DELETE-SEND-COMPLETE	1:1, group	stranger	ON	3rd-party	(virt.) Pixel 6a Pro	mark received sticker as favorite (prerequ. for sending of received stickers) than sent by receiver, delete all traces of sticker from chat, favorites and recent menu
III.20	BLOCK-CONTACT	1:1	stranger	ON	3rd-party	(virt.) Pixel 6a Pro	sticker received, sender blocked
IV.1	UNINSTALL-KEEP	1:1, group	stranger	ON	3rd-party	(virt.) Pixel 6a Pro	sticker received, WhatsApp uninstalled (check "keep app data")
IV.2	UNINSTALL-NOKEEP	1:1, group	stranger	ON	3rd-party	(virt.) Pixel 6a Pro	sticker received, WhatsApp uninstalled (default, "keep app data" unchecked)
IV.3	UNINSTALL	1:1, group	stranger	ON	3rd-party	(virt.) Pixel 3a, Galaxy S9+	sticker received, WhatsApp uninstalled (no uninstall options available)
IV.4	REINSTALL-RECEIVE	1:1, group	stranger	ON	3rd-party	(virt.) Pixel 6a Pro, (virt.) Pixel 3a, Galaxy S9+	sticker received, WhatsApp uninstalled (each uninstall options available), WhatsApp reinstalled, sticker re-received
IV.5	DRIVE-BACKUP	1:1	stranger	ON	3rd-party	(virt.) Pixel 6a Pro, (virt.) Pixel 3a	sticker received, chat unopened, backed up to Google Drive, default uninstall and re-install of WhatsApp, Drive back up restored
IV.6	DRIVE-BU-DELETE-CHAT	1:1	stranger	ON	3rd-party	(virt.) Pixel 6a Pro, (virt.) Pixel 3a	sticker received, chat unopened, chat deleted, backed up to Google Drive, default uninstall and re-install of WhatsApp, Drive back up restored
IV.7	DRIVE-BU-RERECEIVE	1:1	stranger	ON	3rd-party, 1st-party anim.	(virt.) Pixel 6a Pro, (virt.) Pixel 3a	sticker received, chat unopened, backed up to Google Drive, default uninstall and re-install of WhatsApp, Drive back up restored, same sticker received again

References

1. Anglano, C.: Forensic analysis of whatsapp messenger on android smartphones. Digit. Investig. **11**(3), 201–213 (2014)
2. Baden-Württemberg, L.: Strafbare inhalte bei whatsapp und co. Technical report, Polizei Baden-Württemberg (2019)
3. Casey, E.: Digital Evidence and Computer Crime: Forensic Science, Computers, and the Internet. Academic Press, Cambridge (2011)
4. Chang, Y.C.: Law and Economics of Possession. Cambridge University Press, Cambridge (2015)
5. Europol: Operation chemosh: how encrypted chat groups exchanged emoji "stickers" of child sexual abuse (2019)
6. Fayyad-Kazan, H., Kassem-Moussa, S., Hejase, H.J., Hejase, A.J.: Forensic analysis of whatsapp sqlite databases on the unrooted android phones. HighTech Innov. J. **3**(2), 175–195 (2022)
7. Google: Mediastore (2023). https://developer.android.com/reference/android/provider/MediaStore#MEDIA_IGNORE_FILENAME
8. Google: Webp container specification (2023). https://developers.google.com/speed/webp/docs/riff_container
9. Horsman, G.: I didn't see that! an examination of internet browser cache behaviour following website visits. Digit. Investig. **25**, 105–113 (2018)
10. Horsman, G.: Reconstructing streamed video content: a case study on youtube and facebook live stream content in the chrome web browser cache. Digit. Investig. **26**, S30–S37 (2018)
11. Howard, T.E.: Don't cache out your case: Prosecuting child pornograpy possession laws based on images located in temporary internet files. Berkeley Tech. LJ **19**, 1227 (2004)
12. International Centre for Missing & Exploited Children: Child sexual abuse material: Model legislation & global review (2018)
13. Karpisek, F., Baggili, I., Breitinger, F.: Whatsapp network forensics: decrypting and understanding the whatsapp call signaling messages. Digit. Investig. **15**, 110–118 (2015)
14. van Kesteren, M., van Eeten, M., van Wegberg, R.: CSAM data - factcheck of recent European commission statements (2023)
15. Klier, S., Varenkamp, J., Baier, H.: Back and forth – on automatic exposure of origin and dissemination of files on windows. Digit. Threats Res. Pract. (2023). https://doi.org/10.1145/3609232
16. Marin, G.: Possession of child pornography: should you be convicted when the computer cache does the saving for you. Fla. L. Rev. **60**, 1205 (2008)
17. Meng, C., Baier, H.: bring2lite: a structural concept and tool for forensic data analysis and recovery of deleted sqlite records. Digit. Investig. **29**, S31–S41 (2019)
18. Nemetz, S., Schmitt, S., Freiling, F.: A standardized corpus for sqlite database forensics. Digit. Investig. **24**, S121–S130 (2018)
19. Pawlaszczyk, D., Hummert, C.: Making the invisible visible-techniques for recovering deleted sqlite data records. Int. J. Cyber Forensics Adv. Threat Investig. **1**(1–3), 27–41 (2021)
20. Rösler, P., Mainka, C., Schwenk, J.: More is less: on the end-to-end security of group chats in signal, whatsapp, and threema. In: 2018 IEEE European Symposium on Security and Privacy (EuroS&P), pp. 415–429. IEEE (2018)

21. Schmehl, K.: Whatsapp has become a hotbed for spreading nazi propaganda in Germany (2019). https://www.buzzfeednews.com/article/karstenschmehl/whatsapp-groups-nazi-symbol-stickers-germany. Accessed 28 May 2023
22. Statista: Most popular global mobile messenger apps as of January 2022, based on number of monthly active users (2022). https://www.statista.com/statistics/258749/most-popular-global-mobile-messenger-apps/
23. Statista: Most popular social networks worldwide as of January 2023, ranked by number of monthly active users (2023). https://www.statista.com/statistics/272014/global-social-networks-ranked-by-number-of-users/
24. Sticker.ly: Sticker.ly - sticker maker (2023). https://play.google.com/store/apps/details?id=com.snowcorp.stickerly.android. Accessed 30 June 2023
25. TcitNews: Whatsapp expanding features with in-app sticker creation capability (2023). https://tcitnews.com/whatsapp-expanding-features-with-in-app-sticker-creation-capability/. Accessed 10 July 2023
26. WhatsApp: How to create stickers for whatsapp (2018). https://faq.whatsapp.com/1056840314992666/. Accessed 29 Mar 2023
27. WhatsApp: Introducing stickers (2018). https://blog.whatsapp.com/introducing-stickers?lang=en
28. YouTube: How to create your own whatsapp stickers with iphone — whatsapp sticker new update (2023). https://www.youtube.com/watch?v=0UG-JDt0-1o. Accessed 10 July 2023

Machine Learning and Artificial Intelligence in Information Security

A More Secure Split: Enhancing the Security of Privacy-Preserving Split Learning

Tanveer Khan[1]([✉])[iD], Khoa Nguyen[1][iD], and Antonis Michalas[1,2][iD]

[1] Tampere University, Tampere, Finland
{tanveer.khan,khoa.nguyen,antonios.michalas}@tuni.fi
[2] RISE Research Institutes of Sweden, Gothenburg, Sweden

Abstract. Split learning (SL) is a new collaborative learning technique that allows participants, e.g. a client and a server, to train machine learning models without the client sharing raw data. In this setting, the client initially applies its part of the machine learning model on the raw data to generate Activation Maps (AMs) and then sends them to the server to continue the training process. Previous works in the field demonstrated that reconstructing AMs could result in privacy leakage of client data. In addition to that, existing mitigation techniques that overcome the privacy leakage of SL prove to be significantly worse in terms of accuracy. In this paper, we improve upon previous works by constructing a protocol based on U-shaped SL that can operate on homomorphically encrypted data. More precisely, in our approach, the client applies homomorphic encryption on the AMs before sending them to the server, thus protecting user privacy. This is an important improvement that reduces privacy leakage in comparison to other SL-based works. Finally, our results show that, with the optimum set of parameters, training with HE data in the U-shaped SL setting only reduces accuracy by 2.65% compared to training on plaintext. In addition, raw training data privacy is preserved.

Keywords: Activation Maps · Homomorphic Encryption · Machine Learning · Privacy · Split Learning

1 Introduction

Nowadays, machine learning (ML) methods are widely used in many applications due to their predictive and generative power. However, this raises serious concerns regarding user data privacy, leading to the need for privacy-preserving machine learning (PPML) solutions [9]. Split Learning (SL) and Federated

This work was funded by the Technology Innovation Institute (TII) for the project ARROWSMITH and from Horizon Europe for HARPOCRATES (101069535).

L. Fritsch et al. (Eds.): NordSec 2023, LNCS 14324, pp. 307–329, 2024.
https://doi.org/10.1007/978-3-031-47748-5_17

Learning (FL) are two PPML methods that rely on training ML models on decentralized data sources [19]. In FL [22], every client runs a copy of the entire model on its data. The server receives updated weights from each client and aggregates them. The SL [7] model divides the Neural Network (NN) into two parts: the client-side and the server-side. SL is used for training NN among multiple data sources, while mitigating the need to directly share raw labeled data with collaboration parties. The advantages of SL are multifold: *(i)* it allows multiple parties to collaboratively train a NN, *(ii)* it allows users to train ML models without sharing their raw data with a server running part of a NN model, thus preserving user privacy, *(iii)* it protects both the client and the server from revealing their parts of the model, and *(iv)* it reduces the client's computational overhead by not running the entire model [20].

Though SL offers an extra layer of privacy protection by definition, there are no works exploring how it is combined with popular techniques that promise to preserve user privacy (e.g. encryption). In [1], the authors studied whether SL can handle sensitive time-series data and demonstrated that SL alone is *insufficient* when performing privacy-preserving training for 1-dimensional (1D) CNN models. More precisely, the authors showed raw data can be reconstructed from the AMs of the intermediate split layer. The authors also employed two mitigation techniques, adding hidden layers and applying differential privacy to reduce privacy leakage. However, based on the results, none of these techniques can effectively reduce privacy leakage from all channels of the SL activation. Furthermore, both these techniques result in significantly reducing the joint model's accuracy.

In this paper, we focus on training an ML model in a privacy-preserving manner, where a client and a server collaborate to train the model. More specifically, we construct a model that uses Homomorphic Encryption (HE) [4] to mitigate privacy leakage in SL. In our model, the client first encrypts the AMs and then sends the Encrypted Activation Maps (EAMs) to the server. The EAMs do *not* reveal anything about the raw data (i.e. it is *not* possible to reconstruct the original raw data from the EAM).

Contributions: The main contributions of this paper are:

C1. We designed a simplified version of the 1D CNN model presented in [1] and we are using it to classify the ECG signals [16] in both local and SL settings. More specifically, we construct a U-shaped split 1D CNN model and experiment using plaintext AMs sent from the client to the server. Through the U-shaped 1D CNN model, clients do *not* need to share the input training samples and the ground truth labels with the server – this is an important improvement that reduces privacy leakage compared to [1].

C2. We constructed the HE version of the U-shaped SL technique. In the encrypted U-shaped SL model, the client encrypts the AM using HE and sends it to the server. The advantage of HE encrypted U-shaped SL over the plaintext U-shaped SL is that server performs computation over EAMs.

C3. To assess the applicability of our framework, we performed experiments on two heartbeat datasets: the MIT-DB [16] and the PTB-XL [21], with PTB-XL currently being the largest open-source electrocardiography dataset to our knowledge. For the MIT-DB dataset, we experimented with AMs of two lengths (256 and 512) for both plaintext and homomorphically EAMs and we have measured the model's performance by considering training duration test accuracy, and communication cost. We performed similar experiments with PTB-XL dataset, however, only with AMs of length 256.

C4. Moreover, our framework takes advantage of batch encryption, an optimization technique for memory and computation, to improve computing performance over encrypted data. We conducted experiments with and without batch encryption and compared results.

C5. We designed a detailed protocol to prove our construction's and provide proof of its security level under the malicious threat model.

Organization: The rest of the paper is organized as follows[1]: In Sect. 2, we present important published works in the area of SL. The architectures of the proposed models are presented in Sect. 3. The design and implementation of split 1D CNN training protocols are described in Sect. 4, formal protocol construction in Sect. 5, protocol security in Sect. 6, extensive experimental results in Sect. 7, and conclude the paper in Sect. 8.

2 Related Work

One of the primary reasons researchers seek novel techniques is to bridge the large gap between existing privacy solutions and the actual practical deployment of NNs. PPML consists of cryptographic approaches such as HE and Multiparty Computation (MPC), differential privacy as well as distributed ML approaches such as FL, and SL [3]. Google AI Blog introduced FL, where users (e.g. mobile devices) collaboratively train a model [15] under a central server's orchestration (e.g. service provider) without sharing their data. However, in FL, sharing user model weights with server can lead to sensitive information leaks [8].

SL approach [7] is a promising approach in terms of client raw data protection, however, SL provides data privacy on the grounds that only intermediate AMs are shared between the parties. Different studies showed the possibility of privacy leakage in SL. In [19], the authors analyzed the privacy leakage of SL and found a considerable leakage from the split layer in the 2D CNN model. Furthermore, the authors mentioned that it is possible to reduce the distance correlation (a measure of dependence) between the split layer and raw data by slightly scaling the weights of all layers before the split. This scaling works well in models with a large number of hidden layers before the split.

---

[1] Due to space constraints, the necessary background information about 1D CNN, HE and SL are in Sect. A.

The work of Abuadbba *et al.* [1] is the first study exploring whether SL can deal with time-series data. The authors proved that only SL cannot preserve the privacy of the data, and employed two techniques to resolve this privacy problem. However, both suffer from a loss of model accuracy, with the use of *differential privacy degrading the classification accuracy significantly from 98.9% to 50%.*

3   Architecture

In this section, we first describe the non-split version or local model of the 1D CNN used to classify the ECG signal. Then, we discuss the process of splitting this local model into a U-shaped split model. Furthermore, we also describe the involved parties (a client and a server) in the training process of the split model, focusing on their roles and the parameters assigned to them throughout the training process. Notations for all parameters and their descriptions is in Table 1.

Table 1. Parameters and Description in the Algorithms

#	ML Parameters	Description	HE Parameters	Description
1	D	Dataset	$\mathcal{P}$	Polynomial modulus
2	$\mathbf{x}, \mathbf{y}$	Input data samples and ground-truth labels	$\mathcal{C}$	Coefficient modulus
3	n, N	Batch size and number of batches to be trained	Δ	Scaling factor
4	w^i, b^i	Weights and biases in layer i	CKKS	Encryption scheme
5	f^i	Linear or convolution operation of layer i	pk	Public key
6	g^i	Activation function of layer i	sk	Secret key
7	$\mathbf{a}^i$	Output activation maps of g^i	HE.Enc	Homomorphic encryption
8	$\mathbf{z}^i$	Output tensor of f^i	HE.Dec	Homomorphic decryption
9	η	Learning rate	HE.Eval	Homomorphic evaluation
10	Φ	Model's weights	ctx_{pri}	Private context
11	E	Number of training epochs	ctx_{pub}	Public context
12	$\mathcal{L}, J$	Loss function and error	$\bar{\mathbf{a}}^i$	Encrypted activation maps
13	O	Optimizer	$\bar{\mathbf{z}}^i$	Encrypted tensor

3.1   1D CNN Local Model Architecture

We first implement and successfully reproduce the local model results [1]. This model contains two Conv1D layers and two FC layers. The optimal test accuracy that this model achieves is 98.9%. We implement a simplified version where the model has one less FC layer compared to the model from [1]. Our local model consists of all the layer of Fig. 1 without any split between the client and the server. As can be seen in Fig. 1, we limit our model to two Conv1D layers and one linear layer as we aim to reduce computational costs when HE is applied on AMs in the model's split version. Reducing the number of FC layers leads to a drop in the accuracy of the model. The best test accuracy we obtained after training our local model for 10 epochs with a n of 4 is 92.84%. *Although reducing the number of layers affects the model's accuracy, it is not within our goals to demonstrate how successful our ML model is for this task; instead, our focus is to construct a split model where training and evaluation on encrypted data are comparable to training and evaluation on plaintext data.* We also apply the simplified 1D CNN on the PTB-XL dataset, with a small modification due to the difference in the number of input channels compared to the dataset from [16]. The training result on the PTB-XL dataset after 10 epochs with a n of 4 is 74.01%, with the best test accuracy of 67.36%. In Sect. 7, we detail results for the non-split version and compare them with split version.

The training process of the local 1D CNN can be described as following: Suppose we have a heartbeat data sample $\mathbf{x} \in \mathbb{R}^c$, where c is the number of input features or the number of time steps. $\mathbf{x}$ belongs to one out of m ground-truth classes. Each data sample $\mathbf{x}$ has a corresponding encoded label vector $\mathbf{y} \in \mathbb{R}^m$ that represents its ground-truth class. We can write the 1D CNN as a function f_Φ, where Φ is a set of adjustable parameters as denoted in Table 1. Φ is first initialized to small random values in the range $[-1, 1]$. Our aim is to find the best set of parameters to map $\mathbf{x}$ to a predicted output vector $\hat{\mathbf{y}} \in \mathbb{R}^m$, where $\hat{\mathbf{y}}$ is as close as possible to $\mathbf{y}$. $\hat{\mathbf{y}}$ can be a vector of m probabilities, and we pick $\mathbf{x}$ to belong to the class with the highest probability. To find the closest value of $\hat{\mathbf{y}}$ with respect to $\mathbf{y}$, we try to minimize a loss function $\mathcal{L}(\hat{\mathbf{y}}, \mathbf{y})$. Training the 1D CNN is an iterative process to find the best Φ to minimize the loss function. This process consists of two sub-processes called "forward propagation" and "backward propagation". More specifically, forward propagation moves from the input $\mathbf{x}$ throughout the network, reaching the output layer and produces the predicted output $\hat{\mathbf{y}}$. Conversely, backward propagation moves from the network's output layer back to the input layer to calculate the gradients of the loss function $\mathcal{L}$ w.r.t the weights Φ of the network. These weights are then updated according to the gradients. The process of calculating the predicted output, the loss function, the gradients and then updating the weights is called "training". We train the NN with thousands of samples of $\mathbf{x}$'s and corresponding $\mathbf{y}$'s, through many iterations of forward and backward propagation. We do not train the network on each single data example, but use a number of them at a time (defined by the n). The total number of training batches is $N = \frac{|D|}{n}$, where $|D|$ is the size of the dataset. Once the NN goes through all the training batches, it has completed one training epoch. This process repeats for E epochs in total.

3.2 U-Shaped Split 1D CNN Model

In this section, we first present the constructed U-shaped split model. We then report in more detail the roles and access rights of the actors who are involved in the training protocols of the split 1D CNN on both plaintexts and EAMs. The SL protocol consists of two parties: the client and server. We split the local 1D CNN into multiple parts, where each party trains its part(s) and communicates with others to complete the overall training procedure. More specifically, we construct the U-shaped split 1D CNN in such a way that the first few as well as the last layer are on the client-side, while the remaining layers are on the server-side, as demonstrated in Fig. 1. The client and server collaborate to train the split model by sharing the AMs and gradients. On the client-side, there are two Conv1D, two Max Pooling, two Leaky ReLU layers, and a Softmax layer. On server-side, there is only one linear layer. As mentioned earlier, the reason for having only one linear layer on the server-side is due to computational constraints when training on encrypted data.

3.3   Actors in the Split Learning Model

As mentioned earlier, in our SL setting, we have two involved parties: the client and the server. Each party plays a specific role and has access to certain parameters. More specifically, their roles and accesses are described as

- Client: In the plaintext version, the client holds two Conv1D layers and can access their weights and biases in plaintext. In the HE encrypted version, the client generates the HE context and has access to all context parameters ($\mathcal{P}$, $\mathcal{C}$, Δ, pk and sk). Note that for both training on plaintext and EAMs, the raw data examples $\mathbf{x}$'s and their corresponding labels $\mathbf{y}$'s reside on the client side and are never sent to the server during the training process.
- Server: In our model, the computation performed on the server-side is limited to only one linear layer. Hence, the server can exclusively access the weights and biases of this linear layer. The server also has access to the HE parameters except for the secret key sk. The hyperparameters shared between the client and the server are η, n, N, E.

4   Split Model Training Protocols

We first present the protocol for training the U-shaped split 1D CNN on plaintext AMs, followed by training the U-shaped split 1D CNN on EAMs.

4.1   Plaintext Activation Maps

We have used Algorithm 1 and Algorithm 2 to train the U-shaped split 1D CNN reported in Subsect. 3.2. First, the client and server start the socket initialization process and synchronize the hyperparameters η, n, N, E. They also initialize the weights of their layers according to Φ.

During forward propagation, the client forward-propagates the input $\mathbf{x}$ until l^{th} layer and sends $\mathbf{a}^{(l)}$ to the server. The server continues to forward propagate and sends the output $\mathbf{a}^{(L)}$ to the client. Next, the client applies the Softmax function on $\mathbf{a}^{(L)}$ to get $\hat{\mathbf{y}}$ and calculates the error $J = \mathcal{L}(\hat{\mathbf{y}}, \mathbf{y})$.

The client starts the backward propagation by calculating and sending the gradient of the error w.r.t $\mathbf{a}^{(L)}$, i.e. $\frac{\partial J}{\partial \mathbf{a}^{(L)}}$, to the server. The server continues the backward propagation, calculates $\frac{\partial J}{\partial \mathbf{a}^{(l)}}$ and sends $\frac{\partial J}{\partial \mathbf{a}^{(l)}}$ to the client. After receiving the gradients $\frac{\partial J}{\partial \mathbf{a}^{(l)}}$ from the server, the backward propagation continues to the first hidden layer on the client-side. Note that the exchange of information between client and server in these algorithms takes place in plaintext. As can be seen in Algorithm 1, the client sends the AMs $\mathbf{a}^{(l)}$ to the server in plaintext and receives the output of the linear layer $\mathbf{a}^{(L)}$ from the server in plaintext. The same applies on the server side: receiving $\mathbf{a}^{(l)}$ and sending $\mathbf{a}^{(L)}$ in the plaintext as can be seen in Algorithm 2. Sharif *et al.* [1] showed that the exchange of plaintext AMs between client and server using SL reveals important information regarding the client's raw data. Later, in Subsect. 7.4 we show in detail how passing the forward AMs from client to server in the plaintext will result in information leakage. To mitigate this privacy leakage, we propose the protocol, where the client encrypts AMs before sending them to the server (see Subsect. 4.2).

4.2 Encrypted Activation Maps

The protocol for training the U-shaped 1D CNN with a homomorphically EAM consists of four phases: initialization, forward propagation, classification, and backward propagation. The initialization phase only takes place once at the beginning of the procedure, whereas the other phases continue until the model iterates through all epochs. Each phase is explained in detail below.

Initialization. This phase consists of socket initialization, context generation, and random weight loading. The client establishes a socket connection to the server and synchronizes the four hyperparameters η, n, N, E with the server, shown in Algorithm 3 and Algorithm 4. These parameters must be synchronized on both sides to be trained in the same way. Also, the weights on the client and server are initialized with the same set of corresponding weights in the local model to accurately assess and compare the influence of SL on performance. On both, client and server, $\mathbf{w}^{(i)}$ are initialized using corresponding parts of Φ. $\mathbf{a}^{(i)}$, $\mathbf{z}^{(i)}$, and the gradients are initially set to zero. In this phase, the context generated is an object that holds pk and sk of the HE scheme as well as $\mathcal{P}, \mathcal{C}$ and Δ.

Algorithm 1: Client Side

Initialization:
$s \leftarrow$ socket initialized with port and address;
$s.connect$
$\eta, n, N, E \leftarrow s.synchronize()$
$\{w^{(i)}, b^{(i)}\}_{\forall i \in \{0..l\}} \leftarrow$ initialize using Φ
$\{\mathbf{z}^{(i)}\}_{\forall i \in \{0..l\}}, \{\mathbf{a}^{(i)}\}_{\forall i \in \{0..l\}} \leftarrow \emptyset$
$\left\{\frac{\partial J}{\partial \mathbf{z}^{(i)}}\right\}_{\forall i \in \{0..l\}}, \left\{\frac{\partial J}{\partial \mathbf{a}^{(i)}}\right\}_{\forall i \in \{0..l\}} \leftarrow \emptyset$
for $e \in E$ **do**
  for each batch $(\mathbf{x}, \mathbf{y})$ *from* D **do**
    Forward propagation :
    $O.zero\_grad()$
    $\mathbf{a}^0 \leftarrow \mathbf{x}$
    for $i \leftarrow 1$ *to* l **do**
      for $i \leftarrow 1$ *to* l **do**
        $\mathbf{z}^{(i)} \leftarrow f^{(i)}\left(\mathbf{a}^{(i-1)}\right)$
        $\mathbf{a}^{(i)} \leftarrow g^{(i)}\left(\mathbf{z}^{(i)}\right)$
    end
    $s.send\left(\mathbf{a}^{(l)}\right)$
    $s.receive\left(\mathbf{a}^{(L)}\right)$
    $\hat{\mathbf{y}} \leftarrow Softmax\left(\mathbf{a}^{(L)}\right)$
    $J \leftarrow \mathcal{L}(\hat{\mathbf{y}}, \mathbf{y})$
    Backward propagation :
    Compute $\left\{\frac{\partial J}{\partial \hat{\mathbf{y}}} \& \frac{\partial J}{\partial \mathbf{a}^{(L)}}\right\}$
    $s.send\left(\frac{\partial J}{\partial \mathbf{a}^{(L)}}\right)$
    $s.receive\left(\frac{\partial J}{\partial \mathbf{a}^{(l)}}\right)$
    for $i \leftarrow 1$ *to* l **do**
      Compute $\left\{\frac{\partial J}{\partial w^{(i)}}, \frac{\partial J}{\partial b^{(i)}}\right\}$
      Update $w^{(i)}, b^{(i)}$
    end
  end
end

Algorithm 2: Server Side

Initialization:
$s \leftarrow$ socket initialized ;
$s.connect$
$\eta, n, N, E \leftarrow s.synchronize()$
$\{w^{(i)}, b^{(i)}\}_{\forall i \in \{0..l\}} \leftarrow$ initialize using Φ
$\{\mathbf{z}^{(i)}\}_{\forall i \in \{l+1..L\}} \leftarrow \emptyset$
$\left\{\frac{\partial J}{\partial \mathbf{z}^{(i)}}\right\}_{\forall i \in \{l+1..L\}} \leftarrow \emptyset$
for $e \in E$ **do**
  for $i \leftarrow 1$ *to* N **do**
    Forward propagation :
    $O.zero\_grad()$
    $s.receive\left(\mathbf{a}^{(l)}\right)$
    $\mathbf{a}^{(L)} \leftarrow f^{(i)}\left(\mathbf{a}^{(l)}\right)$
    $s.send\left(\mathbf{a}^{(L)}\right)$
    Backward propagation :
    $s.receive\left(\frac{\partial J}{\partial \mathbf{a}^{(L)}}\right)$
    Compute $\left\{\frac{\partial J}{\partial w^{(L)}}, \frac{\partial J}{\partial b^{(L)}}\right\}$
    Update $w^{(L)}, b^{(L)}$
    Compute $\frac{\partial J}{\partial \mathbf{a}^{(l)}}$
    $s.send\left(\frac{\partial J}{\partial \mathbf{a}^{(l)}}\right)$
  end
end

Further information on the HE parameters and how to choose the best-suited parameters can be found in the TenSEAL's benchmarks tutorial. As shown in Algorithm 3 and Algorithm 4, the context is either ctx$_{pub}$ or ctx$_{pri}$ depending on whether it holds the secret key sk. Both the ctx$_{pub}$ and ctx$_{pri}$ have the same parameters, though ctx$_{pri}$ holds a sk and ctx$_{pub}$ does not. The server does not have access to the sk as the client only shares the ctx$_{pub}$ with the server.

Forward Propagation. In the forward propagation the client first zeroes out the gradients for the batch of data $(\mathbf{x}, \mathbf{y})$. He then begins calculating the $\mathbf{a}^{(l)}$ AMs from $\mathbf{x}$, as can be seen in Algorithm 3 where each $f^{(i)}$ is a Conv1D layer.

The Conv1D layer can be described as following: given a 1D input signal that contains C channels, where each channel $\mathbf{x}_{(i)}$ is a 1D array ($i \in \{1, \ldots, C\}$), a Conv1D layer produces an output that contains C' channels. The jth output channel $\mathbf{y}_{(j)}$, where $j \in \{1, \ldots, C'\}$, can be described as

$$\mathbf{y}_{(j)} = b_{(j)} + \sum_{i=1}^{C} w_{(i)} \star \mathbf{x}_{(i)}, \qquad (1)$$

where $\boldsymbol{w}_{(i)}, i \in \{1, \ldots, C\}$ are the weights, $\boldsymbol{b}_{(j)}$ are the biases of the Conv1D layer, and $\star$ is the 1D cross-correlation operation. The $\star$ operation can be described as

$$\mathbf{z}(i) = (\boldsymbol{w} \star \mathbf{x})(i) = \sum_{j=0}^{m-1} \boldsymbol{w}(j) \cdot \mathbf{x}(i+j), \tag{2}$$

where $\mathbf{z}(i)$ denotes the ith element of $\mathbf{z}$, and size of the 1D weighted kernel is m.

In Algorithm 3, $g^{(i)}$ can be seen as the combination of Max Pooling and Leaky ReLU functions. The final output AMs of the lth layer from the client is $\mathbf{a}^{(l)}$. The client then homomorphically encrypts $\mathbf{a}^{(l)}$ and sends the EAMs $\overline{\mathbf{a}^{(l)}}$ to the server. In Algorithm 4, the server receives $\overline{\mathbf{a}^{(l)}}$ and then performs forward propagation, which is a linear layer evaluated on HE encrypted data $\overline{\mathbf{a}^{(l)}}$ as

$$\overline{\mathbf{a}^{(L)}} = \overline{\mathbf{a}^{(l)}} w^{(L)} + b^{(L)}. \tag{3}$$

Upon reception, the client decrypts $\overline{\mathbf{a}^{(L)}}$ to get $\mathbf{a}^{(L)}$, performs Softmax on $\mathbf{a}^{(L)}$ to produce the predicted output $\hat{\mathbf{y}}$ and calculate the loss J, as can be seen in Algorithm 3. Having finished the forward propagation we may move on to the backward propagation part of the protocol.

Backward Propagation. After calculating the loss J, the client starts the backward propagation by initially computing $\frac{\partial J}{\partial \hat{\mathbf{y}}}$ and then $\frac{\partial J}{\partial \mathbf{a}^{(L)}}$ and $\frac{\partial J}{\partial w^{(L)}}$ using the chain rule (Algorithm 3). Specifically, the client calculates:

$$\frac{\partial J}{\partial \mathbf{a}^{(L)}} = \frac{\partial J}{\partial \hat{\mathbf{y}}} \frac{\partial \hat{\mathbf{y}}}{\partial \mathbf{a}^{(L)}}, \quad \frac{\partial J}{\partial w^{(L)}} = \frac{\partial J}{\partial \mathbf{a}^{(L)}} \frac{\partial \mathbf{a}^{(L)}}{\partial w^{(L)}} \tag{4}$$

Following, the client sends $\frac{\partial J}{\partial \mathbf{a}^{(L)}}$ and $\frac{\partial J}{\partial w^{(L)}}$ to the server. Upon reception, the server computes $\frac{\partial J}{\partial b}$ by simply doing $\frac{\partial J}{\partial b} = \frac{\partial J}{\partial \mathbf{a}^{(L)}}$, based on Eq. (3). The server then updates weights and biases of linear layer according to Eq. (5).

$$w^{(L)} = w^{(L)} - \eta \frac{\partial J}{\partial w^{(L)}}, \quad b^{(L)} = b^{(L)} - \eta \frac{\partial J}{\partial b^{(L)}} \tag{5}$$

Next, the server calculates

$$\frac{\partial J}{\partial \mathbf{a}^{(l)}} = \frac{\partial J}{\partial \mathbf{a}^{(L)}} \frac{\partial \mathbf{a}^{(L)}}{\partial \mathbf{a}^{(l)}}, \tag{6}$$

and sends $\frac{\partial J}{\partial \mathbf{a}^{(l)}}$ to the client. After receiving $\frac{\partial J}{\partial \mathbf{a}^{(l)}}$, the client calculates the gradients of J w.r.t the weights and biases of the Conv1D layer using the chain-rule, which can generally be described as:

$$\frac{\partial J}{\partial w^{(i-1)}} = \frac{\partial J}{\partial w^{(i)}} \frac{\partial w^{(i)}}{\partial w^{(i-1)}}, \quad \frac{\partial J}{\partial b^{(i-1)}} = \frac{\partial J}{\partial b^{(i)}} \frac{\partial b^{(i)}}{\partial b^{(i-1)}} \tag{7}$$

Finally, after calculating the gradients $\frac{\partial J}{\partial w^{(i)}}, \frac{\partial J}{\partial b^{(i)}}$, the client updates $\boldsymbol{w}^{(i)}$ and $\boldsymbol{b}^{(i)}$ using the Adam optimization algorithm [12].

5   Formal Protocol Construction

In this section, we formalize the communication between the client and the server. To this end, we design a protocol that is divided in two phases (Setup and Running) and relies on the following five building blocks:

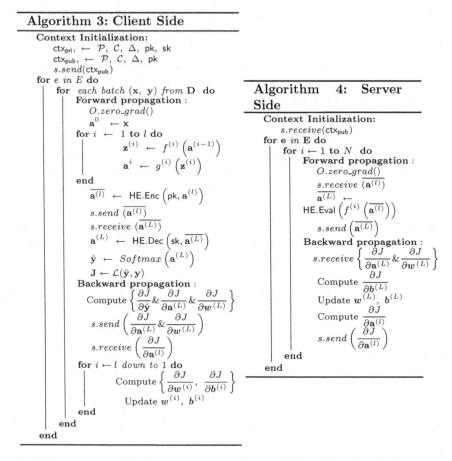

- A CCA2 secure public-key encryption scheme $\mathsf{PKE} = (\mathsf{Gen}, \mathsf{Enc}, \mathsf{Dec})$;
- An EUF-CMA secure signature scheme $\mathsf{Sign} = (\sigma, \mathsf{ver})$;
- A Leveled Homomorphic Encryption scheme $\mathsf{HE} = (\mathsf{KeyGen}, \mathsf{Enc}, \mathsf{Eval}, \mathsf{Dec})$;
- A first and second pre-image resistant hash function H;
- A synchronized clock between the Client and the Server.

Setup Phase. During this phase each entity generates a public/private key pair $(\mathsf{pk}, \mathsf{sk})$ for the CCA2-secure public-key encryption scheme PKE and a sign/verification key pair (σ, ver) for the EUF-CMA-secure signature scheme Sign. Furthermore, the client runs $\mathsf{HE.KeyGen}$ to generate the public, private and evaluation key of the HE scheme. Below we provide a list of all generated keys:

- $(\mathsf{pk_C}, \mathsf{sk_C})$ - public/private key pair for the Client;
- $(\sigma_C, \mathsf{ver_C})$ - sign/verification key pair for the Client;
- $(\mathsf{pk_S}, \mathsf{sk_S})$ - public/private key pair for the Server;
- $(\sigma_S, \mathsf{ver_S})$ - sign/verification key pair for the Server;
- $(\mathsf{pk_{HE}}, \mathsf{sk_{HE}}, \mathsf{evk_{HE}})$ - public, private and evaluation keys generated by Client.

Running Phase. After successfully executing the **Setup** phase, the Client initiates the protocol's running phase by sending
$$m_1 = \langle t_1, \mathsf{PKE.Enc}(\mathsf{pk_S}, \mathsf{evk_{HE}}), \mathsf{HE.Enc}(\mathsf{pk_{HE}}, \mathrm{AMap}), \sigma_C(H_1) \rangle \text{ to the server,}$$
where t_1 is a timestamp, H_1 is a hash such that:
$$H_1 = H(\mathsf{evk_{HE}} \| \mathsf{HE.Enc}(\mathsf{pk_{HE}}, \mathrm{AMap})), \text{ AMap is the AM and } \sigma_C(\cdot) \text{ denotes}$$
the cryptographic signature of C. Upon reception, the Server verifies the freshness of the message by looking at the timestmap t_1 and the signature of the sender. If any of the verifications fail, the Server outputs $\perp$ and aborts the protocol. Otherwise, it first decrypts the evaluation key evk_{HE} using its private key $\mathsf{sk_S}$ and subsequently uses the homomorphic evaluation key $\mathsf{evk_{HE}}$ to operate on Amap. The result of these operations is a homomorphically encrypted output $\mathsf{HE.Enc}(\mathsf{pk_{HE}}, \mathrm{out})$, which is sent back to the Client via: $m_2 = \langle t_2, \mathsf{HE.Enc}(\mathsf{pk_{HE}}, \mathrm{out}), \sigma_S(H_2) \rangle$, where $H(2) = H(t_2 \| \mathsf{HE.Enc}(\mathsf{pk_{HE}}, \mathrm{out}))$. Upon reception, the Client first verifies the freshness of the message and the server's signature. Should the verification fail, the Client outputs $\perp$ and aborts the protocol. Otherwise, the Client first recovers the encrypted output by running $\mathsf{HE.Dec}(\mathsf{sk_{HE}}, \mathsf{HE.Enc}(\mathsf{pk_{HE}}, \mathrm{out})) \rightarrow$ out. This output will be used by the Server to compute the initial gradients grad for the ML model. Having computed grad the Client forwards them to the Server via: $m_3 = \langle t_3, \mathsf{PKE.Enc}(\mathsf{pk}_C, \mathrm{grad}), \sigma_S(H_3) \rangle$, where $H_3 = H(t_3 \| \mathrm{grad})$. Upon receiving m_3, the Server first verifies the freshness and the signature of the message. Should the verification fail, the Server outputs $\perp$ and aborts the protocol. Otherwise, it recovers the gradients by running $\mathsf{PKE.Dec}(\mathsf{sk_S}, \mathsf{PKE.Enc}(\mathsf{pk_S}, \mathrm{grad})) \rightarrow \mathrm{grad}$. Based on grad, the Server can update the parameters of the ML model (i.e. bias and weights), a process resulting to updated gradients grad'. Finally, the Server outsources grad' to the Client via: $m_4 = \langle t_4, \mathsf{PKE.Enc}(\mathsf{pk_C}, \mathrm{grad}'), \sigma_C(H_4) \rangle$, where $H_4 = H(t_4 \| \mathrm{grad}')$. Upon reception, Server verifies freshness and message signature. Should the verification fail, Client outputs $\perp$ and aborts the protocol. Otherwise it decrypts the updated gradients by running $\mathsf{PKE.Dec}(\mathsf{sk_C}, \mathsf{PKE.Enc}(\mathsf{pk_C}, \mathrm{grad}')) \rightarrow \mathrm{grad}'$. The running phase of our protocol is illustrated in Fig. 3.

6   Protocol Security

We prove the security of our protocol in presence of a probabilistic polynomial time (PPT) adversary $\mathcal{ADV}$. We assume that $\mathcal{ADV}$ has the following capabilities:

- $\mathcal{ADV}$ overhears the communication between the Client and the Server;
- $\mathcal{ADV}$ is allowed to tamper with any message she sees, either by changing the contents of the message, or by replacing it with another one.

In our threat model, we assume that $\mathcal{ADV}$ does not block the communication between the Client and the Server.

More formally, we will prove the following proposition:

Proposition 1 (Protocol Soundness). *Let* PKE *be a CCA2-secure public-key encryption scheme and* Sign *an EUF-CMA-secure signature scheme. Moreover, let* $\mathcal{ADV}$ *be a PPT adversary. Then* $\mathcal{ADV}$:

1. *Can not infer any information from the exchanged messages except from the time of sending;*
2. *Can not tamper with the content of any message in a way that goes unnoticed.*

Proof. We examine each assumptions separately, and we will prove that they both hold with overwhelming probability.

A1: Our first assumption is that $\mathcal{ADV}$ can not infer any information from exchanged messages. Assuming that $\mathcal{ADV}$ does not collude with neither Client nor Server, the only way to infer information about messages is to successfully decrypt messages encrypted under PKE or HE. However, assuming security of both of those schemes, this can only happen with negligible probability in the security parameters λ and κ of PKE and HE respectively. Hence, if we denote advantage of $\mathcal{ADV}$ in decrypting exchanged ciphertexts by ϵ, we get: $\epsilon = negl(\lambda) + negl(\kappa)$. So finite sum of negligible functions is still negligible, $\mathcal{ADV}$ can decrypt messages with negligible probability and, our assumption holds with overwhelming probability.

A2: $\mathcal{ADV}$ can try tampering with the exchanged messages in two possible ways:
   – Generate and send her own messages in place of the actual messages;
   – Replay old messages.

Generating her own valid ciphertexts is trivial as every ciphertext is encrypted under a public key. Moreover, $\mathcal{ADV}$ would also need to forge a valid signature of the sender should she wish to create a malicious message that is indistinguishable from a real one. However, given the EUF-CMA security of the signature scheme Sign, this can only happen with negligible probability in the security parameter μ of Sign.

Thus, the only alternative for $\mathcal{ADV}$ is to replay and old message that was transmitted at some time in the past t'. However, since, each exchange message contains the current timestamp both in the first component of the message and in the signed hash, $\mathcal{ADV}$ would once again need to forge a valid signature of the sender since, otherwise, the verification of the signature would pass, though the verification of the timestamp would fail. Hence, if we denote by ϵ_2 the advantage of $\mathcal{ADV}$ in forging a valid signature, we conclude that the overall advantage of $\mathcal{ADV}$ in tampering with the content of any message in an indistinguishable way is:

$$\epsilon_2 = negl(\mu) + negl(\mu) = negl(\mu) \tag{8}$$

Hence, our second assumption holds with overwhelming probability.

7   Performance Analysis

In this work, we evaluate our method on two ECG datasets: the MIT-BIH dataset [16] and the PTB-XL dataset [21].[2]

7.1   Experimental Setup

All models are trained on a machine with Ubuntu 20.04 LTS, processor Intel Core i7-8700 CPU at 3.20GHz, 32Gb RAM, GPU GeForce GTX 1070 Ti with 8Gb of memory. We write our program in the Python version 3.9.7. The NNs are constructed using the PyTorch library version 1.8.1+cu102. For HE algorithms, we employ the TenSeal library version 0.3.10.

In terms of hyperparameters, we train all networks with 10 epochs, a $\eta = 0.001$ learning rate, and a $n = 4$ training n. For split NN with HE AMs, we use the Adam optimizer for client model and mini-batch Gradient Descent for server model. We use GPU for networks trained on plaintext. For U-shaped SL on HE AMs, we train the client model on GPU, and server model on CPU.

7.2   Evaluation

In this section, we report the experimental results in terms of accuracy, training duration and communication throughput. We measure the accuracy of the three NN on the plaintext test set after the training processes are completed.

Networks with Different Activation Map Sizes: The 1D CNN models used on both MIT-BIH and PTB-XL datasets have two Conv1D layers and one linear layer. The AMs are the output of the last Conv1D layer.

For the MIT-BIH dataset, we experiment with two sizes of AMs: $[n, 512]$ (as in [1]) and $[n, 256]$ [10]. We get the AMs of size $[n, 256]$ by reducing the number of output channels in the second Conv1D layer by half (from 16 output channels to 8 output channels). We denote the 1D CNN model with an AM sized $[n, 256]$ as M_1, and the model with an AM sized $[n, 512]$ as M_2.

For the PTB-XL dataset, we change the number of the input channels for the first Conv1D layer to 12, since the input data are 12-lead ECG signals [11]. Besides, we only experiment with 8 output channels for the second Conv1D layer. We denote this network by M_3. Using M_3, the output AM size is $[n, 2000]$.

Training Locally: The result when training the model M_1 locally on the MIT-BIH plaintext dataset is shown in Fig. 4. The NN learns quickly and is able to decrease the loss drastically from epoch 1 to 5. After that, from epoch 6–10, the loss begins to plateau. After training for 10 epochs, we test the trained NN on the test dataset and get 88.06% accuracy. Training the model locally on plaintext takes 4.8 s for each epoch on average.

Figure 5 shows the results when training the model M_2 on plaintext MIT-BIH. After 10 epochs, the model achieves the best training accuracy of 91.66%.

---

[2] Due to limited space, the figures from this section are moved to Sect. B.

The trained model results in 92.84% prediction accuracy. Each training epoch takes 4.8 s on average -the same as model M_1. Even though the two models differ in the output sizes of the AMs, they are relatively small models: the number of parameters is 2061 for M_1, and 3989 for M_2. As both models can fit in the GPU memory, the local training duration becomes similar for both models.

Training M_3 locally on the plaintext PTB-XL dataset results in Fig. 6 achieves a training accuracy of 72.65% after 10 epochs with a test accuracy is 67.68%. This low accuracy is due to small NN with 12013 trainable parameters and limited training epochs (each takes 10.56 s on average).

7.3   U-Shaped Split Learning Using Plaintext Activation Maps

Our experiments, show that training the U-shaped split model on plaintext (reported in Sect. 3.2) produces the same results in terms of accuracy compared to local training for both models M_1, M_2 and M_3. This result is similar to the findings of [1]. Even though the authors of [1] only used the vanilla split model, they also found that compared to training locally, accuracy was not reduced.

We will now discuss the training time and communication overhead of the U-shaped split models and compare them to their local versions. For the split version of M_1, each training epoch takes 8.56 s on average, hence 43.9% longer than local training. Training the split version of M_2 takes 8.67 s per epoch on average, which is 44.6% longer compared to the 4.8 s of local training. The split version of M_3 on the PTB-XL dataset takes 15.55 s per epoch to train and is 47.25% slower than the local version. The U-shaped split models take longer to train due to the communication between the client and the server. The communication cost for one epoch of training split M_1 and M_2 are 33.06 Mb and 60.12 Mb, respectively. M_2 incurs almost twice as much communication overhead compared to M_1 due to the bigger size of the AMs. For M_3, communication overhead is on average 316.9 Mb per epoch, which is much bigger than M_1 and M_2 due to bigger AMs sent from client during training.

These figures show that the similarities are not as strong compared to the MIT-BIH AMs. This is due to the fact that M_3 is a small network trained on a limited number of epochs (72.65% training accuracy after 10 epochs), therefore, the convolution layers are not yet able to produce highly similar AMs compared to the original signals. Still the figures indicate similar patterns between the AMs and the original PTB-XL signals. Nonetheless, to reach any conclusions, we first need to experiment with better NNs that can produce highly accurate predictions on both the train and test splits of the PTB-XL dataset, then quantify similarities between AMs and input signals of these networks.

7.4   Visual Invertibility

In SL, certain AMs sent from client to the server to continue the training process show high similarity with the client's input data, as demonstrated in Fig. 7 for models trained on the MIT-BIH dataset. The figure indicates that, compared to the raw input data from the client (the first row of Fig. 7), some AMs (as plotted in the second and third row of Fig. 7) have exceedingly similar patterns. This phenomenon clearly compromises the privacy of the client's raw data. The authors of [1] quantify the privacy leakage by measuring the correlations between the AMs and the raw input signal by using two metrics: distance correlation and Dynamic Time Warping. This approach allows them to measure whether their solutions mitigate privacy leakage work. Since our work uses HE, said metrics are unnecessary as the AMs are encrypted. Similar to MIT-BIH, we visualize the output AMs produced by M_3 to access their visual similarity compared to original signals. Due to space constraints, we visualize results only for normal class (see Fig. 8) instead of five different classes of heartbeat in PTB-XL dataset.

7.5 U-Shaped Split 1D CNN with Encrypted Activation Maps

We train the split NNs M_1 and M_2 on the MIT-BIH dataset using EAMs according to Sect. 4.2. To encrypt the AMs from the client before sending them to the server, we experiment with five different sets of HE parameters for both models M_1 and M_2. Furthermore, we also employ the batch encryption (BE) feature of the CKKS encryption scheme. BE allows us to encrypt a $N \times N$ matrix into N ciphertexts, with each column encrypted as a ciphertext for memory and computation optimization [2]. We experiment with training the NNs with and without BE. Additionally, we perform experiments using different combinations of HE parameters. Table 2 shows the results in terms of training time, testing accuracy, and communication overhead for the NNs with different configurations on the MIT-BIH dataset. For the U-shaped SL version on the plaintext, we captured all communication between client and server. For training split models on EAMs, we approximate the communication overhead for one training epoch by getting the average communication of training on first ten batches of data, multiply that with total number of training batches.

Results differ between training M_1 and M_2 with different sets of HE parameters. For the M_1 model, the best test accuracy was 85.41%, when using the set of HE parameters with $\mathcal{P} = 4096$, $\mathcal{C} = [40, 20, 20]$, $\Delta = 2^{21}$ (denoted s_1), and without BE. The accuracy drop was 2.65% compared to plaintext training.

However, with BE, s_1 produced only 79% accuracy. Compared to the bigger sets of parameters with $\mathcal{P} = 8192$, s_1 achieves higher accuracy while requiring much lower training time and communication overhead. The result when using the first set of parameters with $\mathcal{P} = 8192$ is close (85.31%), but with a much longer training time (3.67 times longer) and communication overhead (8.43 times higher). We observe that in some cases, training with BE results in better testing accuracy, while in some other, it leads to accuracy reduction. On the other hand, training on EAMs with BE is 23–35% faster. The amount of communication overhead is also significantly reduced (up to 13 times). Interestingly, using the HE parameters with $\mathcal{P} = 2048$ and without BE drastically reduces accuracy to 22.65%, however, with BE, it only reduces accuracy to 70.12%. Hence, the effect of BE in NN training needs further study.

Although M_2 achieves better accuracy than M_1 on plaintext data, it does not provide better results in encrypted version. The best accuracy of M_2 on

Table 2. Training and testing results on the MIT-BIH dataset

Network	Type of Network	HE Parameters				Training duration per epoch (s)	Test accuracy (%)	Communication per epoch (Tb)
		BE	$\mathcal{P}$	$\mathcal{C}$	Δ			
M_1	Local					4.80	88.06	0
	Split (plaintext)					8.56	88.06	33.06e−6
	Split (HE)	False	8192	[60,40,40,60]	2^{40}	50 318	85.31	37.84
			8192	[40,21,21,40]	2^{21}	48 946	80.63	22.42
			4096	[40,20,20]	2^{21}	14 946	85.41	4.49
			4096	[40,20,40]	2^{20}	18 129	80.78	4.57
			2048	[18,18,18]	2^{16}	5 018	22.65	0.58
		True	8192	[60,40,40,60]	2^{40}	33 310	81.22	4.77
			8192	[40,21,21,40]	2^{21}	31 311	84.36	2.81
			4096	[40,20,20]	2^{21}	11 507	79.00	0.67
			4096	[40,20,40]	2^{20}	11 656	80.79	0.69
			2048	[18,18,18]	2^{16}	3 869	70.12	0.16
M_2	Local					4.80	92.84	0
	Split (plaintext)					8.67	92.84	60.12e−6
	Split (HE)	False	8192	[60,40,40,60]	2^{40}	118 518	81.40	238.71
			8192	[40,21,21,40]	2^{21}	n/a	n/a	n/a
			4096	[40,20,20]	2^{21}	31 711	81.38	12.86
			4096	[40,20,40]	2^{20}	31 791	80.12	14.60
			2048	[18,18,18]	2^{16}	12 087	22.65	1.786
		True	8192	[60,40,40,60]	2^{40}	79 637	81.46	17.57
			8192	[40,21,21,40]	2^{21}	56 356	84.46	9.25
			4096	[40,20,20]	2^{21}	20 790	84.69	1.82
			4096	[40,20,40]	2^{20}	20 521	81.65	1.82
			2048	[18,18,18]	2^{16}	8 113	73.82	0.36

encrypted version is 84.69% using s_1 and with BE. Compared to the configuration that achieves best results for M_1 at 85.41%, best configuration for M_2 takes 1.39 times more to train but incurs less communication overhead (about 2.5 times less). This is because the best configuration for M_2 occurs when BE is used, and best configuration for M_1 occurs when BE is not used. In general, training M_2 with EAMs takes 2–3 times longer to train and 3–6 times more communication overhead compared to M_1 with the same HE configuration.

Table 3. Training and testing results on the PTB-XL dataset

Network	Type of Network	HE Parameters				Training duration per epoch (s)	Test accuracy (%)	Communication per epoch (Tb)
		BE	$\mathcal{P}$	$\mathcal{C}$	Δ			
M_3	Local					10.56	67.68	0
	Split (plaintext)					15.55	67.68	316.9e−6
	Split (HE)	True	8192	[40,21,21,40]	2^{21}	72 534	65.42	115.64
			4096	[40,20,20]	2^{21}	24 061	64.22	18.20
			4096	[40,20,40]	2^{20}	22 570	65.23	18.77
			2048	[18,18,18]	2^{16}	7 605	65.33	1.93

The results of training different settings of M_3 on the PTB-XL dataset are reported in Table 3. We only train the split version of M_3 with an EAM using BE. The HE set of parameters $\mathcal{P} = 8192$, $\mathcal{C} = [40, 21, 21, 40]$, $\Delta = 2^{21}$ achieves the best test accuracy at 65.42%. This result is only 2.26% lower than the result obtained by the plaintext version. However, this set of parameters incurs the most communication overhead (115.64 Tb per epoch) and takes the longest to train (72 534 s per epoch). Overall, test accuracies achieved by different HE parameters are quite close to each other, with 65.42% being the lowest. Interestingly, the smallest set of HE parameters $\mathcal{P} = 2048, \mathcal{C} = [18, 18, 18], \Delta = 2^{16}$ achieves second-best accuracy at 65.33%, requiring about 1/10 of the training duration and 1/100 of the communication overhead compared to $\mathcal{P} = 8192$. The two sets of parameters with $\mathcal{P} = 4096$ produce quite similar results, roughly taking same amount of time and communication overhead to train.

Through our experiments, we see that training on EAMs can produce very optimistic results, with accuracy dropping by 2–3% for the best sets of HE parameters. Furthermore, training using BE can significantly reduce the amount of training time and communication overhead needed, while producing comparable results when it come to training without BE. The set of parameters with $\mathcal{P} = 8192$ always achieve the highest test accuracy, though incurring the highest communication overhead and the longest training time. The set of parameters with $\mathcal{P} = 4096$ can offer a good trade-off as they can produce on-par accuracy with $\mathcal{P} = 8192$, while requiring significantly less communication and training time. Experimental results show that with the smallest set of HE parameters $\mathcal{P} = 2048$, $\mathcal{C} = [18, 18, 18]$, $\Delta = 2^{16}$, the least amount of communication and training time is required. In addition, this only works well when used together with BE. When training the network M_3 on the PTB-XL dataset, this set of parameters produces even better test accuracy compared to $\mathcal{P} = 4096$. However, this result may be because the network M_3 is small. The test accuracy on the plaintext version is 67.68%, hence the noises produced by the HE algorithm do not yet have a significant role in reducing the model's accuracy.

Remark 1. As can be seen in Table 2, the accuracy of the same algorithm varies greatly under different CKKS parameters. The parameter selection in CKKS is not evident as a set of the parameter may result in efficient computation for one application but also in poor performance for another application. In addition, CKKS uses approximate arithmetic rather than exact arithmetic, in the sense that once computation is finished the result may slightly differ compared to that of a direct computation [5]. Hence, it is still open to research whether for specific applications, a closed form of relation for the set of parameters can be used to measure the accuracy. However, training both models M_1 and M_2 with a different set of parameters, we observe:

- Training model with BE yields better outcomes than without BE. This pattern can be seen in M_2 and also in M_1 with two exceptions ($\mathcal{P} = 8192, \mathcal{C} = [60, 40, 40, 60], \Delta = 2^{40}$) and ($\mathcal{P} = 4096, \mathcal{C} = [40, 20, 20], \Delta = 2^{21}$).
- Training without BE, higher contexts yield better results than lower. This pattern can be seen in M_2 and also in M_1 with two exceptions ($\mathcal{P} = 4096, \mathcal{C} = [40, 20, 20], \Delta = 2^{21}$) and ($\mathcal{P} = 4096, \mathcal{C} = [40, 20, 40], \Delta = 2^{20}$).
- Also in both models M_1 and M_2, BE is suitable for lower context ($\mathcal{P} = 2048, \mathcal{C} = [18, 18, 18], \Delta = 2^{16}$).

Open Science and Reproducible Research: To support open science and reproducible research, and provide researchers with opportunity to use, test, and extend our work, source code used for the evaluations is publicly available[3].

8   Conclusion

In this paper, we focused on training ML models in a privacy-preserving way. We used the concept of SL in combination with HE and constructed protocols allowing a client to train a model in collaboration with a server without sharing valuable information about the raw data. To the best of our knowledge, this is the first work that uses SL on encrypted data. Our experiments show that our approach has achieved high accuracy, especially when compared with less secure approaches that combine SL with differential privacy. The limitation of our work is having only one client in the protocol. While extending the protocol to multiple clients is an important task, it requires us to rely on a multi-key HE scheme, which is beyond scope of this work and remains to be addressed in future works.

A   Preliminaries

A.1   Convolutional Neural Network

In this work, we employ a 1D CNN [1,13] as a feature detector and classifier for two ECG heartbeat datasets, namely MIT-BIH [16] and PTB-XL [21]. The employed 1D CNN has the following stacked layers:

- Conv1D: Is used to swipe a kernel of adjustable weights over a 1D input signal. The Conv1D outputs the AMs capturing feature information from said input signal. Figure 2 visualizes the Conv1D operation and shows the difference between a Conv1D and a Conv2D layer.
- Leaky ReLU [14]: It is a non-linear function that can be described as $f(x) = x$, if $x \geq 0$, and $f(x) = \alpha x$ if $x < 0$, where α is a small number, such as 0.01.
- Max Pooling: In CNN, Max Pooling compresses the input, focusing on important elements and allowing slight input changes with minimal impact on the pooled version [18].
- Fully Connected (FC): The FC layer has one output unit connected to all input units, unlike the convolution layer, where one output unit in an AM only connects to a small area in the input signal.
- Softmax: A Softmax activation function takes a vector of k real numbers, e.g. $\mathbf{z} = (z_1, \ldots, z_k)\mathbb{R}^k$, and outputs a probability distribution consisting of k probabilities. Each probability in the output vector is calculated as follows:

$$\sigma(\mathbf{z})_i = \frac{e^{z_i}}{\sum_{j=1}^{k} e^{z_j}}. \tag{9}$$

We use the 1D CNN as a supervised learning method, where both the input data and corresponding labels are needed to train our network.

---

[3] https://github.com/khoaguin/HESplitNet.

A.2   Homomorphic Encryption

HE is an emerging cryptographic technique for computations on encrypted data. HE schemes are divided into three main categories according to their functionality: Partial HE [17], leveled (or somewhat) HE [4], and fully HE [6]. Each scheme has its own benefits and disadvantages. In this work, we use the CKKS Leveled HE scheme [4]. CKKS allows users to do additions and a limited number of multiplications on vectors of complex values (and hence, real values too). Prior to the encryption, CKKS encodes a message $\mathbf{z} \in \mathbb{C}^{N/2}$ to a ring of polynomials over the integers $\mathbb{Z}[X]/(X^N + 1)$. Working with polynomials over rings of integers is a good trade-off between security and efficiency compared to standard computations on vectors. During encoding, the vector $\mathbf{z}$ is multiplied by a *scaling factor* Δ to keep a level of precision. The encoded message is encrypted, and the resulted ciphertext is an element $c \in (\mathbb{Z}_q[X]/(X^N + 1))^2$. Ciphertexts can then be added or multiplied together. An issue arises during multiplication, is that the term Δ^2 appears in the ciphertext result. To address this, CKKS deploys a rescaling operation to keep the scaling factor Δ constant. The inverse procedure needs to be followed for the decryption; that is, the ciphertext will be decrypted first, and then the encoded message will be decoded and multiplied by $1/\Delta$ to recover $\mathbf{z}' \in \mathbb{C}^{N/2}$. The number of allowed multiplications is predefined by a list of prime numbers. To build this list, the authors first choose $(p_1, \ldots, p_L, q_0)$ primes, where each $p_\ell \approx \Delta$ and $q_0 > \Delta$. Finally, they set $q_L = \prod_1^L p_l \cdot q_0$, where $q_L = q$ – the order of $\mathbb{Z}_q$ – and the list is $(q_L, \ldots, q_0)$. After each multiplication, an element is deleted from the list. However, according to [4], the security of CCKS is based on the ratio N/q. Hence, to maintain the same level of security as we increase q, we also need to increase N-the degree of the polynomials and hence, computational costs. Summing up, the most important parameters of the CKKS scheme are:

1. **Polynomial Modulus** $\mathcal{P}$: Naturally, this parameter has a direct impact on the scheme's efficiency and security. According to [4], this value needs to be a power of two. Common values include 2048, 4096, 8192, 16384 and 32768.
2. **Coefficient Modulus** $\mathcal{C}$: A list of primes that define current scheme's level. After each multiplication a different prime is used as coefficient modulus. Hence, no more multiplications are allowed when all primes are used.
3. **Scaling Factor** Δ: This is a constant positive number multiplied by the plaintext message during encoding to maintain a certain level of precision.

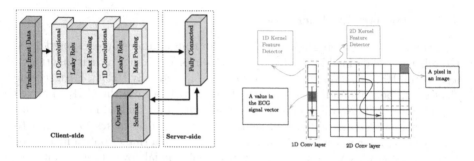

Fig. 1. U-shaped SL   **Fig. 2.** Conv1D vs Conv2D

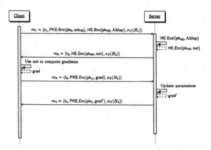

Fig. 3. Running Phase

B   Datasets

MIT-BIH: We use the pre-processed dataset from [1], which is based on the MIT-BIH arrhythmia database [16]. The processed dataset contains 26,490 samples of heartbeat that belong to 5 different types: N (normal beat), left (L) and right (R) bundle branch block, atrial (A) and ventricular (V) premature contraction. To train our network, the dataset is split into a train and test split as matrices of size $[13245, 1, 128]$, meaning that each contain 13,245 ECG samples and, each sample has one channel and 128 timesteps [1].

PTB-XL: According to [21], PTB-XL is the largest open-source ECG dataset since 2020. The dataset contains 12-lead ECG-waveforms from 21837 records of 18885 patients. Compared to PTB-XL, MIT-BIH only contains 2-lead ECG-waveforms obtained from 47 patients. Each waveform from PTB-XL has a duration of 10 s. Two sampling rates are used to collect the data: 100 Hz and 500 Hz. In our experiment, we employ the 100 Hz waveforms. Each 12-lead ECG waveform is associated with one or several classes out of five classes: normal (NORM), conduction disturbance (CD), myocardial infarction (MI), hypertrophy (HYP), and ST/T change (STTC). For waveforms that belong to multiple classes, we choose only the first one and remove the others for simplicity. The dataset is then split into a 90%-10% train-test ratio. In total, we have a training split of

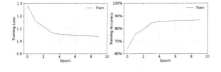

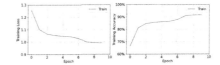

Fig. 4. MIT-BIH $[n, 256]$ **Fig. 5.** MIT-BIH $[n, 512]$

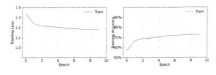

Fig. 6. PTB-XL $[n, 512]$

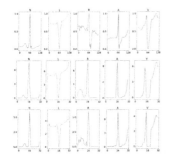

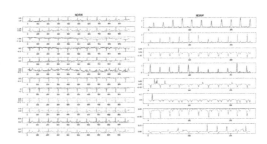

Fig. 7. Top: client input data. Middle: output channels M_1. Bottom: output channels M_2.

Fig. 8. Visual invertibility of the model M_3 on the PTB-XL dataset. Left: input data (NORM class). Right: corresponding activation maps.

size $[19267, 12, 1000]$, with 19,267 ECG waveform samples, of 12 channels (or leads) and 1,000 timesteps each. The test split's size is $[2163, 12, 1000]$.

References

1. Abuadbba, S., et al.: Can we use split learning on 1D CNN models for privacy preserving training? In: Proceedings of the 15th ACM Asia Conference on Computer and Communications Security, pp. 305–318 (2020)
2. Benaissa, A., Retiat, B., Cebere, B., Belfedhal, A.E.: Tenseal: a library for encrypted tensor operations using homomorphic encryption. In: Workshop on Distributed and Private Machine Learning. ICLR (2021)
3. Cabrero-Holgueras, J., Pastrana, S.: SoK: privacy-preserving computation techniques for deep learning. Proc. Priv. Enhancing Technol. **2021**(4), 139–162 (2021)
4. Cheon, J.H., Kim, A., Kim, M., Song, Y.: Homomorphic encryption for arithmetic of approximate numbers. In: Takagi, T., Peyrin, T. (eds.) ASIACRYPT 2017. LNCS, vol. 10624, pp. 409–437. Springer, Cham (2017). https://doi.org/10. 1007/978-3-319-70694-8_15

5. Clet, P.-E., Stan, O., Zuber, M.: BFV, CKKS, TFHE: which one is the best for a secure neural network evaluation in the cloud? In: Zhou, J., et al. (eds.) ACNS 2021. LNCS, vol. 12809, pp. 279–300. Springer, Cham (2021). https://doi.org/10.1007/978-3-030-81645-2_16

6. Gentry, C.: Fully homomorphic encryption using ideal lattices. In: Proceedings of the Forty-First Annual ACM Symposium on Theory of Computing, pp. 169–178 (2009)

7. Gupta, O., Raskar, R.: Distributed learning of deep neural network over multiple agents. J. Netw. Comput. Appl. **116**, 1–8 (2018)

8. Hitaj, B., Ateniese, G., Perez-Cruz, F.: Deep models under the gan: information leakage from collaborative deep learning. In: Proceedings of the 2017 ACM SIGSAC Conference on Computer and Communications Security, pp. 603–618 (2017)

9. Khan, T., Bakas, A., Michalas, A.: Blind faith: privacy-preserving machine learning using function approximation. In: 2021 IEEE Symposium on Computers and Communications (ISCC), pp. 1–7. IEEE (2021)

10. Khan, T., Nguyen, K., Michalas, A.: Split ways: privacy-preserving training of encrypted data using split learning. In: Fletcher, G., Kantere, V. (eds.) Proceedings of the Workshops of the EDBT/ICDT 2023 Joint Conference, Ioannina, Greece, March, 28, 2023. CEUR Workshop Proceedings, vol. 3379. CEUR-WS.org (2023). https://ceur-ws.org/Vol-3379/HeDAI_2023_paper402.pdf

11. Khan, T., Nguyen, K., Michalas, A., Bakas, A.: Love or hate? Share or split? Privacy-preserving training using split learning and homomorphic encryption. In: The 20th Annual International Conference on Privacy, Security & Trust (PST 2023), 21–23 August 2023, Copenhagen, Denmark (2023)

12. Kingma, D.P., Ba, J.: Adam: a method for stochastic optimization. In: International Conference on Learning Representations (ICLR). ICLR (2015)

13. Li, D., Zhang, J., Zhang, Q., Wei, X.: Classification of ECG signals based on 1D convolution neural network. In: 2017 IEEE 19th International Conference on e-Health Networking, Applications and Services (Healthcom), pp. 1–6. IEEE (2017)

14. Maas, A.L., Hannun, A.Y., Ng, A.Y., et al.: Rectifier nonlinearities improve neural network acoustic models. In: Proceedings of the 30th International Conference on Machine Learning, vol. 28, p. 3. Citeseer (2013)

15. McMahan, B., Moore, E., Ramage, D., Hampson, S., Arcas, B.A.: Communication-efficient learning of deep networks from decentralized data. In: Artificial Intelligence and Statistics, pp. 1273–1282. PMLR (2017)

16. Moody, G.B., Mark, R.G.: The impact of the MIT-BIH arrhythmia database. IEEE Eng. Med. Biol. Mag. **20**(3), 45–50 (2001)

17. Paillier, P.: Public-key cryptosystems based on composite degree residuosity classes. In: Stern, J. (ed.) EUROCRYPT 1999. LNCS, vol. 1592, pp. 223–238. Springer, Heidelberg (1999). https://doi.org/10.1007/3-540-48910-X_16

18. Scherer, D., Müller, A., Behnke, S.: Evaluation of pooling operations in convolutional architectures for object recognition. In: Diamantaras, K., Duch, W., Iliadis, L.S. (eds.) ICANN 2010. LNCS, vol. 6354, pp. 92–101. Springer, Heidelberg (2010). https://doi.org/10.1007/978-3-642-15825-4_10

19. Vepakomma, P., Gupta, O., Dubey, A., Raskar, R.: Reducing leakage in distributed deep learning for sensitive health data. In: AI for Social Good Workshop. ICLR (2019)

20. Vepakomma, P., Gupta, O., Swedish, T., Raskar, R.: Split learning for health: distributed deep learning without sharing raw patient data. In: AI for Social Good Workshop. ICLR (2019)

21. Wagner, P., Strodthoff, N., Bousseljot, R.D., Kreiseler, D., Lunze, F.I., Samek, W., Schaeffter, T.: PTB-XL, a large publicly available electrocardiography dataset. Sci. Data **7**(1), 1–15 (2020)
22. Yang, Q., Liu, Y., Cheng, Y., Kang, Y., Chen, T., Yu, H.: Federated learning. Synth. Lect. Artif. Intell. Mach. Learn. **13**(3), 1–207 (2019)

Force: Highly Efficient Four-Party Privacy-Preserving Machine Learning on GPU

Tianxiang Dai[1], Li Duan[1], Yufan Jiang[1,2], Yong Li[1(✉)], Fei Mei[1], and Yulian Sun[1]

[1] Huawei European Research Center, Munich, Germany
{tianxiangdai,li.duan,yufan.jiang,yong.li1,fei.mei,
yulian.sun1}@huawei.com
[2] Karlsruhe Institute of Technology, Karlsruhe, Germany
yufan.jiang@partner.kit.edu

Abstract. Tremendous efforts have been made to improve the efficiency of secure Multi-Party Computation (MPC), which allows $n \geq 2$ parties to jointly evaluate a target function without leaking their own private inputs. It has been confirmed by previous research that Three-Party Computation (3PC) and outsourcing computations to GPUs can lead to huge performance improvement of MPC in computationally intensive tasks such as Privacy-Preserving Machine Learning (PPML). A natural question to ask is whether super-linear performance gain is possible for a linear increase in resources. In this paper, we give an affirmative answer to this question. We propose Force, an extremely efficient Four-Party Computation (4PC) system for PPML. To the best of our knowledge, each party in Force enjoys the *least number of local computations, smallest graphic memory consumption* and *lowest data exchanges* between parties. This is achieved by introducing a new sharing type $\mathcal{X}$-share along with MPC protocols in privacy-preserving training and inference that are *semi-honest* secure in the *honest-majority* setting. By comparing the results with state-of-the-art research, we showcase that Force is sound and extremely efficient, as it can improve the PPML performance by a factor of 2 to 38 compared with other latest GPU-based *semi-honest* secure systems, such as Piranha (including SecureML, Falcon, FantasticFour), CryptGPU and CrypTen.

Keywords: MPC · Privacy-preserving machine learning · Four-party computation

1 Introduction

Values have been constantly generated from machine learning (ML) over mass data collected from different users. On the other hand, the importance of privacy and data security have also been increasingly recognized. Technically, it is a

---

Y. Jiang—Main contributor.

© The Author(s), under exclusive license to Springer Nature Switzerland AG 2024
L. Fritsch et al. (Eds.): NordSec 2023, LNCS 14324, pp. 330–349, 2024.
https://doi.org/10.1007/978-3-031-47748-5_18

Table 1. Comparison of Force and state-of-the-art works against **semi-honest** adversaries, with max boosting factor.

Setting	Ref.	LAN		WAN
		Training	Inference	Inference
2PC	Cheetah - **CPU** [23]	-	1234x	70x
	P-SecureML [40,54]	14x	5.8x	13x
3PC	CryptGPU [50]	6.5x	14x	10x
	P-Falcon [53,54]	2.1x	3.1x	2.4x
4PC	CrypTen [28]	38x	10x	29x
	P-FantasticFour [12,54]	4.7x	7.4x	10x
	Force	1	1	1

Fig. 1. Overview of Force protocols

good starting point to always keep sensitive data at local storage and never reveal them on the Internet in plaintext, but to preserve the usability of data distributed across owners remains challenging.

Secure multi-party computation protocols (MPC) have been designed for multiple parties to jointly compute a function without revealing their own secret inputs. Starting from the two-party case (2PC), frameworks have been proposed [25,27,43] to offer various trade-offs of security and performance. Extending 2PC to three party protocols (3PC), especially by tailoring the secret shares such that a single corrupted party cannot learn anything useful about the complete secret value, leads to a large leap in performance [2,3] in the honest majority setting. Although a giant gap in performance still remains, follow-up works [1,28,50] have proposed algorithmic and engineering optimizations to bring MPC closer to real-world and *high-throughput* applications, such as privacy-preserving machine learning (PPML). Thus, a natural question to ask is: *Can 4PC be non-trivially faster than 3PC?* In this paper, we give an affirmative answer. By introducing a new sharing type $\mathcal{X}$-share and a new set of protocols, our new Force framework for 4PC is not only secure at its cryptographic core, but more importantly, it outperforms cutting-edge semi-honest secure 2PC/3PC/4PC solutions for privacy-preserving machine learning remarkably by a factor of 2 to 38.

More specifically, we made the following contributions:

- **New 4PC Protocols.** Benefiting from a brand new sharing type called $\mathcal{X}$-share (Sect. 4.1), our 4PC matrix multiplication protocol achieves the lowest number of local multiplications and number of ring elements sent/received by each party. Besides, we design novel share conversion and comparison protocols with a new type of correlated randomness, the $\mathcal{X}$-dabit (Sect. 4.3), to achieve the least computational and communication costs. Due to the symmetry property of $\mathcal{X}$-share, we can eliminate the communication in 3PC by turning to the communication-free truncation proposed by SecureML [40] to keep the precision consistent.
- **Extensive Evaluations.** With all the $\mathcal{X}$-share optimized operations as building blocks, shown in Fig. 1, Force greatly improves overall PPML performance. We make fair comparisons between different systems under the same setting. An overview of the evaluation is shown in Table 1. For a better insight, we also include the latest CPU-only framework Cheetah [23].

- **Optimized Graphic Memory Usage.** Unlike [25,34,38,46], which provide inference-only implementations, our aim is to train real-world ML models such as VGG16 [49] with large batch size even for large datasets in MPC over GPU. Given $\mathcal{X}$-share (Sect. 4.1), Force greatly reduce the graphic memory consumption of each party so that it can perform PPML training of one large dataset, ImageNet [48] on large networks like VGG16 with BatchSize = 16, which was not possible in prior solutions.

2   Related Work

2.1   Privacy Preserving Machine Learning

In 2017, SecureML [40] firstly attempted to execute neural networks (NN) in 2PC, using ABY [13] shares with correlated randomness and mixed protocols with pre-processing. Later attempts like miniONN (2017) [37], secureNN (2019) [52], Falcon (2020) [53], Cheetah (2022) [23] and [22,25,34,38,39,46,55] still follow the mixed protocol approach with various optimization for multiplication and approximation methods for other non-linear operations. Recent 4PC systems [5,10,12,29,30,35] also continue with similar approach. All these mainly focus on demonstrating the asymptotic feasibility of PPML and provable security of the system. This might be the primary reason why few of them have taken advantages of GPUs or adapted the solutions for specific ML frameworks.

2.2   PPML on GPU

Research on implementing PPML on GPU can be seen as a tour that starts from two ends and finally meets in the middle.

On one hand, crypto researchers turn to GPUs for faster computation. Pu *et al.* [45] in 2011 implemented Yao's Garbled Circuit (GC) [16] on GPU. Later in 2013, Husted *et al.* [24] and Frederiksen and Nielsen [17] worked on more modern GC protocols on GPUs. cuHE [11] brought homomorphic encryption (HE) onto GPU in 2015. These pioneering works uncovered the potential of GPU-friendly MPC, which could be up to 60 times faster than CPU-based solutions [17].

On the other hand, ML researchers pay more attention to privacy. Google in 2016 proposed secure aggregation and Federated Learning (FL) [4] to train shared models over data distributed across users. TensorFlow added support for differential privacy (DP) [14] in 2019 [19]. Although being quite efficient, FL and DP cannot guarantee the same security as MPC does [26,51].

Finally, the two lines of research meet at CrypTen (2020) [28]. While still having an ABY-style cryptographic core, the underlying MPC protocols in CrypTen are abstracted in a more ML-oriented way so that it can offer PyTorch-like [42] interfaces for ML practitioners, making the PPML framework more approachable for non-cryptographers and extensible for arbitrary number of parties. CrypGPU [50] further extends CrypTen with other GPU-friendly MPC components in a special case: 3PC. In 2022, Watson *et al.* proposed Piranha [54], a modular framework for accelerating generic secret sharing-based MPC protocols over GPU.

With novel engineering optimizations, Piranha can train real PPML model such as VGG [49], which was previously impossible on CryptGPU or CrypTen.

For other approaches to implement PPML such as using designated hardware, we refer the reader to the nice surveys [6, 20, 41].

3   Preliminaries

3.1   Fixed-Point Computation

We define a fixed-point value as an ℓ-bit integer using two's complement representation, consisting of both integer part and decimal part with $\ell - p$ bits and p bits respectively. Normally, addition and subtraction will be directly performed over a $\mathbb{Z}_{2^\ell}$ ring, since the result is supposed to remain below 2^ℓ. Meanwhile, although the multiplication could be performed in the same manner, the result must be divided by 2^p to maintain the same p-bit decimal precision.

3.2   Correlated Randomness

Correlated randomness are random values with special (algebraic) structural relations that are generated during the pre-processing phase [13, 27, 39, 43] to accelerate the online phase in MPC.

Replicated Shared Secrets and Zero Shares. As defined in [1], a secret value $x \in \mathbb{Z}_{2^\ell}$ is said to be *replicated shared* in 3PC, if three random values $x_0, x_1, x_2 \in \mathbb{Z}_{2^\ell}$ are sampled with $x = x_0 + x_1 + x_2$, and the pairs $(x_0, x_1), (x_1, x_2)$ and (x_2, x_0) are owned by each of the three parties respectively. We denote such a sharing type as $[\cdot]_{\mathsf{RS}}$. Addition and subtraction of two replicated shares $[x]_{\mathsf{RS}}$ and $[y]_{\mathsf{RS}}$ can be locally computed by parties. The multiplication of $[x]_{\mathsf{RS}}$ and $[y]_{\mathsf{RS}}$ in 3PC, however, requires parties to interact. More specifically, $\mathbf{P_i}$ is able to compute $z_i = x_i y_i + x_{i+1} y_i + x_i y_{i+1}$, yielding a 3-out-of-3 sharing of xy. In order to recover the replicated share $[xy]_{\mathsf{RS}}$, $\mathbf{P_i}$ has to *re-share* their masked local result $z_i + \alpha_i$ to one of the other two parties, where $\sum \alpha_i = 0$. Such *zero sharing* is the correlated randomness that can be derived from a pseudorandom function $\mathsf{PRF}()$ with pre-shared keys [50]. We also call such a sharing type as replicated share in general, if any share value x_i is held by more than one party.

For Type Conversion : dabit. The dabit (doubly authenticated bit) is a type of correlated randomness proposed by Rotaru and Wood [47] to mainly support secure comparison protocol and sharing type conversion. Let $b \xleftarrow{\$} \{0, 1\}$ be the randomness to be shared, $\sum$ the arithmetic sum in the ring, $\oplus$ the binary XOR operation. Formally, dabit is defined as

$$\mathsf{dabit} := \left([b], \langle b \rangle\right), \text{ such that } b = \sum [b]_i = \oplus \langle b \rangle_i, \ [b]_i \xleftarrow{\$} \mathbb{Z}_{2^\ell} \text{ and } \langle b \rangle_i \xleftarrow{\$} \mathbb{Z}_2.$$

Extended dabit : edabit. Recent work [15] of Escudero *et al.* extends dabit to edabit (extended doubly authenticated bit). Similar to dabit, an edabit is a tuple of shares for $b = (b_0, \cdots, b_{\ell_b - 1}) \xleftarrow{\$} \mathbb{Z}_{2^{\ell_b}}$ defined as

$$\text{edabit} := ([b], \ \langle b \rangle := (\langle b_0 \rangle, \langle b_1 \rangle, \cdots, \langle b_{\ell_b-1} \rangle)),$$

such that $b = \sum [b]_i$, $[b]_i \xleftarrow{\$} \mathbb{Z}_{2^\ell}$ and $b_j = \oplus \langle b_j \rangle_i$, $\langle b_j \rangle_i \xleftarrow{\$} \mathbb{Z}_2$.

3.3 Threat Model

A semi-honest adversary cannot deviate from the protocol description, but may try to infer information about the secret input. As a well studied model, security against semi-honest adversaries [36] in the honest majority setting often leads to 2PC and 3PC protocols with good efficiency [1–3,8,39,40,43,46,50,55], while the ones with *malicious* security [9,18,27,44,53] are still too heavy for large-scale applications in practice [16]. The **honest majority setting** is also adopted by 4PC frameworks with semi-honest or malicious security [5,10,12,28–30,35], where (strictly) less than one half of the parties can be controlled by an adversary.

We assume confidential, authenticated, and peer-to-peer channels between different parties. Thanks to the channel, the adversary can only see, delay or delete encrypted messages and any non-trivial modification can be detected.

Let $\text{REAL}_{\Pi,\mathcal{A},\mathcal{Z}}$ denote the output of an environment machine $\mathcal{Z}$ interacting with the adversary $\mathcal{A}$ executing the protocol Π in the real world. Let $\text{IDEAL}_{\mathcal{F},\mathcal{S},\mathcal{Z}}$ denote the output of $\mathcal{Z}$ interacting with a simulator $\mathcal{S}$ connected to an ideal functionality $\mathcal{F}$ in the ideal world.

Definition 1 (UC security). *Let $\mathcal{F}$ be a four-party functionality and let Π be a four-party protocol that computes $\mathcal{F}$. Protocol Π is said to **uc-realizes** $\mathcal{F}$ **with abort in the presence of static semi-honest adversaries** if for every non-uniform probabilistic polynomial time (PPT) adversary $\mathcal{A}$, there exists a non-uniform PPT adversary $\mathcal{S}$, such that for any environment $\mathcal{Z}$*

$$\text{IDEAL}_{\mathcal{F},\mathcal{S},\mathcal{Z}} \stackrel{c}{\cong} \text{REAL}_{\Pi,\mathcal{A},\mathcal{Z}}.$$

We follow the universally composable framework (UC) described in detail in [7]. More specifically, we use the hybrid model, where provably UC-secure components are abstracted as ideals in the next proof.

4   4PC Protocols

We construct efficient 4PC protocols as building blocks of Force for PPML. In Sect. 4.1, we introduce our new sharing type $\mathcal{X}$-share and how parties perform 4PC fixed-point computations. We highlight that the multiplication based on $\mathcal{X}$-share reduces the local computation of each party to only one multiplication. To the best of our knowledge, this becomes the least computation cost compared to other sharing constructions such as replicated or 2-out-of-2 sharing. In Sect. 4.1 and Sect. 4.3 we show how to perform conversions between share-modes and sharing types (by using a $\mathcal{X}$-dabit transmitted from dabit [47]).

In all the protocol descriptions, we use the term public parameters to denote all security parameters and cipher-suites identifiers, and sid the session identifier.

4.1 $\mathcal{X}$-share and Arithmetic Computation

$\mathcal{X}$-share and Share-Mode. We begin by introducing our new sharing type $\mathcal{X}$-share used in our 4PC computations. $\mathcal{X}$-share can work over both $\mathbb{Z}_{2^{\ell}}$ and $\mathbb{Z}_2$ rings in two modes.

- $[\cdot]_{\text{AC}}$-sharing : We say that a value x is $[\cdot]_{\text{AC}}$-shared among parties $\{\mathbf{P_i}\}$, if $\mathbf{P_A}$ and $\mathbf{P_B}$ hold the same value x_0, $\mathbf{P_C}$ and $\mathbf{P_D}$ hold the same value x_1 such that $x = x_0 + x_1$. We define $[\cdot]_{\text{AC}}^{\mathbf{P_i}}$ to be the share value of $\mathbf{P_i}$.
- $[\cdot]_{\text{AB}}$-sharing : We say that a value x is $[\cdot]_{\text{AB}}$-shared among parties $\{\mathbf{P_i}\}$, if $\mathbf{P_A}$ and $\mathbf{P_C}$ hold the same value x_0, $\mathbf{P_B}$ and $\mathbf{P_D}$ hold the same value x_1 such that $x = x_0 + x_1$. Same as above, we denote the share of $\mathbf{P_i}$ as $[\cdot]_{\text{AB}}^{\mathbf{P_i}}$.

We denote the share-mode as ψ, ϕ, θ, with $\psi, \phi, \theta \in \{\text{AC}, \text{AB}\}$. We say that a value x is $[\cdot]_{\text{4o4}}$-shared among parties $\{\mathbf{P_i}\}$, if $\mathbf{P_i}$ hold share x_i respectively such that $x = \sum x_i$.

Linearity. If the share-modes of both shared values are identical, it is easy to observe that the linear computations can be executed locally with $\mathcal{X}$-share. Given $[\cdot]_{\text{AC}}$-sharing (or $[\cdot]_{\text{AB}}$-sharing) of secret values x, y and public constants e_0, e_1, parties can locally compute $e_0[x]_{\text{AC}} + e_1[x]_{\text{AC}}$. The trick continues when parties have to compute $[x]_{\text{AC}} + e_2$, where e_2 is a public constant.

Now we consider the case if the share modes of secret x and secret y are different, e.g. $[x]_{\text{AC}}$ and $[y]_{\text{AB}}$. In order to keep the output to maintain either $[\cdot]_{\text{AC}}$-sharing or $[\cdot]_{\text{AB}}$-sharing, parties have to jointly change the share mode of y (or x) by executing Π_{chMode} (see Sect. 4.1), then locally compute $[x]_{\text{AC}} + [y]_{\text{AC}}$.

4PC Multiplication. The most important application of $\mathcal{X}$-share is 4PC multiplication. We begin with computing $[z]_{\text{4o4}} = [x]_{\psi}[y]_{\phi}$, where $\psi \neq \phi$. To perform the multiplication of two secret values, parties have to jointly compute:

$$xy = (x_0 + x_1)(y_0 + y_1)$$
$$= x_0 y_0 + x_0 y_1 + x_1 y_0 + x_1 y_1$$

Suppose the secret value x is $[\cdot]_{\text{AC}}$-shared and the secret value y is $[\cdot]_{\text{AB}}$-shared (or reversely), each party can locally compute exactly one out of four terms shown in the above equation. This yields a 4-out-of-4 sharing $[z]_{\text{4o4}} = [x]_{\text{AC}}[y]_{\text{AB}}$. For further computations, parties send their own masked share $[z]_{\text{4o4}}^{\mathbf{P_i}} + r^{\mathbf{P_i}}$ to their reshare partner, where $\sum r^{\mathbf{P_i}} = 0$. Since each *zero sharing* is fresh, parties can freely choose to rebuild either $[z]_{\text{AC}}$ or $[z]_{\text{AB}}$ according to the incoming computations.

Due to the fact that we are using fixed-point numbers to represent both x and y, the re-shared result z has to be truncated to maintain the p decimal bit precision. Remark that after re-sharing, both $[z]_{\text{AC}}$ and $[z]_{\text{AB}}$ yields a 2-out-of-2 sharing, thus we are free to apply the truncation technique Π_{trunc} introduced by

---

Protocol Π_{Mult}

Private inputs: Parties hold $[x]_\psi$, $[y]_\phi$, where $\psi \neq \phi$.
Public inputs: Public parameters, θ.
Outputs: $[z]_\theta$ with $z = xy$.
Preprocessing: $\mathbf{P_i}$ sends (ZeroSGen, $\mathbf{P_i}$, sid) to $\mathcal{F}_{4\text{PC}}^{\text{Pre}}$, receives $r^{\mathbf{P_i}}$ as output.
Protocols:

1. Parties locally compute $[z]_{4\text{o}4} = [xy]_{4\text{o}4}$, where $[z]_{4\text{o}4}^{\mathbf{P_i}} := [x]_\psi^{\mathbf{P_i}} [y]_\phi^{\mathbf{P_i}}$.

2. We denote $\mathbf{P_j}^{\mathbf{P_i}}$ as $\mathbf{P_i}$'s reshare partner.
   - If $\theta = \text{AC}$: $\mathbf{P_A}$ and $\mathbf{P_C}$ set $\mathbf{P_j}^{\mathbf{P_A}} = \mathbf{P_C}$ and $\mathbf{P_j}^{\mathbf{P_C}} = \mathbf{P_A}$, respectively. $\mathbf{P_B}$ and $\mathbf{P_D}$ set $\mathbf{P_j}^{\mathbf{P_B}} = \mathbf{P_D}$ and $\mathbf{P_j}^{\mathbf{P_D}} = \mathbf{P_B}$, respectively.
   - If $\theta = \text{AB}$: $\mathbf{P_A}$ and $\mathbf{P_B}$ set $\mathbf{P_j}^{\mathbf{P_A}} = \mathbf{P_B}$ and $\mathbf{P_j}^{\mathbf{P_B}} = \mathbf{P_A}$, respectively. $\mathbf{P_C}$ and $\mathbf{P_D}$ set $\mathbf{P_j}^{\mathbf{P_C}} = \mathbf{P_D}$ and $\mathbf{P_j}^{\mathbf{P_D}} = \mathbf{P_C}$, respectively.

3. Each $\mathbf{P_i}$ computes $e^{\mathbf{P_i}} := [z]_{4\text{o}4}^{\mathbf{P_i}} + r^{\mathbf{P_i}}$ and sends $e^{\mathbf{P_i}}$ to its reshare partner $\mathbf{P_j}$.

4. Upon receiving $e^{\mathbf{P_j}}$ from $\mathbf{P_j}^{\mathbf{P_i}}$, $\mathbf{P_i}$ sets $[z]_\theta^{\mathbf{P_i}} := e^{\mathbf{P_i}} + e^{\mathbf{P_j}}$.

Fig. 2. Four party multiplication protocol

SecureML [40] to avoid the additional communication overhead and round within the truncation protocols Π_{trunc1} and Π_{trunc2} proposed by ABY3 [39]. A detailed description of our multiplication protocol is shown in Fig. 2.

In contrast to linear operation, an unwilling situation for multiplication is when the share-modes of both secrets x and y are identical. Parties have to execute the Π_{chMode} (Fig. 4) to change the share-mode of either x or y (not both) before multiplication.

Change Share-Mode. Here we present the protocol Π_{chMode} for changing share-modes. We first define correlated randomness called *changeM sharing* or shortly CMS, denoted as $[\![r]\!]_{\psi\text{to}\phi}$.

Suppose parties want to change the share-mode of a shared value x from $[\cdot]_{\text{AC}}$-sharing to $[\cdot]_{\text{AB}}$-sharing, we require parties to already hold $[\![r]\!]_{\text{ACtoAB}}$ after the pre-processing phase. During the execution of Π_{chMode}, $\mathbf{P_A}$ and $\mathbf{P_C}$ simply exchange their own 2-out-of-2 sharing masked with r_0 and r_1, obtaining their new shares $x_0 + x_1 - r_0 - r_1$, while $\mathbf{P_B}$ and $\mathbf{P_D}$ set their shares to be r locally. This yields a fresh $[x]_{\text{AB}}$. The CMS can be generated by computing PRF() with pre-shared keys in the pre-processing stage. We formally define our CMS generation protocol Π_{CMSGen} in Fig. 3, as well as the online protocol Π_{chMode} in Fig. 4.

Division. If parties have to jointly divide a shared value x by a public value γ which is not a power of two, we use the truncation protocol Π_{trunc2} in [39] as a division protocol Π_{Div} to avoid two possible bad events explained in [39]. Π_{Div} consumes a correlated randomness that we call a division share $([r]_\psi, [r']_\phi)$, where $r' = r/\gamma$. The idea behind this protocol is to first reveal $[x]_\psi$ masked with $[r]_\psi$. Parties then compute publicly $(x - r)/\gamma$ and unmask this value by computing $(x - r)/\gamma + [r']_\phi$ locally. Note that we do not require $\phi = \psi$, so the share-mode of the shared division result can be chosen freely.

Protocol Π_{CMSGen}

Private inputs:
$\mathbf{P_A}$ holds k^0_{ACtoAB}, k^1_{ACtoAB}, k^0_{ABtoAC} and k^1_{ABtoAC}. $\mathbf{P_B}$ holds k^0_{ACtoAB}, k^2_{ACtoAB}, k^1_{ABtoAC} and k^2_{ABtoAC}.
$\mathbf{P_C}$ holds k^1_{ACtoAB}, k^2_{ACtoAB}, k^0_{ABtoAC} and k^2_{ABtoAC}. $\mathbf{P_D}$ holds k^0_{ACtoAB}, k^2_{ACtoAB}, k^0_{ABtoAC} and k^2_{ABtoAC}.

Public inputs: Public parameters, sid, $\psi\text{to}\phi$.
Outputs: $[\![r]\!]_{\psi\text{to}\phi}$.
Protocols:

– If $\psi\text{to}\phi = \text{ACtoAB}$:
  1. $\mathbf{P_A}$ computes $r_0 := \text{PRF}_{k^0_{\text{ACtoAB}}}(\text{sid}) - \text{PRF}_{k^1_{\text{ACtoAB}}}(\text{sid})$ then sets $[\![r]\!]^{\mathbf{P_A}}_{\text{ACtoAB}} := r_0$.
  2. $\mathbf{P_C}$ computes $r_1 := \text{PRF}_{k^1_{\text{ACtoAB}}}(\text{sid}) - \text{PRF}_{k^2_{\text{ACtoAB}}}(\text{sid})$ then sets $[\![r]\!]^{\mathbf{P_C}}_{\text{ACtoAB}} := r_1$.
  3. $\mathbf{P_B}$ and $\mathbf{P_D}$ compute:
     $r := \text{PRF}_{k^0_{\text{ACtoAB}}}(\text{sid}) - \text{PRF}_{k^2_{\text{ACtoAB}}}(\text{sid})$ and set $[\![r]\!]^{\mathbf{P_B}}_{\text{ACtoAB}} = [\![r]\!]^{\mathbf{P_D}}_{\text{ACtoAB}} := r$, respectively.
– Otherwise if $\psi\text{to}\phi = \text{ABtoAC}$:
  1. $\mathbf{P_A}$ computes $r_0 := \text{PRF}_{k^0_{\text{ACtoAB}}}(\text{sid}) - \text{PRF}_{k^1_{\text{ACtoAB}}}(\text{sid})$ then sets $[\![r]\!]^{\mathbf{P_A}}_{\text{ACtoAB}} := r_0$.
  2. $\mathbf{P_B}$ computes $r_1 := \text{PRF}_{k^1_{\text{ACtoAB}}}(\text{sid}) - \text{PRF}_{k^2_{\text{ACtoAB}}}(\text{sid})$ then sets $[\![r]\!]^{\mathbf{P_B}}_{\text{ACtoAB}} := r_1$.
  3. $\mathbf{P_C}$ and $\mathbf{P_D}$ compute:
     $r := \text{PRF}_{k^0_{\text{ACtoAB}}}(\text{sid}) - \text{PRF}_{k^2_{\text{ACtoAB}}}(\text{sid})$ and set $[\![r]\!]^{\mathbf{P_C}}_{\text{ACtoAB}} = [\![r]\!]^{\mathbf{P_D}}_{\text{ACtoAB}} := r$, respectively.

Fig. 3. Four party *changeM share* generation protocol

4.2 Boolean Computation

This is the special case for $\ell = 1$ in $\mathbb{Z}_{2^\ell}$. The linearity preserves and parties can simply replace all additions (and subtractions) with XORs and multiplications with ANDs while executing boolean operations.

4.3 Share Conversion

For PPML, non-linear functions (such as ReLU, max-pooling etc.) can be evaluated more appropriate with MPC protocols over boolean inputs [28,39,43,50,54], while other linear functions (multiplication, convolutions etc.) prefer arithmetic shared values. In the following, we show how conversion between sharing types works, and how parties can determine the share-mode of outputs.

$\mathcal{X}$**-dabit.** As an important building block, we extend edabit introduced by Escudero *et al.* [15] to $\mathcal{X}$-dabit. Here $b \xleftarrow{\$} \mathbb{Z}_{2^{\ell_b}}$, and ψ and ϕ can be identical.

$$\mathcal{X}\text{-dabit} := ([b]_\psi, \langle b \rangle_\phi := (\langle b_0 \rangle_\phi, \cdots, \langle b_{\ell_b - 1} \rangle_\phi)) \text{ s.t. } [b]^{\mathbf{P_i}}_\psi \xleftarrow{\$} \mathbb{Z}_{2^\ell}, \langle b_j \rangle^{\mathbf{P_i}}_\phi \xleftarrow{\$} \mathbb{Z}_2$$

To generate $\mathcal{X}$-dabit (in the pre-processing), four parties are assigned into two groups. Then following the protocols proposed by [15] for 2PC setting, each group ends up holding the same randomness and generate shares in both arithmetic and boolean worlds. This allows parties to generate $([b]_\psi, \langle b \rangle_\phi)$, where $\psi = \phi$. To change the share-mode of either $[b]_\psi$ or $\langle b \rangle_\phi$, parties run Π_{chMode} (Fig. 4).

Protocol Π_{chMode}

Private inputs: Parties hold $[x]_\psi$.
Public inputs: Public parameters, ϕ.
Outputs: $[x]_\phi$.
Preprocessing: P_i sends $(\text{CMSGen}, \psi\text{to}\phi\ P_i, \text{sid})$ to $\mathcal{F}_{\text{4PC}}^{\text{Pre}}$, receives $[\![r]\!]_{\psi\text{to}\phi}^{P_i}$ as output.
Protocols:
- If $\psi = \text{AC}$ and $\phi = \text{AB}$:
  1. P_A computes $d_0 := [x]_\psi^{P_A} - [\![r]\!]_{\psi\text{to}\phi}^{P_A}$, then sends d_0 to P_C.
  2. P_C computes $d_1 := [x]_\psi^{P_C} - [\![r]\!]_{\psi\text{to}\phi}^{P_C}$, then sends d_1 to P_A.
  3. Upon receiving d_0 and d_1, P_A and P_C set $[x]_\phi^{P_A} := d_0 + d_1$, $[x]_\phi^{P_C} := d_0 + d_1$ respectively.
  4. P_B and P_D set $[x]_\phi^{P_B} := [\![r]\!]_{\psi\text{to}\phi}^{P_B}$, $[x]_\phi^{P_D} := [\![r]\!]_{\psi\text{to}\phi}^{P_D}$ respectively.
- Otherwise if $\psi = \text{AB}$ and $\phi = \text{AC}$, switch the role of P_C with P_B, do the same as above.

Fig. 4. Four party change share-mode protocol

Protocol Π_{BitToA}

Private inputs: Parties hold $\langle x \rangle_\phi$, where $x \in \{0,1\}$.
Public inputs: Public parameters, ψ.
Outputs: $[x]_\psi$.
Preprocessing: P_i sends $(\mathcal{X}\text{-dabitGen}, \psi, \phi, \ell_b, P_i, \text{sid})$ to $\mathcal{F}_{\text{4PC}}^{\text{Pre}}$ with $\ell_b = 1$, receives $([b]_\psi^{P_i}, \langle b \rangle_\phi^{P_i})$ as output.
Protocols:
1. Parties locally compute and then reveal $h := \langle x \rangle_\phi \oplus \langle b \rangle_\phi$, where $h \in \{0,1\}$.
2. If $h = 0$, parties set $[x]_\psi = [b]_\psi$, otherwise $[x]_\psi = 1 - [b]_\psi$.

Fig. 5. Four party bit to arithmetic protocol

Arithmetic vs. Boolean. We first consider one bit case, where parties have to convert $[x]_\psi$ to $\langle x \rangle_\phi$ with $x \in \mathbb{Z}_2$ (an A2B protocol for one single bit). Note that in this case, parties sample $b \xleftarrow{\$} \mathbb{Z}_2$ in $\mathcal{X}$-dabit. The boolean share of this $\mathcal{X}$-dabit becomes one-bit share among parties. By using such an $\mathcal{X}$-dabit, parties simply open their local shares $[x]_\psi^{P_i}$ masked with $[b]_\psi^{P_i}$, then locally "unmask" the revealed value $x - b$ with $\langle b \rangle_\phi$. Converting $\langle x \rangle_\phi$ to $[x]_\psi$ works in the same manner vice versa. A detailed protocol description (B2A for one bit) is placed in Fig. 5. If $x \in \mathbb{Z}_{2^\ell}$, parties can generate an $\mathcal{X}$-dabit with $\ell_b = \ell$ to support an A2B protocol, and ℓ pieces $\mathcal{X}$-dabits with $\ell_b = 1$ to support a B2A protocol. We refer to [15,47] for more details.

4.4 Secure Comparison

We now introduce our secure 4PC comparison protocol Π_{Comp}. Using the same technique mentioned in [54], parties firstly reveal $[x]_\psi$ by masking it with $[b]_\psi$ (arithmetic part of an $\mathcal{X}$-dabit). Now parties hold $\langle b \rangle_\psi$ (boolean part of an $\mathcal{X}$-dabit) and a public revealed $x - b$ over $\mathbb{Z}_{2^\ell}$. After computing the bit decomposition of $x - b$, parties will jointly compute a parallel prefix adder (PPA) circuit to securely extract the sign bit of $[x]_\psi$. To do so, parties will prepare a shared propagator $\langle p \rangle_\psi = \langle x - b \rangle_\psi \oplus \langle b \rangle_\psi$ and a shared generator $\langle g \rangle_\phi = \langle x - b \rangle_\phi * \langle b \rangle_\phi$,

Table 2. Force compared to the existing works regarding Dot Product (in bits).

Setting	Framework	Preparation	Online			Local	with Trunc	
		Comm	Comm	Rounds	Mult	Comm	Rounds
2PC (S.H.)[a]	P-SecureML [40,54]	TTP[b]	$4n\ell$	1	3	$4n\ell$	1
3PC (S.H.)	CryptGPU [50]	0	2ℓ	1	3	3ℓ	2
	P-Falcon [53,54]	0	2ℓ	1	3	4ℓ	1
4PC (S.H.)	CrypTen [28]	TTP	$8n\ell$	1	2	$(8n+4)\ell$	2
	P-FantasticFour [12,54]	0	4ℓ	1	7	6ℓ	2
	PrivPy [35]	0	4ℓ	1	2	4ℓ	1
4PC (M.)[c]	Trident [10]	3ℓ	4ℓ	1	3	$5\ell(4\ell)$	2(1)
	Swift [29]	3ℓ	3ℓ	2	3	$4\ell(3\ell)$	2(1)
	Tetrad [30]	2ℓ	$4\ell(3\ell)$	2(1)	4	$4\ell(3\ell)$	2(1)
4PC (S.H.)	**Force**	0	2ℓ	1	1	2ℓ	1

[a] Semi-Honest
[b] Trusted Third-Party
[c] Malicious

where $A * B$ denotes a bit-wise AND of A and B, and $\psi \neq \phi$. To prepare such a $\langle g \rangle_\phi$, parties call Π_{chMode} once before computing the PPA. In return now 50% of the secure AND protocols are already executable in an efficient 4PC way. For the rest of AND computations, we choose to let parties call Π_{chMode} once in each round to change the share-mode of the updated propagator. As a result, the overall AND computations can be executed in a 4PC way.

5   Communication and Computation Analysis

We use DotP to denote the dot product computation (convolution) of two secret vectors, for conciseness. And we let n denote the length of a vector. As already mentioned in Sect. 4, parties have to rescale (truncate) the shared output of DotP for consistency in precision. A summary of Force and existing works for DotP at each active party (followed by the truncation) is shown in Table 2.

In 2PC, P-SecureML proposed by [40,54] consumes Beaver Triples to support DotP in the online stage. Instead of implementing a heavy pre-processing computation, P-SecureML simply lets a trusted third party to allocate the shares. Meanwhile, the local truncation technique allows parties to simply truncate the last p bits without any interaction. So the total communication overhead for the online stage is still $4n\ell$ bits.

In 3PC, both CryptGPU [50] and P-Falcon [53,54] use replicated sharing scheme. Parties need to send/receive overall 2ℓ bits after each DotP to reconstruct the replicated share holdings (re-sharing), which yields one communication round. Since a local truncation [40] fails in replicated sharing scheme in 3PC (proven by [39]), parties perform Π_{trunc2} [39] with the help of a pre-computed truncation share $([r],[r'])$, where $r' = r/2^p$. This protocol can be executed combined with re-sharing, which requires parties to exchange 4ℓ bits data in a single communication round. On the other hand, CryptGPU [50] chooses to implement another truncation protocol Π_{Trunc1} [39] to avoid generating truncation share. This results in two rounds and 3ℓ bits communication volume totally.

CrypTen [28] implements 4PC protocols with a 4-out-of-4 sharing scheme. Regardless the triple generation in the pre-processing stage, a party still has to send/receive $8n\ell$ bits and 4ℓ bits within the DotP protocol and the truncation protocol, respectively. Compared to CrypTen, P-FantasticFour [12,54] uses replicated sharing scheme over four shares, which improves the communication overhead to 6ℓ.

Recently some 4PC protocols such as [10,29,30] achieves active security in the honest majority setting (tolerating one malicious corruption). All of those rely on correlated randomnesses generated in the pre-processing stage to accelerate the online computation. While all four parties stay active in the pre-processing stage, some work (such as [29,30]) choose to activate three parties in the online stage to complete the computation. Parties benefit from having continuous multiplication gates with amortized communication overhead of 3ℓ in one round. We point out that in CNN (e.g. [21,49]), a convolution layer is followed directly by an activation layer, which requires parties to execute a comparison protocol. As a result, such a construction requires parties to exchange overall 4ℓ elements in two rounds.

Given $\mathcal{X}$-share in Force, we observe a huge computational and communication complexity reduction and a much simplified connection channel establishment. Without relying on a pre-processing stage[1], parties only have to compute one single multiplication locally for DotP. And in fact, parties exchange their local shares with one single partner instead of two, which yields a simpler peer-to-peer connection. Since the local truncation is compatible with $\mathcal{X}$-share, the total communication overhead of Force is only 2ℓ bits in one round.

6   Accelerated Backward in Training

Backward phase is more complicated than the forward phase: for example, it is possible that parties hold a shared x in $[\cdot]_{\mathsf{AC}}$-sharing, which has to be multiplied by two shared values y in $[\cdot]_{\mathsf{AC}}$-sharing and y' in $[\cdot]_{\mathsf{AB}}$-sharing. Yet, it can get accelerated by $\mathcal{X}$-share. First of all, we exclude this situation from the forward phase (except for the comparison protocol), as the computation moves only in one direction without reusing any shared values in multiple computations. The easiest way to implement the backward phase is to let parties execute Π_{chMode} if needed. Such a naive solution results in an extra round and communication overhead, but it already has a huge performance improvement compared to other frameworks. A more efficient solution is to let parties hold one shared value in both share-modes, which then enables parties to perform 4PC computations everywhere during the backward phase. Such critical values are normally only weights in each layer, meaning that parties are capable to trade a small portion of memory for a huge computation acceleration. Remark that holding a shared value in both share-modes does not leak any information to parties, since local shares of each shared value in different share-modes will be chosen freshly (e.g. $x = x_0 + x_1$ and $x = x_0' + x_1'$).

---

[1] Recall that generating *zero sharing* does not require parties to interact.

7   Evaluation

In this section, we thoroughly evaluate $\mathcal{X}$-share and make in-depth comparisons against other state-of-the-art solutions. We build Force on top of Piranha [54][2], at commit $bd9c8c4$, in C++. We implement the new 4-party sharing type $\mathcal{X}$-share for all relevant PPML operations. Besides, we add support for batch normalization and complex ResNet like ResNet152, while Piranha only supports layer normalization and basic ResNet18.

7.1   Evaluation Setup

Testbed Environment. We run our evaluations on 4 cloud servers, with 2 CPUs, Intel(R) Xeon(R) Platinum 8360Y CPU @ 2.40 GHz, and 12×128 GB of RAM. Each of our servers is equipped with one GPU, NVIDIA Tesla P100-PCIE with 16 GB of video RAM (VRAM). We consider two types of network environments: **LAN** and **WAN**, with 10 Gbps bandwidth + 0.2 ms round-trip latency and 100 Mbps bandwidth + 40 ms round-trip latency, both simulated by the tc tool[3]. Our server is running Ubuntu 18.04.6 LTS with CUDA 10.1.243.

Baseline. We choose as baselines several state-of-the-art systems that have **semi-honest security**, as summarized in Table 1. For 2PC, Cheetah [23] is the most recent PPML work using FHE and correlated oblivious transfer (cOT) on CPUs, which is completely different from ours. We run it on the same server as a baseline of CPU-based PPML. SecureML [40] is the only 2-party system supporting both private inference and training, which is improved by Piranha [54] via porting it to GPU. We refer to the GPU version as P-SecureML. For both 3-party and 4-party, we only consider the **honest-majority** setting. Falcon [53] is the fastest 3-party system on CPU. Piranha [54] ports the **semi-honest** version to GPU with huge boost. We mark it as P-Falcon. CryptGPU [50] is another 3-party system on GPU similar to P-Falcon. We include both of them as baselines. CryptGPU [50] is deployed with the latest Github source code[4], at commit $2ff57b2$. As for 4-party, CrypTen [28] is the only one with **semi-honest security** in an **honest-majority** setting by design. We deploy it using their latest Github source code[5], at commit $efe8eda$. All the other 4-party or more-party systems are for **malicious** adversaries, which are slowed down by heavy verification or validations. For fairness, we should not compare with them. Yet, Piranha [54] re-implemented the **semi-honest** version of FantasticFour [12] on GPU. We include this simplified version and refer to it as P-FantasticFour. We run all the evaluations with 20 bits of fixed-point precision. The calculations are over the 64-bit ring $\mathbb{Z}_{2^{64}}$, except Cheetah [23], which supports maximum 44-bit. All the experiments are performed multiple times, with BatchSize $= 1$, considering that some systems do not support large batch sizes. Then we calculate the benchmarks

---

[2] https://github.com/ucbrise/piranha/.
[3] https://man7.org/linux/man-pages/man8/tc.8.html.
[4] https://github.com/jeffreysijuntan/CryptGPU.
[5] https://github.com/facebookresearch/CrypTen.

by averaging all the results except the first run, to mitigate the influence of system initialization and runtime randomness.

Models and Datasets. For our evaluations, we consider three datasets and three neural networks in different sizes: **Small** ones: CIFAR10 [31] and AlexNet [32]. **Medium** ones: TinyImageNet [33] (Tiny for short) and VGG16 [49]. **Large** ones: ImageNet [48] and ResNet152 [21]. We try to keep the models as much as they are in their original publications. However, due to the various input sizes of different datasets, as well as performance considerations, we slightly adjust the structure similarly to CryptGPU [50] and Falcon [53].

7.2   End-to-End Running Time Evaluation

In Table 3 and 4, we list the running time of an *inference* pass for all datasets and models described in Sect. 7.1 in *LAN* and *WAN* settings. Our Force completely outperforms all the baseline systems in all evaluations. CPU-based Cheetah is slower than all the other GPU-based systems in *LAN*. In *WAN*, Cheetah (implemented in C++) can perform better than the Python-implemented (CryptGPU and CrypTen) in deep network like ResNet152, while still slower than the C++-implemented (P-SecureML, P-Falcon, P-FantasticFour and Force). When comparing all GPU-based systems, the C++-implemented perform much better than the Python-implemented. This could result from the language performance difference. Among those C++-implemented, Force beats the other three Piranha-based systems, P-SecureML, P-Falcon and P-FantasticFour, in all experiments, with the acceleration brought by our novel sharing type $\mathcal{X}$-share.

Benchmarks of a *training* pass are similar, as shown in Table 6. Cheetah is omitted here as it does not support training. Again, our Force completely dominates in all evaluations.

7.3   Linear vs. Non-linear Operations

We group common computation tasks into two categories: linear and non-linear. Linear operations include convolution, matrix multiplication and batch normalization. Non-linear operations include ReLU, pooling and SoftMax.

We plot the running time of different operations during an *inference* pass in Fig. 6. Due to the huge time difference between Cheetah and all other systems, all the experiments other than the two shown are rarely visible as bar charts. Thus we omit them. We can see that the most time-consuming operation in Python-implemented CryptGPU and CrypTen is ReLU, while linear operations cost more in those C++-implemented. CryptGPU can be faster than P-SecureML and P-FantasticFour in linear operations, but slower than P-Falcon and Force. The implementation language still makes a difference here.

Table 3. Running time (Second) of an *inference* pass in *LAN*, BatchSize = 1.

	CIFAR10			Tiny			ImageNet		
	AlexNet	VGG16	ResNet152	AlexNet	VGG16	ResNet152	AlexNet	VGG16	ResNet152
P-SecureML	0.41	1.48	7.89	0.55	2.19	9.44	2.50	15.70	31.46
CryptGPU	1.15	2.91	35.58	1.14	3.83	38.21	2.42	12.74	49.54
P-Falcon	0.29	0.89	5.18	0.35	1.37	6.24	1.12	10.03	20.39
CrypTen	1.05	3.48	26.04	1.25	5.20	29.10	4.59	32.75	62.58
P-FantasticFour	0.72	2.20	12.81	0.87	3.40	15.59	2.72	24.03	49.74
Force	**0.12**	**0.35**	**2.54**	**0.14**	**0.54**	**3.01**	**0.43**	**3.26**	**9.70**
Cheetah	2.67	80.43	66.96	19.74	325.30	263.87	383.97	4026.87	3226.62
PyTorch	0.0008	0.0017	0.0264	0.0009	0.0017	0.0266	0.0009	0.0017	0.0268

Table 4. Running time (Second) of an *inference* pass in *WAN*, BatchSize = 1.

	CIFAR10			Tiny			ImageNet		
	AlexNet	VGG16	ResNet152	AlexNet	VGG16	ResNet152	AlexNet	VGG16	ResNet152
P-SecureML	12.20	57.54	239.81	21.64	121.05	241.73	179.19	1126.83	1907.65
CryptGPU	18.41	44.17	807.32	19.46	65.15	846.11	48.53	359.46	1387.28
P-Falcon	2.85	11.08	91.06	3.80	28.27	119.33	30.79	370.70	730.97
CrypTen	34.37	103.26	721.67	43.47	256.77	876.92	397.49	2203.29	4649.98
P-FantasticFour	7.60	41.39	218.33	13.00	125.80	368.82	135.93	1489.91	2853.29
Force	**2.60**	**6.75**	**75.28**	**2.94**	**14.21**	**85.85**	**13.59**	**155.15**	**324.17**
Cheetah	12.64	233.34	220.16	52.59	908.09	711.77	827.68	11012.47	8101.88

Table 5. Communication volume (MByte) of an *inference* pass, BatchSize = 1.

	CIFAR10			Tiny			ImageNet		
	AlexNet	VGG16	ResNet152	AlexNet	VGG16	ResNet152	AlexNet	VGG16	ResNet152
P-SecureML	65.93	381.39	1178.82	130.16	849.01	2082.17	1186.00	8361.98	15718.33
CryptGPU	2.32	53.59	236.17	13.32	214.12	677.61	226.08	2622.02	7376.14
P-Falcon	3.72	84.48	168.85	20.83	337.62	680.50	350.09	4134.47	8441.19
CrypTen	74.67	579.78	1409.07	178.98	1641.77	3034.04	2005.10	18069.92	27607.43
P-FantasticFour	7.01	159.50	300.42	39.24	637.43	1218.99	659.45	7805.96	15150.84
Force	**1.49**	**33.76**	**79.95**	**8.38**	**134.93**	**316.65**	**140.95**	**1652.33**	**3907.41**
Cheetah	40.10	951.35	773.51	249.24	3792.40	3091.30	4493.92	46450.00	37876.50

Table 6. Running time (Second) of a *training* pass in *LAN*, BatchSize = 1.

	CIFAR10			Tiny			ImageNet		
	AlexNet	VGG16	ResNet152	AlexNet	VGG16	ResNet152	AlexNet	VGG16	ResNet152
P-SecureML	1.62	4.55	29.20	7.53	5.99	27.81	7.41	28.82	65.51
CryptGPU	2.27	5.49	40.24	3.23	8.06	41.37	9.10	38.86	53.28
P-Falcon	0.75	2.44	12.08	0.96	3.04	13.55	4.13	16.14	35.78
CrypTen	13.48	40.86	27.68	18.39	50.34	33.35	FAIL	FAIL	74.07
P-FantasticFour	1.65	4.99	25.65	2.17	6.64	29.96	9.69	37.10	79.78
Force	**0.35**	**1.23**	**6.40**	**0.51**	**1.59**	**7.53**	**2.89**	**8.57**	**22.77**
PyTorch	0.0031	0.0067	0.0659	0.0027	0.0049	0.0637	0.0034	0.0077	0.0683

Table 7. Maximum batch size when training ImageNet in VGG16.

Batch Size	1	2	4	8	16	32
P-SecureML	✓	✓	✓	×	×	×
CryptGPU	✓	×	×	×	×	×
P-Falcon	✓	✓	✓	×	×	×
CrypTen	×	×	×	×	×	×
P-FantasticFour	✓	✓	×	×	×	×
Force	✓	✓	✓	✓	✓	×

Table 8. Inference accuracy comparison of Force and PyTorch.

Inference		CIFAR10	Tiny	ImageNet
AlexNet	PyTorch	69.65%	26.38%	22.84%
	Force	69.69%	26.39%	22.84%
VGG16	PyTorch	88.31%	54.90%	56.41%
	Force	88.34%	54.89%	56.42%
ResNet152	PyTorch	83.99%	65.14%	67.36%
	Force	83.98%	65.15%	67.36%

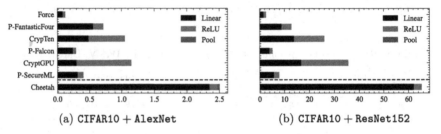

(a) CIFAR10 + AlexNet   (b) CIFAR10 + ResNet152

Fig. 6. Running time of different operations during an *inference* pass in *LAN* setting with BatchSize = 1. X-axis is time in seconds.

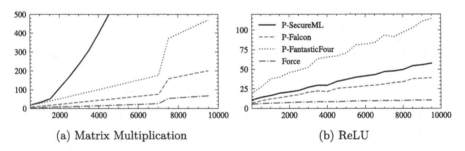

(a) Matrix Multiplication   (b) ReLU

Fig. 7. Micro-benchmark of *matmul* and ReLU in four Piranha-based systems. X-axis is data dimension and Y-axis is time in Milliseconds. For *matmul*, we multiply an $x \times x$ matrix by an $x \times 1$ vector.

To further compare the effect of different sharing types, we make some micro-benchmark of matrix multiplication and ReLU in four Piranha-based systems. We perform *matmul* and ReLU of different input data size and record the average running time. The results are plotted in Fig. 7. Force, with the new sharing type $\mathcal{X}$-share, shows outstanding improvement over the other three. Besides, Force scales much better as the problem size increases.

7.4   Communication Cost

One of the main contribution of Cheetah is low communication cost. We make it even better. As shown in Table 5, we have the minimal communication volume

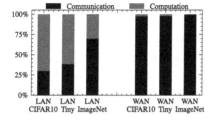
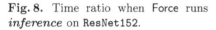
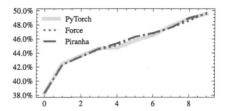

Fig. 8. Time ratio when Force runs *inference* on ResNet152.

Fig. 9. Validation accuracy of 9 training epochs for AlexNet + CIFAR10.

when performing *inference* with BatchSize $= 1$ for all the evaluations. However, we still notice high communication cost during all phases, especially for large datasets and *WAN* settings. As an example, we plot the ratio of communication and computation time of Force in Fig. 8. We can see that as the dataset gets larger, mainly the image dimensions, communication consumes more time. When the network latency is high, like in *WAN*, the whole running time is dominated by communication.

7.5 Memory Efficiency

Compared with RAM, which could easily reach $1TB$ nowadays, VRAM is an extremely limited resource, which is normally 16GB or 24GB per card. To measure the utilization efficiency of VRAM, we run a simple experiment. We train one large dataset, ImageNet, on one of the large models, VGG16, and try to find out the maximum possible batch size. The result is displayed in Table 7. Force is the only system which supports training ImageNet on VGG16 with BatchSize $= 8$ and BatchSize $= 16$. This is achieved by getting rid of Beaver's Triple and reducing the number of local shares to just one. All the other systems can only train with batch size up to 4. CrypTen could not even train with BatchSize $= 1$.

7.6 Accuracy Comparison

To measure the accuracy, we run both inference and training with Force. We first train the models on all the datasets with PyTorch to get pre-trained models. Starting from those pre-trained models, we perform the accuracy evaluation. We run all the evaluation with 26 bits of fixed-point precision, as suggested by Piranha. The inference accuracy on validation sets is shown in Table 8. Force provides almost the same accuracy as the plaintext PyTorch, only with a tiny relative error of less than 0.1% for all models and datasets. For training, we use AlexNet + CIFAR10 as an example. Starting from a pre-trained model, we train AlexNet on CIFAR10 with Piranha, Force and PyTorch for 9 epochs. The validation accuracy is plotted in Fig. 9. After 9 epochs, the accuracy of PyTorch is 49.59%, of Force is 49.71%, which is even 0.12% higher, indicating extremely low accuracy loss.

8   Conclusion

In this paper, we construct a highly efficient 4PC framework Force for PPML. Our implementation and evaluation showcase that Force is by far the most efficient in terms of time, memory consumption and overall performance. It can be meaningful future work to extend Force with malicious security and guarantee of delivery, as well as to generalize it for any number of parties.

References

1. Araki, T., Furukawa, J., Lindell, Y., Nof, A., Ohara, K.: High-throughput semi-honest secure three-party computation with an honest majority. In: Proceedings of the 2016 ACM SIGSAC Conference on Computer and Communications Security, pp. 805–817 (2016)
2. Bogdanov, D., Laur, S., Willemson, J.: Sharemind: a framework for fast privacy-preserving computations. In: Jajodia, S., Lopez, J. (eds.) ESORICS 2008. LNCS, vol. 5283, pp. 192–206. Springer, Heidelberg (2008). https://doi.org/10.1007/978-3-540-88313-5_13
3. Bogdanov, D., Niitsoo, M., Toft, T., Willemson, J.: High-performance secure multi-party computation for data mining applications. Int. J. Inf. Secur. 11(6), 403–418 (2012)
4. Bonawitz, K.A., et al.: Practical secure aggregation for federated learning on user-held data. CoRR abs/1611.04482 (2016)
5. Byali, M., Chaudhari, H., Patra, A., Suresh, A.: Flash: fast and robust framework for privacy-preserving machine learning. Proc. Priv. Enh. Technol. 2, 459–480 (2020)
6. Cabrero-Holgueras, J., Pastrana, S.: SoK: privacy-preserving computation techniques for deep learning. Proc. Priv. Enh. Technol. 2021(4), 139–162 (2021)
7. Canetti, R.: Universally composable security: a new paradigm for cryptographic protocols. In: Proceedings 42nd IEEE Symposium on Foundations of Computer Science, pp. 136–145. IEEE (2001)
8. Catrina, O., de Hoogh, S.: Improved primitives for secure multiparty integer computation. In: Garay, J.A., De Prisco, R. (eds.) SCN 2010. LNCS, vol. 6280, pp. 182–199. Springer, Heidelberg (2010). https://doi.org/10.1007/978-3-642-15317-4_13
9. Chaudhari, H., Choudhury, A., Patra, A., Suresh, A.: Astra: high throughput 3PC over rings with application to secure prediction. In: Proceedings of the 2019 ACM SIGSAC Conference on Cloud Computing Security Workshop, pp. 81–92 (2019)
10. Chaudhari, H., Rachuri, R., Suresh, A.: Trident: efficient 4PC framework for privacy preserving machine learning. In: 27th Annual Network and Distributed System Security Symposium, NDSS 2020, San Diego, California, USA, 23–26 February 2020. The Internet Society (2020)
11. Dai, W., Sunar, B.: cuHE: a homomorphic encryption accelerator library. In: Pasalic, E., Knudsen, L.R. (eds.) BalkanCryptSec 2015. LNCS, vol. 9540, pp. 169–186. Springer, Cham (2016). https://doi.org/10.1007/978-3-319-29172-7_11
12. Dalskov, A., Escudero, D., Keller, M.: Fantastic four: honest-majority four-party secure computation with malicious security. In: 30th USENIX Security Symposium (USENIX Security 2021), pp. 2183–2200 (2021)

13. Demmler, D., Schneider, T., Zohner, M.: ABY-a framework for efficient mixed-protocol secure two-party computation. In: NDSS (2015)

14. Dwork, C., Roth, A., et al.: The algorithmic foundations of differential privacy. Found. Trends® Theor. Comput. Sci. **9**(3–4), 211–407 (2014)

15. Escudero, D., Ghosh, S., Keller, M., Rachuri, R., Scholl, P.: Improved primitives for MPC over mixed arithmetic-binary circuits. In: Micciancio, D., Ristenpart, T. (eds.) CRYPTO 2020. LNCS, vol. 12171, pp. 823–852. Springer, Cham (2020). https://doi.org/10.1007/978-3-030-56880-1_29

16. Evans, D., Kolesnikov, V., Rosulek, M., et al.: A pragmatic introduction to secure multi-party computation. Found. Trends® Priv. Secur. **2**(2–3), 70–246 (2018)

17. Frederiksen, T.K., Nielsen, J.B.: Fast and maliciously secure two-party computation using the GPU. In: Jacobson, M., Locasto, M., Mohassel, P., Safavi-Naini, R. (eds.) ACNS 2013. LNCS, vol. 7954, pp. 339–356. Springer, Heidelberg (2013). https://doi.org/10.1007/978-3-642-38980-1_21

18. Furukawa, J., Lindell, Y., Nof, A., Weinstein, O.: High-throughput secure three-party computation for malicious adversaries and an honest majority. In: Coron, J.-S., Nielsen, J.B. (eds.) EUROCRYPT 2017. LNCS, vol. 10211, pp. 225–255. Springer, Cham (2017). https://doi.org/10.1007/978-3-319-56614-6_8

19. Google LLC: Tensorflow privacy (2019). https://github.com/tensorflow/privacy

20. Hastings, M., Hemenway, B., Noble, D., Zdancewic, S.: SoK: general purpose compilers for secure multi-party computation. In: 2019 IEEE Symposium on Security and Privacy (SP), pp. 1220–1237. IEEE (2019)

21. He, K., Zhang, X., Ren, S., Sun, J.: Deep residual learning for image recognition. In: Proceedings of the IEEE Conference on Computer Vision and Pattern Recognition, pp. 770–778 (2016)

22. Hesamifard, E., Takabi, H., Ghasemi, M., Wright, R.N.: Privacy-preserving machine learning as a service. Proc. Priv. Enh. Technol. **2018**(3), 123–142 (2018)

23. Huang, Z., Lu, W.j., Hong, C., Ding, J.: Cheetah: lean and fast secure two-party deep neural network inference. In: 31st USENIX Security Symposium (USENIX Security 2022), pp. 809–826 (2022)

24. Husted, N., Myers, S., Shelat, A., Grubbs, P.: GPU and CPU parallelization of honest-but-curious secure two-party computation. In: Proceedings of the 29th Annual Computer Security Applications Conference, pp. 169–178 (2013)

25. Juvekar, C., Vaikuntanathan, V., Chandrakasan, A.: Gazelle: a low latency framework for secure neural network inference. In: 27th USENIX Security Symposium (USENIX Security 2018), pp. 1651–1669 (2018)

26. Kanagavelu, R., et al.: Two-phase multi-party computation enabled privacy-preserving federated learning. In: 2020 20th IEEE/ACM International Symposium on Cluster, Cloud and Internet Computing (CCGRID), pp. 410–419. IEEE (2020)

27. Keller, M., Pastro, V., Rotaru, D.: Overdrive: making SPDZ great again. In: Nielsen, J.B., Rijmen, V. (eds.) EUROCRYPT 2018. LNCS, vol. 10822, pp. 158–189. Springer, Cham (2018). https://doi.org/10.1007/978-3-319-78372-7_6

28. Knott, B., Venkataraman, S., Hannun, A., Sengupta, S., Ibrahim, M., van der Maaten, L.: Crypten: secure multi-party computation meets machine learning. Adv. Neural. Inf. Process. Syst. **34**, 4961–4973 (2021)

29. Koti, N., Pancholi, M., Patra, A., Suresh, A.: SWIFT: super-fast and robust privacy-preserving machine learning. In: 30th USENIX Security Symposium (USENIX Security 2021), pp. 2651–2668. USENIX Association (2021)

30. Koti, N., Patra, A., Rachuri, R., Suresh, A.: Tetrad: actively secure 4PC for secure training and inference. In: 29th Annual Network and Distributed System Secu-

rity Symposium, NDSS 2022, San Diego, California, USA, 24–28 April 2022. The Internet Society (2022)

31. Krizhevsky, A., Hinton, G., et al.: Learning multiple layers of features from tiny images (2009)

32. Krizhevsky, A., Sutskever, I., Hinton, G.E.: Imagenet classification with deep convolutional neural networks. In: Pereira, F., Burges, C., Bottou, L., Weinberger, K. (eds.) Advances in Neural Information Processing Systems, vol. 25. Curran Associates, Inc. (2012)

33. Le, Y., Yang, X.: Tiny imagenet visual recognition challenge. CS 231N **7**(7), 3 (2015)

34. Lehmkuhl, R., Mishra, P., Srinivasan, A., Popa, R.A.: Muse: secure inference resilient to malicious clients. In: 30th USENIX Security Symposium (USENIX Security 2021), pp. 2201–2218 (2021)

35. Li, Y., Xu, W.: Privpy: general and scalable privacy-preserving data mining. In: Proceedings of the 25th ACM SIGKDD International Conference on Knowledge Discovery & Data Mining, pp. 1299–1307 (2019)

36. Lindell, Y.: How to simulate it-a tutorial on the simulation proof technique. In: Tutorials on the Foundations of Cryptography, pp. 277–346 (2017)

37. Liu, J., Juuti, M., Lu, Y., Asokan, N.: Oblivious neural network predictions via minionn transformations. In: Proceedings of the 2017 ACM SIGSAC Conference on Computer and Communications Security, pp. 619–631 (2017)

38. Mishra, P., Lehmkuhl, R., Srinivasan, A., Zheng, W., Popa, R.A.: Delphi: a cryptographic inference service for neural networks. In: 29th USENIX Security Symposium (USENIX Security 2020), pp. 2505–2522 (2020)

39. Mohassel, P., Rindal, P.: ABY3: a mixed protocol framework for machine learning. In: Proceedings of the 2018 ACM SIGSAC Conference on Computer and Communications Security, pp. 35–52 (2018)

40. Mohassel, P., Zhang, Y.: Secureml: a system for scalable privacy-preserving machine learning. In: 2017 IEEE Symposium on Security and Privacy (SP), pp. 19–38. IEEE (2017)

41. Papernot, N., McDaniel, P., Sinha, A., Wellman, M.P.: SoK: security and privacy in machine learning. In: 2018 IEEE European Symposium on Security and Privacy (EuroS&P), pp. 399–414. IEEE (2018)

42. Paszke, A., et al.: Pytorch: an imperative style, high-performance deep learning library. In: Advances in Neural Information Processing Systems, vol. 32 (2019)

43. Patra, A., Schneider, T., Suresh, A., Yalame, H.: ABY2.0: improved mixed-protocol secure two-party computation. In: 30th USENIX Security Symposium (USENIX Security 2021), pp. 2165–2182 (2021)

44. Patra, A., Suresh, A.: BLAZE: blazing fast privacy-preserving machine learning. In: 27th Annual Network and Distributed System Security Symposium, NDSS 2020, San Diego, California, USA, 23–26 February 2020. The Internet Society (2020)

45. Pu, S., Duan, P., Liu, J.: Fastplay-a parallelization model and implementation of SMC on CUDA based GPU cluster architecture. IACR Cryptology ePrint Archive, p. 97 (2011)

46. Rathee, D., et al.: Cryptflow2: practical 2-party secure inference. In: Proceedings of the 2020 ACM SIGSAC Conference on Computer and Communications Security, pp. 325–342 (2020)

47. Rotaru, D., Wood, T.: MArBled circuits: mixing arithmetic and boolean circuits with active security. In: Hao, F., Ruj, S., Sen Gupta, S. (eds.) INDOCRYPT 2019. LNCS, vol. 11898, pp. 227–249. Springer, Cham (2019). https://doi.org/10.1007/978-3-030-35423-7_12

48. Russakovsky, O., et al.: Imagenet large scale visual recognition challenge. Int. J. Comput. Vision **115**(3), 211–252 (2015)

49. Simonyan, K., Zisserman, A.: Very deep convolutional networks for large-scale image recognition. In: Bengio, Y., LeCun, Y. (eds.) 3rd International Conference on Learning Representations, ICLR 2015, San Diego, CA, USA, 7–9 May 2015, Conference Track Proceedings (2015)

50. Tan, S., Knott, B., Tian, Y., Wu, D.J.: Cryptgpu: fast privacy-preserving machine learning on the GPU. In: 2021 IEEE Symposium on Security and Privacy (SP), pp. 1021–1038. IEEE (2021)

51. Truex, S., et al.: A hybrid approach to privacy-preserving federated learning. In: Proceedings of the 12th ACM Workshop on Artificial Intelligence and Security, pp. 1–11 (2019)

52. Wagh, S., Gupta, D., Chandran, N.: Securenn: 3-party secure computation for neural network training. Proc. Priv. Enh. Technol. **2019**(3), 26–49 (2019)

53. Wagh, S., Tople, S., Benhamouda, F., Kushilevitz, E., Mittal, P., Rabin, T.: Falcon: honest-majority maliciously secure framework for private deep learning. Proc. Priv. Enh. Technol. **1**, 188–208 (2021)

54. Watson, J.L., Wagh, S., Popa, R.A.: Piranha: a GPU platform for secure computation. In: 31st USENIX Security Symposium (USENIX Security 2022), pp. 827–844 (2022)

55. Zhang, Q., et al.: MORSE-STF: a privacy preserving computation system. CoRR abs/2109.11726 (2021)

Author Index

L. Fritsch et al. (Eds.): NordSec 2023, LNCS 14324, pp. 351–352, 2024.
https://doi.org/10.1007/978-3-031-47748-5

Printed in the United States
by Baker & Taylor Publisher Services